Fiscal Policy and Public Financial Management

Fiscal Policy and Public Financial Management

Edited by

PINAKI CHAKRABORTY
K R SHANMUGAM

OXFORD
UNIVERSITY PRESS

OXFORD
UNIVERSITY PRESS

Great Clarendon Street, Oxford, OX2 6DP,
United Kingdom

Oxford University Press is a department of the University of Oxford.
It furthers the University's objective of excellence in research, scholarship,
and education by publishing worldwide. Oxford is a registered trade mark of
Oxford University Press in the UK and in certain other countries

Published in the United States of America by Oxford University Press
198 Madison Avenue, New York, NY 10016, United States of America

British Library Cataloguing in Publication Data

Data available

Library of Congress Control Number: 2024942659

ISBN 9780198930433

DOI: 10.1093/9780198930464.001.0001

Printed and bound in India by
Replika Press Pvt. Ltd.

Dedicated to

Dr Raja J. Chelliah—a renowned economist and institution builder

Foreword

The reforms introduced in 1991 and subsequently constitute an important landmark in the post-independent economic history of India. The measures introduced at that time focused on stabilization and structural reforms. The crisis that the country had to face was the result of excessive current account deficit and fiscal deficit. The reform of the fiscal system thus became an integral part of the reform process. Dr Raja Chelliah played a critical role in shaping the fiscal reform measures. As Chairman of the Tax Reforms Committee, he spelt out the road map to achieving an efficient tax system. The emphasis was on broadening tax bases by minimizing exemptions and concessions and levying lower and less differentiated rates. He also drew attention to the need for fiscal prudence and minimizing fiscal deficit. Thus, a whole new chapter of the fiscal system was written under Dr Chelliah's guidance. It was only appropriate that he was honoured in 2007 with conferment of the Padma Vibhushan, the second highest civilian honour. Dr Chelliah's contributions to the academic scene in India are also very significant. Not only did he teach in some of the most important universities, but he was also instrumental in the setting up of two important higher education institutions—the National Institute of Public Finance and Policy, and the Madras School of Economics, Chennai. The present book is a way of honouring Dr Chelliah on his centenary birth year—2022. Twenty-four eminent economists, most of whom had the privilege of working with and learning from Dr Chelliah, have contributed to this volume. I am sure that this book will be of great value to policymakers as well as to academics.

C. Rangarajan
Former Chairman, Economic Advisory Council to the Prime Minister
Former Governor, Reserve Bank of India
Chairman, Madras School of Economics

Preface

This book is a collection of essays on various themes related to fiscal policy and public financial management. Specific themes covered in this book are issues related to direct and indirect taxes, public expenditure and debt, fiscal transparency, budget management, fiscal and environmental federalism, climate finance and public sector investment appraisals. The array of issues covered in this book provide important analytical insights into the complexity and challenges of fiscal management in India and emerging issues in public financial management, including climate finance. As editors, we have tried to summarize the main findings of each chapter, while introducing the book in Chapter 1.

This book is also a tribute to Padma Vibhushan Dr Raja J. Chelliah. Dr Chelliah's contribution to India's fiscal policy is enormous. In setting up the National Institute of Public Finance and Policy, New Delhi in 1976, Dr Chelliah laid the foundation for public finance research, policy, and advocacy in India. He also founded the Madras School of Economics (MSE) in 1993, which has evolved as an institute of eminence for research and teaching in Economics in India.

As Chairman of the Tax Reforms Committee, he was the chief architect of tax reforms in India, when the country embarked on its economic liberalization journey in 1991. He also served as a member of the Planning Commission and the Ninth Finance Commission. His book *Fiscal Policy in Underdeveloped Countries* is a profound contribution in the area of public finance, addressing the problems of fiscal policy formulation in developing nations. He obtained his PhD in Economics from the University of Pittsburgh, USA. He taught at the Madras Christian College, the University of Rajasthan, the Osmania University, and also at MSE. He served as Chief, Fiscal Affairs Division, IMF from 1970–75. It is only befitting that 24 economists, most of whom had the privilege of working with and learning from Dr Chelliah, have contributed to this book.

This volume is the outcome of lectures/papers presented by its contributors in a series of training programmes on public finance for officials of the government of Tamil Nadu at the Madras School of Economics (MSE) from 31 August 2021 to 27 December 2021. This programme was orgainzed by the Centre for Public Finance at MSE. The NIPFP faculty actively participated in conducting this training programme.

As editors, we thank all the authors for their contributions. We thank Dr C. Rangarajan for all the guidance and support and his contribution to this volume. We are grateful to him for writing the foreword for the book.

We are also very grateful to two anonymous referees for providing valuable comments on the draft manuscript which enriched the book. We thank Mr Dhiraj Pandey, Editor, and Amrita Brahmo, project editor, Oxford University Press, for their support and guidance. We thank Praveena G. of newgen for timely production of the book.

Pinaki Chakraborty
K. R. Shanmugam

Contents

Contributors

Muralikrishna Bharadwaj is Senior Manager, Ernst & Young India.

Lekha Chakraborty is a Professor at the National Institute of Public Finance and Policy, New Delhi.

Pinaki Chakraborty is the Vice-Chairman of the Institute of Development Studies, Jaipur and Visting Distinguished Professor, National Institute of Public Finance and Policy, New Delhi.

Sanjana Das is an independent scholar, based in New Delhi.

M. Govinda Rao is the Former Director of the National Institute of Public Finance and Policy, New Delhi.

Tarrung Kapur is a Senior Manager, Ernst & Young India.

Amandeep Kaur is an Economist at the National Institute of Public Finance and Policy, New Delhi.

K. S. Kavi Kumar is a Professor at the Madras School of Economics, Chennai.

R. Kavita Rao is Director, National Institute of Public Finance and Policy, New Delhi.

Ranjan Kumar Mohanty is an Assistant Professor at the Xavier Institute of Management, Bhubaneswar.

Sacchidananda Mukherjee is a Professor at the National Institute of Public Finance and Policy, New Delhi.

S. Raja Sethu Durai is a Professor at the School of Economics, University of Hyderabad.

Shanmugam K. R. is Director and Professor, Madras School of Economics, Chennai.

Divy Rangan is a former Research Fellow at the National Institute of Public Finance and Policy, New Delhi.

C. Rangarajan is Chairman, Madras School of Economics (MSE), and formerly Governor, RBI.

Pratap Ranjan Jena is a Professor at the National Institute of Public Finance and Policy, New Delhi.

Amey Sapre is an Associate Professor at the National Institute of Public Finance and Policy, New Delhi.

Ruzel Shrestha is a former Project Associate at the National Institute of Public Finance and Policy, New Delhi.

L. Somasundaram is an Assistant Professor at Bharathidasan Institute of Management, Trichy.

R. Srinivasan is a Member, State Planning Commission, Government of Tamil Nadu, Chennai.

D. K. Srivastava is Chief Policy Advisor, EY India and formerly Director, Madras School of Economics, Chennai.

Ragini Trehan is a Senior Manager, Ernst & Young India.

L. Venkatachalam is a Professor at the Madras Institute of Development Studies, Chennai.

I. Zareena Begum is a Professor at the Madras School of Economics, Chennai.

1

Introducing the Volume on Fiscal Policy and Public Financial Management

Pinaki Chakraborty and K. R. Shanmugam

1.1 Introduction

The scope of Public Finance, as a branch of economics, has expanded with the changing role of government. Though the foundational principles of public finance defined by Musgrave (1957) remain the core, the instruments and options to achieve desired Musgraivian objectives, namely allocation, distribution, and stabilization, have increased greatly over time. In present-day public finance, the subject matter includes not only public revenue/taxation, public expenditure, deficit/public debt financing, and fiscal federalism, but also issues related to climate finance and climate change, environmental federalism, discussion on global public goods having transjurisdictional implications, and legislative control over borrowing. Independent fiscal institutions such as fiscal councils have emerged as major areas of research and policy development.

In the 19th century, the government's role was limited to the provision of public goods and infrastructure. In the 1950s, when many countries were emerging from centuries of colonial rule, the economic role of the government expanded due to socio-economic and redistributive considerations. The structure of public finance in many of these countries, including India, has grown and been influenced by historical accidents, the examples of other countries and the thinking of foreign rulers, and the exigencies of the moment (Chelliah, 1960). After Independence in 1947, India has emerged as one of the major federal countries in the world, though constitutionally India is a Union of States. Fiscal policy and public financial management have received new dimensions and have become

Pinaki Chakraborty and K. R. Shanmugam, *Introducing the Volume on Fiscal Policy and Public Financial Management*
In: *Fiscal Policy and Public Financial Management.* Edited by: Pinaki Chakraborty and K R Shanmugam,
Oxford University Press. © Oxford University Press 2024. DOI: 10.1093/9780198930464.003.0001

increasingly complex. The objective of this book is to deal with this complex theme of fiscal policy and public financial management.

1.2 The Indian Federal System

The Constitutional assignments of revenues and expenditure functions led to vertical fiscal imbalances. Further, due to variations in size, location, and historical development, states have different capacities to raise their revenues. This led to horizontal fiscal imbalances. In order to mitigate these imbalances, the Constitution facilitates the sharing of union taxes under tax devolution (Article 280) and grants-in-aid (Article 275) through the Finance Commission (FC). Until its abolition in 2014, the Planning Commission (PC) (which was appointed through Cabinet Resolution in 1950) used to determine the plan grants to states for balanced regional development. The central ministries also transfer resources to the states through various centrally sponsored and central sector schemes (CSS).

If we consider recent history, major indirect tax reforms happened in the country through the introduction of Goods and Services Tax (GST) in 2017 to harmonise India's indirect tax system. This was preceded by the State level indirect tax reforms through the introduction of Value Added Tax in 2005. The GST was designed as a destination-based tax, and replaced a number of domestic taxes. The GST comprises of a central GST (CGST), a state GST (SGST), and an interstate GST (IGST). The GST Council acts as the governing body and directs every step in the implementation of GST. The Council's decisions over tax rates and further implementation measures are final. The implementation of GST for the last five years has opened up many questions, such as: (i) Since there was a significant loss of fiscal autonomy in deciding GST rates, what would be right balance between fiscal autonomy and tax harmonisation?. (ii) Like GST, which is managed by the GST council, could other indirect taxes like petroleum be subsumed in GST for a broad-base GST? (iii) Since GST is expected to be comprehensive and help widen the tax bases, would this result in more revenues than the pre-GST regime?

Management of deficit at the union and state level is another area of fiscal management which has undergone significant changes over time and particularly in recent years. The most important one is the introduction of rule based fiscal control at the union and state level in early 2000.

The central government was providing loans to the States until 2005–06. The loan component of central assistance to state plans has been discontinued since 2005–06 following the recommendations of the 12th FC. Therefore, as of now, central loans to states are restricted to external loans from multilateral institutions and 50-year interest-free loans to the States started in 2020-21 as a covid response measure.

1.3 Indian Public Finance

Since Independence, the instruments of public finance have evolved to serve changing economic strategy and adapt to the developing economic environment. In the initial four decades, tax and expenditure policies were designed to mobilize resources for the public sector-dominated, heavy industry–based, import-substituting development strategy (Rao, 2022). The direct and the indirect tax systems in India originated in their modern forms with the enactment of the Income Tax Act 1860 and the Customs Act 1978 respectively.

Both direct and indirect taxes have undergone various changes in their structures and rates since Independence. In particular, the economic reforms initiated in the early 1990s in India brought considerable changes in the tax system based on the recommendations of the Tax Reforms Committee (TRC), headed by Dr Raja J. Chelliah. The contribution of indirect taxes was 87 per cent of the general government's total tax revenues in the early 1990s. Based on the recommendations of the TRC, rates of indirect taxes were reduced significantly, and at the same time direct tax rates were also reduced in a phased manner. These changes altered the composition of tax revenues and also simplified the tax structure to a considerable extent.

However, despite reforms, government finances deteriorated after the mid-1990s due to reform-induced losses in revenues from customs and excise duties, poor tax performance (the centre's net tax revenue relative to GDP declined from 6.80 per cent in 1995–96 to 5.77 per cent in 2001–02), low tax buoyancy, and increased spending (general government revenue expenditure increased from 20.27 per cent of GDP in 1996–97 to 23.47 per cent in 2002–03) mainly due to implementing the fifth pay commission's recommendations and rising debt servicing costs. The combined outstanding liabilities of the centre and all states relative to GDP increased from 55.22 per cent in 1996–97 to 89.5 per cent in 2005–06. In response, various fiscal measures, including the implementation of the Fiscal Responsibility and Budget Management (FRBM) Act in 2003 by the central government and subsequently by all state governments were introduced. The centre's tax revenues relative to GDP increased to 8.97 per cent in 2007–08; the combined revenue expenditure relative to GDP came down from 23.47 per cent in 2002–03 to 20.64 per cent in 2007–08; the public debt:GDP ratio declined from 89.50 per cent in 2005–06 to 70.57 per cent in 2014–15.

Though Global financial crisis of 2008 contributed to a significant increase in debt and deficits at the general government level, fiscal consolidation post the financial crisis was significant and there was steady decline in fiscal imbalance at the union and state level in India. However after 2017–18, there was an economic growth slowdown and the COVID-19 pandemic, contributed to a negative growth of -6.6 per cent in 2020–21. The combined total government expenditures relative to GDP increased from 26.42 per cent in 2017–18 to 32.95 per cent in 2020–21. The combined debt again increased from 69.57 per cent to 89.41 per cent during the same period. Though the post-covid fiscal situation has improved, the greater challenge is to bring down the debt to a sustainable level as the combined general government debt continues to remain significantly higher than its pre-covid level.

1.4 Overview of the Book's Chapters

Against the above backdrop, this book is devoted to analysing critical fiscal policy and public finance management issues in India. The book is divided into four parts, covering four broad topics. Each of these topics has three to six chapters. The topics are not mutually exclusive, and often cover common ground. This is due to the nature of the interdependence of these fiscal/public policy issues.

1.4.1 Fiscal Policy and Macroeconomy

The first theme is on Fiscal Policy and Macroeconomy. Controlling public debt is a major policy challenge for India, as both centre and state governments have borrowed heavily over time. Chapter 2, by Shanmugam, deals with the issue of public debt in India. It empirically demonstrates that the current level of public debt in India is unsustainable, and the debt sustainability threshold is about 61.6 per cent. Apart from the roadmap suggested by the 15th FC, there is a need for greater correction of debt, particularly at the union level. Using the simulation exercise, this chapter suggests that the Indian economy (nominal) should grow at 10 per cent and the fiscal deficit target should be 4 per cent from 2023–24 onwards to attain the debt-sustainability target in 2030–31, and that with 12 per cent growth it could reach the target in 2027–28. The relevant policy strategy is revenue augmentation and containing public expenditure including unproductive subsidies, and ensuring high economic growth.

Due to the COVID-19 pandemic, on one hand government spending increased, while on the other revenues contracted significantly. The deficit and debt levels of both centre and state governments increased to unprecedented levels. The war between Russia and Ukraine also aggravated the macroeconomic uncertainties. In Chapter 3, Pinaki Chakraborty discusses post-COVID economic recovery, macroeconomic uncertainties, and fiscal responsibility. The chapter argues that the 2022–23 Union Budget reflects the possibility of significant fiscal consolidation. However, the realization of the proposed fiscal-consolidation strategy, revenue target, and expenditure-allocation priorities would depend on the way the Indian economy navigates these challenges as they unfold.

In Chapter 4, Srivastava, Kapur, and Trehan stress the need for fiscal policy to address two major interlinked objectives, namely (i) obtaining the potential growth consistent with full employment of its resources, and (ii) ensuring stability. The chapter discusses the alternative approaches of measuring potential growth rates and the role of available fiscal instruments to increase growth and reduce the volatility in growth. It also analyses the evolution of the Fiscal Responsibility Legislations in India, and their impact on growth and its volatility in the context of the recent global economic slowdown.

1.4.2 Tax Policy Issues

The book's second part addresses Tax Policy Issues. As the GST is a more efficient tax system with its capacity to raise revenues in the most transparent and neutral manner, many countries have adopted this system. But, due to India's complex federal fiscal arrangement, it could only be introduced in 2017. Srivastava and Bharadwaj, in Chapter 5 on 'GST in India: Transition, Experience, and Future Reforms', highlight the main features of indirect taxes in India prior to the introduction of GST, and explain how this system was introduced after a long federal bargaining with a five rate structures. The paper discusses the experience gained during the first five years of the implementation of GST and highlight its revenue inadequacy, continued tax evasion, and high compliance burden, and continuation of the inverted duty structure. Finally, the paper outlines the nature of reforms that are still required to make India's GST a comprehensive modern indirect tax system.

The Indian GST system is a major departure from the systems in other countries in terms of structure and rates. It was decided to provide compensation from the centre to states for an initial five years to deal with revenue shock arising due to this major transition. GST compensation was also a kind of harmonization cost Government of India wanted to make provision for to move to a simplified indirect tax regime. Chapter 6, by Kavita Rao, analyses the impact on GST revenues inclusive of compensation, once the current regime comes to end. It also identifies states which could experience a fall in revenues at the end of the compensation period, and provides alternative mechanisms for smoothing the states' revenue profile.

An important area of concern in public finance is tax expenditure or revenue foregone that arises due to tax exemptions, tax allowances, tax credits and tax deferral. Sacchidananda Mukherjee (Chapter 7) analyses the tax expenditure relating to union taxes from 2005–06 to 2019–20 in India. He shows that the tax expenditures on direct taxes on account of corporate income tax and personal income tax declined from 32.7 per cent of direct tax collection in 2008–09 to 22.4 per cent in 2019–20. At the same time, the tax expenditures related to union excise duty and customs duty declined from 15.2 per cent to 12.6 per cent of tax collection of these taxes. As a result, the overall tax expenditures of the union government declined from 8.15 per cent of gross value added in 2008–09 to 1.69 per cent in 2019–20. In the post-global financial crisis (GFC) period, successive union budgets raised the standard rate of excise duty gradually to a pre-GFC level, pruned down the exemption list, and consolidated the rate structure of excise duty to prepare for the introduction of GST. This helped the government to contain tax expenditures on indirect taxes.

Another area of concern is tax evasion and unaccounted income. Amey Sapre's Chapter 8 deals with these subjects. It analyses the tax-evasion problem by incorporating a simple game-theoretic framework wherein an individual is confronted with the decision of declaring income for taxation. The game-theoretic results show that the probabilities of audit and penalty rate are inversely related and, beyond a threshold penalty rate, the taxpayer has no incentive to evade.

1.4.3 Fiscal Federalism

The third part of this book pertains to the subject of Fiscal Federalism. With India being a Union of States, its Constitution provides transfer of resource from the centre to the states to mitigate vertical and horizontal imbalances. These transfers are consistent with normative considerations of equity and efficiency. Countries like Canada and Australia also follow equalisation. However, none of the Finance Commissions in India have formulated an explicit methodology on a normative basis to determine the fiscal transfers in India. In their contribution (Chapter 9), Rangarajan and Srivastava explain the Canadian system (which focuses on fiscal capacity equalization), and the Australian model (which considers both fiscal capacity and expenditure equalization), and suggest how the equalization objective can be served by the distance criterion, and how the equalization content can be improved by modifying the area criterion in the existing transfer formula.

Following this, M. Govinda Rao (Chapter 10) explains how Indian fiscal federalism fulfils the broad objectives of ensuring a stable and secure macroeconomic environment, providing public services according to diversified preferences, ensuring a nationwide market for commodities and factors of production, ensuring greater accountability in the provision of public services, promoting and regulating markets to accelerate growth, and creating social conditions for proper state of distribution of income and wealth. The chapter also explains how one can draw lessons from the first- and second-generation federalism theories to identify reform areas. It identifies several reform areas, like redesigning the general and specific purpose transfers to ensure horizontal equity, balanced regional development, and overall stability and integrity of the federation.

In Chapter 11, Lekha Chakraborty, Kaur, and Mohanty argue that the emerging literature on *environmental federalism* deals with the fiscally decentralized determination of environmental quality. The 14th FC designed the world's largest ecological fiscal transfers by including net forest cover as one of the criteria along with the other non-ecological variables—population, area, and income distance. The 15th FC also retained the ecological criterion. Using panel data models, this chapter analyses the relationship between total transfers and forest cover, finding that transfers impact positively on forest cover, reflecting that ecological-based transfers are imperative to sustain ecology and improve environmental outcomes in the country.

Srinivasan and Raja Sethu Durai take up the issue that in the federal system, each level of government should have its own revenue resources to sufficiently finance its own expenditures. Vertical fiscal imbalance (VFI) arises when the own-revenue potential of regional governments is inadequate to meet their own expenditure. It adversely affects the fiscal performance of the regional government. Therefore, the authors examine the VFI for India from 2005 to 2021 and provide empirical evidence that it rose over the period, suggesting a feasible solution rests in the reassignment of commodity taxation powers to the states.

1.4.4 Public Financial Management, and Environmental and Climate Finance

The subject for the book's fourth part, namely Public Financial Management, and Environmental and Climate Finance, is another important area in public financial management (PFM). A sound PFM system rests on the principles of fiscal discipline, strategic resource allocation, and result-oriented operational management. Chapter 13, by

Pratap Ranjan Jena, argues that PFM, conventionally, relates more to public expenditure and thereby to the budgeting system. However, it has evolved over the years by incorporating the management of all facets of public funds. This chapter highlights the PFM systems and reform initiatives and developments in India, including the outcome budget, performance-monitoring and evaluation system, medium-term perspective in expenditure planning, FRBM Act, modified cash-management system, changed budget and accounting classification, adoption of accrual accounting, modernization of internal and external audit, and web-based PFM system.

Venkatachalam (Chapter 14) discusses that wetlands act as *natural capital* and supply highly valuable ecosystem services that are utilized for innumerable consumption and production activities. Since most of these services are non-marketed in nature, their economic importance is not known to the policymakers and the general public. This can lead to the wetlands being subjected to *depletion* and degradation, leading to substantial loss of economic welfare. In order to reverse this situation and protect the wetlands, across the globe, many economic valuation studies have been initiated and their results are used to raise awareness of the need to protect wetlands. The author critically reviews some of these studies to assess current economic valuation of wetland ecosystems, the issues involved in generating such values, and how to strengthen future valuation so that governments can formulate evidence-based policies for an efficient, equitable, and sustainable management of this natural resource.

In Chapter 15 Kavi Kumar provides a broad overview of some of the climate extremes (such as cyclones and drought) in India and discusses the management of climate risk from Indian and global perspectives. He also argues that integrating climate-change risks into mainstream policies requires more flexible, preventive, and forward-looking approaches, and will involve significant legal and institutional policy changes. Among various mainstreaming approaches, climate-proofing existing and planned developmental projects has gained importance.[1]

[1] Recently more than 195 countries agreed at the 27th session of the United Nations Framework Convention on Climate Change (COP27) at Sharm el-Sheikh, Egypt, to set up a loss and damage fund to support poor and vulnerable countries that are victims of extreme weather events worsened by the historical cumulative emissions of developed nations.

There are many publicly funded investment projects. Since resources are scare, economic and financial analyses of these projects are essential to improve the resource allocation in terms of economic efficiency. Chapter 16, by Zareena Begum, explains (with illustrations) how to identify project benefits; estimate net incremental benefits and income; and apply decision criteria such as NPV, cost:benefit ratio, and IRR, inputs, and outputs to the financial model. It further argues that the government must consider the financial cost of the project based on these parameters.

Infrastructure finance is important to achieve welfare targets and service-delivery norms. At least a minimum level of investment has to be made in infrastructure to sustain economic growth. Some of the emerging issues in project finance from a public finance perspective are its governance structure, the ability of users to repay, and its impact on the environment and society. Somasundaram's chapter (17) presents an appraisal mechanism to address these issues. It argues that the cost–benefit analysis (CBA) of the project needs to carry out several complex checks, such as credit risk, feasibility study, and risk assessment. It also uses three case studies to illustrate the application of CBA in publicly funded projects.

In the book's last chapter (18), Lekha Chakraborty, Pinaki Chakraborty, and Ruzel Shrestha analyse forecast errors in the revenue receipts and revenue expenditures of India's subnational governments, and empirically show that the forecast errors have been higher in the case of the former than in the latter. The chapter also shows that in more than 20 states, the sources of error are systemic rather than random in the case of most of the macrofiscal variables.

To conclude, this book covers all contemporary issues relating to fiscal policy and public finance management, specifically concerning India. The contributions have come from economist and scholars who had the opportunity to work and learn from the scholarship and contribution made by Dr. Raja J Chelliah. Essays in this book reflects why the Indian public finance system is a fascinating space to understand complexity of fiscal management and fiscal federalism in developing and emerging economies.

References

Chelliah, Raj J. (1960). *Fiscal Policy in Underdeveloped Countries: With Special Reference to India*. George Allen and Unwin Ltd., London.

Musgrave, R. M. (1959). *The Theory of Public Finance*. McGraw Hill, New York.

Rao, Govinda M. (2022). *Studies in Indian Public Finance*. Oxford University Press, Oxford.

I

FISCAL POLICY AND MACROECONOMY

2

Sustainability of Public Debt in India

An Economic Perspective

K. R. Shanmugam

2.1 Introduction

Deficit financing and public debts are important features of the public finance policy of any national or subnational government.[1] When its revenues fall short of its expenditure, the government borrows to finance its excess expenditures. The fiscal deficit in the budget reflects the net borrowing of the government. The public debt is the total stock of debt accumulated over the years. Many economists believe that debt is one way to raise money for development. Borrowing can enable the government to finance important development programmes and projects (Hakura, 2020). In public economics, intergenerational redistribution/distribution is the justification for the 'golden rule' that there are long-term benefits to deficit financing—future generations will enjoy the benefits of today's loan-funded investments, so they will repay the loans.

If a government uses its debt amounts to finance social and infrastructure development projects, which can trigger economic growth and bring higher income in the future, it would be able to service its debt with increased income. In such a case, rising debt is not a concern. This is true for many governments in developed countries with high debt:GDP ratios. For instance, as per the World Bank's World Development Indicators, the five-year (2017–21) average debt:GDP ratio was 244.43 per cent in Japan, 126.04 per cent in Singapore, 117.87 per cent in the United States, and 104.16 per cent in France. But the situation is different

[1] K. R. Shanmugam is Director and Professor, Madras School of Economics, India; email: shanmugam@mse.ac.in.

K. R. Shanmugam, *Sustainability of Public Debt in India* In: *Fiscal Policy and Public Financial Management*. Edited by: Pinaki Chakraborty and K R Shanmugam, Oxford University Press. © Oxford University Press 2024.
DOI: 10.1093/9780198930464.003.0002

in some other countries. They find it difficult to service their debt obligations. Therefore, fiscal/debt sustainability matters.

Public debt is considered sustainable if the government is able to meet all its current and future obligations without external financial assistance or going into default (IMF, 2011). Alternatively, the debt is sustainable if the current level of debt does not exceed the present value of all future primary surpluses (Blanchard et al., 1991). If the debt:GDP ratio exceeds certain prudent limits, it becomes unsustainable, and this will lead to an excessive burden of debt servicing for the future. Excessive debt (i.e. debt overhang) will lead to debt trap, which is bad for growth, development, and stability; it can negatively affect capital stock accumulation and economic growth via heightened long-term interest rates, higher distortionary tax rates, inflation, and a general constraint on countercyclical fiscal policies which may lead to increased volatility and lower growth rates (Rugy and Salmon, 2020). Sometimes, it can cause the borrowing government to default, which can cause it to lose market access and suffer from a higher cost of borrowing.

Debt unsustainability is not a new phenomenon—many economies have faced this issue over the years, including those of East Asia (1997–2001); Russia (1992–97); Latin America (specifically Mexico, Brazil, and Argentina, 1994–2002); Europe (sovereign debt crisis, 2008 onwards); as well as globally (global financial crisis of 2008 (Srinivas, 2018)); with Sri Lanka being a recent example. Moreover, the spread of COVID-19 has not only caused recession in the world economy but also pushed up the overall amount of debt worldwide to unprecedented levels (Kose et al., 2021).

According to the Economic Survey of India (2021–22), the general government (centre and all states together) debt relative to GDP in India would reach 90 per cent at the end of 2022–23 and the centre's debt alone would be 60.2 per cent. While the New Fiscal Responsibility and Budget Management (FRBM) Review Committee suggested a 60 per cent debt:GDP limit for the country (40 per cent for the centre and 20 per cent for all states together), studies indicate that the combined debt of central and state governments in India is unsustainable (Srivastava et al., 2021; Tiwari, 2012).

Against this backdrop, this study briefly discusses the economic perspectives of public debt and reviews relevant empirical studies on public debt sustainability (Section 2.2). Section 2.3 explains the sources and causes of public debt. In Section 2.4 it presents the trend in public debt and compares this with trends in other major fiscal indicators. In Section 2.5 it empirically analyses the debt sustainability issue, and in Section 2.6 it estimates the debt sustainability threshold for India. Section 2.7 examines the economic growth–debt–growth relationship and asks whether debt level is growth-inducing or -reducing. In Section 2.8, the chapter provides a few simulation exercises using debt dynamics equation to find out when India will achieve the debt sustainability target. In Section 2.9 policy strategies are suggested to control debt and reach sustainable debt level in India.

2.2 Literature Review

2.2.1 Theoretical Views

Conceptually, debt sustainability is a situation where the debt does not accumulate at a rate considerably exceeding the government's capacity to service it (IMF, 2011). On the theoretical front, there are three contrasting views on debt/deficit financing in the literature: Ricardian equivalence theorem, Keynesian, and neoclassical.

The Ricardian equivalence theorem view is that fiscal deficit does not matter except for smoothing the adjustment to expenditure or revenue shocks. Higher deficits today are compensated for by higher taxes in the future, so that the total tax burden remains unchanged. Given that households are forward-looking, they will realize that they need to pay higher taxes in the future so that their total tax burden remains unchanged. As a result, they will reduce their consumption and increase savings to meet their future tax burden. This view rests on the intertemporal budget constraint of the government and on the permanent income hypothesis.

The Keynesian view envisages that deficit financing can boost aggregate demand and thereby stimulate economic growth—that is, an increase in government spending financed by borrowing would cause the output to expand through a multiplier process, and financing in this kind predominantly implies a reallocation of resources from taxpayers to bond-holders. Hence, this is beneficial for the economy.

The neoclassical view considers that deficit financing will adversely affect the economy as the component of revenue deficit in the fiscal deficit implies government dissaving, which if not offset by a corresponding increase in private savings will pull down overall savings, exerting pressure on interest rates, which will eventually distort the rate of growth.

Thus, there is no consensus among economists on whether deficit financing is good or bad or neutral (Rangarajan and Srivastava, 2005). It needs to be resolved empirically—that is, it is necessary to examine whether public debt is beneficial or not, and if beneficial then up to what level? However, on the empirical front also, there is no universal agreement on how public debt sustainability can be assessed (Akhmadeev et al., 2018).

2.2.2 Empirical Models

Traditional studies employed the conventional Domar (1944) stability condition: 'As long as the real economic growth (g) is greater than the real interest rate (r), the government can have a positive primary deficit such that its debt will not rise and so the debt is sustainable'. This debt dynamic equation is given as:

$$d_t = p_t + d_{t-1}\left[\frac{(1+r)}{(1+g)}\right] = f_t + d_{t-1}\left[\frac{1}{(1+g)}\right] \tag{2.1}$$

where d_t is the debt:GDP ratio, p_t is the primary balance relative to GDP, and f_t is the fiscal deficit:GDP ratio. When the primary deficit is zero and $r = g$, the debt:GDP ratio remains constant. If $r > g$, the debt:GDP ratio will rise and is unsustainable.

This approach was extended later to consider the intertemporal budget constraint (IBC) of the government (i.e. outstanding debt today must be equal to the current value of future primary surpluses) and also with additional indicators (growth, liquidity, creditworthiness, fiscal burden, fiscal space, etc.) and renamed as the 'indicator approach' (Blanchard et al., 1991; Pattnaik et al., 2003). However, this approach was criticized as it applied the condition on a year-to-year basis and didn't validate whether the IBC of the government is satisfied or not.

The modern empirical approach utilizes statistical/econometric tests. The seminal work of Hamilton and Flavin (1986) introduced the unit root test to check whether the public debt series (in the US) was stationary or not (i.e. whether the series of public debt contains a bubble term), which later was widely adopted to examine the mean reversal process of debt series (Feve and Henin, 2000; Makrydakis et al., 1999; Uctum and Wickens, 2000). Uctum, Thurston, and Uctum (2006) used a unit root test to check debt sustainability in G7 countries, selected Latin American and Asian countries, and found that the debt was sustainable only in G7 countries.

Trehan and Walsh (1991) employed another test to analyse whether a quasi-difference of public debt ($D_t - \nu D_{t-1}$) with $0 \leq \nu < 1 + r$, (where r is the interest rate) is stationary, and whether public debt and primary surpluses (S_t) are cointegrated. If the public debt is quasi-difference stationary and public debt and primary surpluses are cointegrated (or if total expenditure and revenue receipts are cointegrated), then the public debt is sustainable (Greiner and Fincke, 2009).[2] This approach gained popularity and was accepted in the literature (Quintos, 1995; Martin, 2000; Goyal et al., 2004; Lusinyan and Thornton, 2009; Gabriel and Sangduan, 2011).

Despite their wider applicability, the time series approaches were criticized because: (2) the unit root test is very sensitive to structural breaks and the results could be misleading when structural breaks present (Uctum et al., 2006); (2) rejecting a unit root in real debt or in the debt:GDP ratio is a very difficult task; and (3) the IBC may well be satisfied even if the components of the budget are not cointegrated and even if debts or deficits, revenues or spending, are differencing stationary (Bohn, 2007).

To overcome some of these drawbacks, Bohn (1995) constructed a general equilibrium model with a stochastic version of IBC. Following this stochastic framework, in 1998 he formulated a model-based approach to

[2] If total expenditures and revenues establish long run relationship, then they are cointegrated. Since the deviation between these components leads to deficit and debt, the co-integration between total expenditure and revenues is in general consistent with the co-integration between primary balance and public debt.

test whether the primary surplus:GDP ratio (s_t) is positive and, at least, a linearly rising function of the debt:GDP ratio (d_t) as:

$$s_t = \alpha + \psi d_t + \varepsilon_t \tag{2.2}$$

In (2.2), ε is the random error and α and ψ are parameters to be estimated. A positive and statistically significant value of ψ indicates that debt is sustainable.

Later, Bohn (1998) utilized the Barro (1979) tax-smoothing hypothesis according to which public deficits should be used in order to keep tax rates constant, which in turn minimizes the excess burden of taxation. Hence, normal expenditure can be financed by regular revenues, and deficits will be incurred as a result of financing unexpected spending. Based on this, he derived the following fiscal rule or reaction function:

$$s_t = \alpha + \psi d_t + \phi_1 yvar_t + \phi_2 gvar_t + \varepsilon_t \tag{2.3}$$

In (2.3), *yvar* accounts for fluctuations in revenues and reflects the deviation of real GDP from its trend, computed using the Hodrick–Prescott (HP) filter. Positive values for *yvar* indicate booms and negative values indicate recessions. The *gvar* reflects the deviation of real primary spending from its normal value, with positive values indicating expenditures above the normal level and vice versa (Greiner and Fincke, 2009).[3]

This model received greater attention in the literature because of its intuitiveness (i.e. if governments run into debt today, they will have to take corrective actions in the future by increasing the primary surplus) and robust statistical properties (the positive response of primary surplus to public debt implies a mean-reverting process). Accordingly, it was later extended by researchers by adding other determinants of primary balance, incorporating unobserved heterogeneity factors using panel data structures, and specifying non-linearity and time-varying coefficients in the model.

[3] *yvar* and *gvar* are business cycle variables accounting for fluctuations in GDP and primary spending respectively. They are considered as the other determinants of primary surplus.

In the nonlinear context, the Bohn model can be rewritten as:

$$s_t = \alpha + \psi_t d_{t-1} + \phi_1 yvar_t + \phi_2 gvar_t + \varepsilon_t \tag{2.4}$$

In (2.4), the reaction coefficient ψ_t is time-varying. Mathematically, any nonlinear model can be approximated by a linear model with time-varying coefficients. This approximation is good under certain smoothness assumptions. Empirical estimations using these linear approximations employ the popular penalized spline (p-spline) method. The functional forms or smoothness can be shaped by deviation on individual points (i.e. changing points which are termed as knots). To avoid endogeneity issues, Greiner and Fincke (2009) replaced d_t with d_{t-1}.

Ghosh et al. (2013) introduced the concept of 'fiscal fatigue'. This happens when public debt achieves some threshold and departs from this value when the primary balance does not adjust to debt. Therefore, it is essential to test for the responsiveness of primary balance to lagged levels of debt relative to GDP in different regimes, using the threshold regression method. The threshold model allows coefficients (of region-varying variables) to differ across regions. Those regions are identified by a threshold variable being above or below a threshold value. Later, some argue that higher debt amounts may lead to higher growth or welfare if the debt amounts are invested in development projects (Ghosh, 1998; Greiner and Fincke, 2015). They suggest testing whether the public debt is growth-inducing or not (Greiner and Fincke, 2009).

2.2.3 Empirical Studies

Many studies have emerged to verify whether the public debt is sustainable or not in various countries. For instance, Kaur et al. (2014) used the indicator approach to verify the debt sustainability of Indian states; Hakkio and Rush (1991) and Jha and Sharma (2004) analysed sustainability by verifying the cointegrating relationship between public revenue and expenditure.

Abiad and Ostry (2005) employed the Bohn model to test the debt sustainability of 31 emerging market countries from 1990 to 2002. Greiner and Kauermann (2008) used the p-spline method and found that debt is sustainable in Germany but not in Italy. Griener and Fincke (2009) used the Bohn framework and p-spline techniques to analyse the debt sustainability issue of the United States and six European countries (Austria, France, Germany, Italy, the Netherlands, and Portugal) and six developing countries (Botswana, Costa Rica, Mauritius, Panama, Rwanda, and Tunisia. The debt was found to be sustainable in the United States and five of the European countries (apart from France). Of the six developing countries, debt was found to be sustainable only in Botswana and Rwanda.

Tiwari (2012) used the Bohn framework and spline methodology and found that debt was unsustainable in India from 1970 to 2009. Shanmugam and Renjith (2021) used a panel version of Bohn framework and p-spline techniques to test the debt sustainability of 20 Indian states. Lixin (2019) employed threshold estimation and found that from 1985 to 2015, China's public and external debts were both sustainable. Srivastava et al. (2021) estimate the sustainability threshold for the general government debt:GDP ratio for India using a threshold regression, in which the primary balance:GDP ratio (s_t) is the dependent variable and is related to the lagged debt:GDP ratio (region-varying variable) and other determinants of s_t (region invariant variables). It shows a 59.3 per cent threshold level for India. Shanmugam and Shanmugam (2022) show that the sustainable debt threshold limit for Tamil Nadu state is 18.36 per cent. See Afonso (2005), Neck and Sturm (2008), Fincke and Greiner (2011) and D'Erosmo et al. (2016) for a review of empirical studies.

Studies examining the debt–growth relationship at the international, national, and subnational levels provide four alternative conclusions about the effect of debt on economic growth: (1) growth is independent of debt (e.g. Paniza and Presbitero, 2014), (2) growth is a positive function of debt (e.g. Fincke and Greiner, 2015), (3) growth is a negative function of debt (e.g. Hussain et al., 2015), and (4) the relationship between public debt and economic growth is positive when the debt level is low, and negative if the debt exceeds the sustainability threshold (Kumar and Woo, 2010; Megarsa, 2015)—that is, the relationship is nonlinear (Reinhart and Rogoff, 2010). The advantage of the last approach is that it is useful to computing the threshold level of public debt (see Rugy and Salmon for review).[4] Studies such as

[4] The threshold level of debt is obtained from the regression growth rate = $\alpha + \beta$ debt:GSDP + γ debt:GSDP^2 or from threshold regression model.

Bal and Rath (2014) assessed the debt–growth relation in the Indian context for different time periods, and found no uniformity in their results.

2.3 Sources and Causes of Public Debt

India is a federal country with an asymmetric borrowing power to the union and state governments. The central government debt comprises domestic debt (including market loans-dated securities, floating-rate debt, inflation index bonds, treasury bills, 14-day intermediate treasury bills, cash management bills, securities issued to international financial institutions, market-stabilization scheme, compensation and other bonds, and securities against small savings, etc.) and external debt from multilateral agencies like the IDA (International Development Agency), ADB (Asian Development Bank), etc. Public account liabilities are also considered as central debt, which includes NSSF (National Small Savings Fund); provident funds; and reserve funds of railways, post, and telecommunications, etc.

State governments are only allowed to borrow from the domestic market and raise loans and advances from the central government. They have no power to raise loans outside India except loans for externally aided projects intermediated by the central government. The domestic market debt consists of market loans; loans from financial institutions like commercial banks, NABARD, LIC, NCDC, etc.; ways and advances from RBI; and special securities issued to NSSF, etc. Since 2005–06, due to the recommendations of the twelfth Finance Commission (FC), central loans have been discontinued. The public account debt of the state includes small savings, provident funds, reserve funds, deposits bearing interest, deposits not bearing interest, etc. However, financing of the deficit through public accounts is not under the total control of the state governments.[5]

Governments borrow, in general, for various reasons. The relationship between debt and economic growth in complex. If the actual growth is below potential growth (for structural or cyclical reasons), aggregate

[5] Total (or general) government debt is the sum of central and all states' liabilities to domestic and external lenders. However, while calculating the combined debt, the centre's lending to states is netted out to avoid double counting.

demand has to be increased by more public spending. However, the impact of increased spending stimulus depends on how it is financed. If it is financed through high taxes, this will reduce private disposable income, which in turn will reduce private expenditure that will reduce aggregate demand. The net increase in demand is uncertain in this case. Alternatively, it can be financed through additional borrowings. But the source of borrowing matters: if from the RBI, it is less costly but will increase inflation; if from domestic sources, the interest rate may go up; and if from external sources, the exchange rate may increase. Literature also indicated that political cycle also has its impact on deficit and debt. However, the interrelationship between public debt and growth is also country specific and initial condition of debt and deficit matters.

2.4 Public Debt in India

The outstanding liabilities of the General Government of India was Rs 3,50,730 crore in 1990–91, increasing to Rs 7,70,149 crore in 1996–97. It further increased to Rs 32,50,859 crore in 2005–06, Rs 87,99,111 crore in 2014–15, and further to Rs 177,04,031 crore in 2020–21 (Table 2.1). The debt relative to GDP (2011–12 series) was 60.88 per cent in 1990–91 and declined to 55.22 per cent in 1996–97. Government finances have deteriorated since the mid 1990s in India due to reform-induced loss in revenues from customs and excise duties, poor tax performance and low tax buoyancy, and increased government spending, particularly due to the implementation of recommendations of the fifth pay commission. As a result, the debt:GDP ratio increased continuously to reach a peak of 89.5 per cent in 2005–06.

Thereafter, the debt:GDP ratio declined continuously to 70.57 per cent in 2014–15 due to various fiscal measures, including the implementation of the FRBM (Fiscal Responsibility and Budget Management) Act in 2003 by the Government of India and subsequently by all state governments. It again increased to 75.33 per cent in 2019–20. The COVID-19 pandemic created further trouble and it increased further to 89.41 per cent in 2020–21, registering a 14 percentage-point rise (Figure 2.1). The interest relative to revenue receipts increased from

Table 2.1 Major fiscal indicators for (combined states and centre) India (Rs crore).

Year	GDP(2011–12 Series)		Outstanding liabilities	Primary deficit	Interest payment	Primary expenditure	Revenue expenditure	Revenue receipts
	Current	Constant						
1990–91	576109	2514549	350730	27907	25006	130136	122950	99282
1991–92	662260	2541123	393005	14334	30994	146002	143532	121619
1992–93	761196	2680438	451690	14862	35864	162626	159056	135422
1993–94	875992	2807779	536099	27241	42553	184745	183426	147236
1994–95	1027570	2994747	606434	18129	51933	208705	214615	178012
1995–96	1205583	3221584	686953	18484	58944	234242	245635	207170
1996–97	1394816	3464798	770149	15659	69931	257912	282779	234060
1997–98	1545294	3605116	886772	30438	78551	297171	321144	257994
1998–99	1772297	3828072	1092374	63168	92592	357256	385325	274769
1999–00	1988262	4166694	1300228	73231	110051	410034	448445	327085
2000–01	2139886	4326736	1524933	72123	122792	433872	485388	349979
2001–02	2315243	4535456	1807605	78837	140890	478351	536476	379371
2002–03	2492614	4707984	2096449	74232	154399	514184	585107	423008
2003–04	2792530	5078049	2446870	53583	176373	594246	653977	496699
2004–05	3186332	5480380	2848442	40684	192367	641763	700307	587767
2005–06	3632125	5914614	3250859	30797	206390	735048	789337	696285

(*continued*)

Table 2.1 Continued

Year	GDP(2011–12 Series)		Outstanding liabilities	Primary deficit	Interest payment	Primary expenditure	Revenue expenditure	Revenue receipts
	Current	Constant						
2006–07	4254629	6391375	3633520	−12403	233020	862147	921053	870543
2007–08	4898662	6881007	4020630	−49820	249195	999967	1011221	1007221
2008–09	5514152	7093403	4485502	182270	277638	1246362	1290508	1052670
2009–10	6366407	7651078	5035456	293564	317287	1505274	1541724	1175444
2010–11	7634472	8301235	5623574	178449	351145	1765333	1784314	1548424
2011–12	8736329	8736329	6367621	285199	403235	1978199	2017536	1650846
2012–13	9944013	9213017	7136026	225868	457550	2191713	2272152	1933187
2013–14	11233522	9801370	7994883	216506	537468	2415843	2531370	2169193
2014–15	12467959	10527674	8799111	240181	585714	2607080	2707118	2312342
2015–16	13771874	11369493	9926415	302913	650972	3132740	3078890	2732093
2016–17	15391669	12308193	10584410	340256	724448	3541521	3489074	3132201
2017–18	17090042	13144582	11890383	182341	814757	3701189	3838856	3376416
2018–19	18899668	13992914	13330025	208209	894520	4146227	4269986	3797731
2019–20	20074856	14515958	15121885	493430	955801	4455086	4639603	3851563
2020–21	19800914	13558473	17704031	1552626	1082302	5441614	5685265	3834126

Source: For all fiscal variables, Indian Public Finance Statistics till 2015–16 and RBI from 2016–17 onwards. GDP data from MOSPI (NAS).

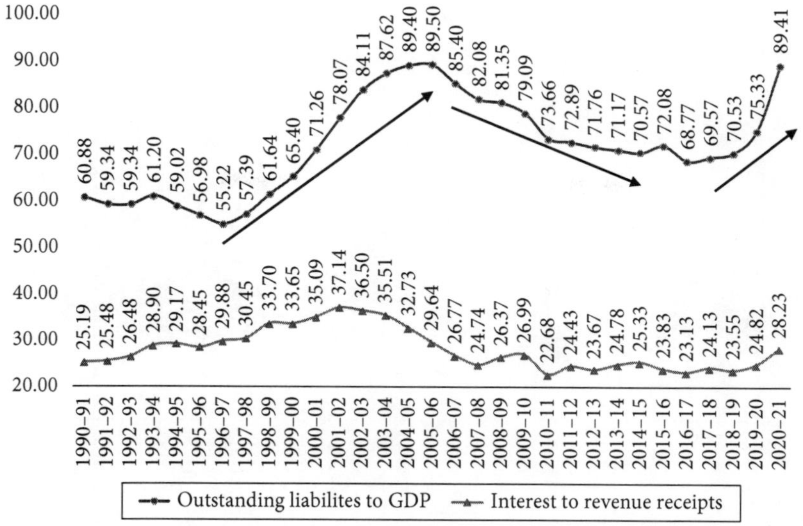

Figure 2.1 Outstanding liabilities to GDP and interest to revenue receipts of India (1990–91 to 2020–21).
Source (basic data): As in Table 2.1.

29.88 per cent in 1996–97 to 37.14 per cent in 2001–02. After that it declined to 22.68 per cent in 2010–11. In 2020–21, it increased to 28.23 per cent (Figure 2.1). The path of interest to revenues clearly indicates that it increased (decreased) whenever the debt:GDP ratio increased (decreased).

The trends in revenue receipts, revenue expenditures, and total expenditures (primary expenditure + interest payment) relative to GDP, as shown in Figure 2.2, explain the movement of the debt:GDP ratio. The gap between the revenue expenditure:GDP ratio and the revenue receipts:GDP ratio was larger from 1996–97 to 2003–04. This was the period when the debt:GDP ratio started increasing continuously. After that, the gap declined till 2007–08 and then started increasing, but still it was less than that during 1996–97 to 2003–04. During this period, the debt:GDP ratio decreased continuously. The gap between revenues and revenue (total) expenditure increased in 2019–20 and again significantly in 2020–21 due to the COVID-19 pandemic. In the pandemic period, the debt:GDP ratio reached 89.41 per cent.

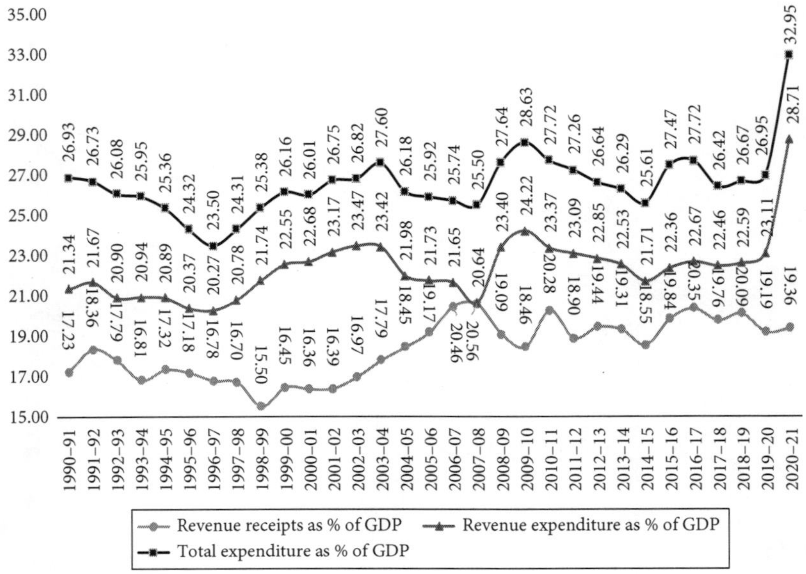

Figure 2.2 Revenue receipts, revenue expenditures and total expenditures relative to GDP in India (1990–91 to 2020–21).

Source (basic data): As in Table 2.1.

It is noticed that GDP (real) growth stagnated between 1996–97 and 2003–04, except in 1999–2000, resulting in increased borrowing. Thereafter, GDP growth picked up and recorded a highest growth of 8.5 per cent in 2010–11 (Figure 2.3). While there was a fall in the growth rate to 4.11 per cent in 2011–12, it then rose continuously to 8.26 per cent in 2016–17. Due to this high growth, which was also supported by austerity measures including the implementation of the FRBM Act, the debt:GDP ratio declined from 89.5 per cent to 68.77 per cent (i.e. it fell by about 20.7 percentage points). After 2016–17 economic growth again slowed, touching the lowest level (–6.6 per cent) in 2020–21 due to the pandemic. During this period, there was a steady increase in debt level, with a sudden spike in 2019–20 and 2020–21. Between 1996–97 and 2002–03 and after 2018–19, revenue receipts growth was low, accentuating the problems of revenue deficit and fiscal deficit (Figure 2.4).

Thus, widening of the fiscal gap is due to prolonged slow economic growth with a consequential fall in revenue receipts. Further

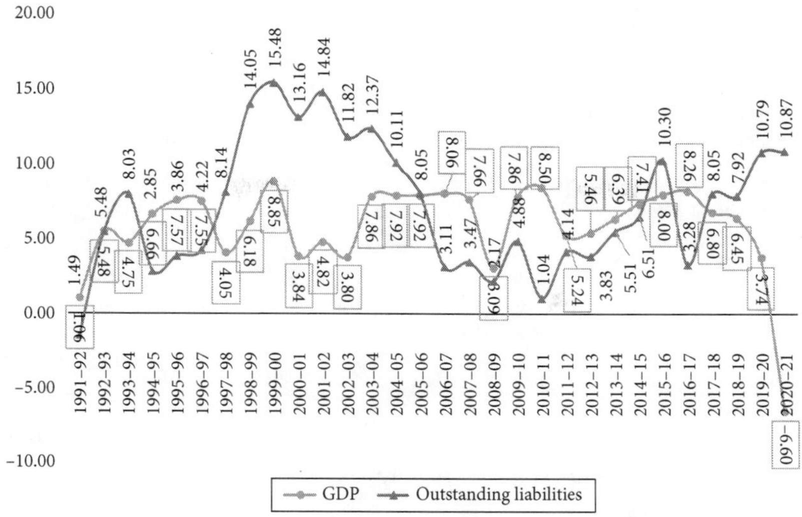

Figure 2.3 Annual growth rates of real GDP and real outstanding liabilities.
Source (basic data): Author's computation using data in Table 2.1.

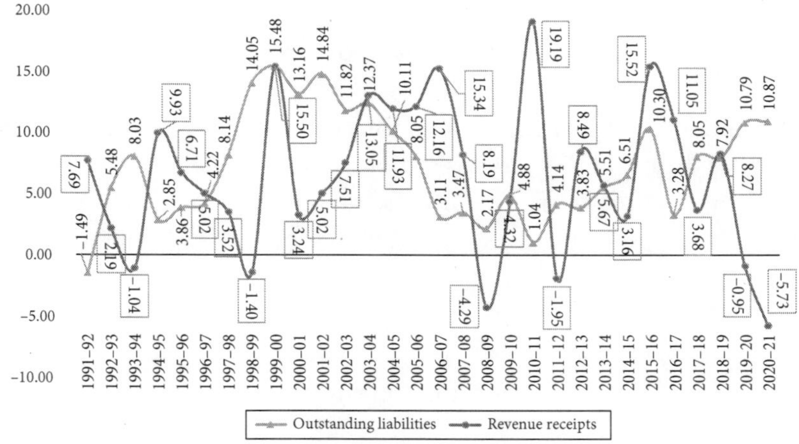

Figure 2.4 Growth rates of real outstanding liabilities and real revenue receipts.
Source (basic data): Author's computation using data in Table 2.1.

restructuring of the debt of power utilities, implementation of GST, the impact of demonetization, and the adverse impact of COVID-19 aggravated the problem. These cumulative effects forced the government (both centre and states) to lend more to fill the gap in the revenue

Table 2.2 Stationary (ADF) test results for debt:GDP ratio (1991–92 to 2020–21).

Augmented Dickey–Fuller test statistics	***t*-statistics**	**Prob.***
	−1.5031	**0.5179**
Test critical values	1 per cent level	−3.679
	5 per cent level	−2.9678
	10 per cent level	−2.6229

Note: *Mackinnon (1996) one-sided p-values.

account. As a result, the interest payment increased. It also seems that the government effort to control revenue expenditures since 2008–09 did not yield results.

2.5 Empirical Tests for Debt Sustainability

2.5.1 Unit Root Test

The simplest modern statistical test on debt sustainability is to check whether the debt:GDP series is stationary or not. Table 2.2 reports the augmented Dickey-Fuller (ADF) test results.[6] The debt:GDP ratio in India has unit root, that is, it is not stationary, indicating that the public debt in India is unsustainable.

2.5.2 Cointegration Test

It examines whether the government revenue and total expenditures relative to GDP are cointegrated or not (Hamilton and Flavin, 1986). Table 2.3 indicates that these two series for combined centre and states governments are not cointegrated at a 5 per-cent level of significance. This means that the debt is not sustainable.

[6] Large accumulation of external debt will severely affect economic growth. However, in India the external debt's share of the total debt is only around 20 per cent. Therefore, this study does not separately analyse external debt sustainability in India.

Table 2.3 Results of Johansen's cointegration (rank) test.*

Unrestricted cointegration rank test (trace)				
Hypothesized no. of CE(s)	**Eigenvalue**	**Trace statistics**	**0.05 Critical value**	**Prob.****
None	0.2609	8.7683	15.4947	0.3873
Atmost 1	0.000009	0.0003	3.8415	0.9889

Note: Trace test indicates no cointegration at 0.05 level; * Max test provides similar results and so not reported. ** Mackinnon (1996) *p*-values.

Table 2.4 *p*-spline estimation results of debt sustainability equation for India (dependent variable: primary deficit to GDP per cent, s_t).

Variables	Notation	Coefficient (*t* value)
Intercept	$\hat{\alpha}$	-8.2350 (-1.633)
Lagged debt:GDP ratio (per cent)	d_{t-1}	0.0687 (1.432)
Real GDP gap	*yvar*	0.000003 (3.553)
Real primary expenditure gap	*gvar*	-0.000008 (-3.375)
edf.		6.38
F (*p*-value)		2.647 (0.028)
R-sq. (adj)		0.787
GCV		0.7849
DW statistics		2.177
N		30

2.5.3 Bohn Model-Based Nonlinear Test

Table 2.4 presents the penalized spline estimation results. As expected, the coefficient of business cycle variable *yvar* (real GDP gap) is positive and that of *gvar* (real primary expenditure gap) is negative. Interestingly, both are statistically significant at a 1 per cent level, indicating that GDP above its normal value has increased the primary surplus in the country while primary spending above its normal value has reduced the primary surplus. As expected, the parameter associated with the lagged debt:GDP ratio is positive, but it is not statistically significant even at a 10 per-cent level, implying that the public debt is unsustainable. Thus, all the three modern statistical tests confirm that the public debt in India is not sustainable.

2.6 Estimating Debt Sustainability Threshold

Table 2.5 presents threshold regression results, in which the lagged debt:GDP ratio (d_{t-1}) is the threshold variable. The sustainable debt:GDP threshold for India is 61.63 per cent, which is slightly higher than the 60 per-cent norm given by new FRBM Review Committee for all India. It is noted that the current level of debt is about 90 per cent of GDP. This is significantly higher than the threshold level. It is observed from Table 2.5 that when debt:GDP increased by one unit, the primary balance increased by about 0.14 unit in region 1 where the debt level was below the threshold and by 0.10 unit in region 2 where the debt exceeded the threshold. *yvar* and *gvar* are regime-invariant variables in this model and their effects are more or less similar to their effects in Table 2.4.

Table 2.5 Threshold regression results (1991–92 to 2020–21).

Dependent variable: primary deficit to GDP per cent (s_t)Threshold variable: lagged debt:GDP ratio per cent (d_{t-1})

Variables	Notation	Coefficient	t-statistics	Prob.
	$d_{t-1} < 61.6361$ (region 1)			
Lagged debt:GDP ratio	d_{t-1}	0.1359	4.7209	0.0001
	$61.6361 \leq d_{t-1}$ (region 2)			
Lagged debt:GDP ratio	d_{t-1}	0.1028	4.6876	0.0001
Region-invariant variables				
Real GDP gap	*yvar*	0.000003	4.7811	0.0001
Real primary expenditure gap	*gvar*	-0.00001	-5.1219	0.00001
Constant	$\hat{\alpha}$	-10.1812	-6.0897	0.00001
Sum squared resid.	SSR	15.442		
Akaike info. criterion	AIC	2.507		

2.7 Examining Debt–Growth Relationship and Debt Threshold

To examine the impact of debt:GDP ratio on (real) growth of economy, the growth rate in percentage is regressed on debt:GDP and its squared term. This nonlinear form is useful to find out the debt threshold, a value up to this debt:GDP ratio is growth-inducing and beyond this it is growth-reducing. Figure 2.5 depicts the nonlinear relation between growth and debt:GDP for India from 1991–92 to 2020–21. The debt:GDP coefficient is positive, while its squared term's coefficient is negative. The threshold level is computed using the formula: threshold = coefficient of debt:GDP / 2 × coefficient of debt:GDP^2 = 0.762 / 2 × 0.006) = 63.5 per cent, which is closer to the debt sustainability threshold value of 61.6 per cent given in the threshold regression model (Table 2.5).

2.8 Simulation Model Examining the Period of Attaining the Debt Threshold Target

As the current level of debt in India is unsustainable and higher than the debt sustainability threshold level of 61.6 per cent, there is a greater need

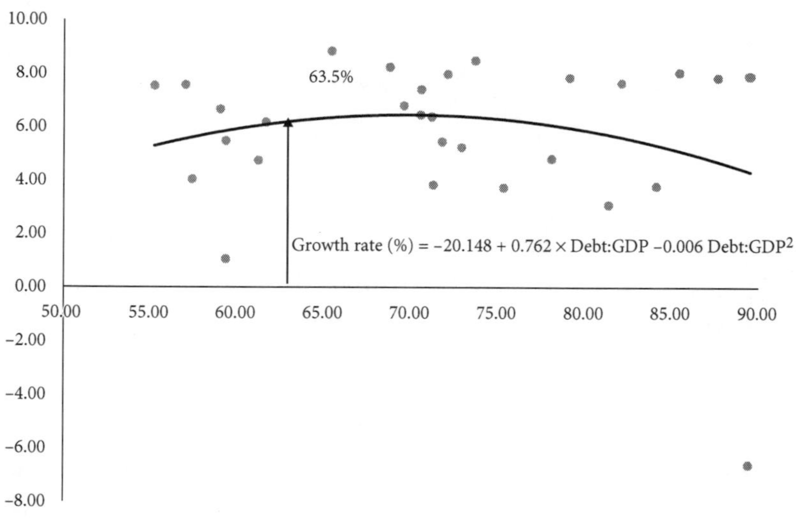

Figure 2.5 Debt threshold for India (1991–92 to 2020–21).
Source (basic data): As in Table 2.1.

to cut down the country's debt ratio by about one third. This section examines whether or not India will achieve a sustainable level of debt, and if it does, when? For this purpose, following debt dynamic equation given in (2.1) defines

$$d_t = f_t + d_{t-1}\left[\frac{1}{(1+g)}\right]$$

In the above equation, the debt:GDP ratio (d_t) at the end of a fiscal year depends on (1) fiscal deficit:GDP ratio (f_t), (2) last year's debt:GDP ratio (d_{t-1}), and (3) nominal growth rate (g_t). Subtracting d_{t-1} on both sides, we get:

$$d_t - d_{t-1} = f_t + d_{t-1}\left[\frac{1}{(1+g)}\right] - d_{t-1} = f_t - d_{t-1}\left[\frac{g}{(1+g)}\right]$$

The left side is the change in debt:debt ratio between two successive years (i.e. between year t and previous year $t-1$).

Using this standard debt dynamic formula, we project or simulate the future debt:GDP level, given assumptions on f_t and g_t and previous year debt (d_{t-1}). We have done a few simulation exercises using different assumptions on these three components to estimate when India will achieve the sustainable level of debt. The following initial values of debt to GDP, fiscal deficit, and nominal growth of the Indian economy from the recent RBI and MOSPI data are used: (1) debt:GDP ratio for 2020–21: 89.41 per cent; (2) fiscal deficit for 2021–22: 13.307 per cent and for 2022–23: 9.62 per cent; and (3) nominal growth for 2021–22: 19.51 per cent.

In fact, the average real GDP growth was 6.31 per cent during 2016–17 to 2019–20, 6.41 per cent during 2011–12 to 2019–20 and 6.8 per cent during 2004–05 to 2019–20 (Table 2.6). From 2004–05 to 2010–11, the average rate was 7.29 per cent and from 2009-10 to 2016-17 it was 7.14 per cent. Thus, the recent trend indicates 6 to 7 per cent average (real) growth of the Indian economy. Assuming an inflation of 4 per cent, the nominal growth will be 10–11 per cent. While in recent years both centre and state governments could not comply with the FRBM norm of a 3 per cent fiscal deficit level, for the purpose of estimation 6 per cent fiscal deficit can be assumed.

Table 2.6 Average annual GDP (real) growth in India.

Period	2017–18 to 2020–21	2016–17 to 2020–21	2016–17 to 2019–20	2011–12 to 2019–20	2004–05 to 2019–20	2004–05 to 2010–11	2009–10 to 2016–17
GDP growth	2.60	3.73	6.31	6.41	6.80	7.29	7.14

Source: Computed by author using data in Table 2.1.

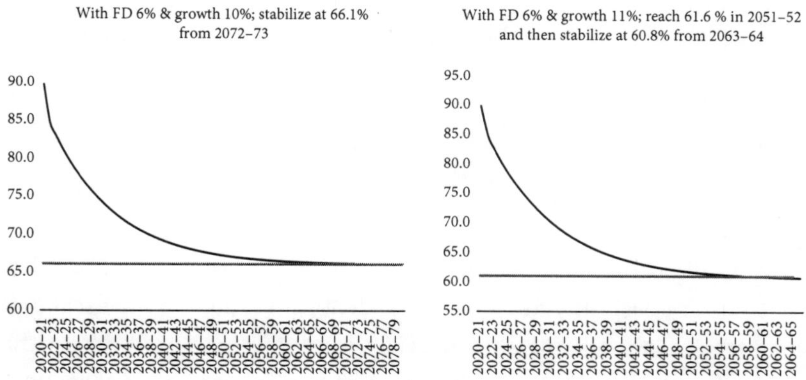

Figure 2.6 Simulation results of debt:GDP ratio, given f_t, g_t, and $d_{t\text{-}1}$.
Source: Author's estimation.

In exercise 1, the nominal annual growth rate is assumed to be 10 per cent from 2022–23 onwards and the fiscal deficit is assumed at 6 per cent from 2022–23 onwards. In exercise 2, the nominal growth of 11 per cent is used; other things remain the same. Simulations based on the above debt dynamics formula (exercise 1) indicate that the debt:GDP ratio will continuously decline every year and reach 66.1 per cent in 2072–73, and then it will stabilize at this level till 2077–78. After that, it will stabilize at 66 per cent and will not reduce further, even after 100 years (Figure 2.6). In exercise 2, the debt:GDP will continuously decline and reach the sustainability threshold level of 61.6 per cent in 2051–52 (i.e. after 30 years).

In exercise 3, when a still higher growth of 12 per cent is used from 2022–23, the debt:GDP ratio will continuously decrease to reach 61.6 per cent in 2036–37 (i.e. after 14 years) and will continue to decline to 56 per

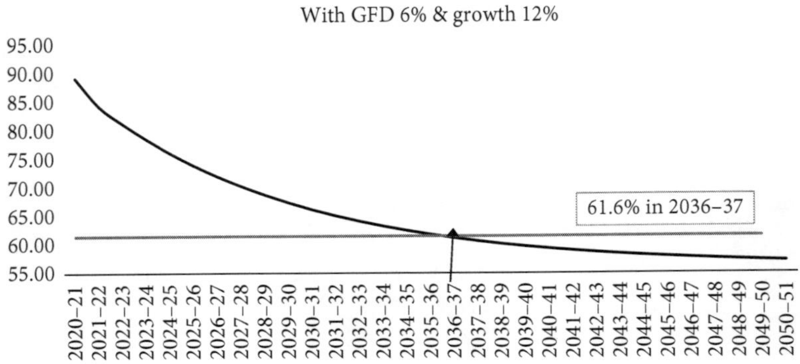

Figure 2.7 Simulation results of debt:GDP ratio, given f_t, d_{t-1}, and $g_t = 12$ per cent.

Source: author's estimation.

cent in 2036–37, and thereafter it will stabilize (Figure 2.7). Beyond 12 per cent growth is a difficult and highly ambitious task, given the historical growth path.

Another possibility for controlling debt is to reducing the fiscal deficit target. If we assume a 5 per cent fiscal target (2.5 per cent for the centre and 2.5 per cent for all states) and 10 per cent nominal growth, the debt:GDP will continuously decline and will reach 61.4 per cent in 2037–38 (Table 2.7). If we assume a 4 per cent fiscal deficit (2 per cent for the centre and 2 per cent for all states), the debt sustainability threshold will be achieved in 2030–31 (Table 2.7). With 11 per cent nominal growth and 5 per cent fiscal deficit, the sustainable debt target will be attained in 2032–33 and with 11 per cent nominal growth and 4 per cent fiscal deficient, it will be achieved in 2028–29—that is, within six years (not shown). When we assume 12 per cent growth, then the sustainable level of debt will be achieved in 2030–31 with a 5 per cent fiscal deficit target and in 2027–28 with a 4 per cent fiscal target (not shown).

Thus, India needs a higher growth strategy and a reduction in fiscal deficit target. Ensuring 10 (11) per cent (nominal) growth of the economy, the country should target a revenue surplus from 2022–23 onwards such that it contains its fiscal deficit to only a 4 per cent level to obtain the sustainable debt level of about 61.6 per cent in 2030–31 (2028–29).

Table 2.7 Simulation results to achieve the sustainable debt:GSDP ratio.

Year	10 per cent growth and 5 per cent fiscal deficit					10 per cent growth and 4 per cent fiscal deficit				
	f_t	d_t	g_t	$1+g_t$	d_t-d_{t-1}	f_t	d_t	g_t	$1+g_t$	d_t-d_{t-1}
2020–21	13.3071	89.4	−1.365	−0.365	13.3071	13.307	89.4	−1.3646	−0.3646	13.3071
2021–22	9.62	84.4	0.1951	1.1951	−4.97618	9.62	84.4	0.1951	1.1951	−4.97618
2022–23	5	81.8	0.1	1.1	−2.6758	4	80.8	0.1	1.1	−3.6758
2023–24	5	79.3	0.1	1.1	−2.43255	4	77.4	0.1	1.1	−3.34164
2024–25	5	77.1	0.1	1.1	−2.21141	4	74.4	0.1	1.1	−3.03785
2025–26	5	75.1	0.1	1.1	−2.01037	4	71.6	0.1	1.1	−2.76168
2026–27	5	73.3	0.1	1.1	−1.82761	4	69.1	0.1	1.1	−2.51062
2027–28	5	71.6	0.1	1.1	−1.66146	4	66.8	0.1	1.1	−2.28238
2028–29	5	70.1	0.1	1.1	−1.51042	4	64.7	0.1	1.1	−2.07489
2029–30	5	68.7	0.1	1.1	−1.37311	4	62.9	0.1	1.1	−1.88627
2030–31	5	67.5	0.1	1.1	−1.24828	**4**	**61.1**	**0.1**	**1.1**	**−1.71479**
2031–32	5	66.3	0.1	1.1	−1.1348					
2032–33	5	65.3	0.1	1.1	−1.03164					
2033–34	5	64.4	0.1	1.1	−0.93785					
2034–35	5	63.5	0.1	1.1	−0.85259					
2035–36	5	62.8	0.1	1.1	−0.77508					
2036–37	5	62.0	0.1	1.1	−0.70462					
2037–38	**5**	**61.4**	**0.1**	**1.1**	**−0.64057**					

Source: Author’s estimation.

2.9 Strategies to Control Debt and Reach a Sustainable Level

The analyses suggest the following policy viewpoints:

1. Although the current level of debt:GSDP (i.e. about 90 per cent) is within the limit set by the Fifteenth Finance Commission considering the pandemic, it is not a sustainable debt level for India. Our analysis clearly indicates that a debt level beyond 63.5 per cent is growth-reducing. Maintaining a sustainable level of debt will be growth-inducing, which will help the country to increase its own revenues further, if they are buoyant.
2. Reducing the debt level to a sustainable level will also bring down the cost of debt servicing due to reduced interest payments. From Figure 2.1, it is observed that in 2016–17, the debt:GDP ratio was about 68.7 per cent and the interest (Rs 7,24,448 crore) to revenue receipts was 23.13 per cent (i.e. 4.7 per cent of GDP). When the debt:GDP increased to 89.41 per cent in 2020–21, the interest (Rs 10,82,302 crore) to revenue receipts increased to 28.23 per cent (i.e. 5.5 per cent of GDP). The difference in interest is Rs 3,57,854 crore. Thus, reduction of the debt:GDP ratio will automatically reduce the interest relative to GDP.
3. The country should aim to attain a 12 per cent or above nominal growth rate. Higher buoyancy in tax revenues and additional resources to control the debt level would require critical sectoral growth enhancing strategies to to increase revenue mobilisation.
4. Apart from aiming for higher growth, debt sustainability is possible only if the fiscal deficit is brought down to 4 per cent of GDP from 2023–24 onwards. The centre's fiscal deficit should not exceed 2 per cent of GDP and all states' fiscal deficit should not exceed 2 per cent. The appropriate policy strategy is revenue augmentation or containing expenditures including unproductive subsidies.
5. Considering the fact that the Public Sector Undertakings are already fiscally stressed, it is absolutely necessary to restructure their finances so that debt sustainably is achieved.

We hope that this study is useful to policymakers and other stakeholders, helping them to understand the debt dynamic in India and take appropriate policy strategies, in order to attain and maintain debt sustainability so that the economy can grow faster and fiscal stability is maintained.

References

Abiad, M. A., and Ostry, M. J. D. (2005). 'Primary Surpluses and Sustainable Debt Levels in Emerging Market Countries'. *IMF Policy Discussion Paper*, 5(6), 3–18.

Afonso, A. (2005). 'Fiscal Sustainability: The Unpleasant European Case'. *FinanzArchiv/ Public Finance Analysis*, 61(1), 19–44.

Akhmadeev, R. G., Bykanova, O. A., and Turishcheva, T. B. (2018). 'Brics' Foreign Debt Burden and Its Impact on Core Institutional Basis'. *Journal of Reviews on Global Economics*, 7, 345–359.

Bal, D. P., and Rath, B. N. (2014). 'Public Debt and Economic Growth in India: A Reassessment'. *Economic Analysis and Policy*, 44(3), 292–300.

Barro, R. J. (1979). 'On the Determination of the Public Debt'. *Journal of Political Economy*, 87(5, Part 1), 940–971.

Blanchard, O. J., Chouraqui, J. C., Hagemann, R., et al. (1991). *The Sustainability of Fiscal Policy: New Answers to an Old Question* (NBER Working Paper, R1547), National Bureau of Economic Research, Cambridge.

Bohn, H. (1995). 'The Sustainability of Budget Deficits in a Stochastic Economy'. *Journal of Money, Credit and Banking*, 27(1), 257–271.

Bohn, H. (1998). 'The Behavior of US Public Debt and Deficits'. *Quarterly Journal of Economics*, 113(3), 949–963.

Bohn, H. (2007). 'Are Stationarity and Cointegration Restrictions Really Necessary for the Intertemporal Budget Constraint?' *Journal of Monetary Economics*, 54(7), 1837–1847.

D'Erosmo, P., Mendoza, E. G., and Zhang, Jing (2016). 'What is Sustainable Public Debt?' *Handbook of Macroeconomics* 2: 2493–2597.

Domar, E. D. (1944). 'The Burden of the Debt and the National Income'. *American Economic Review*, 34(4),798–827.

Feve, P., and Henin, P. (2000). 'Assessing Effective Sustainability of Fiscal Policy within the G-7'. *Oxford Bulletin of Economics and Statistics*, 62, 75–195.

Fincke, B., and Greiner, A. (2011). 'Debt Sustainability in Germany: Empirical Evidence for Federal States'. *International Journal of Sustainable Economy*, 3(2), 235–254.

Fincke, B., and Greiner, A. (2015). 'Public Debt and Economic Growth in Emerging Market Economies'. *South African Journal of Economics*, 83(3), 357–370.

Gabriel, V. J., and Sangduan, P. (2011). 'Assessing Fiscal Sustainability Subject to Policy Changes: A Markov Switching Cointegration Approach'. *Empirical Economics*, 41, 371–385.

Ghosh, A. R., Kim, J. I., Mendoza, E. G., et al. (2013). *Fiscal Fatigue, Fiscal Space and Debt Sustainability in Advanced Economies* (NBER Working paper 16782), National Bureau of Economic Research, Cambridge.

Ghosh, S. (1998). 'Can Higher Debt Lead to Higher Welfare? A Theoretical and Numerical Analysis'. *Applied Economic Letters*, 5 (2) 111–116.

Goyal, R., Khundrakpam, J. K., and Ray, P. (2004). 'Is India's Public Finance Unsustainable? Or, Are the Claims Exaggerated?' *Journal of Policy Model*, 26, 401–420.

Greiner, A., and Fincke, B. (2009). *Public Debt and Economic Growth* (vol. 11). Springer Science and Business Media.

Greiner, A., and Fincke, B. (2015). *Public Debt, Sustainability and Economic Growth*. Springer International Publishers.

Greiner, A., and Kauermann, G. (2008). 'Debt Policy in Euro Area Countries: Evidence for Germany and Italy Using Penalized Spline Smoothing'. *Economic Modelling*, 25(6), 1144–1154.

Hakkio, C. S., and Rush, M. (1991). 'Is the Budget Deficit Too Large?' *Economic Inquiry*, 29, 429–445.

Hakura, Dalla (2020). 'What Is Debt Sustainability?' *Finance & Development*, September, IMF's Strategy, Policy and Review Department, 60–61. https://www.imf.org/en/Publications/fandd/issues/2020/09/what-is-debt-sustainability-basics.

Hamilton, J., and Flavin, M. (1986). 'On the Limitations of Government Borrowing: A Framework for Empirical Testing'. *American Economic Review*, 76(4), 808–819.

Hussain, M. E., Haque, M., and Igwike, R. S. (2015). 'Relationship Between Economic Growth and Debt: An Empirical Analysis for Sub-Saharan Africa'. *Journal of Economics and Political Economy*, *2*(2), 262.

IMF (2011). *Modernizing the Framework for Fiscal Policy and Public Debt Sustainability Analysis* (IMF policy papers), Washington, DC.

Jha, R., and Sharma, A. (2004). 'Structural Breaks, Unit Roots, and Cointegration: A Further Test of the Sustainability of the Indian Fiscal Deficit'. *Public Finance Review* 32(2), 196–219.

Kaur, B., Mukherjee, A., Kumar, N., et al. (2014). 'Debt Sustainability at the State Level in India'. *Indian Economic Review*, 53, 93–129.

Kumar, M. and Woo, J. (2010) *Public Debt and Growth* (IMF Working Papers, no. 10/174), International Monetary Fund, Washington, DC.

Kose, M. A., Ohnsorge, F., and Sugawara, N. (2021). *A Mountain of Debt: Navigating the Legacy of the Pandemic*. World Bank Document.

Lixin, Sun (2019). 'The Structure and Sustainability of China's Debt'. *Cambridge Journal of Economics*, 43(3), 695–715.

Lusinyan, L., and Thornton, J. (2009). 'The Sustainability of South African Fiscal Policy: An Historical Perspective'. *Applied Economics*, 41(7), 859–868.

MacKinnon, J. G. (1996). 'Numerical Distribution Functions for Unit Root and Cointegration Tests'. *Journal of Applied Econometrics*, Vol.11, 601–618.

Makrydakis, S., Tzavalis, E., and Balfoussias, A. (1999). 'Policy Regime Changes and the Long-run Sustainability of Fiscal Policy: An Application to Greece'. *Economic Modelling*, 16, 71–86.

Martin, G. (2000). US Deficit Sustainability: 'A New Approach Based on Multiple Endogenous Breaks'. *Journal of Applied Econometrics*, 15, 83–105.

Megarsa, K. A. (2015). 'The Laffer Curve and the Debt–Growth Link in Low-income Sub-Saharan African Economies'. *Journal of Economic Studies*, 42(5), 878–892.

Neck, R., and Sturm, J. E. (2008). 'Sustainability of Public Debt: Introduction and Overview', in R. Neck and J. E. Sturm (eds.) *Sustainability of Public Debt*, MIT Press, Cambridge, MA, 1–13.

Panizza, U., and Presbitero, A. F. (2014). 'Public Debt and Economic Growth: Is there a Causal Effect?' *Journal of Macroeconomics*, 41, 21–41.

Pattnaik, R. K., Prakash, A., and Mishra, B. S. (2003). *Sustainability of Public Debt in India: An Assessment in the Context of Fiscal Rules* (in 6th Workshop on Public Finance, Bank of Italy, Italy, 679–735).

Quintos, C. (1995). 'Sustainability of the Deficit Process with Structural Shifts'. *Journal of Business & Economic Statistics*, 13(4), 409–417.

Rangarajan, C., and Srivastava, D. K. (2005). 'Fiscal Deficits and Government Debt: Implications for Growth and Stabilization'. *Economic and Political Weekly*, 40(27), 2919–2933.

Reinhart, C. M., and Rogoff, K. (2010). 'Growth in a Time of Debt'. *American Economic Review: Papers and Proceedings*, no.100, 573–578.

Rugy, V., and Salmon, J. (2020). *Debt and Growth: A Decade of Studies.* Policy Brief, Mercatus Centre, George Mason University, Fairfax, VA.

Shanmugam, K. R. and Renjith, P. S. (2021). 'Empirical Analysis on Sustainability of Public Debt in Indian States'. *London Journal of Research in Humanities and Social Studies*, 21(10), 31–45.

Shanmugam, K. R. and Shanmugam, K. (2022). *Sustainability and Threshold Value of Public Debt in Tamil Nadu* (Madras School of Economics, Working Paper no. 226) Chennai, India.

Srinivas,V. (2018). Major Financial Crisis from Great Depression to Great Recession. chrome-extension://efaidnbmnnnibpcajpcglclefindmkaj/https://taxboard.rajasthan.gov.in/images/MAJOR_FINANCIAL_CRISIS_2OTH_CENTURY.pdf.

Srivastava, D. K., Bharadwaj, M., Kapur, T., et al. (2021). 'Examining Sustainability of Government Debt in India: Post COVID Prospects'. *Journal of Advanced Studies in Finance*, 12(1): 51–62. DOI: 10.14505/jasf.v12.1(23).05.

Tiwari, A. K. (2012). 'Debt Sustainability in India: Empirical Evidence Estimating Time-varying Parameters'. *Economics Bulletin*, 32(2), 1133–1141.

Trehan, B., and Walsh, C. E. (1991). 'Testing Intertemporal Budget Constraints: Theory and Applications to US Federal Budget and Current Account Deficits'. *Journal of Money, Credit and Banking*, 23(2), 206–223.

Uctum, M., and Wickens, M. (2000). 'Debt and Deficit Ceilings, and Sustainability of Fiscal Policies: An Intertemporal Analysis'. *Oxford Bulletin of Economics and statistics*, 62, 197–222.

Uctum, M., Thurston, T., and Uctum, R. (2006). 'Public Debt, the unit Root Hypothesis and Structural Breaks: A Multi-country Analysis'. *Economica*, 73(289), 129–156.

3

Post-COVID Economic Recovery, Macroeconomic Uncertainties, and Fiscal Responsibility

Pinaki Chakraborty

3.1 Introduction

While the global economy is battling the economic shock due to the COVID-19 pandemic, the wars between Russia and Ukraine, and Palestine and Israel, have increased global macroeconomic uncertainties manifold.[1] A recent blog (Gudmundsson2022) published by the IMF notes that inflation 'has been higher than expected in many economies, while financial markets remain volatile and geopolitical tensions have increased'.[2] It further notes that with reduced growth momentum, 'the world needs strong international cooperation to end the pandemic, navigate monetary tightening and shift focus to fiscal sustainability'.[3] The likely impact of the wars on emerging market economies including India will only be known as they unfold. The war between Palestine and Israel has increased geo-political tension in West Asia. Recently, the IMF's Deputy Managing Director, while speaking on the future of the international monetary system, observed that

[1] This chapter is an updated and revised version of the article published in the Special Issue of *Economic and Political Weekly*, on the Union Budget 2022–23, dated 26 March 2022, edited by Pinaki Chakraborty.

[2] https://blogs.imf.org/2022/02/24/economic-indicators-signal-diminished-growth-momentum-at-start-of-year/ (accessed 17 February 2024).

[3] https://blogs.imf.org/2022/02/24/economic-indicators-signal-diminished-growth-momentum-at-start-of-year/ (accessed 17 February 2024).

Pinaki Chakraborty, *Post-COVID Economic Recovery, Macroeconomic Uncertainties, and Fiscal Responsibility*
In: *Fiscal Policy and Public Financial Management*. Edited by: Pinaki Chakraborty and K R Shanmugam,
Oxford University Press. © Oxford University Press 2024. DOI: 10.1093/9780198930464.003.0003

> After years of shocks—including the COVID-19 pandemic and Russia's invasion of Ukraine—countries are reevaluating their trading partners based on economic and national security concerns. Foreign direct investment flows are also being redirected along geopolitical lines. Some countries are reevaluating their heavy reliance on the dollar in their international transactions and reserve holdings.
>
> All of this is not necessarily bad. Given the recent history of events, policymakers are increasingly—and justifiably—focused on building economic resilience. But if the trend continues, we could see a broad retreat from global rules of engagement and, with it, a significant reversal of the gains from economic integration.[4]

Alfred Kammer et al. (2022) dated 15 March 2022,[5] mentioned that the impact on the global economy will flow through three channels:

> One, higher prices for commodities like food and energy will push up inflation further, in turn eroding the value of incomes and weighing on demand. Two, neighbouring economies to Ukraine and Russia will grapple with disrupted trade, supply chains, and remittances as well as a historic surge in refugee flows. And three, reduced business confidence and higher investor uncertainty will weigh on asset prices, tightening financial conditions and potentially spurring capital outflows from emerging markets.

We recognize that realization of the proposed fiscal consolidation strategy, revenue target, and expenditure-allocation priorities accorded in the Union Budget 2022–23 would depend on the way the Indian economy navigates these challenges as they unfold. In this chapter, I give an overview of the macrofiscal issues emerging in light of the Union Budget 2022–23, discussing economic recovery, the availability of fiscal space, issues related to revenue versus capital spending, and fiscal rule in times of economic uncertainty.

[4] https://www.imf.org/en/News/Articles/2024/05/07/sp-geopolitics-impact-global-trade-and-dollar-gita-gopinath

[5] https://blogs.imf.org/2022/03/15/how-war-in-ukraine-is-reverberating-across-worlds-regions/ (accessed: 17 February 2024).

3.2 Fiscal Rules in Times of Economic Uncertainty

The general government debt[6] to GDP ratio for the advanced economies is hovering around 120 per cent of GDP (See Figure 3.1). For the emerging and middle-income economies, the ratio is around 60 per cent. It increased to around 90 per cent of GDP for India. Though the debt:GDP ratio stabilized during the fiscal year 2021, the IMF Fiscal Monitor (2021) observed that 'The pandemic will leave a lasting mark on government finances, inequality, poverty, and the level of GDP in many countries'. It further noted that 'following this one-time jump, debt in the coming years is expected to remain persistently higher than the levels projected before the pandemic—in advanced economies it is projected to be almost 20 percentage points higher through 2026'.

This increase in the debt:GDP ratio across countries resulted in a reassessment of conventional wisdom on fiscal rule and accumulation of public debt. In a recent paper, Ardanaz et al. (2021) observed that in 75 advanced and emerging economies

> with either no fiscal rule or with a rigid fiscal rule, a fiscal consolidation of at least 2 percent of GDP is associated with an average 10 percent reduction in public investment. Instead, in countries with flexible fiscal rules, the negative effect of fiscal adjustments on public investment vanishes, which implies that flexible rules protect public investment during consolidation episodes.

Blanchard et al. (2021) state that 'The European Union's fiscal rules have been suspended until at least the end of 2021. When they are reinstated, they will need to be modified, if only because of the high levels of debt. Proposals have been made—and more are to come— suggesting various changes and simplifications.' They go on to discuss 'how one should think about debt sustainability in the current and likely future EU economic environment'. According to Oliver et al. (2021), it is an illusion

[6] General government consists of all government units and all nonmarket non-profit institutions that are controlled by government units (IMF Fiscal Monitor, 2021).

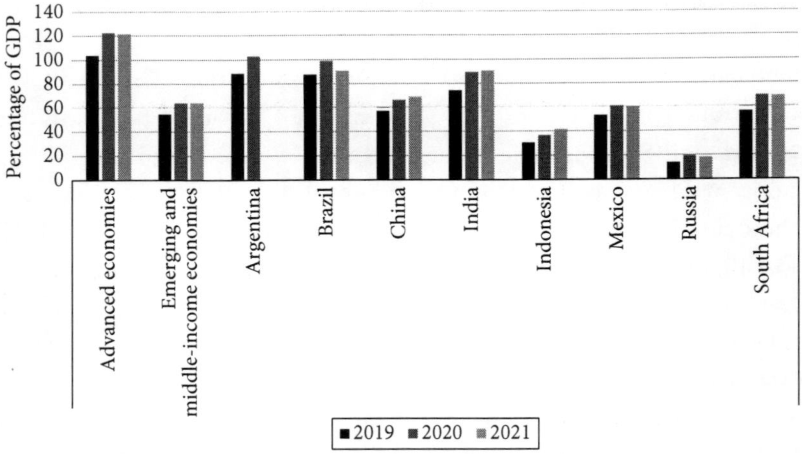

Figure 3.1 General government debt (percentage of GDP).
Source: IMF Fiscal Monitor, April 2021. (https://www.imf.org/en/Publications/FM/Issues/2021/03/29/fiscal-monitor-april-2021, accessed 17 February 2024).

to think that EU fiscal rules can be simple. But it is also an illusion to think that they can ever be complex enough to accommodate most relevant contingencies. This leads us to propose the abandonment of fiscal rules in favor of fiscal standards, i.e., qualitative prescriptions that leave room for judgment together with a process to decide whether the standards are met. Central to this process would be country-specific assessments using stochastic debt sustainability analysis, led by national independent fiscal councils and/or the European Commission.

Gbohoui and Medas (2021) argued that

> The COVID-19 pandemic and the global economic contraction will put rule-based fiscal frameworks to the test. The severity of the shock will likely result in a temporary large deterioration in the fiscal deficit and public debt. Many countries are already activating escape clauses to deviate or suspend the fiscal rules. It will be important to ensure the use of this flexibility is temporary and done transparently, including explaining the size of the deviation and process to return to the rule, to preserve the credibility of the fiscal framework.

The Government of India's Economic Survey 2020–21 (2021) observed that 'Amidst the Covid-19 crisis, fiscal policy has assumed enormous significance across the world. Naturally, the debate around higher Government debt to support a fiscal expansion is accompanied by concerns about its implications for future growth, debt sustainability, sovereign ratings, and possible vulnerabilities on the external sector.' The Survey further noted that 'For India and other EMEs, which have consistently grown their GDP at high rates over the last few decades, the relationship between debt and growth exhibits a clear direction of causality: Higher growth lowers debt-to-GDP ratios but lower debt does not necessarily lead to higher growth.'

3.3 Economic Recovery, Uncertainties, and Fiscal Space

The preceding discussion shows that post-COVID fiscal consolidation is emerging as a major issue as countries deal with large deficits and debt, high inflation, and uneven economic recovery. Though in the short run flexibility for the creation of fiscal space needs to be provided through higher borrowing, when we take a medium-term view there is a need to return to a sustainable fiscal management for macro-stability and growth (Chakraborty, 2021). Though the economic shock in terms of GDP contraction due to the COVID-19 pandemic reversed in the fiscal year 2021–22, a stable and sustained recovery is needed. The Medium-Term Fiscal Policy cum Fiscal Policy Strategy Statement presented as a part of the Union Budget 2022–23 mentioned that

> in line with the commitment made in the budget for FY 2021–22, the Government would pursue a broad path of fiscal consolidation to attain a level of fiscal deficit lower than 4.5 per cent of GDP by FY 2025–26. The Government would continue with its efforts to attain sustained, broad based economic growth, and take such measures as

may be necessary to protect the lives/livelihoods of the people, while adhering to the path of fiscal rectitude.

The Monthly Economic Report (MER), for February 2022, published by the Department of Economic Affairs, Ministry of Finance, observed that 'The Geo-political Crisis is still evolving and these are early days to make a plausible forecast of its impact on India's economy year ahead'.[7] However, the MER draws optimism from the upturn in GST revenues and improvement in the performance of various high-frequency data on the economy, and stable and sustainable balance-of-payment account and significant foreign exchange reserves. All these should, according to the MER, act as a cushion to deal with the uncertainties induced by war.

It is important to note that, since the time the Union Budget 2022–23 was presented, there have been considerable discussions on the allocation priorities attached to capital expenditure, and many argued that it was at the cost of development expenditure in the revenue account. As mentioned earlier, the increased allocation for capital spending in this year's budget needs to be seen in the context of the decline in capital formation in the country in recent years. As evident from Figure 3.2, between 2011–12 and 2019–20, the gross fixed capital formation (GFCF) as a percentage of GDP declined from 34.91 to 29.15 per cent. The GFCF as a percentage of GDP for the year 2020–21 (second revised estimates) is 27.3 per cent of GDP, for the year 2021–22 (first revised estimates) is 28.9 per cent of GDP, and for the year 2022–23 (second advanced estimates) is 29.2 per cent of GDP.[8] The Second Advance Estimates of National Income, 2022–23, released on 28 February 2023 by the Ministry of Statistics and Programme Implementation, show that

> (T)he rate of GCF[9] to GDP is 31.4 per cent during 2021–22 as against 27.9 per cent in the year 2020–21. The rates of capital formation in the years 2011–12 to 2019–20 and 2021–22 have been higher than the rate of saving because of positive net capital flow from RoW.[10]

[7] MER_FEB 2022_F.pdf (dea.gov.in) (accessed 17 February 2024).
[8] https://pib.gov.in/PressReleasePage.aspx?PRID=1903091 (accessed 28 February 2023).
[9] GCF is GFCF + CIS (change in stocks) + valuables.
[10] https://pib.gov.in/PressReleasePage.aspx?PRID=1903091 (accessed 28 February 2023).

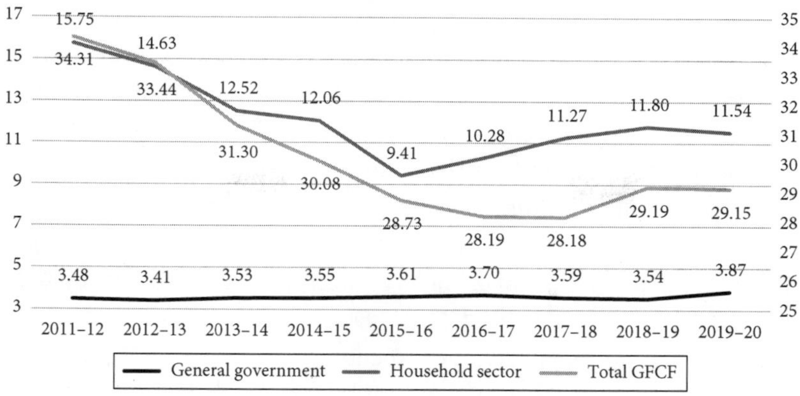

Figure 3.2 Gross fixed capital formation as a percentage of GDP, current prices, 2011–12 series.

Source: National Accounts Statistics, 2021.

The household sector GFCF as a percentage of GDP also showed a steady decline during this period. However, there was a marginal increase in the general government (centre and gtate) GFCF during the period.

Given the economy's savings–investment profile and macroeconomic uncertainties due to the pandemic, private and household investments are likely to be reactive to the general economic environment, and it is safe to assume that people's decision to save and invest may have been seriously impacted by the pandemic. But for the government, making the capital investment in such uncertain times assumes a much higher priority and is equally indispensable for achieving a strong and sustainable recovery from the pandemic.

The fiscal stance taken in the post-pandemic budgets for higher capital spending (including that of 2022–23, 2023–24 and 2024–25) is likely to further enhance the general government's share in overall capital formation. The 2022–23 Union Budget projects an increase in Capex by Rs 3.14 lakh crore, as compared to the budgeted numbers of the previous fiscal period. However, it is also important to recognize that around two-thirds of the general government's capital expenditure is undertaken by states, and in this context the announcement of the Rs 1 lakh crore interest-free loans to the states to increase public investment has been a significant step. The 50-year interest-free loan to the states for the fiscal year 2022–23 is important for two reasons: (i) as it is meant for capital spending, it cannot be diverted to finance revenue deficit and thus has the potential to augment capital spending at the state level and thereby the overall capital spending in the country; (ii) in the year 2021–22, 13 states had reported revenue deficit in their accounts and this loan facility (which is over and above the FRBM limit) can prevent the downside fiscal risk of reduction in capital expenditure at the state level. Allocation priorities for this interest-free loan have also been indicated in the budget. One such priority is the states' share of contributions to PMGSY (Pradhan Mantri Gram Sadak Yojana, implementing good road connectivity to villages) from this fund. Since states taken together have a higher share in the country's public capital spending, effective absorption of this additional borrowing facility will be critical for higher public investment. This also has the risk of substitution of states' own capital spending in the face of rising revenue deficit of States-an issue we discuss in the next section.

3.4 Fiscal Space for Capital Spending at the State Level, and Additional Borrowing

As evident from Figure 3.3, Capital expenditure (as percent of GSDP) aggregated across states declined from 2.64 per cent in 2016–17 to 2.03 per cent in 2019–20. It is, however, budgeted to increase to 2.27 per cent in 2020–21 RE and further to 2.75 per cent in 2021–22 BE. This budgeted increase in capital expenditure may not happen if the estimated deficit in the revenue account increases. An increase in revenue deficit would result in the diversion of borrowed resources to finance revenue expenditure. Also, the fiscal risk of a large number of states slipping into revenue deficit in the year 2021–22 is known now and has the potential to reduce states' own capital spending. As is evident from Figure 3.4, the number of states reporting revenue deficit has increased from 10 to 24, between 2017–18 and 2020–21 (the first year of the COVID pandemic) (see Table 3.4 in this chapter's Appendix). Though the number of states reporting revenue deficit is expected to decline as per 2020–21 (RE) and 2021–22 (BE) to 13 and nine respectively (see also Table 3.4), it will depend on several other factors including the realization of the revenue growth assumed in various state budgets for these two years.

Another important issue in the context of state-level capital expenditure is the quality of the budgetary forecast. If we consider the issue of

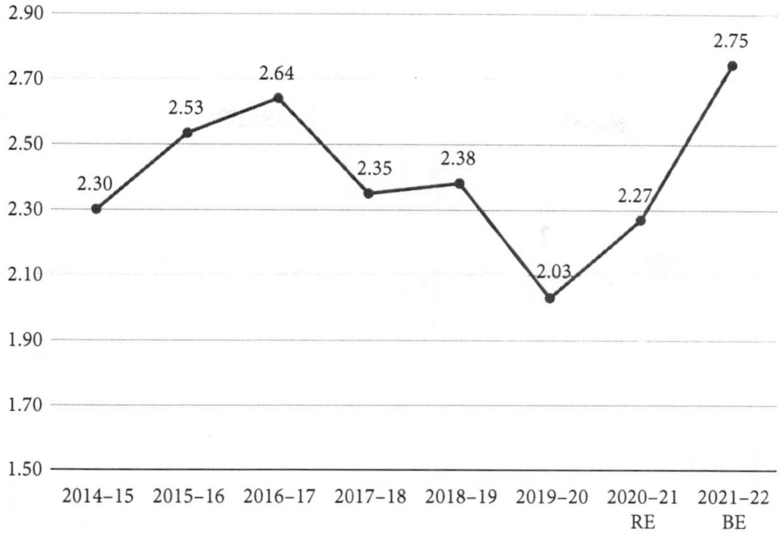

Figure 3.3 All-state capital expenditure: 2014–15 to 2021–22 (BE) (as a percentage of GSDP).

Source: Various state budget documents (2016–17 to 2021–22 BE).

capital expenditure in the federal context of India, states have a ceiling on capital expenditure due to the hard budget constraint imposed by FRBM, unless they generate a revenue surplus. Again, if we examine 2020–21 (BE) against RE of 28 states (for which all state data are available), the decline in capital expenditure was 16 per cent. The Budget 2021–22 (BE) shows an increase in capital expenditure by 34 per cent compared to 2020–21 (RE). These numbers, I believe, need to be deconstructed into two components: (i) deviation in a normal year, and (ii) deviation in an abnormal period induced by COVID. In other words, some normative judgement is necessary to understand the credibility of budget forecasts in times of crisis. It cannot be judged by just looking at the deviation between RE and BE. This applies to revenue expenditure as well. This additional borrowing of 1 lakh crore for on-lending to the states may help reduce volatility in capital expenditure at the state level. However, if a large number of states slip into revenue deficit, this additional allocation over and above the FRBM limit may provide fiscal space for maintaining capital spending at least at the pre-covid level.

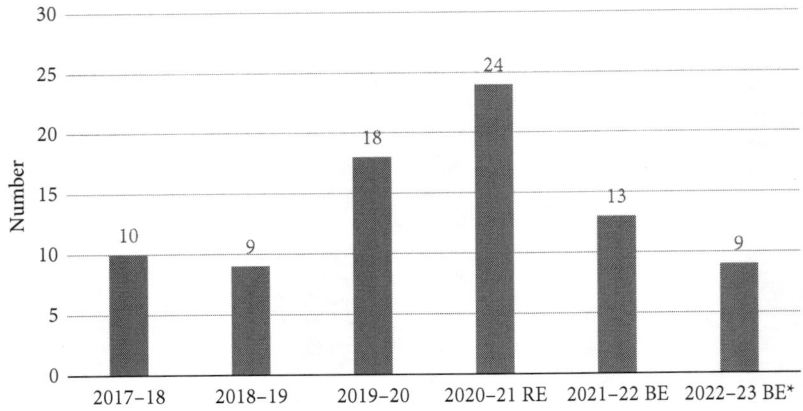

Figure 3.4 Number of states reporting revenue deficit.

Source: RBI's report on state finances, state budgets.

Note: * for 2022–23 BE, information available for 16 states that presented their budgets as of 22 March 2022. The names of the states that reported revenue deficit are available in Table 3.4 in the Appendix.

3.5 Fiscal Consolidation, Debt, and Fiscal Rule

The Fifteenth Finance Commission (FC-XV) Report (2020) envisions a next-generation fiscal architecture and a system of intergovernmental fiscal transfers to enable India to utilize the opportunity presented by the crisis, to be ready and agile, and to thrive in what lies ahead (FC XV: Para. 1.73). The FC-XV has argued that the upward increase in union and state debt positions is unavoidable at a time when growth destruction must be mitigated and income support extended (FC-XV: Para. 1.37). However, in the medium term, fiscal policies must be embedded in caution rather than exuberance, in restraint rather than profligacy (Para. 1.38). What emerges will depend on the actual quantum of fiscal shock due to COVID and the fiscal requirements of COVID response and recovery. The FC-XV has taken a view that though necessary flexibility needs to be provided, there is a need to return to sustainable fiscal management for macro-stability and growth when we take a medium-term view.

The Commission provided a range of debt deficits targets instead of an annual fixed target, considering the prevailing uncertainties related to economic recovery (see Table 3.1). The indicative debt–deficit path for the union as assessed by the Commission is presented in Table 3.2. The

Table 3.1 Range of Union government's fiscal deficit (percentage of GDP).

Scenarios of economic recovery	2021–22	2022–23	2023–24	2024–25	2025–26
Slower than assessed economic recovery	6.5	6.0	5.5	5.0	4.5
As per the assessed economic recovery	6.0	5.5	5.0	4.5	4.0
Faster than assessed economic recovery	6.0	5.5	5.0	4.0	3.5

Source: Fifteenth Finance Commission Report (2020).

Table 3.2 Indicative debt–deficit path for the Union governments (percentage of GDP).

Indicators	2020–21	2021–22	2022–23	2023–24	2024–25	2025–26
Revenue deficit	5.9	4.9	4.5	3.9	3.3	2.8
Fiscal deficit	7.4	6.0	5.5	5.0	4.5	4.0
Total liabilities	62.9	61.0	61.0	60.1	58.6	56.6

Source: Fifteenth Finance Commission Report (2020).

Commission estimated a sharp rise in debt:GDP ratio in 2020–21 owing to the contraction in nominal GDP by 6 per cent,[11] along with the fall in revenues and increase in expenditure needs. The Commission recognized that it would be impossible to pursue the FRBM as specified in the FRBM Act. According to the Commission's estimates, a fiscal deficit at 3 per cent of GDP will not be able to cover even the revenue account imbalances till 2024–25 and will barely cover them in 2025–26.

In India, between 2020–21 (the first year of the COVID-19 pandemic) and 2022–23, the fiscal challenges eased, but they remain present as we navigate economic recovery in uncertain times. It is difficult to predict the impact of the ongoing war between Russia and Ukraine on the fiscal situation as we move during the fiscal year 2022–23. Between 2020–21

[11] The contraction in nominal GDP estimated by the NSO as per the second advances estimates for 2020–21 is 3.8 per cent, which is lower than that projected by the FC-XV.

Table 3.3 Central government deficits and liabilities (percentage of GDP).

Year	Fiscal deficit	Revenue deficit	Primary deficit	Total liabilities
2011–12	5.9	4.5	2.8	51.7
2012–13	4.9	3.7	1.8	51.0
2013–14	4.5	3.2	1.1	50.5
2014–15	4.1	2.9	0.9	50.1
2015–16	3.9	2.5	0.7	50.1
2016–17	3.5	2.1	0.4	48.3
2017–18	3.5	2.6	0.4	48.2
2018–19	3.4	2.4	0.4	48.1
2019–20	4.7	3.3	1.6	50.9
2020–21	9.2	7.3	5.7	61.0
2021–22 RE	6.7	4.6	3.3	57.5
2022–23 BE	6.3	3.8	2.7	57.9

Source: *Handbook of Statistics on Indian Economy* (RBI) and Union Budget Documents 2022–23.

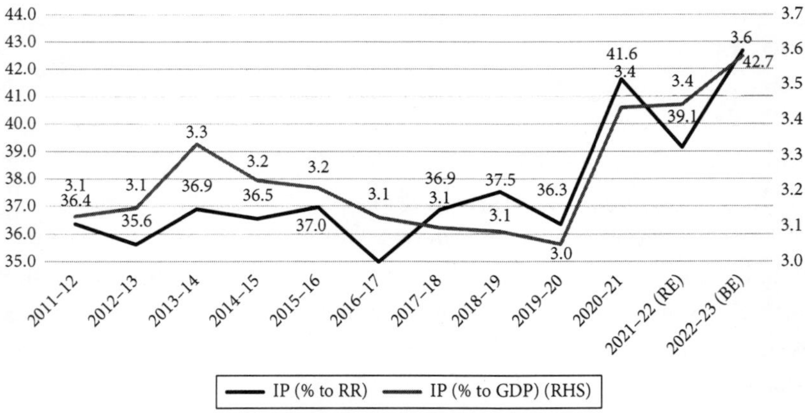

Figure 3.5 Interests payments to Revenue Receipts and GDP Ratio.
Source: *Handbook of Statistics on Indian Economy* (RBI) and Union Budget Documents 2022–23.

and 2022–23 (BE), the reduction in revenue deficit has been substantial, from 7.3 per cent to 3.8 per cent of GDP (see Table 3.3). Compositionally, revenue deficit continues to be more than 55 per cent of the fiscal deficit, and management of such a deficit has important considerations for revenue expenditure—(i) interest payments, and (ii) allocation under various centrally sponsored and central sector schemes. In 2021–22 (RE), the interest payment is 25.7 per cent of the revenue expenditure and 39.14 per cent of revenue receipts. As a percentage of GDP, it increased from 3.1 to 3.6 per cent of GDP from 2012–13 to 2022–23 (BE) (See Figure 3.5). This implies a corresponding reduction in the fiscal space for primary expenditure for discretionary development spending.

3.6 Conclusions

Considering India's recovery from the shock of the pandemic, the need for a careful approach to fiscal expansion cannot be overemphasized. Rebalancing fiscal expenditure between redistribution and growth in a time like this is extremely challenging. The focus on capital spending as an instrument of choice carries the underlying assumption that it will create a virtuous circle of higher growth and larger development spending and revenue-led fiscal consolidation. If that does not happen, and pressure to increase revenue expenditure goes up, we may end up with a higher deficit, larger debt, and reduced space for primary spending due to enhanced debt-servicing costs.

References

Ardanaz, M., Cavallo, A., Izquierdo, A., et al. (2021). Growth-friendly Fiscal Rules? Safeguarding Public Investment from Budget Cuts through Fiscal Rule Design, *Journal of International Money and Finance*, 111, March 2021, 102319.

Blanchard, O., Leandro, A., and Zettelmeyer, J. (2021). *Redesigning EU Fiscal Rules: From Rules to Standards*, Peterson Institute for International Economics, WP 21-1, Washington, DC.

Chakraborty, P. (2021). COVID-19 Context and the Fifteenth Finance Commission: Balancing Fiscal Need and Macroeconomic Stability, *Economic and Political Weekly*, 56(33), 33–39, August.

Department of Economic Affairs (2022). Monthly Economic Report, February, Ministry of Finance, Government of India.

Economic Survey 2020–21 (2021). Ministry of finance, Government of India, https://www.indiabudget.gov.in/economicsurvey/

Fifteenth Finance Commission Report (2020). Finance Commission in COVID Times, https://fincomindia.nic.in/ShowContentOne.aspx?id=9&Section=1.

Gbohoui, W., and Medas, P. (2021). 'Fiscal Rules, Fiscal Discipline, and Shocks'. *Fiscal Affairs*, International Monetary Fund, Washington, DC.

Gudmundsson, T. (2022). 'Economic Indicators Signal Diminished Growth Momentum at Start of Year', IMFBlog, 24 February, https://www.imf.org/en/Blogs/Articles/2022/02/24/economic-indicators-signal-diminished-growth-momentum-at-start-of-year.

IMF Fiscal Monitor (2021). 'Strengthening the Credibility of Public Finances'. International Monetary Fund, https://www.imf.org/en/Publications/FM/Issues/2021/10/13/fiscal-monitor-october-2021.

Kammer, A., Azour, J., Selassie, A. A., et al. (2022). 'How War in Ukraine is Reverberating across World's Regions'. IMFBlog, 15 March, https://www.imf.org/en/Blogs/Articles/2022/03/15/blog-how-war-in-ukraine-is-reverberating-across-worlds-regions-031522.

Appendix

Table 3.4 States with revenue deficit.

	2017–18	2018–19	2019–20	2020–21 RE	2021–22 BE	2022–23 BE*
No. of states that reported a revenue deficit	10	9	18	24	13	9
Names of the states that reported a revenue deficit	Andhra Pradesh, Assam, Haryana, Kerala, Punjab, Rajasthan, Tamil Nadu, Tripura, Uttarakhand, West Bengal	Andhra Pradesh, Haryana, Kerala, Meghalaya, Punjab, Rajasthan, Tamil Nadu, Uttarakhand, West Bengal	Andhra Pradesh, Assam, Chhattisgarh, Goa, Haryana, Kerala, Madhya Pradesh, Maharashtra, Meghalaya, Nagaland, Punjab, Rajasthan, Sikkim, Tamil Nadu, Telangana, Tripura, Uttarakhand, West Bengal	Andhra Pradesh, Bihar, Chhattisgarh, Goa, Gujarat, Haryana, Himachal Pradesh, Jharkhand, Karnataka, Kerala, Madhya Pradesh, Maharashtra, Mizoram, Nagaland, Punjab, Rajasthan, Sikkim, Tamil Nadu, Telangana, Tripura, Uttar Pradesh, Uttarakhand, West Bengal	Andhra Pradesh, Chhattisgarh, Haryana, Himachal Pradesh, Karnataka, Kerala, Madhya Pradesh, Maharashtra, Punjab, Rajasthan, Tamil Nadu, Tripura, West Bengal	Andhra Pradesh, Haryana, Himachal Pradesh, Karnataka, Kerala, Madhya Pradesh, Maharashtra, Rajasthan, West Bengal
No. of states that reported a revenue surplus	18	19	10	4	15	7

Source: RBI Report on state finances (2021).

Note: * information as per the budget documents of 16 states whose budget has been presented.

4

Fiscal Policy for Growth and Stabilization

Theory and Application in India

D. K. Srivastava, Tarrung Kapur, and Ragini Trehan

4.1 Introduction

Two major objectives of fiscal policy in a developing country like India pertain to growth and stabilization. The growth objective can be stated as pushing actual growth towards potential growth. Correspondingly, the economy should be nudged to produce an output level which is consistent with full employment of its resources. Similarly, the stabilization objective is to use fiscal policy instruments with a view to minimizing volatility of actual growth around potential or trend growth. Clearly, these two objectives are interlinked. Some other complementary objectives of fiscal policy may pertain to achieving a more equitable income distribution, reducing poverty to an acceptable minimum, and ensuring adequate provision of publicly provided public and merit goods like health and education. Governments also play a major role in building up a country's infrastructure, which requires long-term capital investment. This results in government-owned assets, and such investment can be financed by borrowing, which leads to the creation of liabilities. One dimension of fiscal policy relates to conditions that affect the sustainability of government liabilities.

This chapter is divided into five sections. Following the introductory section, Section 4.2 discusses the concept of potential growth and methodologies that have been used in the existing literature to estimate it. Section 4.3 discusses the available fiscal policy instruments and their role in increasing growth and minimizing the variations of actual growth

D. K. Srivastava, Tarrung Kapur, and Ragini Trehan, *Fiscal Policy for Growth and Stabilization* In: *Fiscal Policy and Public Financial Management*. Edited by: Pinaki Chakraborty and K R Shanmugam, Oxford University Press.
 DOI: 10.1093/9780198930464.003.0004

from potential growth. This section also discusses the concept of fiscal multipliers. Section 4.4 discusses the role that fiscal policy can play in dealing with economic cycles. Further, in the context of macroeconomic stabilization, the evolution of FRLs in India and their impact on growth and its volatility has also been analysed. Section 4.5 provides concluding observations.

4.2 Measuring Potential Growth

One key responsibility of the government is to ensure that a growth level is reached that is consistent with maintaining full employment of a country's resources without creating an accelerating rate of inflation. Such a growth level is often referred to as the non-accelerating inflation rate of unemployment (NAIRU).

Recognizing that resources such as capital stock and labour supply grow year after year, output and employment should also grow accordingly so as to ensure continued full employment of resources. This may be subject to some allowance being made for the existence of frictional unemployment which may be inevitable with the coexistence of surplus employment opportunities in some sectors and surplus human resources in some others that are unable to neutralize themselves due to mismatch of available skills vis-à-vis skills in demand and informational constraints.

Capital stock grows because of growth in investment, which is financed by growth in savings and net inflow of capital from abroad. Figure 4.1 shows actual and trend growth in net fixed capital stock (NFCS) in India at constant 2011–12 prices. We note that on a trend basis, the rate of growth of real NFCS fell during the decade of 2010–11 to 2019–20. It was at about 6.8 per cent in 2019–20 before the onset of COVID-19.

Labour supply grows when additional human resources join the labour force due to population growth and its evolving age structure, leading to an increase in the share of working age population (WAP). In India, we note that the growth of working age population fell during the decade of 2011–20. It was estimated at 1.4 per cent in 2020 (Figure 4.2).

These trends indicate that India's trend GDP growth rate may fall because of both the fall in the growth of real NFCS and that of the working

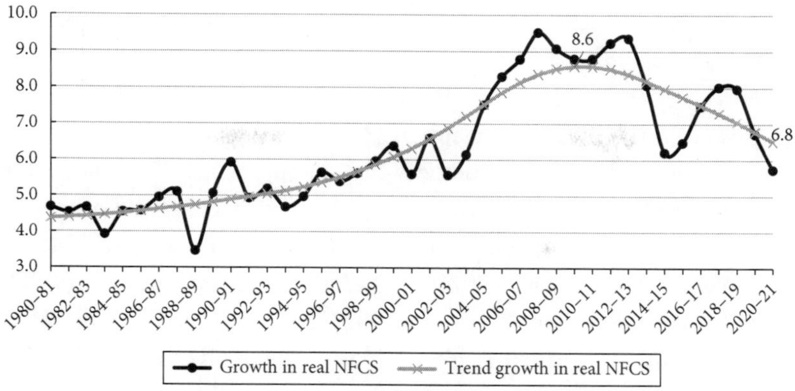

Figure 4.1 Growth in real net fixed capital stock (per cent, annual).
Source: (basic data): MoSPI.

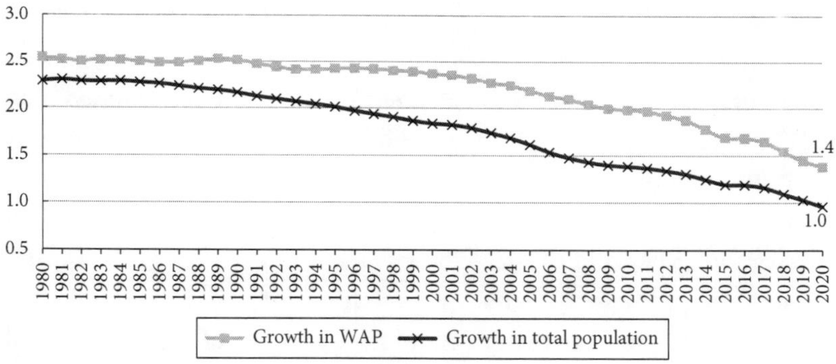

Figure 4.2 Growth in India's total and working age population (WAP) (per cent, annual).
Source (basic data): UN World Population Prospects 2022.

age population, unless counterbalanced by technological progress and reduction in unemployment rate. Technological progress is an important determinant of growth, since factor productivity increases as technology improves or is adopted from other countries where more advanced technologies are already available.

Thus, maintaining potential growth becomes a dynamic concept where fiscal instruments need to be used so as to ensure full employment of the growing capital stock and supply of labour, while taking into account improvement in their productivity resulting from technological progress.

Three key approaches to measuring potential growth which have been suggested in the literature relate to: (1) the estimation of trend growth rate, (2) the total factor productivity-based approach, and (3) the sector-differentiated incremental investment ratio approach. Some of the important works in this field in India's context are summarized in Table 4.1.

In Figure 4.3, we have estimated India's actual and trend real GDP growth over the period 1951–52 to 2022–23. We notice that there is a significant volatility of actual growth around the trend growth. This volatility was relatively high in the years prior to the early 1990s. The fluctuations around the trend growth rate have remained, but their amplitude as a percentage of trend growth rate came down from the 1990s until the onset of COVID-19 in 2020–21. This volatility refers to the problem of stabilization which we have discussed in Section 4.4 of this chapter. We also notice that the trend growth rate, which was relatively low at 4 per cent or less up to the early 1970s, then started to steadily increase, reaching a peak of close to 7.0 per cent by 2007–08. It remained close to 7.0 per cent until 2009–10, after which it fell, reaching 5.1 per cent by 2019–20, the pre-COVID year. With the deleterious impact of the pandemic in 2020–21, India's trend growth continued to fall, reaching a 40-year low of 4.6 per cent in 2022–23.

The time profile of a country's growth performance can be decomposed between trend growth rate and the deviation of the trend growth rate from the actual growth rate. This deviation reflects the extent to which an economy is characterized by growth volatility. Using trend growth rate as a measure of potential growth implies that it does not have a normative element. It does not indicate optimal levels of growth which could potentially have been achieved by pursuing a policy configuration different from what might have been followed historically. Other measures of potential growth may include such elements of optimality which may be potentially achievable by suitable policy reforms. In historical contexts, such policy reforms may only relate to counterfactual experiments. This is the reason why, in Table 4.1, some of the estimated potential growth rates are higher than the trend growth rate.

For example, in Rangarajan and Srivastava (2017), where a sectorally differentiated incremental investment ratio approach was followed,

Table 4.1 Fiscal multiplier estimates: Distinguishing between capital and revenue expenditure multipliers.

Policy variables	Expenditure multipliers: Aggregate and sectoral by Srivastava and Bharadwaj (2018)	Expenditure multiplier estimates by Patra et. al (2019, RBI)	Expenditure multiplier estimates by Bose and Bhanumurthy (2013)	Expenditure multiplier estimates by Goyal and Sharma (2015)#
Capital expenditure	2.90	3.25	2.45	2.38
Revenue expenditure	2.04	0.45	–	1.69
Transfer payments	–	–	0.98	–
Other revenue expenditure*	–	–	0.99	–

Source: Authors' compilation and EY Economy Watch March 2022 (In-focus section on expansionary potential of the Centre's 2019 budget—sectoral impact), https://assets.ey.com/content/dam/ey-sites/ey-com/en_in/topics/tax/economy-watch/2018/ey-economy-watch-march-2018.pdf (accessed 12 October 2021).

Note: * Other revenue expenditure of the government is the revenue expenditure after netting out the transfer payments. # Cumulative multipliers in the presence of supply shocks plus endogenous monetary response.

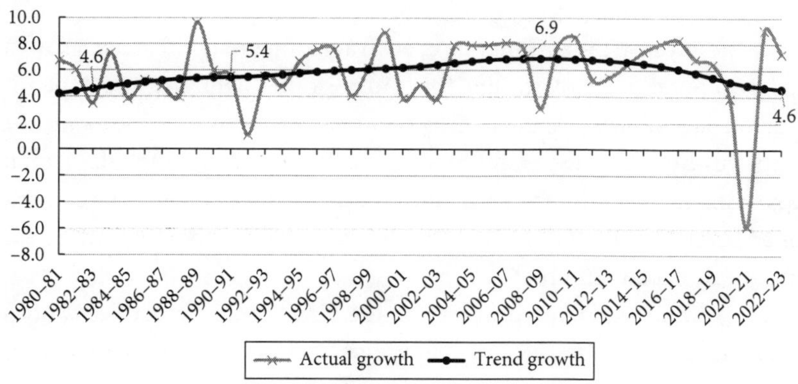

Figure 4.3 Real GDP growth in India (actual and trend).

Source (basic data): MoSPI.

Note: Trend GDP is calculated using Hodrick-Prescott filter.

alternative scenarios provide a range of potential growth rates for within-sample and beyond-sample years. These growth rates range from 7.6 per cent to 8.1 per cent in the base run for the period 2014–15 to 2029–30. At the upper end, this growth rate is shown to potentially range from 7.6 per cent to 9.6 per cent depending on an augmentation of the overall savings ratio (Simulation 2). Details of alternative potential growth estimates linked with different simulations in this study are given in Table 4.2.

The base run in these estimates was derived by assuming that both the gross capital formation (GCF) and the GDP deflators grow at 4 per cent per annum. The incremental output:capital ratios are taken at 2014–15 levels, which are also the maximum except for agriculture and construction. For agriculture and construction, separate rules were applied. For the buoyancy of net product taxes, actuals for 2014–15 and 2015–16 were used after which it was kept at 1 for the remaining forecast period. The actual levels of growth in nominal savings were used for 2014–15 and 2015–16, after which a growth rate of 12.5 per cent was applied for the remaining period. This was also the growth rate applied for net capital inflows from abroad from 2016–17 onwards. Details regarding assumptions for the different simulations, as they differ from the base run, may be referred to in the 2017 study.

4.3 Main Instruments of Fiscal Policy

Fiscal policy instruments may be used in a manner to uplift actual growth close to potential growth. For this purpose, the nature of the expenditure- and revenue-side instruments and how these may be used must be distinguished. The expenditure-side fiscal instruments include overall government expenditure as divided between revenue and capital expenditures. These may include subsidies and tax expenditures. These may be direct and indirect.

The revenue-side instruments include direct and indirect taxes, non-tax resources and non-debt capital receipts including disinvestment. One important consideration in the formulation of fiscal policy is to recognize the importance of the budget constraint which ensures that total government expenditure cannot exceed the total resources. Formally, the budget constraint may be stated as follows.

Table 4.2 Estimation of India's potential growth: A review of literature.

Authors and year	Methodology	Key features
Donde and Saggar (1999); Ranjan et. al. (2007); Bordoloi et al. (2009); Mishra (2013)	Uses statistical filters to estimate the potential output	While most of these studies have estimated potential output/growth for selected historical periods, some have used specific assumptions regarding TFP growth and other determinants for specified future periods to make projections.
Goyal and Arora (2012); Mishra (2013)	Uses structural VAR methods or other statistical filters for estimating potential growth	
Ranjan et. al. (2007)	Uses a production function approach for deriving the contribution of total factor productivity	
Rodrik and Subramanian (2004)	Projects a potential growth of over 7.0 per cent for India up to 2025 using TFP growth at 2.5 per cent and capital share of 0.35	
Poddar and Yi (2007)	India's potential growth could be about 8 per cent until 2020 taking TFP growth at 3.3 per cent	
Economic Survey of India 2015–16	Uses a determinants-cum-convergence approach based on the empirical finding that institutions are a key determinant of long-term growth	Estimates India's potential growth to be in the range of 8 to 10 per cent up to 2029–30
Burns (2016)	Uses the production frontier approach, but unlike many other estimates of total factor productivity, in Burns's study the TFP estimates are net of the effects of structural change.	Provides estimates of potential output growth for a sample of 26 Asian economies including India for the period 2015–40. India's potential output growth, which was 6.7 per cent in 2010–15, falls to 4.1 per cent in 2035–40

(continued)

Table 4.2 Continued

Authors and year	Methodology	Key features
Rangarajan and Srivastava (2017)	Considers sectoral disaggregation in determining India's potential growth. Rangarajan and Srivastava highlight the relative roles of (a) growth of investible resources comprising domestic savings and net capital inflow, (b) differential prices of investment goods vis-à-vis consumption goods and services, (c) sectoral incremental capital:output ratios, (d) the changing weights of sectoral outputs in total output due to sectoral growth rate differentials, and (e) the buoyancy of net product taxes in determining India's potential growth.	Estimates India's potential growth to be in the range of 7.6–8.1 per cent (as per base run) for the period 2014–15 to 2029–30

Source: Authors' compilation based on several research articles as listed in column 1) of the table (see References for further details).

$$G = TR + NTR + NDCR + FD \quad (4.1)$$

where G refers to total government expenditure, TR refers to total tax revenues, NTR refers to non-tax revenues, $NDCR$ refers to non-debt capital receipts, and FD refers to fiscal deficit.

Fiscal deficit provides an element of dynamics in the formulation of fiscal policy since incurring fiscal deficit year after year leads to accumulation of government debt on which interest payments are made. This links current expenditure to past fiscal deficits. We may write the definition of fiscal deficit as:

$$FD = PD + IP = B - B_{-1} \quad (4.2)$$

where FD refers to fiscal deficit, PD refers to primary deficit, and IP refers to interest payment. B refers to government liabilities at the end of a given period, and B_{-1} refers to government liabilities at the end of the previous period.

With a view to uplifting actual growth to potential growth, if the latter is higher than the actual growth, aggregate demand would need to be stimulated. This can be done directly by increasing that part of government expenditure which can be considered as autonomous. The final impact of an initial increase in autonomous expenditure tends to be higher than the initial injection of stimulus. This relationship between final and initial increases in autonomous expenditure is captured by what is called the 'autonomous expenditure multiplier'. Thus, if the value of this multiplier is 5, it would imply that total increase in aggregate demand is five times the initial increase in autonomous expenditure. The impact of such intervention can be improved by looking at components of government's autonomous expenditure that are to be increased. Generally, the multiplier associated with capital expenditure tends to be higher than that associated with revenue expenditure (refer to Table 4.3). However, the impact of increasing revenue expenditure may show its results quickly by increasing aggregate demand, whereas that of increasing capital expenditure may be spread over a longer period of time.

The extent to which total expenditures can be increased is subject to the government budget constraint. This implies that any increase in government expenditure must be suitably financed. If it is financed through additional taxation, there will be a two-sided impact on aggregate demand. First, when government expenditure increases, total expenditure increases directly. Second, if taxation increases to finance this increase in government expenditure, private disposable income would be reduced, which would reduce private expenditure and therefore aggregate demand.

If increase in government expenditure is financed by additional government borrowing resulting in an increase in fiscal deficit, then its impact will depend on how the fiscal deficit is financed—that is, by way of borrowing from (1) central bank, (2) within the domestic market, or (3) external sources. In the first case, money supply will increase, leading to higher inflation. In the second case, domestic interest rates may go up, leading to lower investment. In the third case, current account deficit will increase, which may lead to an exchange rate depreciation. Thus, the impact of fiscal instruments that are used to stimulate the economy when it is operating below potential needs to be studied in a macroeconometric framework where the relevant interdependencies are properly taken into account.

For illustration purposes, the derivation of the autonomous expenditure multiplier is explained below.

$$Y = E = C + I + G \tag{4.3}$$

where Y is aggregate income, E is aggregate expenditure, C is private consumption expenditure, I is investment expenditure, and G is government expenditure.

$$C = C_0 + bY, \quad 0 \leq b \leq 1$$

where C_0 is autonomous consumption expenditure and b is the marginal propensity to consume (MPC)

$I = I_0$ implying that private investment is autonomous

$G = G_0$ implying that government expenditure is autonomous.

$$\text{Thus, } Y = (C_0 + I_0 + G_0) + bY \text{ or } Y = A + bY \tag{4.4}$$

If A is changed to $A + \Delta A$, then Y will also change. Suppose it changes to $Y + \Delta Y$; then we can write

$$Y + \Delta Y = A + \Delta A + b(Y + \Delta Y) \tag{4.5}$$

Now (4.5) minus (4.4) gives

$$\Delta Y = \Delta A + b\Delta Y \text{ or } \Delta Y(1-b) = \Delta A \text{ or } \frac{\Delta Y}{\Delta A} = \frac{1}{(1-b)} \tag{4.6}$$

Thus, the autonomous expenditure multiplier is related to the MPC. The higher the MPC, the lower the denominator in equation (4.6) will be, and the higher the multiplier. Thus, if $b = 0.8$, the fiscal multiplier is equal to 5.

Many of the assumptions of this simple model are relaxed to give rise to more elaborate derivations. One such derivation is that of automatic fiscal stabilizer. If the increase in government expenditure is to be financed by additional taxation, the value of the autonomous expenditure multiplier would be reduced. Thus, if

$$T = tY, \ [0 < t < 1] \tag{4.7}$$

where t is the average tax rate and T is the volume of tax revenues

$$C = C_0 + b(Y - T)$$

$$\text{Thus, } C = C_0 + b(Y - tY) \tag{4.8}$$

It can be shown that

$$\frac{\Delta Y}{\Delta A} = \frac{1}{1 - b + bt} \tag{4.9}$$

For any positive value of t, the magnitude of multiplier is lower than that of the simple autonomous expenditure multiplier. The higher the tax rate, the lower the multiplier. Thus, in equation (4.9), if $b = 0.8$ and $t = 0.25$, the multiplier is reduced to 2.5.

Estimation of the optimal extent of stimulus is facilitated by the use of macroeconometric models, which quantify the impact of fiscal multipliers which may be compared with monetary multipliers. In summary, we may note that different kinds of expenditures may have different magnitudes of associated multipliers and different time lags for their full effect on the economy to take place.

Often, the efficacy of monetary multipliers and that of fiscal multipliers are compared. Optimally, both instruments should be utilized in combination depending on the nature of correction required. In Table 4.3, we have summarized some estimates of the magnitude of fiscal multipliers for the Indian economy in recent years, especially highlighting the differential magnitudes of capital and revenue expenditure multipliers. Multiplier estimates differ based on the methodology used and assumptions made. It may be noted that capital expenditure multipliers

Table 4.3 Growth of GDP under alternative policy configurations.

	Base run	Simulation 1	Simulation 2	Simulation 3	Simulation 4
Changes introduced		**Differential GCF and GDP deflators**	**Growth rate of saving**	**Output: capital ratio**	**Buoyancy of net indirect taxes**
2014–15	7.6	7.6	7.6	7.6	7.6
2015–16	8.0	8.0	8.0	8.0	8.0
2016–17	8.0	8.0	8.0	8.0	8.0
2017–18	8.0	8.0	8.0	8.0	8.1
2018–19	8.0	8.1	8.1	8.0	8.1
2019–20	8.0	8.1	8.1	8.1	8.1
2020–21	8.0	8.2	8.2	8.1	8.2
2021–22	8.0	8.2	8.3	8.2	8.2
2022–23	8.0	8.2	8.4	8.2	8.2
2023–24	8.1	8.3	8.6	8.2	8.2
2024–25	8.1	8.3	8.7	8.3	8.2
2025–26	8.1	8.3	8.9	8.3	8.2
2026–27	8.1	8.4	9.0	8.4	8.2
2027–28	8.1	8.4	9.2	8.5	8.3
2028–29	8.1	8.4	9.4	8.5	8.3
2029–30	8.1	8.5	9.6	8.6	8.3

Source (basic data): Rangarajan and Srivastava (2017).

are higher than revenue expenditure multipliers according to most of the studies cited here.

4.4 Fiscal Policy for Stabilization

In this section, we consider the role of fiscal policy for meeting the stabilization objective in the context of macro-fiscal policies. We may note that GDP growth may be below the corresponding potential growth due to structural or cyclical reasons. If the problem is structural in nature, fiscal policy should be used to remove the structural constraints in the economy. If the problem is cyclical, fiscal policy should be used in its countercyclical role. This is the main purpose of using fiscal instruments for stabilization.

If actual growth is above potential growth, the economy may be overheated, and aggregate demand may need to be reduced. On the other hand, if the actual growth is below potential growth, aggregate demand would need to be increased. For increasing aggregate demand, if additional borrowing is undertaken, sourced from the central bank, it is often considered politically least costly because there is no additional tax burden. However, this may lead to inflation after a lag which may prove to be politically costly. Alternatively, if such borrowing is done by domestic sources, then interest rates may go up, investment may come down, and growth may come down after a lag, thereby making the intervention self-defeating or less effective. Thus, the issue of time lag and magnitude of impact is also of considerable importance in managing cyclical variations in GDP growth.

In understanding countercyclical interventions of fiscal policy, the relevant literature has made a distinction between economic and political economy motives for undertaking such interventions. The political economy motive is also of considerable importance in understanding why, in many countries, debt and deficit relative to GDP grow to unsustainable levels.

Governments often resort to higher expenditures in order to woo the voters. These politically motivated higher expenditures may be broad-based with the intention of benefitting the population at large or targeted with the intention of benefitting particular segments of voters. Since borrowing-financed increases are politically most convenient almost throughout the world, governments have become more indebted over time. Similarly, governments also implement tax regime-related concessions such as lower rates, higher deduction limits, etc. Since political parties forming a government change from time to time, their perspectives are often myopic. Progressively, government debt relative to GDP crosses prudent limits, becoming unsustainable, leaving an excessive burden of debt servicing for future generations. For this reason, many governments enact FRLs in order to curb the tendency of the government of the day to borrow excessively, that is, beyond sustainable limits. Well-known examples of FRLs are the Maastricht Treaty norms, India's FRLs for central and state governments, and comparable norms for many other countries. Details of the Maastricht Treaty norms and India's FRLs are given in Tables 4.4, 4.5, and 4.6.

In the practical application of the Maastricht Treaty norms, the European economies that are the members of the European Economic Community have shown different degrees of success in meeting

Table 4.4 Maastricht Treaty norms and Stability and Growth Pact (SGP).

Maastricht Treaty norms	Stability and Growth Pact (SGP)
General government fiscal deficit targeted at 3 per cent of GDP Public debt targeted at 60 per cent of GDP Examples: Germany, Italy, France	Defined a detailed list of procedural steps, including sanctions, aimed at correcting an excessive deficit Under this pact all the Member States: • committed to maintaining a budgetary position of 'close to balance or surplus' over the medium term, and • committed to regularly submit stability and convergence programmes detailing all information necessary to carry out multilateral fiscal surveillance Country-specific medium-term budgetary objectives (MTOs) were set The fiscal compact establishes a structural deficit floor for the MTO of 0.5 per cent of GDP for countries with debt above 60 per cent of GDP, and of 1 per cent of GDP for countries with debt significantly below 60 per cent of GDP The extent of annual adjustment for achieving the MTO depends on the economy's cyclical position, debt level, and the risks to public finance sustainability

Source (basic data): Lledó et al. (2017).

sustainability norms. Some countries like Germany have shown extraordinary success by keeping their debt:GDP ratio at low and prudent levels in spite of facing major global cyclical economic challenges. Some of the weaker economies, such as those of Greece, Spain, and Italy, have shown much less satisfactory results in meeting sustainability norms (see e.g. Srivastava et al. (2020)).

India's debt and deficit sustainability norms also constitute an important example, since it is a major federal country. While the central government has taken a lead in initiating its FRL, states in India subsequently enacted their individual legislations. Table 4.5 indicates the major landmarks in the evolution of the centre's Fiscal Responsibility and Budget Management Act (FRBMA) since its inception in 2003.

Table 4.5 The centre's FRBMA, and the main amendments to it since inception.

Year	Change	Comments
2003	FRBMA introduced	Fiscal deficit targeted at 3 per cent of GDP
July 2004	FRBMA rules notified	Achieving the FD target of 3 per cent of GDP by 2008–09; reduction of 0.3 per cent of GDP per year by the central government. Revenue deficit elimination by 2008–09
Union Budget 2012–13	FRBMA amended through Finance Act	Concept of effective revenue deficit introduced
May 2013	FRBM rules amended	Achieving zero effective revenue deficit by 2014–15; revenue deficit to be reduced to 2 per cent of GDP
May 2015	FRBM	Target dates for achievement of all three deficit indicators extended to March 2018
April 2018	FRBM Act amended	Debt targets for central and general government at 40 per cent and 60 per cent of GDP by end of 2024–25; limit fiscal deficit to 3 per cent of GDP by 31 March 2021; revenue deficit target given up
April 2018	FRBM rules amended	Centre's fiscal deficit: Annual reduction margin of 0.1 per cent or more of GDP

Source (basic data): Department of Economic Affairs, Ministry of Finance, Government of India.

Table 4.6 summarizes the progress of Indian states in adopting their individual FRLs. Most of the states adopted their FRLs after the recommendations of the Twelfth Finance Commission (FC 12). By September 2010, all states had adopted their respective FRLs.

In the discussion below, we illustrate the evolution of fiscal imbalances after the enactment of the FRLs in India. Figure 4.4 shows that states have, by and large, successfully achieved the fiscal deficit target of 3 per cent of GDP (with marginal exceptions). The largest exception is on account of the impact of COVID in 2020–21. The central government, on the other hand, achieved the 3 per cent target only once in 2007–08. It is remarkable that centre made a concerted effort during the period 2012–13 to 2018–19 to reduce its fiscal deficit closer to the target level of 3 per cent of GDP. It is also clear that major departures for the centre's fiscal deficit occurred due to exogenous adverse events in 2008–09 and 2020–21. Thus, it is largely because of the need for the central government to play a leading role in macro-stabilization that major departures from its fiscal deficit target occurred.

Figure 4.5 shows that states considered together have managed to remain closely aligned to the revenue account balance line, with marginal departures on both sides from time to time. The only major exception to this trend emerged in the COVID year of 2020–21. In contrast, the centre

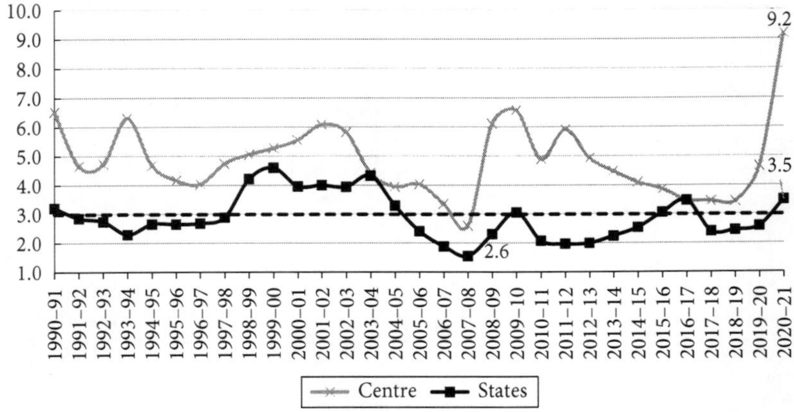

Figure 4.4 Fiscal deficit relative to GDP (per cent): Centre and states.
Source: IPFS, Union Budget (various issues) and RBI.

Table 4.6 State-wise adoption of FRLs: A time profile.

#	State	Date	Comment	#	State	Date	Comment
1	Karnataka	Sept. '02	Before centre's FRBM	15	Manipur	Aug. '05	After FC 12 recommendations (continued)
2	Tamil Nadu	May '03		16	Chhattisgarh	Sep. '05	
3	Kerala	Aug. '03		17	Assam	Sep. '05	
4	Punjab	Oct. '03	After centre's FRBM and before FC 12 recommendations	18	Uttarakhand	Oct. '05	
5	Uttar Pradesh	Feb. '04		19	Arunachal Pradesh	Mar. '06	
6	Gujarat	Mar. '05		20	Meghalaya	Mar. '06	
7	Maharashtra	Apr. '05		21	Bihar	Apr. '06	
8	Himachal Pradesh	Apr. '05		22	Goa	May '06	
9	Rajasthan	May '05	After FC 12 recommendations	23	Jammu and Kashmir	Aug. '06	
10	Madhya Pradesh	May '05		24	Mizoram	Oct. '06	
11	Andhra Pradesh	Jun. '05		25	Jharkhand	May '07	
12	Odisha	Jun. '05		26	Nagaland	Jan. '10	
13	Tripura	Jun. '05		27	West Bengal	Jul. '10	After FC 12 recommendations
14	Haryana	Jul. '05		28	Sikkim	Sept. '10	

Source: State Finances: A Study of Budgets, Reserve Bank of India (2015).

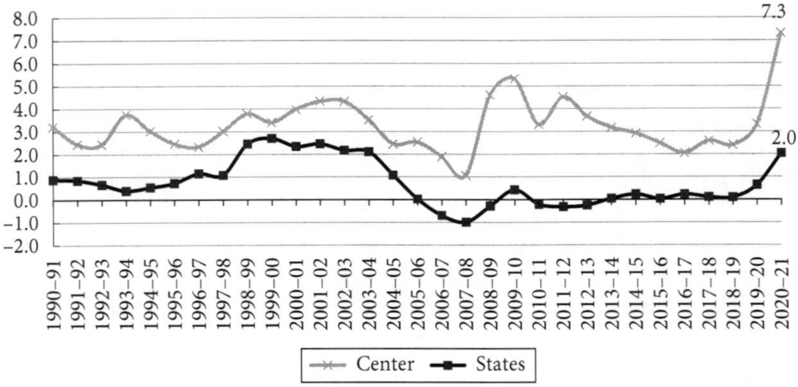

Figure 4.5 Revenue deficit relative to GDP (per cent): Centre and states.
Source: IPFS, Union Budget (various issues) and RBI.

has incurred large deficits on its revenue account, with notably high levels during the crisis years of 2008–09, 2009–10, and more recently 2020–21.

In the context of debt, we may consider two sets of benchmarks. According to the centre's FRBMA 2018, it is 40 per cent and 20 per cent of GDP for the centre and states respectively. FC 12 considered a symmetrical debt target of 28 per cent of GDP for both central and state governments. In a recent work (Srivastava et al., 2021), it was pointed out that the debt and GDP combination of 40 per cent and 20 per cent is not a valid one if the fiscal deficit to GDP target is equal for both the centre and states at 3 per cent. However, as Figure 4.6 indicates, the centre has kept missing its debt target, whether 40 per cent or 28 per cent of GDP, year after year, whereas states have almost always achieved it.

The literature on fiscal federalism has argued that the central government has to play a dominant role in macro-stabilization. This is partly due to the fact that macro-stabilization often involves using the monetary instruments over which state governments do not have control, and partly due to the fact that the objective is to affect aggregate or country-wide demand and not just regional demand. It is, however, arguable that in India's context, states may also have a significant role to play in complementing the centre's efforts to achieve stabilization. Three main reasons can be cited for this. First, in India, it is the state governments which incur the relatively larger share of total government expenditures after fiscal transfers. Second, some of the Indian states are inordinately

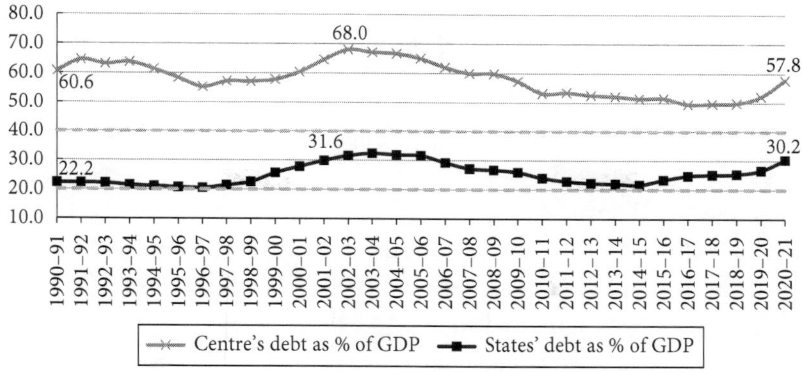

Figure 4.6 States' and centre's debt as percentage of GDP.
Source (basic data): MoSPI, RBI, author's estimates.

large (in fact, many states are larger than individual countries). Third, it is useful to distinguish between two types of economic cycles in India, namely agricultural and non-agricultural. Agricultural cycles have an average periodicity of three years, and non-agricultural cycles of about six years (see Srivastava et al. (2021)). Further, as per the Constitution of India, the subject of agriculture is within the jurisdiction of the state governments. In a fiscal federal framework characterized by cooperation and coordination, identifying a stabilization role for the state governments would not only lead to sharing the burden of fiscal imbalances but also prove to be more effective.

4.5 Concluding Observations

In this chapter, alternative concepts of potential growth have been discussed, making a distinction between potential growth measured as trend growth, and potential growth estimated using econometric methods involving different approaches to considerations of factor productivity. An analysis has been undertaken of the distinction between the revenue and expenditure sides of managing government budgets, and the role of the government budget constraint. The concept of fiscal multipliers has also been discussed at length, to highlight the factors that determine the final impact of an initial fiscal intervention. The issue of dealing with economic cycles and the role that the fiscal policy can play in this context has been discussed in detail with illustrations drawn from the Indian economy. Within the context of the subject of stabilization, the evolution of FRLs in India and their impact on growth and its volatility has also been analysed.

The central government enacted its FRBMA in 2003. This act was amended from time to time, most recently in 2018. Most of the state governments enacted their FRLs between 2005 and 2008. At present, all state governments have subjected themselves to their respective FRLs. Since these enactments, two major global crises (in 2008–09 and in 2020–21) upset India's fiscal consolidation efforts. In both cases, the slippage was largely on account of the central government and comparatively much less on account of the state governments. This may be considered justifiable since the central government, in theory and in practice, has had to play a proactive role in achieving stabilization. The more recent COVID crisis in 2020–21 forced the combined government debt:GDP ratio to sharply increase to an estimated level of 88.4 per cent, largely because of the contraction in both real and nominal GDP growth. In the emerging post-COVID global economic scenario, India must aim to raise its growth rate closer to its potential while restoring fiscal consolidation, so that sustained growth and stability in government finances can be achieved. For this purpose, the centre's FRBMA needs to be recast.

References

Blanchard, Olivier Jean (2002) *Macroeconomics* (third edition), Prentice Hall, Hoboken, NJ.

Bordoloi, S., Das, A., and Ramesh, J. (2009). 'Estimation of Potential Output in India'. Reserve Bank of India Occasional Papers, 30(2), 37–73.

Bose. S., and Bhanumurthy, N. R. (2013). 'Fiscal Multipliers for India'. NIPFP working paper no. 125, National Institute of Public Finance and Policy, New Delhi.

CAG report on compliance of FRBMA (2003). For the Years 2015–16 and 2016–17, https://cag.gov.in/cag_old/content/report-no32-2017-compliance-audit-fiscal-responsibility-and-budget-management-act2003 (accessed 23 August 2021).

European Central Bank (2019). 'Taking Stock of the Functioning of the EU Fiscal Rules and Options for Reform'. Occasional Paper Series. https://www.ecb.europa.eu/pub/pdf/scpops/ecb.op231~c1ccf67bb3.en.pdf.

European Council (1997). Resolution of the European Council on the Stability and Growth Pact Amsterdam, 17 June 1997. *Official Journal* C 236 (August),

1–2, https://eur-lex.europa.eu/LexUriServ/LexUriServ.do?uri=CELEX:31997Y0802(01):EN:HTML (accessed 5 July 2021). European Council, Amsterdam.

FRBM Review Committee Report (January 2017). Responsible Growth: A Debt and Fiscal Framework for 21st-century India, https://dea.gov.in/sites/default/files/Volumepercent201percent20FRBMpercent20Reviewpercent20Committeepercent20Report.pdf (accessed 13 January 2022). Department of Economic Affairs, Government of India, New Delhi.

Goyal, A., and Arora, S. (2012). 'Deriving India's Potential Growth from Theory and Structure', IGIDER Working Paper No. 018, IGIDR, Mumbai.

Goyal, A., and Sharma, B. (2015). Government Expenditure in India: Composition, Cyclicality and Multipliers. IGIDR Working Paper 32. IGIDR, Mumbai.

IMF, Finance and Development Basics (2021), https://www.imf.org/external/pubs/ft/fandd/2013/09/basics.htm (accessed 24 July 2021).

Lledó, V., Yoon, S., Fang, X., et al. (2017). Fiscal Rules at a Glance. International Monetary Fund, 2–77.

Mishra, P. (2013). 'Has India's Growth Story Withered?' *Economic and Political Weekly* 48(15), 51–59.

Patra, M. D., Mitra, P., Bhattacharyya, I., et al. (2019). Estimable Fiscal Multipliers for India, Reserve Bank of India, Mumbai.

Poddar, T., and Yi, E. (2007). India's Rising Growth Potential. Global Economic Paper No. 152. Goldman Sachs Global Research Centers, New York.

Rangarajan, C., and Srivastava, D. K. (2017). Underlying Drivers of India's Potential Growth, *Economic and Political Weekly*, 52(25–26), 69–77.

Ranjan, R., Rajeev, J., and Sarat, C. D. (2007). 'India's Potential Economic Growth: Measurement Issues and Policy Implications', *Economic and Political Weekly*, April, 1563–1572.

Reserve Bank of India (2019). 'Fiscal Rules and Cyclicality of Fiscal Policy: Evidence from Indian States', RBI occasional papers, no. 40(2), 2019, https://www.rbi.org.in/Scripts/bs_viewcontent.aspx?Id = 3841#AP1 (accessed 2 September 2021).

Rodrik, D., and Subramanian, A. (2004). 'From Hindu Growth to Productivity Surge: The Mystery of the Indian Growth Transition'. Paper presented at the IMF Jaques Polak Annual Research conference, 4–5 November, Washington DC.

Srivastava, D. K., Bharadwaj, M., Kapur, T., et al. (2021). Covid's Economic Impact: Should India Recast its Fiscal and Monetary Policy Frameworks? *Journal of International Economics and Finance*, 1(1), 53–71.

Srivastava, D. K., Kapur, T., Bharadwaj, M., et al. (2020). 'Impact of Covid-19 on Global Debt: A Study of Countries in the G-20 group'. *Modern Economy*, 11, 2101–2121.

II

TAX POLICY ISSUES

5

Goods and Services Tax in India

Transition, Experience, and Future Reforms

D. K. Srivastava and Muralikrishna Bharadwaj

5.1 Introduction

India is a federal fiscal system consisting of a central government, a set of state governments, and a large number of local governments.[1] Under constitutional arrangements, in this multi-tier system, each tier of the government has been assigned specific revenue powers. These powers may relate to taxation as well as non-tax revenues. Taxation may be direct or indirect. Most direct taxes such as personal income tax or corporate income tax have been assigned to the central government. Indirect taxes have been divided between the central and the state governments. The evolution of indirect taxes in India has been such that indirect taxes levied at the production or the manufacturing stage in the form of excise duties were assigned to the central government, whereas taxes at the retail stage such as sales tax were assigned to state governments. Such a system suffered from various infirmities. Apart from overlapping jurisdictions, major problems arose in the taxation of inter-state movement of goods and services. Service tax was introduced in the mid-1990s as a central tax—that is, four-and-a-half decades after the inception of the Constitution. Initially it was levied on a limited number of services. Over time, its scope was increased and made more comprehensive. In this stage-wise and fragmented evolution of indirect taxes in India, major problems such as cascading of taxes, multiplicity of tax rates, and

[1] This chapter is based on the session on GST delivered as a part of a training course on Public Finance for Group A Officers of the Government of Tamil Nadu, run by the MSE from 31 August to 4 September 2021.

D. K. Srivastava and Muralikrishna Bharadwaj, *Goods and Services Tax in India* In: *Fiscal Policy and Public Financial Management.* Edited by: Pinaki Chakraborty and K R Shanmugam, Oxford University Press.
 DOI: 10.1093/9780198930464.003.0005

creation of fiscal barriers in the working of an all-India common market arose. Indirect tax reforms were initiated from the 1980s. These aimed at gradually bringing in the taxation of value-added in the process of production and sale of goods and services. Eventually, the central and state governments agreed to bring in a Goods and Services Tax (GST) in 2017, replacing a number of erstwhile indirect taxes under their separate jurisdictions. The resulting experience with the working of GST clearly indicates that it still requires many additional reforms before India's system of indirect taxes can be called an efficient, least distortionary, and revenue-productive system consistent with the requirements of the challenges of a growing economy.

This chapter is divided into five sections. Following the introductory section, Section 5.2 deals with the features of indirect taxes in India prior to the introduction of GST in 2017. It also summarizes the key features of the international experience with VAT and GST and gives a brief description of the issues with reference to the determination of a revenue-neutral rate (RNR) in India. Section 5.3 discusses the experience gained with GST during the period from 2017 to 2022. It discusses the role of the GST Council, the evolutionary nature of the GST tax structure, areas that remain outside the ambit of GST, and GST's revenue performance. Section 5.4 outlines the nature of reforms that are still required in order to make India's GST a comprehensive and modern-day indirect tax system. Section 5.5 provides concluding observations.

5.2 Domestic Indirect Taxes in India: Transition to GST

In order to evaluate the evolution of the system of indirect taxes in India's federal set-up, it is useful to make reference first to the characteristics of a good tax system and assess how India's tax system endeavoured to meet these characteristics as it evolved. In their well-known public finance text, Musgrave and Musgrave (1973) describe a good tax system as having the following as characteristics:

a. **Adequacy of revenue:** The tax system should be revenue productive in a manner that the government is able to finance the provision of public and merit goods to the desired extent.

b. **Equitable distribution:** The tax system should be such that everybody pays their fair share of taxes according to their ability to pay. This issue should be considered in terms of final incidence of tax.
c. **Minimum distortions:** Taxes should be chosen so as to minimize interference with economic decisions relating to allocation of resources in markets that may otherwise be efficient. In fact, taxes impose excess burdens, and the design of the tax system should be such that these are minimized.
d. **Facilitation of stabilization and growth objectives of fiscal policy:** The tax structure should facilitate the use of fiscal policy for stabilization and growth by suitably providing for automatic stabilizers as well as supporting the saving performance of the economic agents.
e. **Fair administration:** The tax system should permit a fair, transparent, non-arbitrary, and easily understandable administration for the taxpayers.
f. **Minimum administration and compliance costs:** The tax system should involve minimum costs of administration for the government and compliance costs for the taxpayer.

5.2.1 The Pre-GST Universe of Domestic Indirect Taxes

Under constitutional arrangements, the central government was given the power to levy central excise duties on the manufacturing of goods. The concept of taxation of services came in much later. Apart from basic excise duties, various additional or special duties of excise were introduced from time to time. Thus, additional duties of excise were levied on sugar, tobacco, and specified textile items such as cotton, woollen, and man-made fabrics, and special additional duties of excise were levied on motor spirits. Two important considerations arose in relation to domestic taxation of goods produced within India vis-à-vis imported goods, and taxation of goods which were produced in one state but sold in another. These considerations led to such taxes as additional duties of customs, which were levied on all imported goods as a countervailing duty (CVD) with respect to central excise duty, and special additional duties (SAD) of customs which were levied as countervailing duty with respect to VAT/state sales tax. A key characteristic of India's indirect tax system was the taxation of inter-state sales. The power to levy this tax was vested with the central government. However, this tax was administered, and its revenues were retained, by the state governments. At first, the idea was to levy this tax more with a view to keeping an account of the inter-state transactions of goods. Its rate was also kept low at 1 per cent. However, gradually this rate was increased to 4 per cent and the revenue importance of this tax grew enormously for the state governments. It became one of the main reasons for cascading and fragmentation of an all-India market. Another layer of problem was introduced with the levy of the service tax. In modern economic systems it is difficult to make a distinction between goods and services, and a separate service tax without any credit given to taxation of goods that were used in the production of services and vice-versa also led to cascading and distortions. By the late 1990s, the landscape of India's indirect tax system had become characterized by multiplicity of taxes, multiplicity of rates for the same tax, cascading of taxes, undue emphasis on the origin principle of taxation, and fragmentation of a genuine all-India common market. At this time, this landscape may be described by the existence of central and state indirect taxes as summarized in Table 5.1.

A number of critical shortcomings of such a fragmented system of indirect taxes may be noted as summarized below.

1. Issues pertaining to definition of manufacturing
2. Problems of valuation
3. Excessive categorization
4. Excessive litigation
5. Cascading
6. Blocking of input taxes
7. Non-transparency in incidence of taxation
8. Absence of all-India common market with CST leading to inter-jurisdictional barriers
9. Issues pertaining to definition of manufacturing

In the case of central excise duties, the main issues arose because the tax was levied on the 'manufacturing' of goods. Since manufacturing did not involve any sales, the goods that were manufactured had no price that could be related to the market. As such, any value attached to the

Table 5.1 List of central and state domestic indirect taxes in India: Pre-GST.

Domestic central indirect taxes	Domestic state indirect taxes
Central excise duties (basic): Levied on non-petroleum goods and petroleum products	State VAT/sales tax
Additional duties of excise: Levied on sugar, tobacco, and specified textile items such as cotton, woollen, and man-made fabrics	Sales tax on motor spirit
Special additional duties of excise: Levied on motor spirit	State excise duties
Additional duties of customs (CVD): Levied on all imported goods in the nature of countervailing duty with respect to central excise duty	Motor vehicle tax
Central sales tax/inter-state sales tax: Levied by the centre, but revenues accrued to the states	Stamp duty and registration fees
Special additional duties of customs (SAD): levied as countervailing duty with respect to VAT/state sales tax	Entertainment tax (other than those levied by local bodies)
Service tax:	Hotel and luxury tax
Taxed by the central government under its residuary powers	Advertisement tax
Issues of cross-cascading (goods are inputs into services and services are inputs into goods)	Entry tax
Fragmentation of value-added tax space	Taxes on lottery, betting, and gambling

Source: Authors' compilation based on https://pib.gov.in/newsite/printrelease.aspx?relid=161273 (accessed 2 June 2021).

manufactured goods by the concerned department faced a lot of litigation. Such litigation pertained to what would constitute manufacturing and how should it be evaluated. It also led to taxation at the location of manufacturing rather than where the manufactured goods were sold. The idea of a good indirect tax system is that inputs should not be taxed, and outputs should be taxed where they are sold. Only the value added that takes place in the process of the production of goods should be taxed, and any tax on inputs paid at earlier stages of manufacturing should be rebated. The nature of the production of goods is such that a final good may be produced after it passes through several intermediate stages of value added. These may all be specialized jobs or works and may be undertaken in different premises. But every time a manufactured good,

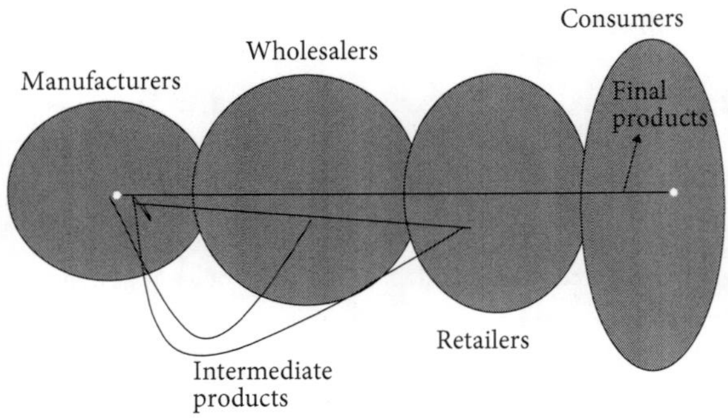

Figure 5.1 Diagrammatic representation of the process of cascading in an indirect tax system.
Source: Authors' depiction.

even if it was not successfully converted into a final good, left a factory or premises, the excise authorities would tax it, and in the subsequent stages taxes would be levied on the already paid tax. Thus the process of cascading—that is, taxation of taxes paid on inputs—became an integral part of the system of excise duties. This process is explained diagrammatically in Figure 5.1.

5.2.2 Fragmentation of Commodity Tax Space

A second problem arose because of the interface between inter-state sales tax and the artificial distinction between value added up to manufacturing and value added up to the final sale of goods. This led to fragmentation of the common market and the overlapping of central and state jurisdictions. This is represented in Figure 5.2.

5.2.3 Distinction between Goods and Services

A third problem arose because of the artificial distinction between goods and services. A distinction can be made between goods that are produced by only using other goods, and services that are produced by only

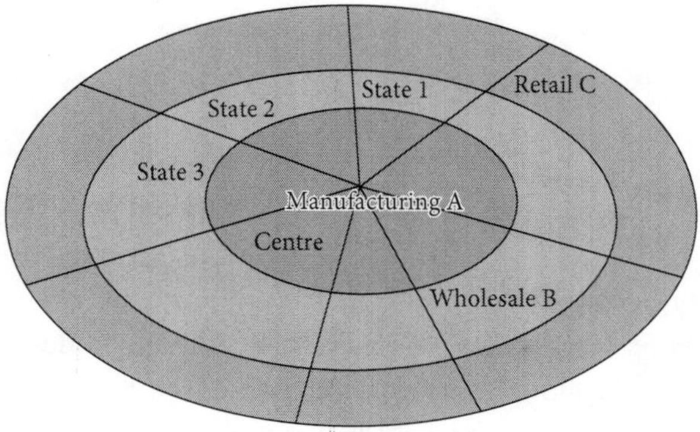

Figure 5.2 Diagrammatic representation of fragmentation of commodity tax space.
Source: Authors' depiction.

Table 5.2 Goods and services produced out of goods and services: Alternative combination.

Inputs/outputs		Output/production and sale	
		Goods	**Services**
Inputs	Goods	Goods where inputs are only goods	Services where inputs are only goods
	Goods and services	**Goods where inputs are goods and services**	**Services where inputs are goods and services**
	Services	Goods where inputs are only services	Services where inputs are only services

Source: Authors' depiction.

using other services. In general, however, in the production of goods, both goods and services are used, and in the production of services also, both goods and services are used. Thus, as shown in Table 5.2, boxes that could contain goods produced only out of goods, and services produced only out of services, were nearly empty. Even if rebates on input taxation were to be given, it would remain limited to these narrow boxes of economic space. In the bigger boxes (where goods were produced out of goods and services, and services were produced out of goods and services), a lot of cascading remained unavoidable since rebates could not be given across taxes.

5.2.4 Issues Relating To Taxation of Capital Assets

A fourth problem arose because of the distinction between capital assets such as real estate vis-à-vis goods that could be produced and sold within a given accounting period. Capital assets could consist of accumulated investment of goods and services but would yield a flow of services over a period of time. These capital assets could be interpreted either as goods or services interchangeably as compared to the flow of goods that are produced and sold within an accounting period. Other related problems arose because of goods that were produced but remained unsold within an accounting period, leading to a problem of taxation of inventories, and correspondingly there was the problem of taxation of goods that were sold in a given period but produced in an earlier period where taxes might have been paid on inputs in the earlier periods.

5.2.5 Taxation of Agriculture Vis-à-Vis That of Manufacturing and Services

A fifth problem arose because of the distinction between taxation of agriculture vis-à-vis that of manufacturing and services. Agriculture as a subject under the Indian Constitution belongs to the State List but involves the use of various manufactured goods and produced services. Agricultural output/income was often not taxed, whereas its inputs were taxed, making it difficult to provide for any scheme of input tax rebate. Many tax reformers visualized as a solution the introduction of a value-added tax system covering both goods and services. Such a tax system was called VAT in many countries and GST in some other countries.

5.2.6 Other issues

Some other issues also arose from time to time. These are briefly described below.

1. Defining whether a particular transaction constituted a sale of goods often became complex, particularly when dealing with software products and intangibles like a right to distribute/exhibit films or time slots for broadcasting advertisements.
2. Local- or other state-level taxes like octroi, entry tax, lease tax, worker's contract tax, entertainment tax, and luxury tax were not integrated into the state VAT regime, which goes against the basic premise of VAT which is meant to have uniformity in the tax structure.
3. Multiplicity of tax rates according to different goods within a state and across states led to considerable heterogeneity across states because of their different schedules.

5.2.7 International Experience with VAT/GST

Many unitary countries and a number of federal countries had already embarked upon VAT/GST before India. India was a relative latecomer in bringing about the GST characterized by the principles of value-added taxation. As of 2020, 170 countries and territories have been operating with a system of VAT/GST; a list of selected major countries is given in Table 5.3.

International practices indicate that in adopting VAT/GST, many countries have adopted a two-rate or three-rate structure.

Figure 5.3 shows that these two groups of countries account for 77 per cent of those that have adopted VAT/GST.

5.2.8 Determining Revenue-Neutral Rates (RNR), and Issues of Transitional Compensation

In the discussions leading up to the transition to GST, considerable effort was focused on determining a revenue-neutral rate (RNR). The idea was that GST should be able to produce at least the same level of revenues as were being obtained by the erstwhile taxes that were to be merged into the GST. The RNR could be considered as a

Table 5.3 List of countries and respective years of adoption of VAT/GST.

	Country	Implementation	Standard rate (per cent)	Reduced rate (per cent)	Increased rate (per cent)	Number of rates
1	Argentina	1974	21	2.5, 5, 10.5	27	5
2	Australia	2000	10	0		2
3	Bangladesh	1991	15	5, 7		3
4	Belgium	1971	21	0, 6, 12		4
5	Brazil	1964	17, 18	4, 7, 12	25, 30	7
6	Canada	1991	5, 13, 15			3
7	China	1994	13	1, 3, 6, 9		5
8	Denmark	1967	25	0		2
9	France	1968	20	2.1, 5.5, 10		4
10	Germany	1968	19	7		2
11	Hungary	1988	27	5, 18		3
12	India	2017	12, 18	0, 5	28	5
13	Indonesia	1985	10	0	10–125	–
14	Iran	2008	9	0	12 + 3, 20 (5 or 10)	–
15	Italy	1973	22	0, 4, 5, 10		5
16	Japan	1989	10	8		2
17	South Korea	1977	10			1
18	Luxembourg	1970	17	3, 8, 14		4
19	Mexico	1980	16	0		2
20	Nepal	1997	13	0		2
21	Netherlands	1969	21	9		2
22	New Zealand	1986	15	0		2
23	Philippines	1988	12	0, 5		3
24	Romania	1993	19	5, 9		3
25	Russia	1991	20	0, 10		3
26	Saudi Arabia	2018	5	0		2
27	Singapore	1994	7	0		2
28	South Africa	1991	15	0		2
29	Spain	1986	21	4, 10		3
30	Sri Lanka	1998	8	0	15	3
31	Switzerland	1995	7.7	2.5, 3.7		3

Table 5.3 Continued

	Country	Implementation	Standard rate (per cent)	Reduced rate (per cent)	Increased rate (per cent)	Number of rates
32	Thailand	1992	10	0, 7		3
33	Turkey	1984	18	1, 8		3
34	UAE	2018	5	0		2
35	UK	1973	20	0, 5		3
36	Venezuela	1993	16	8	31	3
37	Zimbabwe	2004	14.5	0		2

Source: OECD; https://www.oecd-ilibrary.org/sites/1ca62ced-en/index.html?itemId=/content/component/1ca62ced-en (accessed 25 August 2021).

single-rate construct, meaning that it is that single-rate GST which would produce the same level of revenues as that from the merged taxes. However, instead of a single rate, a multiple-rate GST was being considered. Such a rate structure was to be devised around the single-rate RNR. At this point, it also became clear that even if the transition was to be made consistent with a suitable RNR, some states would lose while other states might gain because revenue neutrality was for the system as a whole. Since under the constitutional provisions the gaining states would not compensate the losing states, a separate compensation system had to be planned for. This became necessary at least for a limited period, if the net losing states were to be persuaded to join the comprehensive GST reform. For this purpose, a compensation mechanism was devised. This mechanism consisted of (a) a formula to estimate growth of revenues with respect to which the amount of compensation could be measured, and (b) a mechanism for financing the needed compensation. Thus, with respect to (a), it was decided that an annual growth rate of 14 per cent would be applied to the 2015–16 base revenue of individual states with respect to the state taxes merged in the GST for a period of five years from the point of transition. With respect to (b), a compensation cess on selected items was levied.

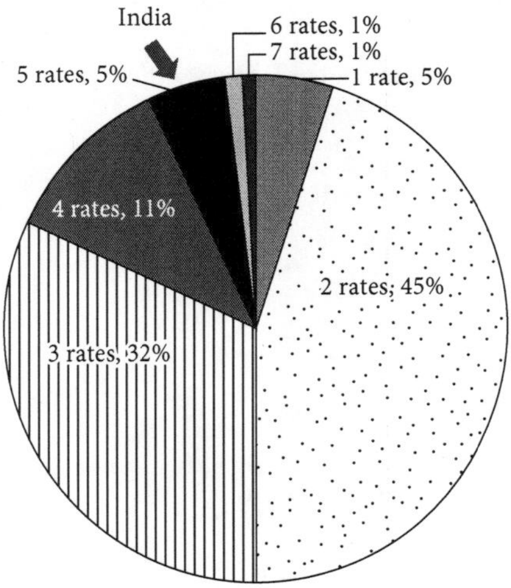

Figure 5.3 Distribution of countries according to the number of VAT rates; about 45 per cent of countries have a two-rate structure of VAT/GST.

Source: OECD; https://www.oecd-ilibrary.org/sites/1ca62ced-en/index.html?itemId=/content/component/1ca62ced-en (accessed on 25 August 2021).

Note: Total number of countries = 168, as Iran and Indonesia are excluded.

In the pre-GST system, the net producing states obtained substantial revenues from the levy of CST or inter-state sales tax. Once CST was to be abolished with the implementation of GST, the expectation was that, after a transition period, the access of the states to the service tax base would compensate them for the loss of CST as well as the sharing of the goods tax base with the central government. This was called the *Grand Bargain* by the Kelkar Committee on Indirect Taxes and the Report of the Thirteenth Finance Commission. Some of the major states that were considered the likely net losers included states with large manufacturing bases such as Maharashtra, Gujarat, Tamil Nadu, Andhra Pradesh, and Karnataka. Some of the expected net gainers included the net consuming states like Uttar Pradesh, Bihar, Madhya Pradesh, Rajasthan, and the erstwhile special-category states.

Thus, given the reluctance of states to agree to implement the GST, as an incentive to cover their likely revenue losses particularly in the initial years, a compensation scheme was designed. However, given the fact that states were not adequately compensated by the central

Table 5.4 Cesses merged under GST Compensation Cess.

1	Rubber Act 1947—cess on rubber
2	Industries (Development and Regulation) Act 1951—cess on automobiles
3	Tea Act 1953—cess on tea
4	Coal Mines (Conservation and Development) Act 1974—cess on coal
5	Beedi Workers' Welfare Cess Act 1971—cess on beedis
6	Water (Prevention and Control of Pollution) Cess Act 1977—cess levied on water consumed by certain industries and by local authorities
7	Sugar Cess Act 1982; Sugar Development Fund Act 1982—cess on sugar
8	Jute Manufacturers Cess Act 1983—cess on jute goods manufactured or produced or in part of jute
9	Finance (2) Act 2004—education cess on excisable goods
10	Finance Act 2007—secondary and higher education cess on excisable goods
11	Finance Act 2010—clean energy cess
12	Finance Act 2015—Swachh Bharat cess
13	Finance Act 2016—infrastructure cess and Krishi Kalyan cess

Source: https://pib.gov.in/newsite/PrintRelease.aspx?relid=164456 (accessed 31 July 2021).

government when CST rates were progressively reduced under the earlier system, there was insistence by the states for the GST compensation mechanism to be constitutionally provided for, or made part of the GST Act. Accordingly, financing of compensation was provided for by the levy of a compensation cess on selected items, so that it could be automatically financed. The list of cesses for this purpose is given in Table 5.4.

Cesses in general are to be discouraged in a GST regime. However, a set of erstwhile cesses in India were continued even after the implementation of GST as summarized in Table 5.5.

5.3 Experience with GST: Key Features

GST was eventually introduced in India with effect from 1 July 2017 after a constitutional amendment (101st amendment). A number of innovations had to be brought in, including the constitution of a GST council.

Table 5.5 Cesses that have continued to be levied under the GST regime.

1	The Finance (2) Act 2004 – education cess on imported goods
2	The Finance Act, 2007 – secondary and higher education cess on imported goods
3	Cess on crude petroleum oil under the Oil Industry Development Act 1974
4	Additional duty of excise on motor spirit (road cess)
5	Additional duty of excise on high speed diesel oil (road cess)
6	Special additional duty of excise on motor spirit
7	NCCD on tobacco and tobacco products and crude petroleum oil

Source: https://pib.gov.in/newsite/PrintRelease.aspx?relid=164456 (accessed 31 July 2021).

5.3.1 The Role of the GST Council

With respect to the taxes merged in GST, the revenue autonomy—that is, the autonomy of the entities levying the taxes to change their rates, classification schemes, deductions, exemptions etc.—was effectively vested in the GST Council. This applied to both the central and the state governments. However, the provisions pertaining to the GST Council and the dynamics of its working have largely implied that it is extremely difficult for any individual state to change any tax rate or other GST-related provisions by itself. The weighting scheme and the voting pattern are such that the central government can almost always get its decisions implemented while no individual state can do so. As per Article 279(A) of the Constitution pertaining to the GST Council, the weight attached to the vote of the central government is 1/3 and that to the state governments/UTs in aggregate is 2/3. Since the number of states and UTs that are members of the GST Council add to 31, an individual state/UT accounts for 0.0215, that is 2.15 per cent, as compared to the centre's weight of 33.33 per cent. These numbers are based on the assumption that all members of the GST Council are present and voting. Further, this article provides that:

> Every decision of the Goods and Services Tax Council shall be taken at a meeting, by a majority of not less than three-fourths of the weighted votes of the members present and voting, in accordance with the following principles, namely:—(a) the vote of the Central Government shall have a weightage of one-third of the total votes cast, and (b) the

votes of all the State Governments taken together shall have a weightage of two-thirds of the total votes cast, in that meeting.

Thus, even if all states join together, they will only have an aggregate vote of 66.7 per cent—less than the required 75 per cent majority for carrying a decision through. As such, states, individually or together, cannot carry forward any GST reform on their own. Thus, effectively, the centre has a veto power. On the other hand, if the states were to form a group in order to hold a centre's move, they will require a minimum of 12 votes. If we examine these provisions from the viewpoint of the centre, they will require the support of 19.4 states/UTs with legislature—that is, at least 20 states/UTs with legislature (because $1/3 + 20 \times (2/3) \times (1/31) = 0.33 + 0.43 = 0.76$, thus crossing the 75 percent benchmark)—for a piece of legislation to be passed. This may prove to be an uphill task as long as there are 12 states/UTs forming governments by opposition parties, provided they form a group. These provisions, therefore, make any reform to GST extremely difficult. This is why the GST Council keeps going via the rule of unanimity. But unanimity leads to agreement on lowest common denominators. Such agreement is usually arrived at when rates are lowered rather than increased or rationalized. Further, incremental changes may go through relatively more smoothly, whereas the major reforms that India's GST actually requires are very difficult to negotiate.

An important recent development in this context came from a recent Supreme Court judgment which has clarified that decisions of the GST Council are not binding on the participating governments and at best have only a persuasive value (see this chapter's Appendix). This has opened up the possibility of the GST tax rate structure evolving towards a heterogeneous structure across states over time.

5.3.2 The GST structure

Major central taxes which were merged in the GST included: (1) union excise duties (except those pertaining to specified petroleum products), (2) service tax, (3) additional duties of excise, (4) excise duty on medicinal and toiletries preparation, (5) additional duties of customs (CVD), (6) special additional duties of customs (SAD), and (7) selected surcharges and cesses. Major state taxes which were merged in the GST included: (1) state VAT (except on specified petroleum products), (2) entry tax, (3) entertainment tax (other than those levied by local bodies), (4) hotel and luxury tax, (5) central sales tax (except on specified petroleum products), (6) advertisement tax, (7) taxes on lottery, betting, and gambling, and (8) state surcharges.

In India, the GST rate for various taxable goods and services is divided into four parts, as shown in Table 5.6. A low rate of tax of 5 per cent is levied on essential items, whereas a high rate of 28 per cent is levied on demerit and luxury goods and services. The standard GST rates are 12 per cent and 18 per cent. Further, a special rate of 3 per cent is levied on gold, silver, and jewellery. Precious stones (other than diamonds) and semi-precious stones attract a GST rate of 0.25 per cent.

As discussed earlier, the artificial attempt to seek unanimity in GST Council decisions has led over time to all participants agreeing to the lowest common denominators. As such, in the long list of GST rate revisions, the overwhelming trend has been towards lowering the GST rates. As the rates are lowered, revenues may also be adversely affected if the base-increasing effect is less than the revenue-reducing impact of the rate reductions. In Table 5.7, we highlight that in 51 GST Council meetings held up to 2 August 2023, 622 rate revisions were undertaken out of which 578 related to reduction of rates.

In recent years, the trend of downward revision in GST rates has been reversed to some extent. The GST Council had set up a Group of Ministers (GoM) in September 2021 to consider rationalization of the GST rates with a view to increasing GST revenues. The GoM recommendations were considered in the 47th meeting of the GST Council,

Table 5.6 GST rate structure: Standard rates.

	Special (gold and other precious metals)	Lower rate	Standard rate	Services/ selected goods rate	Demerit rate
GST rates	1.5 per cent/ 3 per cent	5 per cent	12 per cent	18 per cent	28 per cent

Source: Authors' compilation based on https://cbic-gst.gov.in/gst-goods-services-rates.html (accessed 20 February 2022).

Table 5.7 List of GST rate revisions: First to 50th GST Council meetings.

Change in GST rate(s)	First to tenth revision, till 37th GST Council meeting on 20 September 2019	Eleventh to Fifteenth revision, till 44th GST Council meeting on 27 June 2021	Sixteenth to Twentieth revision, till 37th GST Council meeting on 18 February 2023	Twenty-first revision as on 50th GST Council meeting* held on 11 July 2023	Total
28% to 18%, 12%, 5%, 0%, Nil	277	1	0	0	278
18% to 12%, 5%, 0%, Nil	117	6	7	3	133
12% to 5%, 0%, Nil	69	12	12	1	94
8% to 1%	1	0	0	0	1
5% to 0%, Nil	24	2	1	0	27
Applicable rate to 3%, Nil	2	0	2	0	4
3% to 0.25%, 0%, Nil	5	0	0	0	5
Exemption (incl. IGST)	5	22[†]	0	4	31
15%[‡] to 1%, 3%	2	0	0	0	2
Total items with lower GST rates	502	44[§]	24[¶]	8	578
Total items with higher GST rates	4	6	30	4	44
Total items affected	**506**	**50**	**54**	**12**	**622**

Source: Author's compilation; GSTN, PIB.

Notes:

* Fifty-first GST Council meeting did not involve any rate revisions.

† Twenty of these items were exempted from IGST on imports even if imported on payment basis during the 43rd GST council meeting, held on 28 May 2021. Earlier, on 3 May 2021, these had been exempted if imported on free-of-cost basis for free distribution.

‡ Rate of GST compensation cess.

§ Includes a category of items whose GST rates are reduced to 5% upon the recommendation of MoHFW and Dept of Pharma during the 44th GST council meeting, held on 27 June 2021.

¶ Includes (a) retro-fitment kits for vehicles used by the disabled whose rate was reduced to 5% from more the applicable rate as per PIB PR dated 17 September 2021, and (b) IGST exemption on goods supplied at Indo-Bangladesh border haats during the recommendation of the 45th GST Council meeting, held on 17 September 2021.

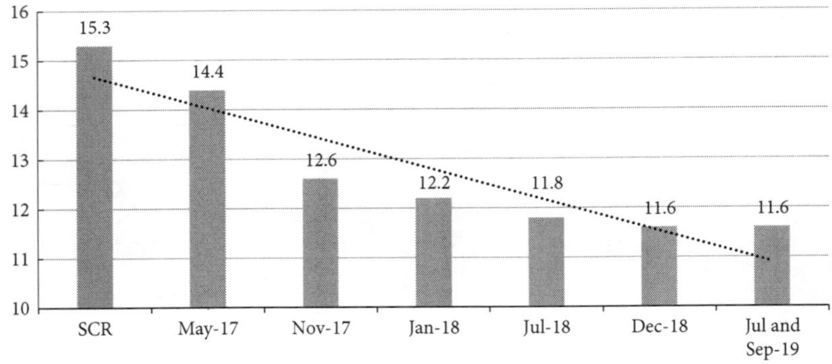

Figure 5.4 Weighted average (effective) GST rate.
Source (basic data): *RBI Bulletin*, September 2019.
Note: SCR refers to Subramanian Committee recommendation.

and accordingly 42 rate increases were implemented. The rate revisions included: (a) rate increases on 21 goods/services (excluding withdrawal of exemptions), (b) withdrawal of complete exemption on 15 goods/services, and (c) reduction in rates of six goods/services. Most of the upward-rate revisions were undertaken with the objective of correcting the still-continuing inverted duty structures. These rates were made applicable with effect from 18 July 2022. Similarly, in the 50th GST Council Meeting, held on 11 July 2023, the GST rate on online gaming, horse racing, and casinos was increased to 2 per cent% from 18 per cent, with the applicable base extended to cover the full face value.

A recent RBI study (*RBI Bulletin* September 2019) has estimated the effective weighted average GST rate which has fallen over time as compared to the effective RNR at the time of transition. The RNR was estimated at 14.4 per cent in May 2017 just prior to the introduction of GST in July 2017 (Figure 5.4).

5.3.3 Areas left uncovered in GST

Major goods that could not be included in the present GST include petroleum products, alcoholic liquor, real estate, electricity, and agriculture. These items are of significant revenue importance for both the central and the state governments. The continuation of taxation of these products outside of GST provides a limited degree of residual revenue autonomy to both the central and the state governments. Given the lack-lustre revenue performance of GST, neither the central government nor the state governments are in favour of including these left-out items in GST. Incomplete GST reforms appear to have entered a gridlock, which none of the participating governments are willing to break out of, at least in the short to medium term. We have argued that there is only one way the GST reforms can be completed while ensuring revenue adequacy as well as revenue autonomy for the participating governments (see Srivastava (2022)). This is to integrate environmental and demerit taxes into GST by including a non-rebatable cess in the GST scheme of taxation and giving a degree of autonomy for the participating governments to fix the rate of this cess. Such a cess or additional non-refundable levy may be implemented by both the centre and the states, and the rate of such a cess can be different for the central and individual states with a view to raising revenues consistent with their current revenues from the petroleum products and state excise duties on alcoholic liquor.

5.3.4 Revenue Performance

The growth of GST revenues and their buoyancy with respect to GDP at current prices indicate a massive erosion as compared to the pre-GST performance of the taxes merged in GST. As shown in Table 5.8, the growth of taxes merged in GST from 2014–15 to 2016–17 was 12.46 per cent. This fell to 6.21 per cent from 2017–18 to 2021–22. Correspondingly, the buoyancy of GST vis-à-vis that of the merged taxes fell from 1.13 to 0.5 during the relevant period. These are comparisons based on GST performance excluding the GST compensation cess. Similar trends are seen even if we include the compensation cess, as shown in Table 5.9.

5.3.5 Working and Revenue Underperformance of the GST Compensation Cess

There have been many issues in the design and working of the compensation cess mechanism. The decision to finance it through an elaborate

Table 5.8 Assessing GST's Performance (excluding GST compensation cess).

Year	Subsumed taxes/GST collections excluding GST compensation cess	GST revenues		
		Growth	Buoyancy	Notes
2011–12	5,09,076			Pre-GST
2012–13	6,33,921	24.5	1.8	
2013–14	6,96,299	9.8	0.8	
2014–15	7,50,110	7.7	0.7	
2015–16	8,57,228	14.3	1.4	
2016–17	9,88,997	15.4	1.3	
2017–18	9,24,252	−6.5	−0.6	Part GST
2018–19	9,76,939	5.7	0.5	
2019–20	10,02,244	2.6	0.4	
2020–21	9,77,824	−2.4	–	COVID year
2021–22	12,88,296	31.8	1.6	
Average over FY18–FY22		**6.21**	**0.50***	
Average over FY15–FY17		**12.46**	**1.13**	
FY18–FY22 minus FY15–FY17		**−6.25**	**−0.37**	

Source: Respective state budgets, Union Budgets, CGA, RBI (State Finances: A study of state budgets).

Notes: (1) State revenues include revenues of all states and Union Territories with legislature. For 2020–21 and 2021–22 the revenues of states are RE and BE, respectively. (2) For the centre's 2021–22 revenues, data have been sourced from the CGA.

*Excludes the buoyancy for the COVID year of FY21 because of negative nominal growth and tax revenues.

scheme of cesses defeated the very first objective of making the transition to GST, which was to discontinue the multiple cesses mainly on central taxes. The compensation cess mechanism worked by replacing one set of cesses with another and a larger one, which was also distortionary in some cases. One important example is the clean energy cess/coal cess which has been merged in the GST compensation cess. This defeated the very purpose of compensating the states that suffered the environmental hazards due to coal mining. Instead, now these revenues are to be shared amongst all the states that would be entitled for receiving the GST compensation according to the agreed formula. Thus, a targeted cess was replaced by a generalized revenue-sharing device.

Table 5.9 Assessing GST's performance (including GST compensation cess).

Year	Subsumed taxes/ GST collections including GST compensation cess	GDP growth	GST revenues		
			Growth in revenues	Buoyancy	Notes
2011–12	5,09,076				Pre-GST
2012–13	6,33,921	13.8	24.5	1.77	
2013–14	6,96,299	13.0	9.8	0.76	
2014–15	7,50,110	11.0	7.7	0.70	
2015–16	8,57,228	10.5	14.3	1.37	
2016–17	9,88,997	11.8	15.4	1.31	
2017–18	9,86,864	11.0	−0.2	−0.02	Part GST
2018–19	10,72,020	10.6	8.6	0.81	
2019–20	10,97,797	6.2	2.4	0.39	
2020–21	10,63,016	−1.4	−3.2	-	COVID year
2021–22	13,92,879	19.5	31.0	1.59	
Average over FY18–FY22			**7.74**	**0.69***	
Average over FY15–FY17			**12.46**	**1.13**	
FY18–FY22 minus FY15–FY17			**−4.72**	**−0.11**	

Source: Respective state budgets, Union Budgets, CGA, RBI (State Finances: A study of state budgets).

* Excludes the buoyancy for the COVID year of FY21 because of negative nominal growth and tax revenues.

Notes: (1) State revenues include revenues of all states and Union Territories with legislature. For 2020–21 and 2021–22 the revenues of states are RE and BE, respectively. (2) For the centre's 2021–22 revenues, data have been sourced from the CGA. (3) GST compensation cess revenues by the centre have been included in the total revenues. However, borrowings by the centre in lieu of shortfall in GST compensation cess have been excluded.

A second difficulty in the implementation of the cess pertained to its inadequate revenues. Thus, the agreed compensation at the rate of 14 per cent growth on the 2015–16 base of the merged taxes could not be financed by the proceeds of the compensation cess. As per the 15th FC estimates, the total requirement for compensation would be Rs 7.10 lakh crore at the end of June 2022. At that time, the estimated balance in the compensation fund would be Rs 2.25 lakh crore. Therefore, the compensation cess would have to be extended up to 2025–26 in order to raise the balance amount of Rs 4.85 lakh crore. In order to finance these unpaid amounts, the GST Council will have to continue with the cess but not necessarily the compensation mechanism. Already, the GST Council has decided to extend the compensation cess up to March 2026 for financing the unpaid amounts for 2020–21 and 2021–22, including repayment and servicing of loans raised by the central government to pay due compensation as an interim measure.

If the compensation provisions are discontinued, a good number of states will suffer a major revenue shock. Some of the major losers in spite of the compensation mechanism have been Tamil Nadu, Kerala, and Andhra Pradesh (Table 5.10).

5.4 GST Reforms: Reforming the Reformed System

India's GST is still an incomplete story. In particular, a large share of sales pertaining to petroleum products, agricultural products, electricity, and real estate remains outside the purview of GST. In terms of revenue importance, the share of taxation of petroleum products and alcoholic beverages by the central and state governments amounted to 60.8 per cent in 2019–20 and 83.3 per cent in 2020–21 of GST revenues excluding compensation cess (Table 5.11).

Given the revenue importance of these exclusions, neither the central nor the state governments are likely to vote in favour of including these products in GST due to the need for maintaining a degree of revenue autonomy. The only way in which GST can be reformed and made fully or near fully comprehensive is to ensure that all participating governments have adequate revenue autonomy. For this purpose, one clear, and perhaps the only, way out is to incorporate the idea of integrating environmental and demerit taxes in GST through the mechanism of a non-rebatable cess on polluting and demerit inputs and outputs. The findings of an earlier study (Srivastava and Kavi Kumar (2012)) in this context were presented to the 13th Finance Commission and the Commission on Centre–State Relations (Puncchi Commission). In their respective reports, they had emphatically endorsed this idea as indicated below.

Table 5.10 Perspective on state-wise gainers and losers under GST.

State	Average share (per cent) in SGST + state's share in IGST(2017–18 to 2019–20)	Share (per cent) in taxes merged into GST (2015–16)	Excess of GST share (per cent) over share in merged taxes
(1)	(2)	(3)	(4) = (2) - (3)
Tamil Nadu	7.63	11.43	−3.8
Kerala	4.02	5.62	−1.6
Andhra Pradesh	4	5.11	−1.1
Telangana	4.5	5.18	−0.68
Uttarakhand	0.9	1.14	−0.25
Karnataka	8.12	8.34	−0.22
Himachal Pradesh	0.68	0.89	−0.21
Puducherry	0.13	0.32	−0.19
Delhi	3.81	3.97	−0.17
Gujarat	6.73	6.88	−0.15
Goa	0.49	0.55	−0.06
Punjab	2.56	2.62	−0.06
Jammu and Kashmir	1.03	1.08	−0.05
Haryana	3.55	3.58	−0.04

Source (basic data): RBI (State Finances: A Study of Budgets 2020) for SGST revenues covering 2017–18 and 2018–1,9 and taxes merged into GST and respective state budget documents for data on SGST revenues for 2019–20.

> The taxation of petroleum products and natural gas would be rationalized by including them in the tax base. HSD, MS, and ATF could be charged GST and an additional levy by both the Central and State Governments. No input credit would be available against either CGST or SGST on the additional levy. A similar treatment would be provided to alcohol and tobacco. Such an arrangement would ensure protection of existing revenues while taking care of environmental concerns.
>
> (Para. 5.28 of the Report of the Thirteenth Finance Commission)

In view of the dire need to arrest environmental degradation it is necessary to integrate environmental considerations within the framework of GST. Environmental taxes act as an indirect mechanism to control

Table 5.11 Taxes on petroleum products and alcoholic beverages relative to GST revenues (taxes merged in GST in the pre-GST years).

Year	Including GST compensation cess	Excluding GST compensation cess
2011–12	49.1	
2012–13	45.3	
2013–14	43.5	Same as in previous column
2014–15	45.5	
2015–16	50.9	
2016–17	53.1	
2017–18	56.3	60.1
2018–19	54.3	59.6
2019–20	55.5	60.8
2020–21	76.3	83.3

Source: Respective state budgets, Union Budgets, CGA, RBI (State Finances: A study of state budgets).

> pollution and are likely to induce appropriate environmental decisions. We therefore recommend that polluting inputs and outputs may be subjected to a special non-rebatable levy by both the Centre and the States. In addition, petroleum products, alcoholic beverages and tobacco products may also be subjected to a non-rebatable levy.
>
> (Para. 9.5.02 of the Report of the Commission on Centre–State Relations—Volume III)

This reform can serve the purpose of not only restoring revenue buoyancy but also protecting revenue autonomy of the central and individual state governments. This is because the GST core rate may be fixed at a suitable level, but it is the non-rebatable cess which can be used to calibrate with upward and downward adjustments. Both the centre and the states may be given a flexibility in determining the applicable rate of cess in their respective jurisdictions.

The GST Council may have to play a critical role in continuing with GST reforms so that it is transformed into a truly comprehensive value-added tax system. Recently, the compensation cess mechanism was extended to cover the payment of compensation arrears up to June 2022. In addition, states have been asking for its continuation so that some of the states that may continue to lose on this account may be compensated for that loss in the medium term. If such an arrangement were to be agreed to, the compensation cess mechanism should be continued with significant modifications as compared to the original scheme. In particular, the 14 per cent annual growth may not be relevant and should be recalibrated. An effort should also be made to progressively reduce the number of compensation cesses that have been introduced. These should eventually be eliminated, except for those that relate to demerit and polluting goods.

5.5 Concluding Observations

GST was introduced in India with effect from 1 July 2017 after a long period of deliberations between the central and state governments. The objective of implementing GST was to remove various infirmities of India's system of domestic indirect taxes. These infirmities included multiplicity of tax rates, distortions affecting market allocation of resources, cascading, predominance of the origin principle adversely affecting tax revenues of the consuming states, and fragmentation of a genuine common market across India. The first five years of the implementation of GST showed its revenue inadequacy, continued tax evasion and high compliance burden, and continuation of the inverted duty structure. Only more recently has GST revenue growth shown a tangible improvement.

Future GST reforms should include (1) further rationalization of the GST rates, reducing to at best a two- or three-rate structure; (2) bringing into its ambit demerit and polluting goods with the provision of a non-rebatable levy to make up for the consequent revenue loss; (3) further strengthening of the IT platform and reduction in compliance requirements; and (4) strengthening GST data and sharing it with not only the central and state governments but also other stakeholders. One expectation from GST related to its positive impact on efficiency and thereby growth. So far, there has not been any evidence of such a positive impact. However, as the system matures and after some of the residual areas like petroleum products and alcoholic liquor are brought in GST's ambit, it may eventually prove to have a positive impact on growth and employment.

References

Centre–State Financial Relations and Planning (2010). Report of the Commission on Centre–State Relations (vol. 3). https://interstatecouncil.gov.in/wp-content/uploads/2015/06/volume3.pdf. Government of India, Delhi.

Chadha, R (2009). 'Moving to Goods and Services Tax in India: Impact on India's Growth and International Trade'. Trade Working Papers no. 23071, East Asian Bureau of Economic Research.

Compliance Audit Report of the Comptroller and Auditor General of India on Goods and Services Tax (2021). Central Excise and Service Tax Revenue (Report No. 1 of 2021) for the Year ended March 2019. https://cag.gov.in/en/audit-report/details/113428.

Compliance Audit Report of the Comptroller and Auditor General of India (2020). Report No.11 of 2019—Compliance Audit of Union Government, Department of Revenue (Indirect Taxes—Goods and Services Tax). https://cag.gov.in/uploads/media/AR-no-11-of-2020-E-05f80987f0fd291-60966608-20201116151607-20201225150521.pdf.

GSTN (2020). A Statistical Report on Completion of 3 Years of GST; https://icmai.in/upload/Taxation/Statistical_Report_GST_10072020.pdf (accessed 1 August 2021).

GSTN (2021). A Statistical Report on Completion of 4 years of GST; https://tutorial.gst.gov.in/offlineutilities/gst_statistics/4YearReport.pdf (accessed 10 August 2021).

Keen, Michael (2015). 'Targeting and Indirect Tax Design', in Benedict J. Clements, Ruud A. de Mooij, Sanjeev Gupta, Miet al. (eds), Inequality and Fiscal Policy, International Monetary Fund, Washington, DC.

Kotha, A. P., Agarwal, V., Sengupta, A. et al. (2018). 'Cesses and Surcharges: Concept, Practice and Reform', submitted to the Fifteenth Finance Commission. Report, Vidhi Centre for Legal Policy.

Leemput, E. V., and Wiencek, E. A. (2017). 'The Effect of the GST on Indian Growth'. International Finance Discussion Paper Notes. Board of Governors of the Federal Reserve System, International Finance Discussion Paper Note, Washington DC.

Mehta, Diva, and Mukherjee, Sacchidananda (2021). 'Emerging Issues in GST Law and Procedures: An Assessment'. NIPFP working paper no. 21/347. National Institute of Public Finance and Policy, New Delhi.

Mukherjee, Sacchidananda (2020). 'Plugging Loopholes in Taxation of Interstate Sales'. *Economic and Political Weekly*, 55(19), 18–20.

Musgrave, R. A., and Musgrave, P. B. (1973). *Public Finance in Theory and Practice*. McGraw-Hill.

Rao, Kavita (2014). 'Revenue Implications of GST and Estimation of Revenue Neutral Rate: Estimates for 2011–12', National Institute of Public Finance and Policy, New Delhi.

Report of the Task Force on Goods and Services Tax submitted to the Thirteenth Finance Commission (2009). https://fincomindia.nic.in/writereaddata/html_en_files/oldcommission_html/fincom13/discussion/report291209.pdf (accessed 25 June 2021).

Report of the Thirteenth (2009) and Fifteenth (2020) Finance Commissions https://fincomindia.nic.in/asset/pdf/commission-reports/13fcreng.pdf;

https://fincomindia.nic.in/commission-reports-fifteenth (accessed 17 May 2021).

Report on the Revenue Neutral Rate and Structure of Rates for the Goods and Services Tax (GST) (2015). Government of India, Ministry of Finance (4 December 2015). http://www.gstcouncil.gov.in/sites/default/files/CEA-rpt-rnr.pdf (accessed 2 December 2021).

Srivastava, D. K. (2022). 'Intergovernmental Fiscal Relations in India: Time for the Next Generation of Reforms'. Madras School of Economics Working Paper 222, July. Madras School of Economics, Chennai.

Srivastava, D. K., and Kavi Kumar, K. S. (2012). 'Integrating Eco-Taxes in the Goods and Services Tax Regime in India'. Madras School of Economics, monograph no. 16/2012, Madras School of Economics, Chennai..

Srivastava, D. K., and Kumar, K. K. (eds) (2014). *Environment and Fiscal Reforms in India*. SAGE Publications, New Delhi.

Appendix

Supreme Court Judgment: in the case *of Union of India & Anr. v M/s Mohit Minerals Pvt. Ltd.*, delivered on 19 May 2022.

i. The recommendations of the GST Council are not binding on the Union and States for the following reasons:
   a. The deletion of Article 279B and the inclusion of Article 279(1) by the Constitution Amendment Act 2016 indicates that the Parliament intended for the recommendations of the GST Council to only have a persuasive value, particularly when interpreted along with the objective of the GST regime to foster cooperative federalism and harmony between the constituent units;
   b. Neither does Article 279A begin with a non-obstante clause nor does Article 246A state that it is subject to the provisions of Article 279A. The Parliament and the State legislatures possess

simultaneous power to legislate on GST. Article 246A does not envisage a repugnancy provision to resolve the inconsistencies between the Central and the State laws on GST. The 'recommendations' of the GST Council are the product of a collaborative dialogue involving the union and states. They are recommendatory in nature. To regard them as binding edicts would disrupt fiscal federalism, where both the union and the States are conferred equal power to legislate on GST. It is not imperative that one of the federal units must always possess a higher share in the power for the federal units to make decisions. Indian federalism is a dialogue between cooperative and uncooperative federalism where the federal units are at liberty to use different means of persuasion ranging from collaboration to contestation; and

c. The Government while exercising its rule-making power under the provisions of the CGST Act and IGST Act is bound by the recommendations of the GST Council. However, that does not mean that all the recommendations of the GST Council made by virtue of the power Article 279A (4) are binding on the legislature's power to enact primary legislations;

ii. On a conjoint reading of Sections 2(11) and 13(9) of the IGST Act, read with Section 2(93) of the CGST Act, the import of goods by a CIF contract constitutes an 'inter-state' supply which can be subject to IGST where the importer of such goods would be the recipient of shipping service;

iii. The IGST Act and the CGST Act define reverse charge and prescribe the entity that is to be taxed for these purposes. The specification of the recipient—in this case the importer—by Notification 10/2017 is only clarificatory. The Government by notification did not specify a taxable person different from the recipient prescribed in Section 5(3) of the IGST Act for the purposes of reverse charge;

iv. Section 5(4) of the IGST Act enables the Central Government to specify a class of registered persons as the recipients, thereby conferring the power of creating a deeming fiction on the delegated legislation;

v. The impugned levy imposed on the 'service' aspect of the transaction is in violation of the principle of 'composite supply' enshrined under Section 2(30) read with Section 8 of the CGST Act. Since the Indian importer is liable to pay IGST on the 'composite supply', comprising of supply of goods and supply of services of transportation, insurance, etc. in a CIF contract, a separate levy on the Indian importer for the 'supply of services' by the shipping line would be in violation of Section 8 of the CGST Act.

6

GST, End of Compensation Regime, and Stress on State Finances

R. Kavita Rao

6.1 Introduction

The introduction of GST in India constitutes a major departure from the then existing regime of taxation of goods and services. Apart from a change in the structure and the level of taxes on different sectors, the change in regime also brought in a significant change in the operational autonomy of tax policy for both the union government and the state governments. The expectation at the time of introduction of GST was for the regime to acquire stability and buoyancy within a few years. With this in mind, the union government proposed to assure a reasonable growth in revenues for the state governments for a period of five years.

The period since the introduction of GST has been one of considerable turmoil in the economy. The COVID-19 pandemic in its many waves has disrupted the economy and resulted in lower economic growth and slower growth in tax revenues. With the economic shocks, the revenue performance of the union and states has been correspondingly poorer than in the pre-GST period. Further, the GST regime is soon going to complete five years in operation. Therefore, there are two big challenges the governments face in going forward: first, there is need to raise the level and the rate of growth of revenues to ensure that the regime provides adequate revenues in the medium term; and second, in the short run, there is a potential shortfall of revenues for states which needs to be addressed to ensure short-run viability. There is considerable discussion on the first aspect, with a focus on the need for recalibration of the rates of tax for GST. The present chapter is an attempt to present the contours

R. Kavita Rao, *GST, End of Compensation Regime, and Stress on State Finances* In: *Fiscal Policy and Public Financial Management*. Edited by: Pinaki Chakraborty and K R Shanmugam, Oxford University Press.
 DOI: 10.1093/9780198930464.003.0006

of the second challenge and explore options available to the GST Council on this front.

The rest of this chapter is organized as follows: Section 6.2 highlights the differences in revenue performance of states pre and post GST, alongside figures of GST compensation claimed by the states during this period. Section 6.3 explores the impact on GST revenues inclusive of compensation, once the current regime comes to an end. In particular, it identifies states which could experience a decline in revenue in 2022–23. In light of the challenges that states would face to find offsetting revenues, Section 6.4 explores some alternative mechanisms for smoothing the revenue profile of the states.

6.2 Revenue Performance Under GST

The volatility in economic activity in the country and the resultant volatility in revenue collections implies that in order to understand the revenue performance of GST, one cannot look at the gross collections per se. Figure 6.1 below presents the ratio of GST collections to GDP. As is evident from the figure, the ratio has remained around 6 per cent or slightly higher for most of the period.

Trends in gross revenue collections in Figure 6.2 show that the revenue from SGST including IGST settlement seems to be consistently lower than the revenue attributable to the union government (here defined as

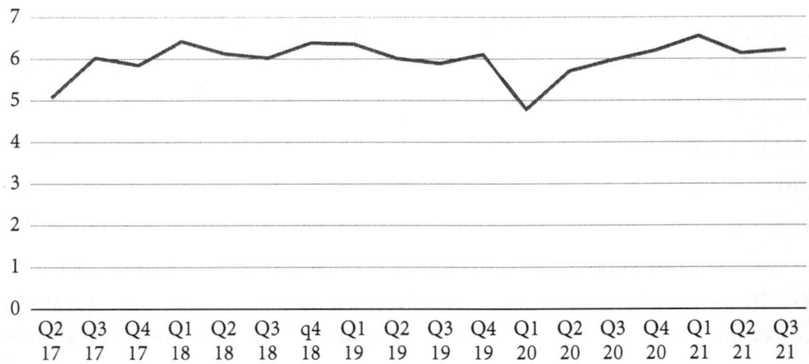

Figure 6.1 GST revenue as a percentage of GDP.

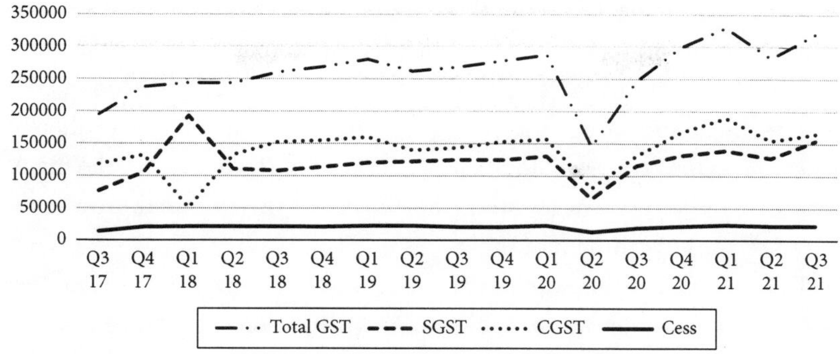

Figure 6.2 GST collections (Rs crore).

Source: https://www.gst.gov.in/download/gststatistics (accessed on 20 March 2022).

Note: Revenue from GST compensation cess is kept separate from the other revenue collections.

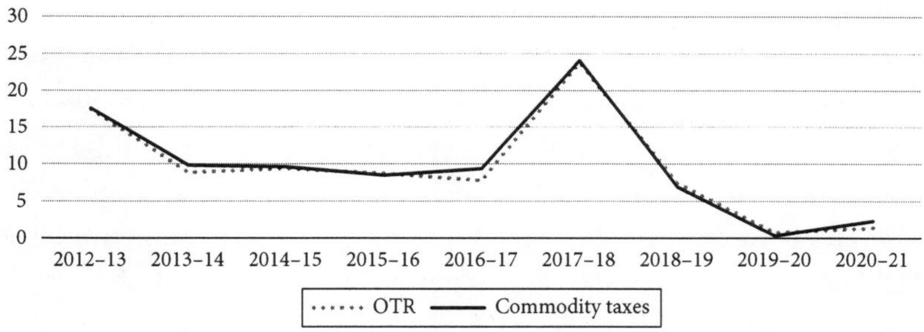

Figure 6.3 All states: Growth of OTR and commodity taxes.

Source: Using RBI state finances data.

Note: For all years data for accounts are used, except for 2020–21, where RE is used.

all GST revenue net of cess and SGST with IGST settlement). Staggering of the settlement process can be one reason for this observed difference between revenues to union and state governments.

Turning to revenue collections for the states, it is illustrative to compare the growth in revenue collections pre and post GST. Given that the revenues attributable to the taxes subsumed in GST are not readily available for years other than 2015–16, a comparison of own tax revenues (OTR) of the states taken together and revenues from taxes on commodities and services are presented as close approximations (Figure 6.3). It is evident that the average rate of growth prior to GST appears to be higher than that in the years subsequent to the introduction of GST.

Further, as Table 6.1 shows, the average growth in revenue for taxes on commodities and services varies considerably across states. Two features are evident from this table. One, for some states, implementation of GST resulted in an increase in the average growth rate, while in others, there is a decline when compared to the pre-GST period. Two, most of the major states report growth of less than 14 per cent—the nominal growth assured by the government of India.

To get a sense of the extent of dependence of the states on the resources provided as compensation, Table 6.2 provides trends in total compensation paid to states by year, along with total revenue states earned through SGST and IGST settlement. The table clearly shows that compensation dues have become quite large in comparison to the revenues generated through GST.

To help understand the dimensions of the role played by GST compensation in state finances, Figure 6.4 provides a comparison of the ratio of GST compensation received to fiscal deficit for 2020–21. The figure suggests that the size of the compensation is considerable and ending the compensation regime in the absence of any other measures could considerably affect the ability of states to maintain their spending programmes without taking recourse to expenditure compression in some way. The problem is more pronounced for states like Himachal Pradesh, Punjab, Karnataka, and Odisha.

6.3 Projected Implications for State Revenues for the Year 2022–23

In an attempt to facilitate the adoption of GST, the union government agreed to a proposal to provide an assurance in growth of revenue for the states for a period of five years from the date of introduction of GST. The assurance implied a 14 per cent rate of growth of revenue for the states, with 2015–16 being the reference year. However, the compensation period comes to an end in June 2022. In other words, from July 2022, the states are on their own so far as GST revenues are concerned. What is the implication of this for state revenues from GST?

Using some assumptions, we attempt to present a picture of the likely scenario of states revenues from GST. The revenue collections used

Table 6.1 Average growth of revenue from taxes on commodities and services (per cent).

States with lower growth			States with higher growth		
	Pre GST	Post GST		Pre GST	Post GST
Bihar	13.3	11.2	Andhra Pradesh	2.0	6.7
Chhattisgarh	12.6	4.4	Arunachal Pradesh	18.4	34.6
Goa	10.5	3.4	Assam	10.2	12.5
Gujarat	8.6	7.2	Manipur	11.5	31.3
Haryana	11.8	7.9	Meghalaya	11.5	21.5
Himachal Pradesh	11.7	3.0	Nagaland	12.0	23.2
Jammu and Kashmir	11.0	10.4	Tripura	11.0	12.3
			Uttar Pradesh	10.7	11.3
Jharkhand	13.8	11.1			
Karnataka	12.6	3.3			
Kerala	11.6	2.1			
Madhya Pradesh	12.1	4.4			
Maharashtra	9.7	9.5			
Mizoram	21.1	18.3			
NCT Delhi	9.7	−1.2			
Odisha	11.2	9.8			
Puducherry	9.4	0.2			
Punjab	10.5	2.1			
Rajasthan	13.0	11.5			
Sikkim	19.0	10.2			
Tamil Nadu	8.4	6.0			
Telangana	28.5	12.2			
Uttarakhand	14.4	−0.3			
West Bengal	14.1	8.0			

Source: Computed using RBI State Finances Database.

Note: Pre GST is the average growth over the period 2011–12 to 2016–17. Post GST is the average growth over the period 2017–18 to 2020–21. For Andhra Pradesh and Telangana, the pre-GST period is taken to be 2014–15 to 2016–17, given the reorganization of erstwhile Andhra Pradesh.

pertain to the period April to February 2021–22. The average of the levels achieved in the last six months was used as an estimate of the revenue for March 2022. With this assumption, we get an estimate of the likely revenue for 2021–22 for individual states.

Table 6.2 GST revenue and compensation received for all states together (Rs crore).

	Compensation dues	Total SGST revenue
2017–18	49,276	3,76,186
2018–19	81,887	4,53,736
2019–20	1,65,302	5,03,704
2020–21	2,87,134	4,52,398
2021–22	2,59,000	5,48,303

Source: PIB press releases, https://www.gst.gov.in/download/gststatistics (accessed 20 March 2022).

Note: Compensation dues for 2021–22 are estimates and revenue for 2021–22 is up to February 2022.

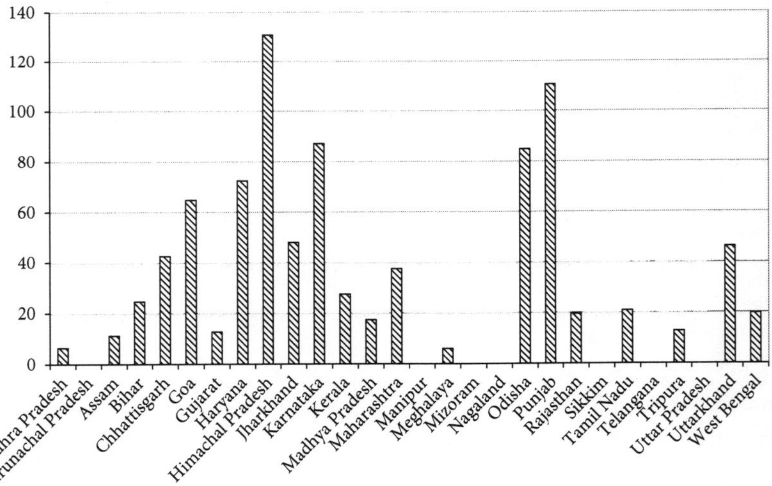

Figure 6.4 Ratio of compensation received to fiscal deficit (2020–21).

Source: RBI state finances.

Note: Figure for compensation reported in the revised estimates for 2020–21 could be underestimates since some of the claims have been settled only in 2021–22. Some states have not reported compensation figures in the RE figures.

Using the revenue from the basket of taxes subsumed in GST in 2015–16, as the benchmark and assuming 14 per cent growth annual growth in revenue, one can derive the amount of compensation due to individual states. These figures could be slight overestimates since they do not take into account any revenues the states have earned from the subsumed taxes by way of resolution of disputes.

For the next financial year, there is a challenge. Compensation on account of shortfall in revenue is available only for the first three months. The likely revenue from GST for the states can be derived by using some assumptions on the rate of growth of revenue for the next financial year.

For states which did not require any compensation on revenues, the revenue for 2022–23 would merely be the rate of growth applied to revenues of 2021–22. On the other hand, for states which have need of compensation, revenue can be derived as follows:

$$GST_{i,t} = 0.25 * R_{i,t} + 0.75 * GST_{i,t-1} * gr \qquad (6.1)$$

where
$GST_{i,t}$ is the revenue from GST in the ith state in the tth year,
gr is the rate of growth of GST revenue, and
$R_{i,t}$ is the protected revenue for the ith state in the tth year.

$$R_{i,t} = R_{i,0} * (1.14)^{t+2} \qquad (6.2)$$

where $t = 0$ for 2015–16.

Table 6.3 provides two alternative scenarios for 2022–23–one assuming rate of growth of revenue of 14 per cent in 2022–23 and the second assuming a higher rate of 20 per cent. In each case, the column headed 'Estimated revenue' is the revenue estimated for 2022–23 and the column titled 'Shortfall' captures the shortfall with reference to the protected revenue for 2021–22. In other words, it captures the extent to which revenues in 2022–23 would be lower than those in 2021–22. The table shows that for a growth rate of 14 per cent, 14 states would report a shortfall. As would be expected, with a higher growth in revenue of 20 per cent, the number would decline to ten. The amount of shortfall too declines. In addition, another eight to ten states would record rates of growth of revenue of less than 10 per cent.

This is a challenging situation that needs to be addressed. States experiencing a fall in the revenue collections would be forced to curtail some of their expenses to make ends meet.

Table 6.3 Estimates of revenue shortfall in 2022–23 (Rs crore).

	Scenario 1: Growth rate of 14 per cent		Scenario 2: Growth Rate of 20 per cent	
	Estimated revenue	Shortfall	Estimated revenue	Shortfall
Andhra Pradesh	28,632	1,819	29,682	769
Arunachal Pradesh	1,242	0	1,307	0
Assam	12,357	781	12,810	328
Bihar	23,479	4,223	24,299	3,403
Chhattisgarh	12,192	3,957	12,591	3,557
Delhi	29,058	7,782	30,035	6,806
Goa	3,631	1,158	3,750	1,038
Gujarat	56,692	6,647	58,726	4,613
Haryana	29,814	3,617	30,881	2,550
Himachal Pradesh	6,047	1,930	6,246	1,732
Jharkhand	11,845	2,226	12,258	1,813
Karnataka	66,044	13,292	68,330	11,006
Kerala	29,774	7,148	30,788	6,135
Madhya Pradesh	27,918	5,730	28,882	4,765
Maharashtra	1,22,925	9,881	1,27,403	5,403
Manipur	1,242	0	1,307	0
Meghalaya	1,330	67	1,379	18
Mizoram	796	0	838	0
Nagaland	941	0	990	0
Odisha	20,675	3,578	21,400	2,853
Puducherry	1,423	981	1,462	943
Punjab	22,320	9,445	23,018	8,747
Rajasthan	33,845	3,818	35,061	2,602
Sikkim	715	0	752	0
Tamil Nadu	57,520	7,860	59,567	5,813
Telangana	34,740	618	36,038	0
Tripura	1,528	203	1,582	149
Uttar Pradesh	66,528	6,757	68,930	4,355
Uttarakhand	7,984	2,905	8,241	2,649
West Bengal	38,381	5,733	39,740	4,374

Source: Own estimates.

6.4 Options for Correcting This Situation

Broadly there are four kinds of options available to deal with the above challenge. These can be classified into short-term and long-term solutions. Some implications of these are discussed in this section.

1. **Long-Term Solutions**: Improving the revenue productivity of GST can be thought of as having three components—rationalizing the rates of tax to increase the weighted average tax rate, expanding the base for the tax by bringing within the tax base activities which were hitherto excluded, and improving administration to expand the coverage of the tax. There have been references to improved collections attributable to administrative measures by the central and state tax administrations in the financial year 2021–22.[1] These measures would contribute to improvements in revenue collection but the extent of improvement is not predictable.
   a. *Recalibration of GST rates*: Increase in GST collections through recalibration of the tax rates and improvement in compliance through effective administration are required for the long-term sustainability of the regime. As shown in a comparison of scenario 1 and scenario 2 in Table 6.3, if the growth of revenue increases, the number of states which would experience a decline in revenue would be smaller. The Report of the Fifteenth Finance Commission in its chapter on Resource Mobilization highlights the observation that the weighted average tax rate under GST has declined from 14.4 per cent at the time of introduction of GST to about 11.6 per cent.[2] The GST Council set up a Group of Ministers headed by the Chief Minister of Karnataka to 'simplify rate structures, reduce classification related disputes and raise revenues'.[3] Academic studies too have provided some

[1] https://indianexpress.com/article/explained/november-gst-collection-surge-explained-7650750/.

[2] https://www.rbi.org.in/Scripts/PublicationsView.aspx?id = 19240, https://fincomindia.nic.in/ShowContentOne.aspx?id = 9&Section = 1.

[3] https://gstcouncil.gov.in/sites/default/files/GoM-Dynamic/OM-GoM-on-Rate-Rationalization.pdf.

opinions on this front.[4] A quick and ready calculation of the impact of increase in the weighted average tax rate from 11.6 per cent to say 13 per cent suggests a 12 per cent increase in revenue. This in turn would leave only six states with revenue less than in 2021–22. Raising rates of tax, however, could be a faced with political and economic challenges, especially given the context of a nascent recovery in the economy. For this reason, it can be considered a long-term solution implemented in a phased or gradual manner. In implementing such a restructuring, increase in rate of tax can be moderated by keeping the CGST rate unchanged and allowing for increase of SGST alone, if the purpose is to provide some additional space to the states.

b. *Expanding the base for GST*: While this is a very commonly discussed option in the debate on rationalizing the GST regime, there are limitations to this approach from the point of view of raising additional revenue. Briefly put, the major segments remaining outside the base for GST are certain petro products like petrol, diesel, crude oil, and natural gas, and alcoholic beverages for human consumption. Historically both the union government and state governments have been dependent on the revenues raised from these sectors. At present, the rates of tax on these sectors are quite high. Bringing these goods within the ambit of GST can be visualized in two ways: first, only GST is applicable on these goods; second, a two-part tariff is put in place, like the present regime for tobacco products. Since the effective tax on these products is higher than the peak rate available within the GST regime, bringing them within the ambit of GST would result in a lower tax incidence and therefore reduction in revenue collection. Electricity is one other activity which continues to remain outside the base of GST. While the tax rate on electricity is not very high, it is largely used as an input for many sectors in the economy. This feature of the sector underlines the need to bring it into the base for GST for reasons of improving efficiency of the GST regime, not to raise additional resources. In other words,

[4] https://nipfp.org.in/publications/working-papers/1956/.

expansion in the base through changes in the tax design does not offer much scope for raising the revenue productivity of GST.

2. **Short-Term Solutions:** An alternative option can be to consider an extension in the compensation regime by a few more years. The purpose of the extension could be to safeguard the fiscal position of the states from being witness to a decline in revenue. Given the volatility in economic growth, assurances of a high rate of growth of protected revenue might be considered unsustainable. An acceptable compromise in growth of protected revenue needs to be reached. This could protect the concerns of the states which face a decline in revenue or a very slow rate of growth of revenue. One such benchmark is protecting the revenue to the extent of the inflation rate—that is, if the expected rate of inflation is 5 per cent, this could in turn be the rate of growth of protected revenue. Alternatively, the GST Council could seek to protect revenues with a moderately higher growth of say 8 per cent. Table 6.4 shows the number of states which would require compensation and the amounts of compensation payout for a period of five years under alternative assumptions about revenue growth (14 per cent and 20 per cent) and growth in revenue to be compensated (5 per cent and 8 per cent) against the present rate of 14 per cent. These estimates are presented as an aid to a discussion on the feasibility of such an alternative scenario. It is clear from the table that the number of years for which the compensation would be required as well as the amount of compensation and the number of states requiring compensation fall quite sharply in most scenarios, except scenario 3 which refers to the higher rate of compensation with a lower rate of growth of revenue.

Given that the timeline for the imposition of the compensation cess has been extended by another five years, for servicing the back-to-back debt to honour the compensation commitments, it is useful to examine whether this time period would be adequate eliminating the need for compensation. Looking at Table 6.5, it is possible to argue that this time line can be further extended to create space for such an extended compensation regime. It should be noted that if the timeline for imposition of the compensation cess is extended to 2029–30, most of the scenarios

Table 6.4 Estimated consequences of alternative compensation schemes (revenue in Rs crore).

	Last year		2022–23	2023–24	2024–25	2025–26	2026–27
Scenario 1	2029–30	Revenue	2,51,885	2,04,250	1,46,729	85,226	44,771
ROG of revenue 14 per cent ROG of compensation 5 per cent		No. of states	25	25	24	20	13
Scenario 2	2026–27	Revenue	2,16,663	1,23,551	44,254	13,716	3,787
ROG of revenue 20 per cent ROG of compensation 5 per cent		No. of states	25	24	14	7	2
Scenario 3	2029–30	Revenue	2,71,209	2,52,753	2,27,199	1,93,191.5	1,52,042
ROG of revenue 14 per cent ROG of compensation 8 per cent		No. of states	25	25	25	25	23
Scenario 4	2026–27	Revenue	2,35,987	1,70,333	91,686	40,187	16,445
ROG of revenue 20 per cent ROG of compensation 8 per cent		No. of states	25	25	20	13	7

Table 6.5 Net outstanding debt from back-to-back loans (Rs crore).

	2021–22	2022–23	2023–24	2024–25	2025–26	2026–27	2027–28	2028–29	2029–30
Revenue from cess	90,442	1,03,104	1,17,538	1,33,994	1,52,753	1,74,138	1,98,518	2,26,310	2,57,993
Scenario 1	2,69,208	4,36,834	5,54,124	6,05,648	5,80,516	4,91,785	3,49,377	1,58,684	
Scenario 2	2,69,208	3,82,768	3,88,780	2,99,040	1,60,003				
Scenario 3	2,69,208	4,37,313	5,72,528	6,65,733	7,06,171	6,84,075	5,11,484	2,98,566	46,991
Scenario 4	2,69,208	4,02,091	4,54,886	4,12,580	3,00,014	1,42,321			

Note: Revenue from cess assumed to increase by 14 per cent per annum.

discussed here can be financed fully. This could be one alternative way to protect the revenues of the states. Further, this time frame is sensitive to the rate of growth of revenue. Work on the long-term solutions alongside can provide the necessary boost to revenue, to ensure that the time period for extended compensation can be kept low.

If the extension of the compensation regime is not found to be suitable, a final option is to explore alternative ways for states to raise revenues. While exploring beyond the scope of GST is outside the purview of this chapter, it might be worth raising the possibility of allowing for a degree of flexibility in the rates of tax within the GST regime. While flexibility does bring an element of complexity into the regime, it could relieve the union government of its responsibility to ensure a minimum rate of growth of revenue to the states from GST.

6.5 Conclusions

The change in the GST regime can result in some disruptions to the performance of state tax revenues, since revenues from GST account for a significant part of the own-tax revenues of states. Economic uncertainties arising from impact of the multiple rounds of COVID-19 have exacerbated the stress in state finances. There is the need for some short- and medium-term interventions to ensure that GST remains a buoyant source of revenue for the union and the states. While extension in the compensation regime has not been accepted by the union government, one supporting initiative has been put into place—augmented support for capital expenditure by state governments in the form of interest-free loans. Growth in GST revenues too have been robust, with year-on-year growth remaining high at over 20 per cent, creating confidence in the capacity of the regime to generate reliable revenues. The need for rationalization of the regime in the medium term remains, but with robust growth in revenues within the present regime, the GST Council has earned itself some time before rationalization becomes essential.

7

Tax Expenditures on Union Taxes in India from 2005–06 to 2019–20

Sacchidananda Mukherjee

7.1 Introduction

Tax expenditure or revenue foregone is a presumptive loss of revenue on account of preferential tax treatments that deviate from the general tax structure (Chen, 2015). It arises due to tax exemptions, tax allowances, tax credits, tax rate relief, and tax deferral (Heady and Mansour 2019). Assessment of tax expenditures on account of preferential tax treatment or provisions of various tax incentives or tax preferences (e.g. special tax rates, exemptions, deductions, rebates, deferrals, and credits) has gained interest in public finance literature over the past two decades (Redonda et al., 2019). However, literature on tax expenditure is still sparse, at least in India. Tax expenditures are often considered as pervasive and growing around the world (OECD, 2010). If not published by the government, tax expenditures often remain invisible in public finance management (PFM) (Burman and Phaup, 2012). Often, estimates of tax expenditures are not integrated with budget documents, and as a result it is considered to be less transparent, prone to corruption, and vulnerable to encouraging lobbying by politically active groups (Fuest and Riedel, 2009; Burman and Phaup, 2012; Hunter and Nelson, 1989). Lack of transparency in PFM often obscures the fiscal vulnerabilities of the governments. It is widely considered that tax expenditures are allocated based on certain political criteria/ideology as the incumbent political party (or alliance) wants to appease certain sections of taxpayers in exchange of their political support (Marjit et al., 2020; Das and Raja, 2008). This is often referred to in the literature as 'political clientelism', where political parties or elected legislatures trade benefits to individuals or groups of voters/

Sacchidananda Mukherjee, *Tax Expenditures on Union Taxes in India from 2005–06 to 2019–20* In: *Fiscal Policy and Public Financial Management.* Edited by: Pinaki Chakraborty and K R Shanmugam, Oxford University Press.
 DOI: 10.1093/9780198930464.003.0007

citizens in exchange for their political support (Hicken, 2011; Das and Raja, 2008).

Over the years, more countries have started publishing tax expenditure estimates. There was a rise in countries' average tax expenditures (as a percentage of GDP and tax revenue) on corporate income tax (CIT), compared to a fall in tax expenditure on personal income tax (PIT) in the period 2005–10 to 2011–19 (Table 7.1). India's tax expenditure on CIT (as a percentage of tax revenue) was relatively high during 2005–10 as compared to other regions of the world. Though India contained its tax expenditure on CIT during 2011–19, it is still higher than other regions in the world, except East Asia and Pacific, and North America. According to the world's average, tax expenditure on PIT is higher than on CIT. However, in India it is the opposite. During 2011–19, all countries except high-income ones reduced their average tax expenditure on CIT (as a percentage of tax revenue) vis-à-vis 2005–10; and in PIT, all countries except upper middle-income ones reduced tax expenditure (as a percentage of tax revenue) during 2011–19 vis-à-vis 2005–10.

The union government of India has been publishing revenue foregone statement or tax expenditures as part of the budget documents since 2004–05. The present chapter assesses the trends and patterns in tax expenditures on four union taxes: CIT, PIT,[1] Union excise duty (UED), and customs duty (CD), from 2005–06 to 2019–20. These taxes together have contributed on average 86.6 per cent of gross tax revenue (GTR) (including states' share in union taxes) of the union government during 2005–20.

The government of India initiated reforms by setting sunset clauses in various tax incentives schemes on union taxes in the Union Budget 2015–16, and as per our knowledge, this is not yet highlighted in Indian public finance literature—the present study attempts to fill this gap. Moreover, existing studies highlight only tax expenditures on CIT (Rao and Mukherjee, 2017; Rao et al., 2016). The present study covers all union taxes and attempts to understand their dynamics with specific regard to tax collection as well as gross value added (GVA).

[1] In this paper PIT excludes Hotel Receipts Tax (0023), Interest Tax (0024), Fringe Benefit Tax (0026), Other Taxes on Income and Expenditure (0028), Land Revenue (0029), Stamps and Registration fees (0030), Gift Tax (0033), Security Transaction Tax (0034), and Banking Cash Transaction Tax (0036).

Table 7.1 Average tax expenditures on corporate income tax and personal income tax.

Region	Corporate income tax				Personal income tax			
	Percentage of tax revenue		Percentage of GDP		Percentage of tax revenue		Percentage of GDP	
	2005–10	2011–19	2005–10	2011–19	2005–10	2011–19	2005–10	2011–19
World	**3.60**	**3.77**	**0.58**	**0.64**	**8.85**	**7.15**	**1.39**	**1.22**
East Asia and Pacific	3.33	5.55	0.59	0.75	16.27	8.80	1.98	1.36
Europe and Central Asia	2.38	3.54	0.53	0.75	8.23	7.86	1.80	1.62
Latin America and Caribbean	4.68	4.69	0.66	0.70	4.12	3.13	0.58	0.49
Middle East and North Africa	2.94	3.81	0.68	0.75	1.02	3.84	0.29	0.73
North America	6.72	6.88	0.78	0.79	43.29	43.52	4.83	4.96
South Asia	5.06	1.99	0.53	0.22	2.74	1.55	0.29	0.16
Sub-Saharan Africa	2.15	1.61	0.37	0.29	3.79	1.83	0.92	0.44
High Income	*3.59*	*4.42*	*0.68*	*0.84*	*13.10*	*10.47*	*2.12*	*1.82*
Upper Middle Income	*4.60*	*4.20*	*0.59*	*0.60*	*3.37*	*3.58*	*0.45*	*0.61*
Lower Middle Income	*2.46*	*2.35*	*0.36*	*0.36*	*1.29*	*1.00*	*0.15*	*0.16*
Low Income	*4.72*	*1.46*	*0.41*	*0.17*	*N.A.*	*1.32*	*N.A.*	*0.15*
India	**10.12**	**5.00**	**1.06**	**0.54**	**4.47**	**3.12**	**0.47**	**0.35**

Source: Compiled from Global Tax Expenditures Database (https://gted.net/, last accessed 10 March 2022).

7.2 Analysis of Tax Expenditures on Union Taxes

Aggregate tax expenditure on union taxes decreased from 8.15 per cent of gross value added (GVA) in 2008–09 to 1.69 per cent of GVA in 2019–20.[2] This was possible due to continuous reductions of tax expenditures on

[2] GVA at basic prices (at current prices, 2011–12 series).

indirect taxes since 2010–11. Overall annual tax expenditures remained stable at an average of 1.63 per cent of GVA during 2017–18 to 2019–20. Tax expenditures on union taxes can be divided into three phases: phase 1 (2005–06 to 2007–08), phase 2 (200809 to 2014–15) and phase 3 (2015–16 to 2019–20) (Figure 7.1). In phase 1, average annual tax expenditure was 6.2 per cent of GVA (Table 7.2). The rise in tax expenditures on indirect taxes during 2008–09 to 2009–10 is attributed to fiscal stimulus measures adopted by the union government to tackle the global financial crisis (GFC) in terms of reducing tax rates on UED and CD. In phase 2, average annual tax expenditure was 6.5 per cent of GVA and post 2009–10 on average each year tax expenditures has declined by 0.65 per cent of GVA. In 2011–12, tax expenditure increased marginally from 6.49 per cent in 2010–11 to 6.58 per cent. In phase 3, average annual tax expenditure was 1.9 per cent of GVA and on average tax expenditure in each year has declined by 0.63 per cent of GVA. The largest fall in tax expenditures were observed in 2010–11 and 2015–16. An in-depth analysis of tax expenditure on each tax may help to bring out new insights. The experience of the union government of India in cutting down tax expenditures may help state governments in India to reduce their tax expenditures, which is yet to be assessed.

With reduction of tax expenditures on union taxes, there is no sign of improvement in tax collection (Table 7.3). GTR of union taxes both

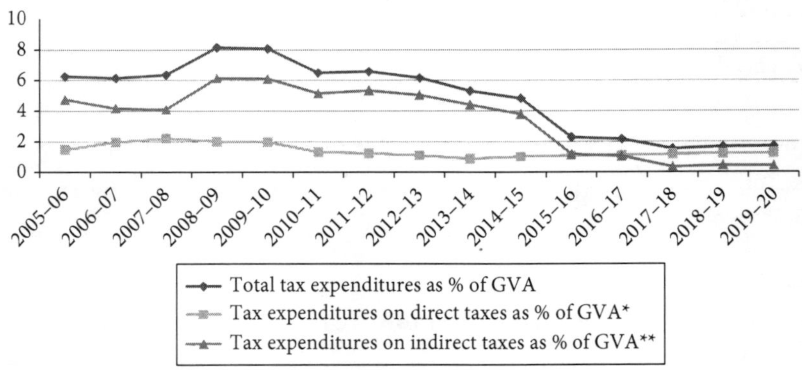

Figure 7.1 Overall tax expenditure of Union taxes (as a percentage of GVA).
Source: Computed by author based on Union Budget documents (various years).
Note: *Direct taxes include CIT and PIT only, **indirect taxes include UED and customs only.

Table 7.2 Average annual tax expenditure on Union taxes (percentage of GVA).

Tax Head	2005–06 to 2007–08	2008–09 to 2014–15	2015–16 to 2019–20
A. Direct Taxes (a + b)	**1.9**	**1.4**	**1.2**
(a) Corporate Income Tax	1.2	0.9	0.6
(b) Personal income tax (i + ii)	**0.7**	**0.5**	**0.6**
(i) Firms/AOPs/ BOIs	0.1	0.1	0.0
(ii) Individuals	0.6	0.5	0.5
B. Indirect taxes (c + d)	**4.4**	**5.2**	**0.7**
(c) Union excise duty	**2.0**	**2.4**	**0.2**
(i) Area based exemptions	0.2	0.2	0.1
(ii) General exemptions	1.8	2.2	0.2
(d) Customs duty (i – ii)	**2.4**	**2.8**	**0.5**
(i) Customs duty (gross)	3.6	3.4	0.7
(ii) Input tax neutralisation or exemption schemes	1.2	0.6	0.2
C. Total tax expenditure, Union government (A + B)	**6.2**	**6.5**	**1.9**

Source: Computed by author based on Union Budget documents (various years).

Table 7.3 Average annual gross tax revenue of Union taxes (percentage of GVA).

Tax head	2005–06 to 2007–08	2008–09 to 2014–15	2015–16 to 2019–20
Gross tax revenue (GTR)	12.1	11.1	11.8
A. Corporation tax	3.7	4.0	3.5
B. Taxes on income other than corporation tax	2.0	2.1	2.6
C. Union excise duties	3.0	1.8	1.9
D. Customs	2.2	1.7	1.1
E. GST on imports (IGST + cess)			1.5
GTR, selected (sum of A to E)	10.8	9.6	9.9

Source: Computed by author based on Union Budget documents (various years).

at the aggregate level as well as for selected taxes does not show any improvement with reductions of tax expenditures.

During phase 1, on average, total tax expenditure was 57.8 per cent of GTR (from selected taxes). It was 67.4 per cent during phase 2 and 18.8 per cent during phase 3 (Table 7.4). Major reduction in tax expenditure was observed in indirect taxes during phase 3. The introduction of GST from 1 July 2017 helped to contain tax expenditure on account of Union excise duty. As a step towards introduction of GST, withdrawal of various tax incentive/exemption schemes under UED has been initiated since 2015–16. Major reduction in tax expenditures on direct taxes was observed during phase 2.

In addition to reductions in tax expenditures on direct and indirect taxes, there was a structural shift in tax expenditure from indirect to direct taxes during phase 3 (Table 7.5). Average share of indirect taxes in total tax expenditure (TTE) went up in phase 2 due to reduction of

Table 7.4 Average annual tax expenditures on Union taxes (percentage of gross tax revenue from selected taxes).

Details	2005–06 to 2007–08	2008–09 to 2014–15	2015–16 to 2019–20
A. Direct taxes (a + b)	**17.4**	**14.2**	**11.9**
(a) Corporate income tax	11.0	8.8	6.0
(b) Personal income tax (i + ii)	**6.5**	**5.4**	**5.9**
(i) Firms/AOPs/ BOIs	0.7	0.7	0.4
(ii) Individuals	5.8	4.7	5.5
B. Indirect taxes (c + d)	**40.4**	**53.2**	**6.9**
(c) Union excise duty	**18.2**	**24.4**	**2.3**
(i) Area-based exemptions	1.5	1.8	0.7
(ii) General exemptions	16.7	22.5	1.6
(d) Customs duty (i – ii)	**22.2**	**28.8**	**4.6**
(i) Customs duty (gross)	33.3	35.1	7.1
(ii) Input tax neutralisation or exemption schemes	11.2	6.2	2.5
C. Total tax expenditure (A + B)	57.8	67.4	18.8

Source: Computed by author based on Union Budget documents (various years).

Note: Includes CIT, PIT, UED and customs duty (including IGST and GST compensation cess from imports).

Table 7.5 Average composition of tax expenditures on Union taxes (percentage share).

Composition	2005–06 to 2007–08	2008–09 to 2014–15	2015–16 to 2019–20
A. Direct taxes (a + b)	**30.4**	**20.7**	**65.1**
(a) Corporate income tax	19.1	12.8	32.6
(b) Personal income tax (i + ii)	**11.4**	**7.9**	**32.5**
(i) Firms/AOPs/ BOIs	1.2	1.1	2.2
(ii) Individuals	10.1	6.9	30.4
B. Indirect taxes (c + d)	**69.5**	**79.3**	**34.9**
(c) Union excise duty	**31.4**	**36.3**	**10.2**
(i) Area-based exemptions	2.6	2.8	3.1
(ii) General exemptions	28.8	33.5	7.2
(d) Customs duty (i – ii)	**38.1**	**43.0**	**24.7**
(i) Customs duty (gross)	57.5	52.2	37.0
(ii) Input tax neutralisation or exemption schemes	19.4	9.2	12.3
C. Total tax expenditure (A + B)	100.0	100.0	100.0

Source: Computed by author based on Union Budget documents (various years).

tax expenditure on direct taxes during this phase. In phase 3, the share of direct taxes in TTE went up with reduction of tax expenditures on indirect taxes.

The rise in tax expenditures on indirect taxes during 2008–09 to 2009–10 is attributed to a cut in the effective UED rate as part of the fiscal stimulus package announced to counter the general economic slowdown due to the GFC. The effective UED rate was reduced by 4 percentage points on 7 December 2008, and on 24 February 2009 the mean excise duty rate of 10 per cent was further reduced to 8 per cent. While the standard UED rate was 16 per cent, the effective duty rate on most excisable goods was reduced to 10 per cent and subsequently to 8 per cent, in December 2008 and February 2009, respectively. The effective rate of 8 per cent continued throughout 2009–10. This resulted in a rise in tax expenditure during 2008–10, as the standard UED rate of 16 per cent remained unchanged.

As a part of the fiscal stimulus package of the union government, there was also a reduction in the effective rate of custom duty on many revenue-important items (e.g. crude petroleum, edible oils, steel). In addition, revenue impact of reduction of effective UED rates on customs collections is also observed through the countervailing duty (CVD) channel. In 2010–11, the difference between the standard UED rate and the effective rate decreased from 8 per cent to 6 per cent, which helped to contain tax expenditures on account of UED. Further, commensurate increase in the effective rates applicable to refined petroleum products also helped to contain tax expenditure on account of UED. Re-imposition of 5 per cent customs duty on crude petroleum with effect from 27 February 2010, and increasing CVD rate by 2 per cent, helped to contain tax expenditure on account of customs duty.

As compared to 2007–08, tax expenditures on direct taxes went down by 1.2 per cent of GTR (selected) in 2008–09 and 1.8 per cent in 2009–10 (Figure 7.2). There was no reduction of statutory CIT rates during 2008–10. Moreover, annual growth rates in CIT and PIT collections went down to 10.6 per cent and 3.3 per cent respectively in 2008–09. In 2009–10, annual growth rate of CIT and PIT collections improved marginally

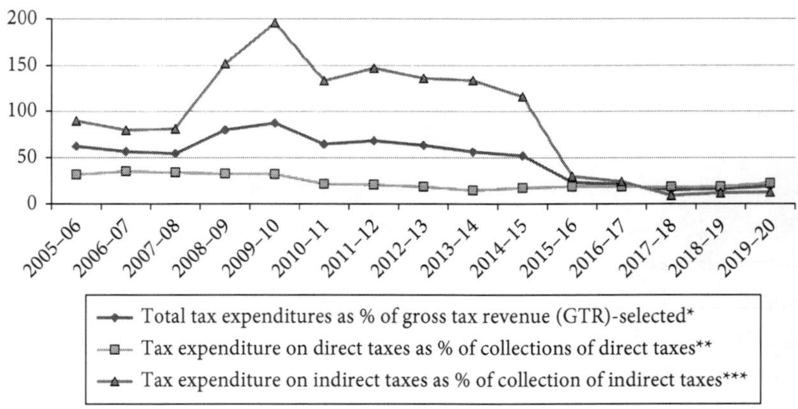

Figure 7.2 Overall Tax expenditure of Union taxes.

Source: Computed by author based on Union Budget documents (various years).

Notes: *GTR of selected taxes, namely CIT, PIT, UED, customs duty (including GST on imports).

**Revenue corresponding to CIT and PIT only.

***Revenue corresponding to UED, customs duty.

to 14.7 per cent and 15.5 per cent respectively. Post GFC, annual growth rate in CIT and PIT collections never reached the growth rate that was prevailing prior to GFC.

7.2.1 Tax Expenditures on Direct Taxes

Tax expenditure on direct taxes has been stable and hovering between 1 and 1.5 per cent of GVA since 2010–11 (Figure 7.3). The rise in tax expenditure on direct taxes (as a percentage of GVA) was observed during 2006–10 and is attributed to rise in tax expenditures on both CIT and PIT. However, there was no reduction in tax rates in either CIT or PIT as a part of fiscal stimulus measures taken up by the union government to counter GFC during the second half of 2008–09 (Figure 7.3). This therefore demands a detailed assessment of the reasons for the rise in tax expenditures on CIT during 2006–10.

Tax expenditure on direct taxes has gone down over the years, and has been hovering around 19 per cent of direct tax revenue since 2014–15 (Figure 7.4). In general, tax expenditure on PIT is higher than on CIT. In the Union Budget of 2015–16, it was announced that the statutory CIT

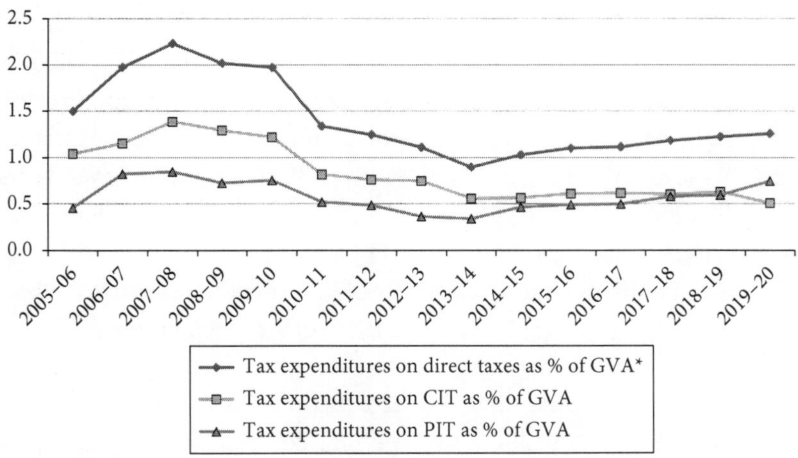

Figure 7.3 Tax expenditures on direct taxes.

Source: Computed by author based on Union Budget documents (various years).

Note: *Direct taxes include CIT and PIT only.

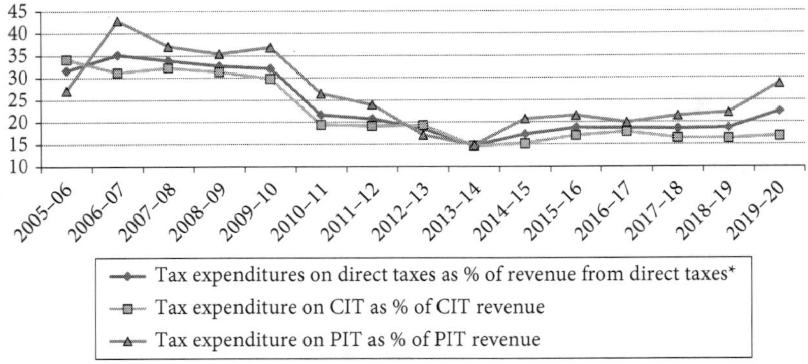

Figure 7.4 Tax expenditures on direct taxes as a percentage of direct tax revenue.

Source: Computed by author based on Union Budget documents (various years).

Note: *Direct taxes include CIT and PIT only.

rate would be reduced from 30 per cent to 25 per cent over four years, along with phasing out of some tax exemptions and deductions by 31 March 2017. Sunset clauses for various tax-exemption schemes, especially the profit-linked, investment–linked, and area-based, helped the government to contain tax expenditures on CIT as well as PIT.

Tax expenditures on direct taxes (as percentages of tax revenue) fell after 200910 (Figure 7.4). Out of the 15 years (i.e. 2005–20) of our analysis, annual growth rate in tax expenditure on CIT exceeds the annual growth rate in CIT collection in six years (2007–08, 2012–13, 2014–15 to 2016–17, 2019–20) (Figure 7.5). In PIT, the annual growth rate in tax expenditure on PIT exceeds the annual growth rate in PIT collection for seven years (2006–07, 2009–10, 2014–15 to 2015–16, 2017–18 to 2019–20) (Figure 7.6). A rising trend in tax expenditures on PIT has been observed since 2014–15. The difference between the growth rate of tax expenditures and tax collection needs to be minimized for consolidation of tax expenditures.

7.2.1.1 Tax Expenditures on Corporate Income Tax

From 2005–07 to 2019–20, on average, CIT contributed 32.8 per cent of GTR. During the period, on average one-fifth (20.6 per cent) of total tax expenditures of the union government was on CIT. If we consider only

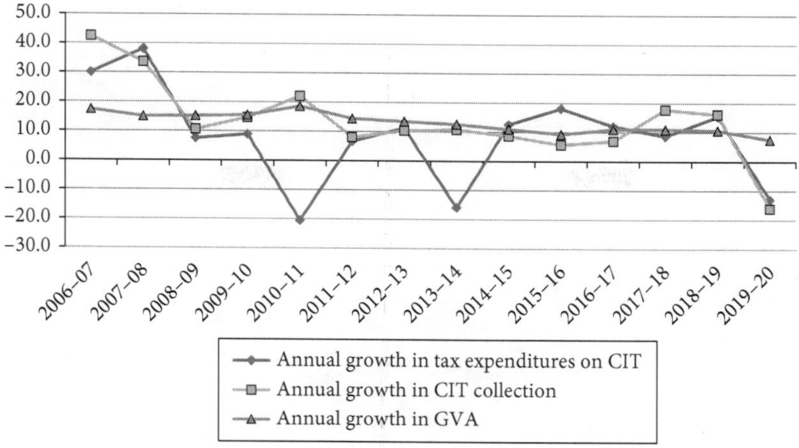

Figure 7.5 Annual growth rate in CIT collection, tax expenditure on CIT and GVA (per cent).

Source: Computed by author based on Union Budget documents (various years).

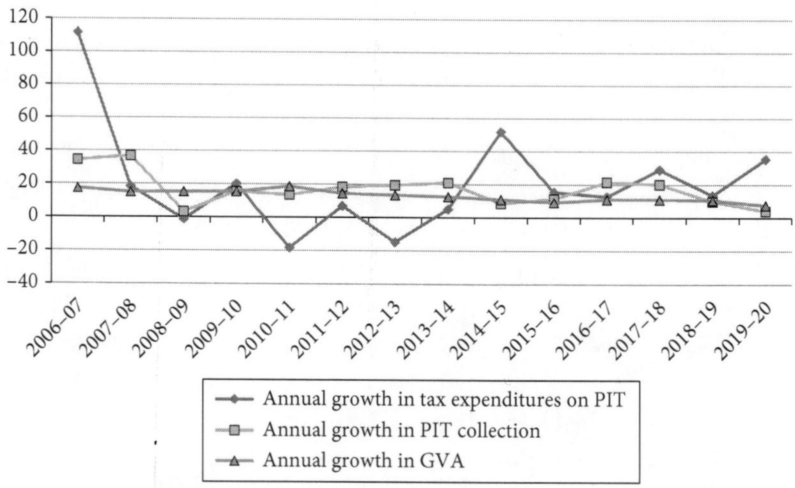

Figure 7.6 Annual growth rate in PIT collection, tax expenditure on PIT and GVA (per cent).

Source: Computed by author based on Union Budget documents (various years).

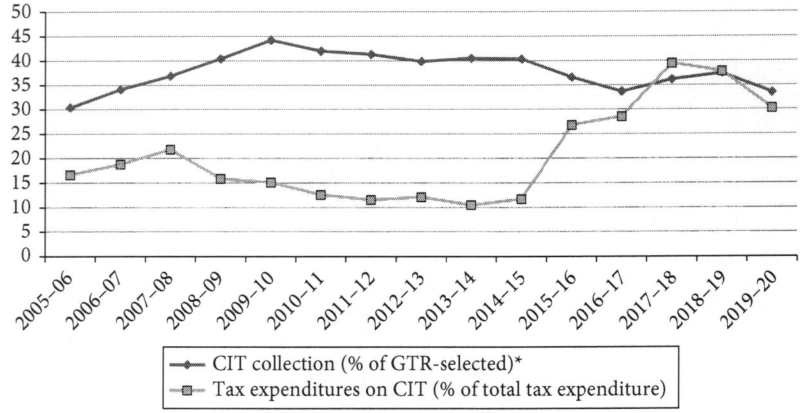

Figure 7.7 CIT collection and tax expenditures on CIT.
Source: Computed by author based on Union Budget documents (various years).

GTR of selected union taxes, average contribution of CIT stands at 37.8 per cent during 2005–07 to 2019–20.[3] Figure 7.7 shows that since 2010–11, there has been a falling trend in the share of CIT in GTR (selected), except during 2017–19. A falling trend in CIT collection (as per cent of GVA) has also been observed since 2008–09 (Figure 7.21 in Appendix). The rise in the share of CIT in total tax expenditure is mainly on account of the falling share of indirect taxes in the total tax expenditure. Tax expenditure on CIT shows stable trends since 2013–14 both as percentage of CIT collection and as percentage of GVA (Figure 7.8).

Stable statutory CIT rate and gradual reductions of tax expenditure on CIT resulted in a rise of effective CIT rate over time (Figure 7.9). The effective tax rate of CIT went up from 19.26 per cent in 2005–06 to 27.81 per cent in 2018–19. Fall in effective CIT rate in 2019–20 to 22.54 per cent is related to the concessional CIT rate of 22 per cent offered to existing domestic companies and 15 per cent CIT rate for newly incorporated domestic companies,[4] provided they satisfy certain conditions,

[3] Since there is no information on tax expenditures on UED after introduction of GST (i.e. 1 July 2017), we avoided taking central GST (CGST) and corresponding IGST (integrated GST) settlement on CGST account in our analysis.

[4] Which make fresh investment by 31 March 2023 for manufacturing, production, research, or distribution of such article or thing manufactured (https://pib.gov.in/Pressreleaseshare.aspx?PRID=1585641, last accessed 10 March 2022).

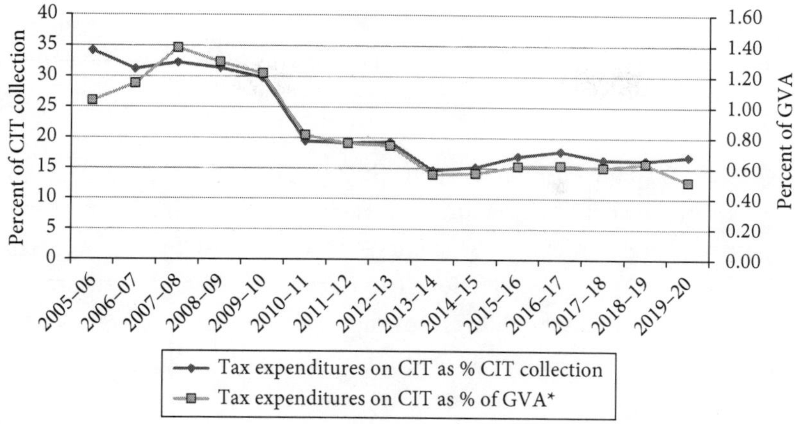

Figure 7.8 Tax expenditure on CIT.
Source: Computed by author based on Union Budget documents (various years).

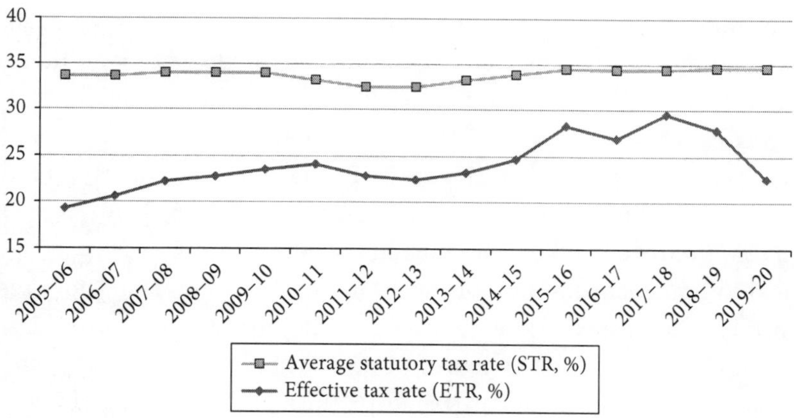

Figure 7.9 Statutory and effective tax rates of CIT (per cent).
Source: Computed by author based on Union Budget documents (various years).

including that they do not avail any specified incentives or deductions. Containing tax expenditures on CIT helped to achieve the improvement in ETR, apart from maintaining a stable statutory CIT rate.

7.2.1.1.1 Structure of Tax Expenditure on CIT

The structure of tax incentives and associated tax expenditure on CIT has gone through changes over time. For example, shares of 'accelerated depreciation' and 'deduction/weighted deduction for expenditure on scientific research' have gone up, whereas the shares of 'area-based exemptions' and 'export promotion' have gone down (Table 7.6).

7.2.1.2 Tax Expenditures on Personal Income Tax

Apart from the corporate sector, businesses often organized as partnership firms (hereafter firms), associations of persons (AOPs), or bodies of individuals (BOIs). Tax collections from firms, AOPs, and BOIs are accounted for under 'Taxes on Income other than Corporation Tax'. But we have captured the tax expenditures on these heads under 'PIT' along with tax expenditures on individuals. Tax expenditure on PIT constituted on average 16.82 per cent of total tax expenditure of the union government from 2005–07 to 2019–20 (Figure 7.10). However, there has been an upward trend in the share of tax expenditure on PIT since 2014–15, and part of this is attributed to the falling share of indirect taxes on total tax expenditure. Average share of PIT collection in selected GTR was 22.44 per cent during the same period. There is also an upward trend in the share of PIT collection in selected GTR (Figure 7.21 in Appendix).

Tax expenditure on PIT (both as percentage of PIT collection and GVA) shows a similar trend (Figure 7.11). There was a downward trend in tax expenditure on PIT during 2006–14. Since 2014–15, there has been an upward trend in tax expenditure on PIT, and a part of this may be related to improvement in capturing information through mandatory reporting of permanent account number (PAN) for various transactions, extending tax deducted at source (TDS) (withholding of tax) system, digitalization of public finance database, third party reporting of information through annual information return (AIR) submissions, etc.

Tax expenditures on individual taxpayers hold the largest share in the composition of tax expenditure on PIT. On average, tax expenditure on firms/AOPs/BOIs contributed 1.5 per cent of total tax expenditure of the union government and 8.7 per cent of tax expenditure on PIT during 2005–20. The structural shift in tax expenditures on firms, AOPs, and BOIs is observed as the shares of area-based exemptions, deductions of profits related to development of housing projects have gone down over the years, whereas the shares of accelerated depreciation and deductions of profits related to cooperative societies have gone up.

Table 7.6 Average composition of tax expenditures on corporate income tax (as a percentage of total tax expenditure on CIT).

Nature of incentive	2005–06 to 2007–08	2008–09 to 2014–15	2015–16 to 2019–20
Area-based exemptions	8.15	7.94	4.89
Accelerated depreciation	**13.03**	**39.14**	**44.23**
Donations to charitable trusts and institutions, political parties, scientific research, and rural development	6.84	0.70	2.37
Export promotion	*29.05*	*22.08*	*19.23*
Deduction of profits of undertakings engaged in power sector	11.28	9.97	11.63
Deduction of profits of undertakings engaged in telecommunications	11.35	2.87	0.26
Deduction of profits of undertakings engaged in minerals and natural gas production	9.58	5.13	1.89
Deduction of profits of undertakings engaged in the health sector, R&D, and environmental management	0.13	0.12	0.02
Deduction of profits of undertakings engaged in infrastructure	3.02	3.63	4.98
Deduction of profits of undertakings engaged in transportation of foodgrains, processing, preservation and packaging of fruits and vegetables	0.06	0.19	0.23
Deduction of profits of undertakings engaged in the housing sector	2.12	0.82	0.12
Deduction of profits of undertakings engaged in economic upliftment, new employment, financial services, SSI industries, start-ups, and special businesses	0.43	1.21	2.98
Deduction/weighted deduction for expenditure on scientific research	**4.96**	**6.19**	**7.16**
Total	100.00	100.00	100.00

Source: Computed by author based on Union Budget documents (various years).

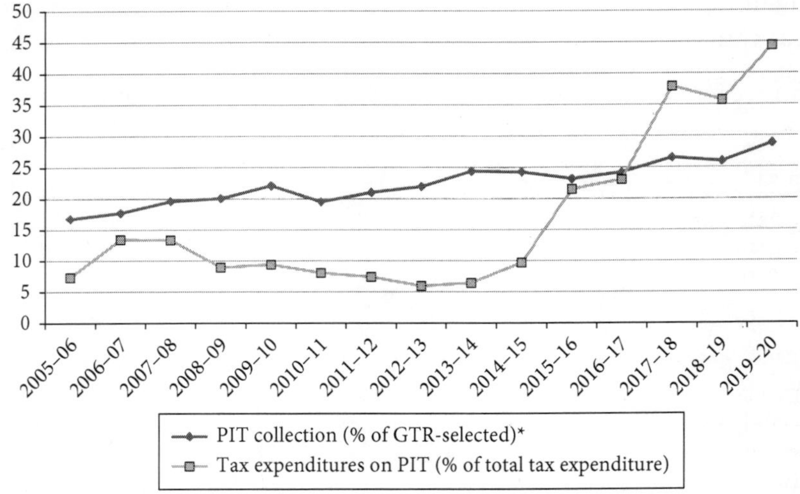

Figure 7.10 Tax expenditure on PIT and PIT collection.
Source: Computed by author based on Union Budget DOCUMENTS (various years).

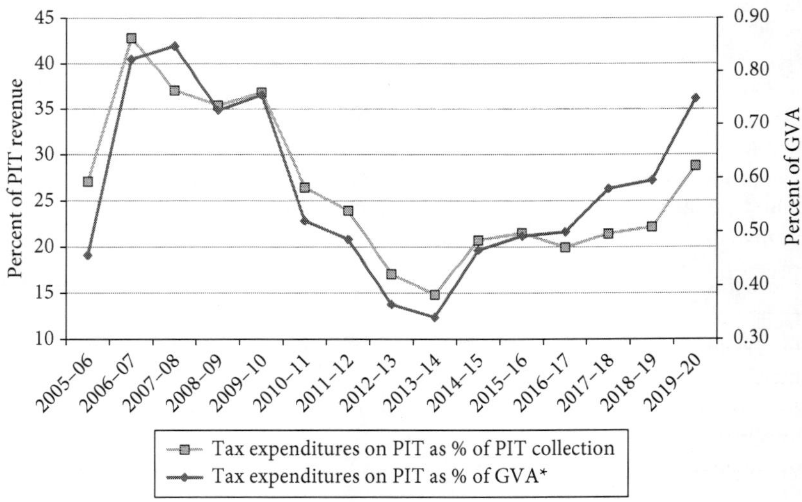

Figure 7.11 Tax expenditure on PIT, as a percentage of PIT revenue and GVA.
Source: Computed by author based on Union Budget documents (various years).

7.2.1.2.1 Composition of Tax Expenditures on Individual Taxpayers

On average, tax expenditure on individual taxpayers constituted 15.36 per cent of total tax expenditure of the union government from 2005–06 to 2019–20. The average share of individuals in total tax expenditure went up from 6.52 per cent during 2005–16 to 41.81 percent in 2019–20. The structural composition of tax expenditure on individuals went through changes over the period (Table 7.7).

Table 7.7 Average composition of tax expenditures on individual taxpayers (percentage share).

Nature of incentives	2005–06 to 2007–08	2008–09 to 2014–15	2015–16 to 2019–20
Investment in specific instruments and payments	73.16	81.88	72.41
Contribution to provident funds and new pension scheme	0.39	0.66	3.54
Export promotion	0.11	0.28	0.09
Area-based exemptions	1.36	0.83	0.12
Donations to charitable trust and institutions, political parties, and R&D	0.78	1.34	1.17
Deduction in case of a person with disability	0.18	0.34	0.44
Deduction on account of health insurance premium, expenditure for medical treatment of a dependent disabled person, expenditure for medical treatment of specified diseases	1.50	2.96	4.89
Income tax rebate specific to income slab	0.00	0.99	10.53
Deduction of income from certain specific business, industrial activities	2.57	0.66	0.04
House rent allowance (HRA)	0.14	0.38	1.25
Interest on education and home loans	0.14	0.71	0.99
Interest income from savings bank account	0.00	0.77	1.41
Royalty income	0.02	0.03	0.02
Senior citizens	11.05	4.97	3.07
Women	8.55	3.18	0.00
Others (employment generation, environmental management, profits and gains from housing projects, infrastructure projects)	0.05	0.03	0.03
Total	100.00	100.00	100.00

Source: Computed by author based on Union Budget documents (various years).

Note: Excluding tax expenditures on Firms, AOPs, and BOIs.

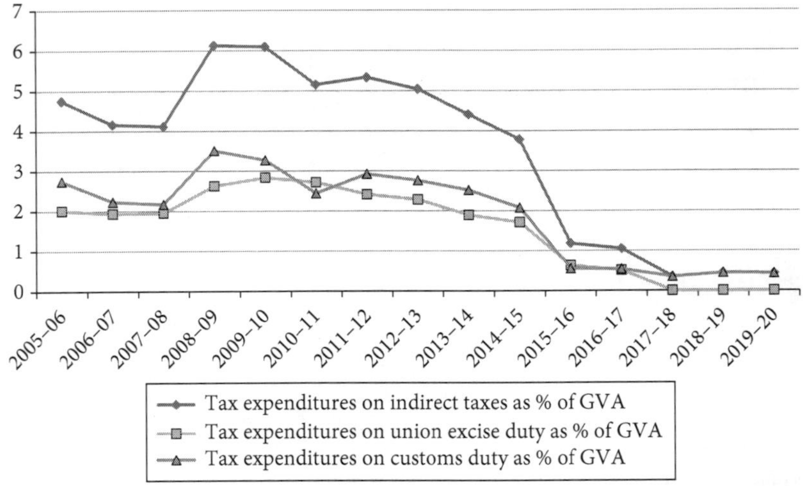

Figure 7.12 Tax expenditures on indirect taxes (as a percentage of GVA).
Source: Computed by author based on Union Budget documents (various years).
Notes: *Indirect taxes include UED and customs duty.
**Revenue from customs duty.

7.2.2 Tax Expenditure on Indirect Taxes

India's success in containing tax expenditures on indirect taxes is a remarkable. However, tax expenditures in the GST regime are yet to be assessed. A major reduction in tax expenditure on indirect taxes has happened since 2015–16, as India was preparing to roll out a harmonized tax system on goods and services (Mukherjee, 2021). Tax expenditure on indirect taxes (as a percentage of GVA) went up from an average of 4.3 per cent during phase 1 to 5.1 per cent in phase 2 and then fell to 0.7 per cent in phase 3 (2015–16 to 2019–20) (Table 7.8). Reductions of effective rates of UED and customs as a part of the fiscal stimulus package to moderate the impacts of the GFC had an impact on rising tax expenditures on indirect taxes of the union government during 2008–10 (Figure 7.12). Post-GFC successive union budgets raised the standard rate of excise duty gradually to pre-GFC levels,[5] pruned down the exemption list, and

[5] Please refer Para. 177 of the Budget Speech of the Union Budget 2012–13, https://www.indiabudget.gov.in/budget2012-2013/budget.asp.

Table 7.8 Tax expenditures on indirect taxes (percentage of GVA and indirect tax revenue).

	2005–06 to 2007–08	2008–09 to 2014–15	2015–16 to 2019–20
Tax expenditures on indirect taxes as percentage of GVA	4.3	5.1	0.7
Tax expenditures on Union excise duties (UED) as percentage of GVA*	2	2.4	0.2
Tax expenditures on customs duties as percentage of GVA*	2.4	2.8	0.5
Tax expenditure on indirect taxes as percentage of revenue of indirect taxes (per cent)†	83.3	144.8	17.5
Tax expenditure on UED as percentage of revenue from UED (per cent)	65	129.1	9.2
Tax expenditure on customs duty as percentage of revenue from customs duty (per cent)	111	162	24.2
GTR - selected as percentage of GVA	10.8	9.6	9.9

Source: Computed by author based on Union Budget documents (various years).

Note: * Tax expenditure on UED is not available beyond 2016–17 from the Union budget documents.

† Indirect taxes include UED and customs duty.

consolidated the rate structure of excise duty (or CenVAT) to prepare for the introduction of GST. This helped the government to contain tax expenditures on indirect taxes. However, containing tax expenditure on indirect taxes was slow during phase 2 as compared to phase 3.

Tax expenditure on indirect taxes went up from an average of 83.3 per cent of indirect tax collection (on account of UED and customs duty) during 2005–08 to an average of 144.8 per cent during 2008–15 (Table 7.8). The rise in tax expenditure during 2008–15 is the result of reductions in UED and customs duty rates as a part of fiscal stimulus measures to tackle the GFC (Figure 7.13). Post-GFC, the containing tax expenditure (as a percentage of indirect tax revenue) was slow and as a result on average tax expenditure (as a percentage of revenue from indirect taxes) was 144.8 per cent of revenue during phase 2. During 2015–20, average tax expenditure on indirect taxes fell to 17.5 per cent.

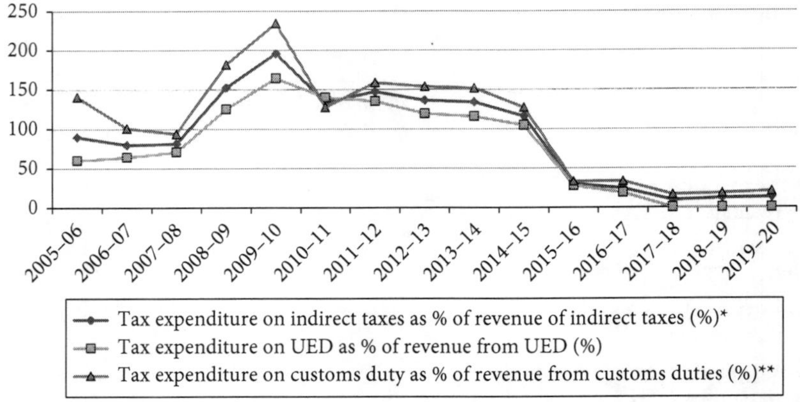

Figure 7.13 Tax expenditures on indirect taxes (as a percentage of revenue from indirect taxes).

Source: Computed by author based on Union Budget documents (various years).

Notes: *Indirect taxes include UED and customs duty only, **Revenue from customs duties includes GST on imports.

7.2.2.1 Tax Expenditures on Union Excise Duty

On average, UED contributed 22.2 per cent of GTR (selected taxes) from 2005–06 to 2016–17. The share of UED in GTR went up from an average of 18.8 per cent during phase 2 (2008–15) to 24.9 per cent during 2015–17. The average share of tax expenditure on UED in total tax expenditure was 36.3 per cent during phase 2 and it went down to 25.6 per cent during 2015–17 (Figure 7.14). Later, UED was subsumed into GST. UED continues for only those items where the Goods and Services Tax (GST) Council has not yet recommended the date of levying GST (i.e. petrol, diesel, aviation turbine fuel, crude petroleum, compressed natural gas, and tobacco products) where the union government has provision to levy UED in addition to the GST. Since there is no comprehensive estimate of tax expenditure is available for the GST, overall tax expenditure of the union government is incomplete beyond 2016–17.

During 2010–11 to 2014–15, annual growth rates in tax expenditure on UED and UED collection show similar trends, which resulted in stability in tax expenditure on UED as a percentage of UED collection (Figure 7.15). In 2015–16, the growth rate in UED collection improved, whereas the growth rate in tax expenditure on UED fell; as a

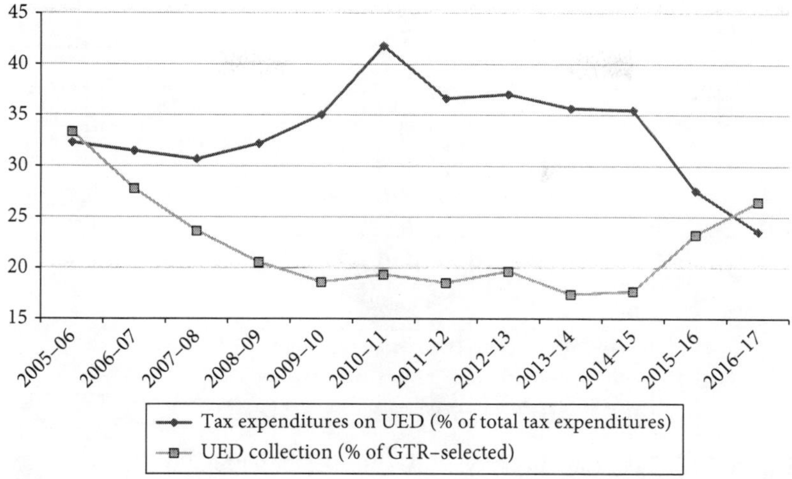

Figure 7.14 Tax expenditure on UED and UED collection.
Source: Computed by author based on Union Budget documents (various years).

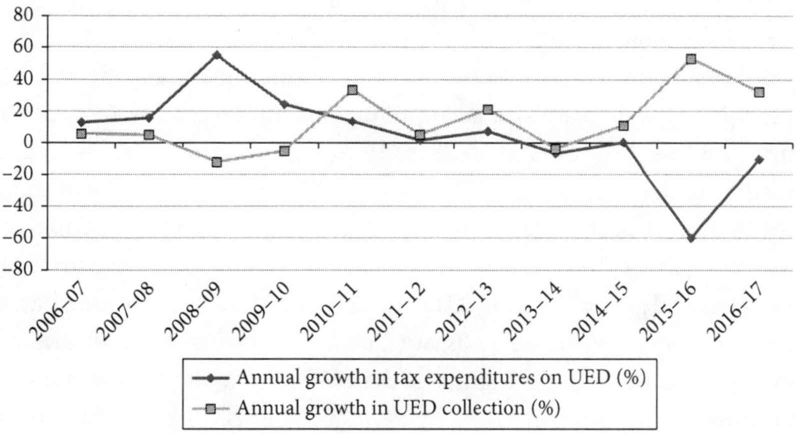

Figure 7.15 Annual growth rate in tax expenditure on UED and UED collection.
Source: Computed by author based on Union Budget documents (various years).

result, we observe a substantial fall in tax expenditure on UED. The rise in tax expenditure on UED in 2008–09 was related to reductions in effective tax rates of UED as a part of the fiscal stimulus measure. Higher tax expenditure coupled with negative growth in UED collection during

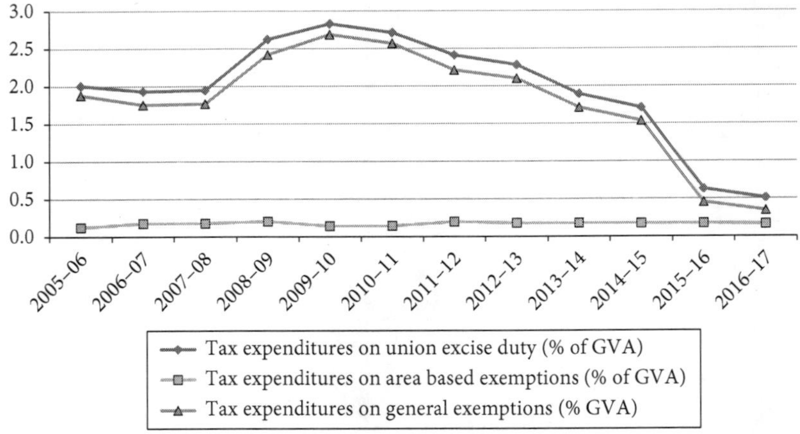

Figure 7.16 Tax expenditure on UED (as a percentage of GVA).
Source: Computed by author based on Union Budget documents (various years).

2008–10 resulted in rising tax expenditure on UED as a percentage of UED collection.

Tax expenditures on UED consist of two components—general UED exemptions and area-based exemptions. General exemption went down from 2.69 per cent of GVA in 2009–10 to 1.54 per cent in 2014–15 and further to 0.35 per cent of GVA in 2016–17 (Figure 7.16). The average share of area-based exemptions in total tax expenditure on UED remained stable at 7.87 per cent during 2005–15. However, it went up to an average of 30 per cent during 2015–17. The rise in the share of area-based exemptions during 2015–17 is attributed to a falling share of general exemptions. In the GST regime, if the decision on any tax exemption/incentive scheme is not taken by the GST council, the corresponding revenue impact is to be borne by the concerned government offering tax incentive/exemption scheme. To avoid the complication in determining tax liabilities and input tax credit adjustments, instead of up-front tax exemptions, tax refunds are provided where the refunds are adjusted with the respective share of the government responsible for offering the tax incentive/exemption (Mehta and Mukherjee, 2021).

In the budget documents, the union government publishes the amount of refund issued against Central GST (CGST) and Integrated GST (IGST) (CGST portion) to industrial units located in the North Eastern

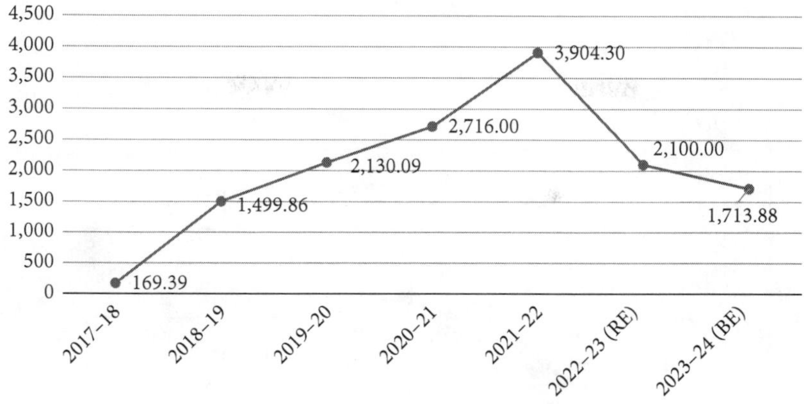

Figure 7.17 Refund of central GST and integrated GST to industrial units located in north-eastern region and Himalayan states (Rs crore).
Source: Computed by author based on Union Budget documents (various years).

Region and the Himalayan States. Figure 7.17 shows that tax expenditure on this account went up from Rs 169.4 crore in 2017–18 to Rs 3,904.3 crore in 2021–22. From 2014–15 to 2016–17, average annual tax expenditure on area-based UED exemption was Rs 21,639 crore. Therefore, it is to be highlighted that there is a substantial fall in tax expenditure on area-based exemptions in the GST regime. Revenue foregone due to general tax exemptions in the GST regime is yet to be assessed.

7.2.2.2 Tax Expenditures on Customs Duty

On average customs duty contributed 19 per cent of GTR (selected taxes) during 2005–06 to 2019–20. Since countervailing duty and special additional duty on customs (SAD) have been subsumed into GST, we include GST collection on imports (IGST and GST compensation cess) along with basic customs duty (BCD) collection to make the series comparable. The share of tax expenditure on customs duty in total tax expenditure went down from an average of 43 per cent during phase 2 to average 24.7 per cent during phase 3 (Figure 7.18). Improvement in the share of customs collection (as a percentage of GTR- selected) is observed in the GST regime.

Tax expenditures on Customs Duty consist of two components—gross tax expenditures on customs duty and input tax neutralization or

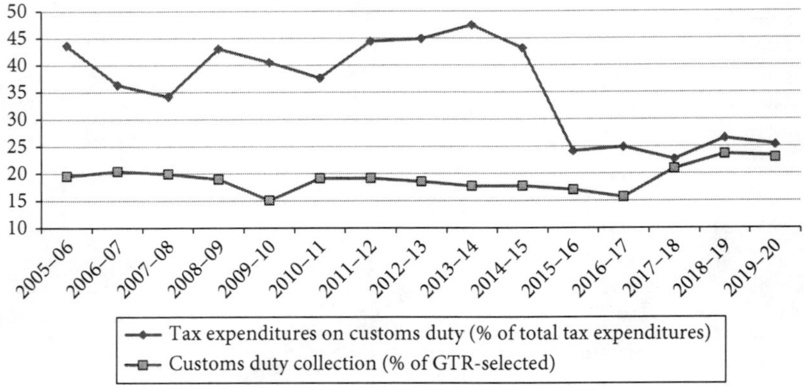

Figure 7.18 Tax expenditure on customs duty and customs duty collection.
Source: Computed by author based on Union Budget documents (various years).

exemption schemes. To avoid exportation of taxes to destination countries, zero rating of exports is a common practice across the world. Prior to the introduction of GST in India, due to overlapping jurisdiction of indirect taxes between the union and state governments, it was difficult to assess the burden of input taxes on exported goods and services (Mukherjee, 2021). As a result, various schemes were employed to provide access to duty-free imports of inputs as well as capital goods to exporters, for example: Advanced License Scheme, tax exemptions of inputs used for exports in Export Oriented Units, Electronic Hardware Technology Park, Software Technology Park, Special Economic Zone, Export Promotion Capital Goods Scheme, Duty Free Import Authorization Scheme, Duty Free Replenishment Certificate, and Duty Entitlement Pass-Book Scheme. In the GST regime, the following schemes are available for exporters to avoid exportation of taxes to destination countries:

- LUT Bond Scheme: Exporters can export goods without paying any GST by obtaining a Letter of Undertaking bond.
- IGST Refund: Exporters can export goods on payments of IGST and later, claim the refund for the same from the customs department.
- 0.1 per cent GST Benefit for Merchant Exporters: Merchants can procure goods for exports from domestic suppliers at a 0.1 per cent concessional GST rate.

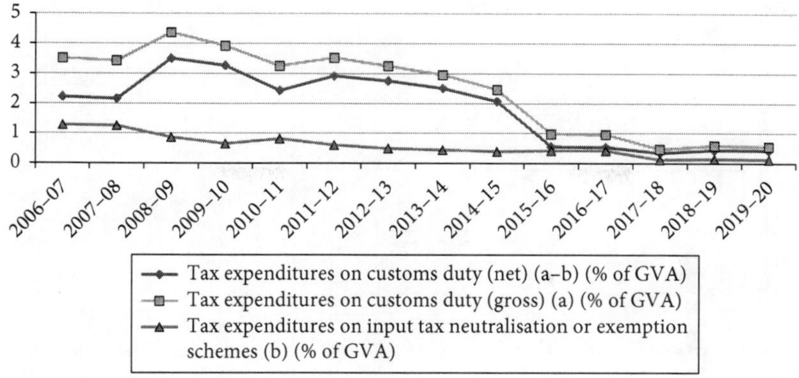

Figure 7.19 Tax expenditures on customs duty (as a percentage of GVA).
Source: Computed by author based on Union Budget documents (various years).

In addition, Remission of Duties and Taxes on Export Products scheme was rolled out at the start of 2021 to ensure that the exporters receive refunds on the embedded taxes and duties which are non-recoverable even in the GST regime (e.g. Mandi tax, State VAT, Coal cess, Central Excise duty on fuel, electricity duty, etc.).

Average tax expenditure on customs duty was around 2.7 per cent of GVA during 2005–15 (Figure 7.19). During 2015–20, average tax expenditure on customs duty went down to 0.5 per cent of GVA (Table 7.8). This shows that gradually tax expenditure on customs duty has been reduced in India. The possibility of further reduction of tax expenditure on customs duty must be explored, especially on items which are not covered under any free or preferential trade agreements/treaty.

During 2006–20, annual growth in customs duty collection fell below the annual growth in tax expenditure on customs duty for six years (2008–10, 2011–12, 2016–17, and 2018–20 (Figure 7.20). The impact of GFC was restricted not only to a fall in tax collections, but also to a rise in tax expenditures during 2008–10.

7.3 Conclusions

Tax expenditure is often viewed as a potential loss of tax revenue which otherwise would have been collected by the government. With the fall

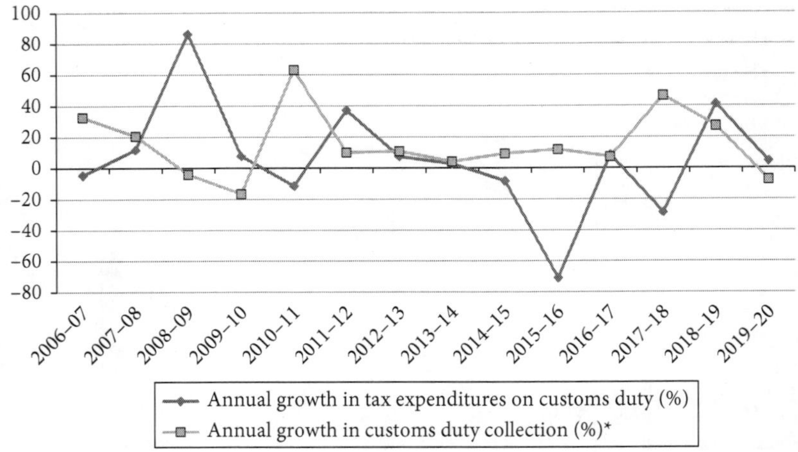

Figure 7.20 Annual growth in tax expenditure and tax collection—customs duty.

Source: Computed by author based on Union Budget documents (various years)

Note: *includes GST on imports.

in tax expenditures in India, we have not observed any improvement in tax collection (as a percentage of GVA) in union taxes during 2006–07 to 2019–20. However, we observed a significant rise in tax expenditures on indirect taxes in India during 2008–10, attributed to cuts in tax rates of UED and customs duty as part of fiscal stimulus measures adopted by the union government to cope up with the GFC. Therefore, any measure to provide fiscal stimulus by cutting effective tax rates may have revenue impact in terms of lower tax collection and rising expectations of taxpayers for tax incentives/exemptions. With the recovery of the economy, timely withdrawal of tax exemptions/incentives is important to achieve macroeconomic stability. However, withdrawals of tax incentives often take longer and face resistance from taxpayers. Impact assessments of tax incentive/exemption schemes are lacking in India and it would be prudent to initiate such appraisals.

Reduction in tax expenditures on indirect taxes was slow post-GFC. However, the introduction of GST on 1 July 2017 helped the union government eliminate tax exemptions on UED. As a step towards the introduction of GST, the union government reduced tax expenditures on indirect taxes from 2015–16. Average annual tax expenditure on indirect taxes was reduced from 4.7 per cent of GVA during 2010–15 to 0.7 per cent of GVA during 2015–20. Though comprehensive assessment of tax expenditures in the GST regime is awaited, available data show that area-based tax expenditures in the GST regime are much lower than during the pre-GST regime.

As mentioned, before the introduction of GST, it was hard to assess the burden of input taxes on exported goods and services. So various schemes were proposed to allow access to duty-free imports of inputs and capital goods to exporters. Strengthening of the tax base of indirect taxes in the GST regime facilitated zero rating of Indian exports. This has also helped to contain tax expenditures on customs duty.

In addition to the overall reduction in tax expenditures, structural composition of tax expenditure underwent changes over the period. The priorities of the government change over time, and tax incentives are one way to assess government priorities. A significant reduction in tax expenditures on direct taxes was observed during 2010–15, whereas in indirect taxes it was during 2015–20. Average annual tax expenditure on union taxes (as a percentage of gross tax revenue of selected taxes) fell from an average of 70 per cent during 2006–10 to 61 per cent during 2010–15, and further to 18.4 per cent during 2015–20.

Cuts in tax expenditure on CIT helped to reduce the difference/gap between the statutory and effective CIT rates. However, tax expenditure on PIT (as a percentage of GVA and of PIT revenue) has shown a rising trend since 2014–15.

References

Burman, L. E., and Phaup, M. (2012). 'Tax Expenditures, the Size and Efficiency of Government, and Implications for Budget Reform', *Tax Policy and the Economy*, 26(1), 93–124.

Chen, D. (2015). 'The Framework for Assessing Tax Incentives: A Cost Benefit Analysis Approach'. Paper for workshop on Tax Incentives and Base Protection, New York, 23–24 April 2015.

Chetty, R., Hendren, N., Kline, P., et al. (2015). 'The Economic Impact of Tax Expenditures: Evidence from Spatial Variation across the US'. Available at: https://www.irs.gov/pub/irs-soi/14rptaxexpenditures.pdf (accessed 10 March 2022).

Dash, B. B., and Raja, A.V. (2008). 'Do Political Determinants affect Revenue Collection? Evidence from Indian States', National Institute of Public Finance and Policy, New Delhi.

Daude, C., Gutiérrez, H., and Melguizo, Á. (2014). 'The Political Economy of Tax Incentives for Investment in the Dominican Republic: Doctoring the Ball'. OECD Development Centre Working Paper 322. https://doi.org/10.1787/5jz3wkh45kmw-en.

Fuest, C., and Riedel, N. (2009). 'Tax Evasion, Tax Avoidance and Tax Expenditures in Developing Countries: A Review of the Literature'. Report prepared for the UK Department for International Development (DFID), 44.

Heady, C., and M. Mansour (2019). 'Tax Expenditure Reporting and Its Use in Fiscal Management: A Guide for Developing Economies'. Fiscal Affairs Department, International Monetary Fund, Washington, DC.

Hicken, A. (2011). 'Clientelism', *Annual Review of Political Science*, 14, 289–310.

Hunter, W. J., and Nelson, M.A. (1989). 'Interest Group Demand for Taxation', *Public Choice* 62(1), 41–61.

Marjit, S., Sasmal, R., and Sasmal, J. (2020). 'Composition of Public Expenditure and Growth of Per Capita Income in Indian States: A Political Perspective', *Journal of Social and Economic Development*, 22(1), 1–17.

Mehta, D., and Mukherjee, S. (2021). 'Emerging Issues in GST Law and Procedures: An Assessment', Working Paper 347, NIPFP, New Delhi.

Mukherjee, S. (2021). 'India: The Challenges of Implementing VAT in a Federal State', in Robert F. van Brederode (ed.), *Virtues and Fallacies of VAT: An Evaluation after 50 Years*, Kluwer Law International, UK, 575–602.

OECD (2010). *Tax Expenditures in OECD Countries*, OECD, Paris. Available at: https://www.oecd-ilibrary.org/governance/tax-expenditures-in-oecd-countries_9789264076907-en (last accessed 10 March 2022).

Rao, R. K., and Mukherjee, S. (2017). 'Corporate Tax Concessions in India: Are they Equitable?', *Asia-Pacific Tax Bulletin*, 23(4), August 2017.

Rao, R. K., Tandon, S., and Mukherjee, S. (2016). 'Corporate Tax: A Brief Assessment of some Exemptions', Working Paper 165, NIPFP, New Delhi.

Redonda, Agustin, de Sarralde, Santiago Diaz, Hallerberg, Mark, et al. (2019). 'Tax Expenditure and the Treatment of Tax Incentives for Investment', *Economics*, 13 (2019-12): 1–11.

Appendix

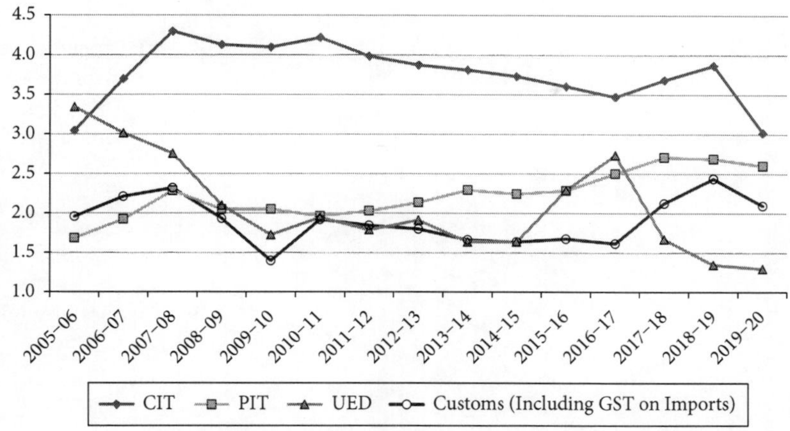

Figure 7.21 Trends in tax collections (as a percentage of GVA).

Source: Computed by author based on Union Budget documents (various years).

8

Tax Evasion and Unaccounted Incomes

A Theoretical Approach

Amey Sapre

8.1 Introduction

In this chapter I develop a theoretical analysis of the problem of tax evasion. I take a renewed approach to analysing the decision-making problem of an individual confronted with the choice of declaring either the entire income or a part thereof for paying taxes. The work primarily builds on existing theoretical approaches that have modelled a variety of problems ranging from decisions under uncertainty to experimental approaches in understanding compliance, predictive audits, and network effects. Tax evasion, as has commonly been understood, is about engaging in illegal methods to escape from paying taxes. The act of evasion also implies that individuals (or firms) deliberately misreport their incomes, expenditure, or other gains to do so. In the context of behavioural attributes or studies, such deliberate acts of tax evasion are seen as forms of *non-compliance* and open a new and separate line of research.

The formal approach to analysing tax evasion at an individual level began with the seminal works of Allingham and Sandmo (1972) and Srinivasan (1973). Other notable ideas in this area were introduced by Mossin (1968), Stiglitz (1969), Mirrlees (1971), and Yilthzaki (1974), eventually leading to the formalization of the decision under uncertainty model. Later formulations included works of Gordon (1987), Graetz et. al (1986), Liu (1986), and Mittone (2006) that brought several social interactions into consideration. The framework was built on the proposition that taxpayers abide by the axioms of utility theory and maximize expected utility, and that audits (or detection of evasion) conducted by tax authorities were random in nature. Hence, gains could be made by

Amey Sapre, *Tax Evasion and Unaccounted Incomes* In: *Fiscal Policy and Public Financial Management.*
Edited by: Pinaki Chakraborty and K R Shanmugam, Oxford University Press.
DOI: 10.1093/9780198930464.003.0008

under-reporting incomes. The key limitation of this approach is that such a simplified model over-predicts the extent of evasion when evaluated with objective probabilities of audits, rather than subjective beliefs of taxpayers. Recent research in areas of behavioral economics has shown that a large number of audits are 'risk based' and only a small proportion are done on a random basis. This approach has motivated several applications in predictive audits, agent-based modelling, and other experimental settings (see Hashimzade et al. (2012) for a survey).

From the tax authorities' side, the costs of tax administration play a significant role in determining the number or extent of scrutiny or even prosecutions of offenders. In the conventional set-up, such direct costs of administering a tax system have received little attention as the analysis is largely summarized in either the tax effort or the efficiency of the tax system as a whole (see e.g. Chattopadhyay and Das Gupta (2002)). Similarly, there are no established feedback mechanisms on how taxpayers perceive the administration's ability or cost of audits, which in turn can influence their decision on engaging in evasion. These are primarily summarized in the subjective beliefs of taxpayers about the probability of being audited and the efforts made by the administration.

The key underlying aspect of the engagement of taxpayers and the tax authorities is that the authorities may not necessarily commit to an audit rule before taxpayers report their incomes (or file tax returns). However, given optimal audits, the authority may well follow procedures to audit reported incomes below (or above) a certain threshold and selectively audit the others. In case no such committed rule exists, the interaction between a taxpayer and the authorities becomes complicated and can be taken as strategic in nature.

8.1.1 Motivation and Extensions

Theoretical research in the domain of tax evasion has touched upon several dimensions. However, a common theme of all foundational papers was to model a one-period decision. Within this framework, findings of the seminal papers highlighted that the level of tax evasion primarily depends on two factors, namely (1) penalty or punishment for tax evasion, and (2) the probability of audit. Similarly, extensions in the existing framework explain the factors or variables that affect non-compliance and/or compliance in paying taxes. However, even within a static framework, the results in most of the cases have been conflicting. In order to broaden the existing framework, it is useful to ask whether further modifications provide more useful insights.

The first question in extending the framework is whether the decision to under-report income (hence tax evasion) can be considered over repeated interactions. This is clearly plausible as, given an income stream, an individual faces the decision of reporting the true income in every single time period. The analysis of a series of decisions also allows us to characterize the accumulation of unreported income. In the static framework, the unreported income is only in a single period, which, in principle, does not allow us to infer the size of unreported income over time. Once we conceptualize that, over time, under-reporting of true income generates a flow of unaccounted incomes and saved tax thereof, we have an extended problem as compared to the existing static one-period problem.

The extensions also have a qualitative nature. In Allingham and Sandmo (1972) and Srinivasan (1973) the role of the tax authority was not modelled explicitly. The tax authority plays a passive role as there is no strategic engagement of the authority in the taxpayers' decision of whether or not to evade taxes. Another important aspect not emphasized in the literature is the tax authority's cost of audit. As the tax authority is primarily concerned with collection of tax revenue and penalties in cases of evasion, the net outcome of conducting an audit can be conceptualized as gains from collecting tax and penalties, vis-à-vis, incurring the cost of audit. We can now ask the question: do the results of the static model change if we incorporate these two aspects in the static model? And further, do the results change if we consider the decision in a repeated scenario? In what follows, the extensions are built into a simple game-theoretic framework.

8.2 Basic Structure: A Short Review

Theoretical models with exogenous income provided the foundation in the area of tax evasion. The initial contributions of Sharon (1967),

Allingham and Sandmo (1972), and Srinivasan (1973) provided the basic set-up to analyse the individual's decision of reporting income for taxation. The general set-up of the model specifies how an individual maximizes expected utility from reporting part of income for taxation with the uncertainty of being caught of evasion.

The decision problem of the individual is set as under

$$E(u) = (1 - p)u[y - tR] + pu[y - tR - \pi(y - R)] \tag{8.1}$$

where $E(u)$ is the expected utility. The expression summarizes the expected utility of the individual in the two possible states, namely let-off or undetected with probability $(1 - p)$, and caught with probability (p). The decision variable for the individual is R, that is, the reporting of a fraction of the actual or true income. In general, to draw inferences one would require specific forms of the utility function and the risk preferences of the taxpayer. Nevertheless, we can consider the major implications of the basic model. First, the predictions about the effect of different parameters such as tax rate, penalty, and the probability of detection depend largely on the choice of utility functions. Allingham and Sandmo (1972) made use of the Arrow–Pratt measure of risk aversion and assumed decreasing absolute risk aversion. Also, with regard to marginal tax rate, the model predicts that a rise in tax rate has an ambiguous effect on tax evasion. The prediction is due to the ambiguity in the magnitudes of income and substitution effects. With higher taxes, the income effect is negative as the individual is left poorer, but the substitution effect works in favour of tax evasion.

Further, changes in the probability of detection and the penalty structure change the results considerably. Yitzhaki (1974) modified the set-up to change the way the penalty was imposed. Yitzhaki argued that if the penalty were imposed on the evaded tax (i.e. (πt $(y - R)$), instead of the unreported income $(y - R)$), then the model would not have any substitution effect. With this change, only the income effect remains, which establishes a negative relation between the tax rate and the amount of evasion.

Srinivasan (1973) presented a similar model of tax evasion, but with modifications in the objective of the individual. In his model, individuals chose to maximize expected income instead of utility, which implied that individuals were treated as risk-neutral. Another assumption made was that individuals chose to report a proportion of their true income in order to maximize expected income. An important conclusion of this model was that, with a constant marginal tax rate and with probability of detection as an increasing function of the *actual* income, individuals will report a larger fraction of income for taxation as their actual incomes rise.

Christiansen (1980) was among the early studies to modify the Allingham and Sandmo framework by introducing an association between the penalty and the probability of audit (or detection). The analysis shows that, given the nature of the functions, in some cases an increase in penalty might lead to an increase in tax evasion. Another modification was made by Witte and Woodbury (1985), wherein two separate probabilities were introduced, namely civil and criminal, instead of a single probability of audit. The approach was to introduce additional parameters to explain non-compliance, rather than a singular instance of audit. Cross and Shaw (1981, 1982) extended the framework further to consider a case of tax evasion and avoidance. They argued that evasion and avoidance are joint decisions and can act as substitutes or complimentary options under different scenarios.

In a series of papers, Hashimzade and Myles (2017) and Hashimzade et al. (2012, 2014, 2015, 2016) explored a variety of behavioural economics aspects on audits, predictive analysis on audits, agent-based approach to model tax compliance, and effect of social networks on tax compliance. On a related issue, Pestieau et al. (1994) analysed the effects of tax audit and compliance on occupational choices the taxpayer. They argued that individuals have different risk preferences; risk-averse individuals would choose safe occupations, while less averse people would prefer entrepreneurship. Similarly, the level of information with taxpayers, levels of scrutiny, and risk preferences have also been common in several empirical applications. For instance, Das-gupta et al. (2004) analysed the effect of tax reform on compliance. Using data on tax audits of different assessment units, they found evidence consistent with the predictions of the Allingham and Sandmo (1972) model. A similar line of research is available in Mookherjee and Png (1989) and Mookherjee (1990, 2004, (2008).

More recently, Rao and Tandon (2016) used prospect theory to model and revisit the compliance problem. Their starting point of the analysis is the decision to file a tax return, instead of the conventional approach of modelling reporting of income. They conduct a simulation exercise of different policy parameters of the model and find a threshold beyond which individuals choose to file their tax returns. Their work introduces a new dimension to the existing set of problems by considering an additional step of filing a tax return. An important finding is that not all individuals find it optimum to file a tax return and that on low incomes, individuals may not prefer to file one.

Given the vast literature on the problem of tax evasion, it is useful to summarize the main findings before attempting to develop a renewed approach to the problem. Broadly, the general theme that emerges from the literature is that variables such as tax structure or rates, effectiveness of tax administration, penalty structure, and audit probability, among others, qualitatively explain the individual's decision of *non-compliance* (involvement in tax evasion). The first lesson is that the foundation of tax evasion models is based on the theory of risk and uncertainty. The second is that individuals are perceived as maximizing expected incomes or expected utility, which is based on two possible states, one of successful evasion and the other in which evasion is detected.

8.3 Tax Evasion: A Game-Theoretic Approach

8.3.1 Formulation

The basic framework is similar in spirit to Allingham and Sandmo (1972) and Srinivasan (1973), but differs in formulation. In this set-up, an individual has an exogenously given income and has to make the decision whether or not to engage in tax evasion by under-reporting income. To begin with, the variables used to formulate the model are as follows.

y denotes the income of the individual in a given time period; α ($0 \leq \alpha \leq 1$) denotes the fraction of income reported to tax authorities; τ ($0 < \tau < 1$) denotes the tax rate on income; p ($0 < p < 1$) denotes the probability of auditing & detecting the instance of tax evasion; c ($c > 0$) denotes the of conducting an audit of the individual; d, ($0 < d < 1$) denotes the cost probability of engaging in tax evasion for the individual and N time periods

The first distinction from the conventional set-up is to explicitly incorporate the role of the tax authorities in conducting an audit. In the earlier models, the role of the tax authorities was taken as passive, and the cost of audit was also not included in the model. A second departure is by introducing a repeated interaction between a representative taxpayer and the tax authority. In earlier formulations, the model of decision under uncertainty provides a limited characterization of the decision and the strategies available to the stakeholders involved. The game-theoretic formulation also allows us to extend the problem to a multi-period set-up, thereby changing the decision-making process from a static to a dynamic scenario. However, some basic features of the earlier models continue to be used as building blocks. Following Yilthzaki (1974), the penalty in the case of a person caught of tax evasion is levied on evaded tax.

To formulate the problem, consider first a single-period decision-making situation. The individual earns an income (y) and decides whether or not to evade taxes by under-reporting income. Given an income, the individual engages in tax evasion by choosing to report a fraction ($0 < \alpha < 1$) of the income to tax authorities. The remaining fraction ($1 - \alpha$) remains unreported and escapes tax liability. Thus, in a single period, the individual has a tax liability only on reported income, that is ($\tau \alpha y$).

In the second case, the individual does not engage in tax evasion and thus chooses to report the entire income for taxation. From the tax authorities' side, the purpose of conducting audits is primarily to ensure tax compliance and to uncover tax evasion in case of willful tax defaulters. Also, in case of tax evasion, the authorities are empowered to levy penalties that contribute to additional tax revenues. However, conducting tax audits involves significant monetary and human resource costs and, given a resource-constrained tax authority, it can be safely assumed that not all tax-payers are audited. This subjective yet practical view allows taxpayers' the possibility of a successful evasion in any given time period. If we consider that a taxpayer faces an audit with probability (p), a penalty of ($\pi > 1$) is levied on the amount of evaded tax if the taxpayer is found to be engaging in tax evasion. Thus, if we conceptualize the choices available to the individual and the tax authority in a strategic setting, the outcomes of a single time period can be explained using a game tree.

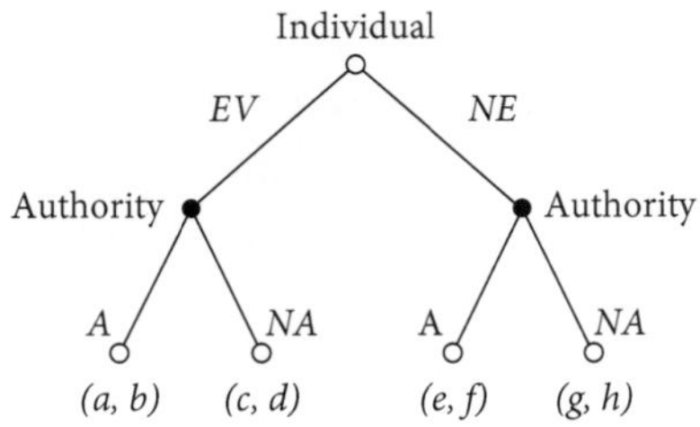

Figure 8.1 One period game (choices of taxpayer and tax authority).

The individual has two available choices, $\{EV, NE\}$, namely to evade or not to evade taxes. For each choice, the individual can be audited by the tax authority with probability (p) or can be let off with probability $(1-p)$. These two outcomes are denoted by $\{A, NA\}$ on each node. With four possible outcomes, the payoffs for each can be summarized under different scenarios for both the taxpayer and the authority.

8.3.2 Case 1: Basic Game

The simplest case is the original problem in the literature where the individual compares the expected value of income from evasion and from no evasion. Let (d) denote the probability that the individual evades taxes by underreporting income. The payoffs (or the income remaining with the individual) for each strategy can be given by

$$\begin{array}{ll} \{EV, A\} = y - (\tau \alpha y) - \pi[\tau(1-\alpha)y] & \{EV, NA\} = y - \tau(\alpha y) \\ \{NE, A\} = y - \tau y & \{NE, NA\} = y - \tau y \end{array} \tag{8.2}$$

$\{EV, A\}$ denotes the outcome where the individual decides to underreport income and is audited. The payoff in this situation is the income left after paying the tax on the reported income and the penalty on evaded tax. For the outcome $\{EV, NA\}$, the individual evades taxes by underreporting income, but escapes the audit (with probability $(1-p)$). Tax is paid only on the reported income and the taxpayer successfully evades taxes on unreported income. In the other two outcomes, $\{NE, A\}$ and $\{NE, NA\}$, the taxpayer reports his/her full income and thus does not evade taxes, irrespective of being audited or not. From the view of the tax authorities, each strategy leads to different payoffs in terms of tax collections. For each choice, the tax collections can be summarized as:

$$\begin{array}{ll} \{EV,A\} = (\tau\,\alpha y) + \pi[\tau(1-\alpha)y] - c & \{EV,NA\} = \tau(\alpha y) \\ \{NE,A\} = (\tau\,y) - c & \{NE,NA\} = \tau\,y \end{array} \tag{8.3}$$

In the first case, the tax authorities collect the tax paid on reported income and the penalty on evaded tax. The authority also incurs a monetary cost of audit, and in the net payoff the cost of audit is deducted from the total tax collection. For ease of exposition, it is assumed that the (tax and) penalty exceed the cost of audit. In the second case, tax collection is only on the reported income as the taxpayer is not audited and successfully evades taxes by under-reporting income. In the last two cases, tax collection is on actual or full income as the taxpayer does not under-report income. However, in the case of an audit, the tax authorities incur a cost and that is deducted from the tax collection. The payoffs can be summarized and tabulated in a 2 × 2 game matrix with the strategies for the taxpayer and the authorities.

	(p) **Audited**	$(1-p)$**Not audited**
(d) Evade	$y-(\tau\alpha y)-\pi[\tau(1-\alpha)y], (\tau\alpha y)+\pi[\tau(1-\alpha)y]-c$	$(1-\tau\alpha)y, \tau(\alpha y)$
$(1-d)$ Do not evade	$(1-\tau)y, (\tau y)-c$	$(1-\tau)y, \tau y$

Nash Equilibrium: One-Period-Stage Game

The payoff structure has the following implications. First, rational and selfish individuals will evade taxes if not audited and will comply in case they are audited. Second, tax authorities will conduct audits if taxpayers evade taxes, and will not conduct audits in cases where taxpayers comply. The consequence of such a payoff structure is that neither the taxpayer nor the authority has a best or a fixed strategy, that is, there is no best action for either party, regardless of the decision of the other. Thus, in this setting, the game does not have a 'pure' strategy equilibrium. Therefore, to make their best decision, each party has to decide on a mix of strategies. In order to find the best set of choices for both players, we need to find the mix strategy Nash equilibria of the game. We first derive the best response functions of the taxpayer and of the authority. Consider the argument for each player as follows.

Taxpayer's best response: The taxpayer faces two possibilities, namely being audited and not being audited, with probabilities (p) and ($1 - p$). If $p = 0$ (i.e. the tax payer is not audited), the best choice in this situation is to evade taxes, since the payoff $(1 - \tau\alpha)y > (1 - \tau)y$. If $p = 1$ (i.e. the taxpayer is audited), then the best choice is not to evade taxes since the payoff $(1 - \tau)y > y - (\tau\alpha y) - \pi[\tau(1 - \alpha)y]$. We can now ask the question: for what probability of audit is the taxpayer indifferent between evading and not evading taxes? To compute, for a given value of p, the expected payoff of evasion is $p[y - (\tau\alpha y) - \pi[\tau(1 - \alpha)y]] + (1 - p)[(1 - \tau\alpha)y]$, while the expected payoff of not evading taxes is $p[(1 - \tau)y] + (1 - p)[(1 - \tau)y]$. The individual is indifferent between the two choices when the value of both outcomes is equal. This implies:

$$\begin{aligned} &p[y-(\tau\alpha y)-\pi[\tau(1-\alpha)y]]+(1-p)[(1-\tau)\alpha y] \\ &\quad = p[(1-\tau)y]+(1-p)[(1-\tau)y] \end{aligned} \tag{8.4}$$

Simplifying and rewriting the expression in terms of p, we have; $p^* = 1/\pi$.

Tax authority's best response: The tax authority has to decide whether or not to audit the taxpayer. If the taxpayer evades (i.e. ($d = 1$)), the best choice for the authority is to audit, since the payoff in terms of tax collection is higher ($\tau y(\alpha + \pi - \pi\alpha) - c > \tau(\alpha y)$). However, if ($d = 0$), then the best choice is not to audit the taxpayer as the payoff $(\tau y) > (\tau y) - c$. Similar to the taxpayer's expected income, the expected tax collection for the authority in case of auditing is; $d[\tau y(\pi + \alpha(1 - \pi)) - c] + (1 - d)[\tau(y) - c]$, while for not auditing the payoff is $d[(\tau\alpha y)] + (1 - d)[\tau y]$. The authority is indifferent in conducting an audit if:

$$\begin{aligned} &d[\tau\alpha y]+\pi[\tau(1-\alpha)y]-c]+(1-d)[(\tau y)-c] \\ &\quad = d[(\tau\alpha y)]+(1-d)[(\tau y)] \end{aligned} \tag{8.5}$$

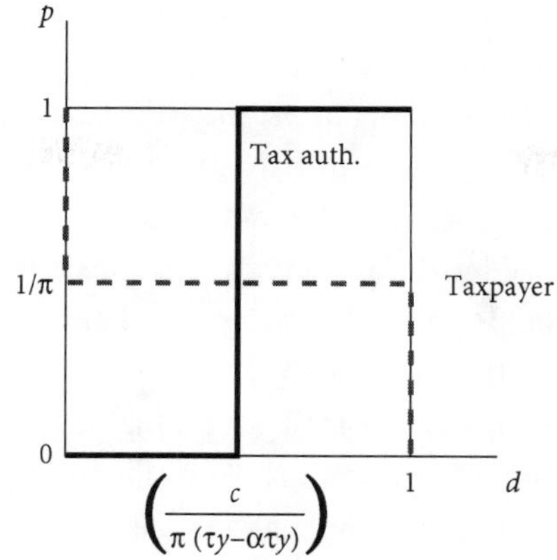

Figure 8.2 Best response function of taxpayer and tax authority.

Simplifying the expression, the value of (d) is; $d^* = c/\pi(\tau y - \alpha\tau y)$. Combining the best responses of each player, we can graph the responses in the (d, p) space. In Figure 8.2, the dashed line plots the best response of the taxpayer. The solid line represents the response of the tax authorities. The equilibrium point is at the intersection of the two best response functions in the (p, d) space, that is, $(p^*, d^*) = (1/\pi, c/(\pi(\tau y - \alpha\tau y))$, thus giving us the following proposition;

Proposition 1: *Given the set of actions and payoffs for the individual and the tax authority, the strategy profile* $(p^*, d^*) = (1/\pi, c/\pi(\tau y - \alpha\tau y)$ *is a unique mixed strategy Nash equilibrium of the game.*

The equilibrium values p^* and d^* can be obtained after equating equations 8.2 and 8.3 (the best response functions of the taxpayer and the tax authority). The equilibrium value is depicted in Figure 8.1. In this mixed-strategy equilibrium, the taxpayer is honest on some occasions and dishonest on others. This fact is also clear from the payoffs as the best response in the case of being audited is not to evade taxes, but in the case of no audit, the payoff of evading taxes is higher, that is, $(1 - \tau\alpha)y > (1 - \tau)y$. Alternatively, from the expression that gives the value of (d), we can note that the value of (α) is positive. Rearranging the expression in terms of (α) gives; $\alpha = \dfrac{d\tau y\pi}{d\tau y\pi - c}$, which is positive based on the condition that tax revenue (τy) times penalty is higher than the cost of audit for the authority.

From the equilibrium values of (p, d) we can determine that if the probability of audit were to fall below $(1/\pi)$, the individual could improve his/her payoff by evading taxes, since the best response in that case is $d = 1$. Conversely, for audit probability values higher than $(1/\pi)$, the individual's best response is not to evade taxes, that is, $(d = 0)$. In a specific case, if we consider the penalty on tax evasion to be 100 percent, implying that the taxpayer has to pay an equal amount of evaded tax by way of penalty, then the threshold value of p equals 1/2 $(\pi = 2)$ in case of 100 per cent penalty on evaded tax). Qualitatively, the result gives new insights into the tax-evasion problem. The mixed-strategy equilibrium has a counter-intuitive implication that higher penalties may not lead to a decrease in evasion. The reason is that the mixed-strategy equilibrium is optimal only when both parties make each other indifferent between their respective actions. In case both parties are not indifferent between the two decisions, the player can take advantage by exploiting the other, thus giving incentive to change the decision. The result of the mixed-strategy equilibrium is consistent with the earlier formulations of Allingham and Sandmo (1972), Srinivasan (1973), and Sandmo (2004). The result also provides a range of values of the probability of evasion, which in the earlier models was not explicitly available. Also, the result is achieved under much simpler and more general conditions, since in the earlier formulations the choice of utility functions clearly limited the scope of signing the derivatives to obtain a clear prediction. In addition, an important aspect of the game-theoretic model is that it actively models the role of tax administration.

The key variables that operate through the probability of audit are the penalty rate and the cost of the audit. In earlier models, the cost of audit was not included, thereby leaving a wide scope for interpretation of the results. Incorporating the role of cost of audit clearly influences the decision-making on the part of the taxpayer. Also, qualitative understanding of the penalty rate, which is taken to act as a deterrent on tax evasion, is equally important. Since the probability of audit is inversely related to the penalty rate, it provides a logical answer to the question of evasion. If penalty rates are high, they are expected to lead to lower numbers of audits and tax assessments. Conversely, if penalty rates are lower, taxpayers may perceive a lower burden of penalty on being caught of tax evasion, and thus lower penalty rates may not act as a deterrent. It follows that to compensate for the low deterrence, the frequency of audits must increase.

In the literature, the interactions between the taxpayer and the administration have also been explored. Given the subjective nature of probability, evasion may actually increase if taxpayers believe that audit costs are significantly high. Intuitively, a similar logic applies to deciding on the extent of under-reporting. If audit costs are high, in turn leading to fewer audits, taxpayers are likely to under-report their income by a greater extent. As earlier, the penalty structure and the cost of audit are the key variables that influence the decision of the taxpayer on evasion. The penalty structure also operates as an incentive to the tax authorities as they can recover additional revenue apart from tax collections on declared incomes. If recoveries from penalties are assumed to be higher than the cost of audit (i.e. $\pi[\tau(1-\alpha)y] > c$), then there are clear incentives for conducting audits in cases where taxpayers choose to evade. What other insights can be obtained from the tax evasion game? We can now extend the basic model to consider if the taxpayer can successfully accumulate undisclosed income and evade taxes over repeated interactions.

8.3.3 Case 2: Accumulation and no Disclosure

To build on the existing result, consider a repeated version of the one-period game. Since tax-evasion decisions are not limited to a single occurrence, a taxpayer has to decide on disclosing income in every period. In this setting, the taxpayer compares the gains from evading against not evading over many periods. As there are incentives to evade taxes, it is the taxpayer's presumption that, unless audited, it is gainful to evade taxes for as long as possible. The mechanism at work is that a taxpayer can successfully under-report income at any period and not disclose it in any future time period. Thus, in every period, the taxpayer discloses only the current-period income and escapes tax liability on any previously undisclosed income. On the other hand, the tax authorities have the same choice as earlier, that is, whether or not to audit the tax payer.

However, in a repeated interaction, we assume that if the taxpayer is caught of evading, the tax authorities will audit the individual in every subsequent period. The underlying logic is that once an evader is found, tax authorities are more likely to audit to prevent further evasion. The principle is similar to a one-step deviation, wherein players choose a pair of strategies and continue with them up until one of the players defects and, post defection, continue to defect thereafter. To formulate the situation, consider that a taxpayer can be caught evading at any period. Once caught, the taxpayer will be audited for every period, and thus will not evade henceforth. For successful evasion throughout, the taxpayer must not be caught in any period. Therefore, the individual has to consider the payoffs of evading and being caught at least once, vis-à-vis not evading at all. The set-up is as follows.

Let *Vc* denote the payoffs from the strategy where the taxpayer evades and is caught, that is, [*EV*, *A*]. Let *Ve* denote the payoffs when the taxpayer successfully evades, that is, the strategy [*EV*, *N A*] ,and *Vne* the payoff when the taxpayer does not evade. To begin with, consider a set-up in *N* periods. The situation unfolds in each period, particularly when the taxpayer is not audited and thus successfully evades in the period. In other words, the taxpayer can either successfully evade in period 1, or get caught. Similarly, the taxpayer can successfully evade in the first two periods, or get caught, and so on. Continuing to *N* periods,

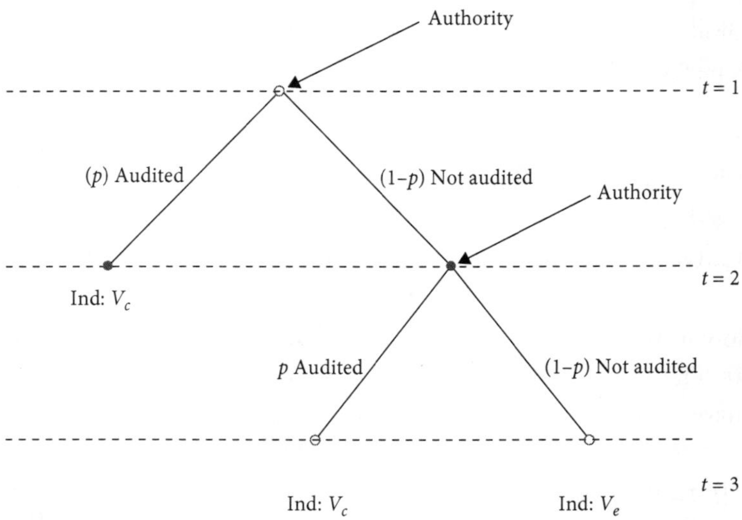

Figure 8.3 Timing and sequence of taxpayers.

Figure 8.3 shows the sequence of the taxpayer moving over each time period depending on whether the individual was audited (and caught) in the previous period.

The payoffs are derived as follows.

For $t = 1$, the payoff of the taxpayer is $p[Vc + (N - 1)Vne] + (1 - p)Ve$. The expression captures the expected value under the scenario that the taxpayer either is caught in the first period with probability (p) thus giving the payoff of Vc and Vne for all future time periods, or is not audited in the first period thus successfully evading with probability $(1 - p)$ and the payoff Ve.

For $t = 2$, the situation is dependent on whether the taxpayer successfully evaded in the previous period. The payoff is $(1 - p)[p(Vc + (N - 2)Vne)]$, that is, the probability of not being caught in the previous period times the payoff of the second period. The sequence $(N - i)$; $i = 1, 2, \ldots N$ captures the payoff the taxpayer will get for the rest of the period in the event of being caught.

For $t = N$, the general expression is $(1 - p)^{N-1}[p(Vc + (N - N)Vne) + (1 - p)Ve]$, where ($p$) and $(1 - p)$ are respectively the probabilities of being caught and let off (i.e. not audited). As earlier, the payoff after being caught in any period is the payoff of non-evasion (i.e. Vne), as the taxpayer does not engage in evasion thereafter. For evasion to be gainful, the taxpayer must compare the sum of this stream with the other alternative of not evading in any period (i.e. $Vn\ e$). Expanding it to N periods, we get

$$pV_e\left[\frac{1-(1-p)^N}{1-(1-p)}\right]+(1-p)V_e\left[\frac{1-(1-p)^N}{1-(1-p)}\right]+ \quad (8.6)$$
$$pV_{ne}[(N-1)+(1-p)(N-2)+(1-p)^2(N-3)+\cdots+1-p^{N-1}(N-1)]$$

Solving the expression requires simplifying the right-hand side in two parts. First, reducing the second part (equation 8.5) of the sequence, we have

$$pV_{ne}[(N-1)+(1-p)(N-2)+(1-p)^2(N-3)+\cdots+1-p^{N-1}(N-1)] \quad (8.7)$$

Rearranging by excluding the last term and shifting backwards, we obtain

$$pV_{ne}[(N-1)+(1-p)(N-2)+(1-p)^2(N-3) \\ +\cdots+(1-p)^{N-2}(N-(N1))] \tag{8.8}$$

Rearranging the sequence further in reverse order of terms, we have

$$pV_{ne}[1.(1-p)^{N-2}+2(1-p)^{N-3} \\ +\cdots+(1-p)^2(N-3)+(1-p)(N-2)+(N-1)] \tag{8.9}$$

Writing the series as a sum of the components, we get

$$pV_{ne}\left[\sum_{i=1}^{N-1} i(1-p)^{N-1-I}\right] \tag{8.10}$$

Solving the expression ($\forall i \in 1 \ldots N-1$) and denoting the sum within the parentheses by S, we have

$$S=1.(1-p)^{N-2}+2(1-p)^{N-3}+\cdots+(N-2)(1-p)+(N-1) \tag{8.11}$$

Multiplying both sides by $(1-p)$, we have

$$(1-p)S=2(1-p)^{N-2}+3(1-p)^{N-3}+\cdots+(N-1)(1-p)+(1-p)^{N-1} \tag{8.12}$$

Subtracting the above expression from the previous expression, we obtain

$$pS=-(1-p)^{N-2}-(1-p)^{N-3}-\cdots-(1-p)^{N-1}+(N-1) \tag{8.13}$$

Rearranging,

$$-pS=1+(1-p)+(1-p)^2+\cdots+(1-p)^{N-2}+(1-p)^{N-1}-N \tag{8.14}$$

which reduces to

$$-pS=\left[\frac{1-(1-p)^{N}}{1-(1-p)}\right]-N \text{ or } S=\left[\frac{N}{p}-\frac{1-(1-p)^{N}}{p^{2}}\right] \qquad (8.15)$$

Combining the reduced form of the second part with the earlier expression (8.6) gives us the comparison

$$\begin{aligned} &pV_{e}\left[\frac{1-(1-p)^{N}}{1-(1-p)}\right]+(1-p)V_{e}\left[\frac{1-(1-p)^{N}}{1-(1-p)}\right] \\ &+pV_{ne}\left[\frac{N}{p}-\frac{1-(1-p)^{N}}{p^{2}}\right]\geq NV_{ne} \end{aligned} \qquad (8.16)$$

The expression captures the payoff of the entire sequence of the repeated game, dependent on the period in which the individual is caught and henceforth does not evade, versus the payoff of not evading in any period. Rearranging this inequality, we can write by cancelling out p from the last square term

$$[pV_{c}+(1-p)V_{e}]\left[\frac{1-(1-p)^{N}}{p}\right]\geq NV_{ne}-V_{ne}\left[N-\left(\frac{1-(1-p)^{N}}{p}\right)\right] \qquad (8.17)$$

Solving by cancelling out the term $\left[\frac{1-(1-p)^{N}}{p}\right]$ from both sides, we obtain

$$(pVc+(1-p)Ve)\geq Vne \qquad (8.18)$$

Substituting the values of the payoffs from the earlier payoff matrix, we have

$$\begin{aligned} &Vc=(y-\tau\,\alpha y-\pi[\tau(1-\alpha)y]), \\ &Ve=(y-\tau\,\alpha y) \text{ and } Vne=(y-\tau\, y) \end{aligned} \qquad (8.19)$$

Simplifying, the expression becomes

$$p(y-\tau\,\alpha y-\pi(\tau(1-\alpha)y))+(1-p)(y-\tau\,\alpha y)\geq y-\tau\, y \qquad (8.20)$$

Rearranging, we obtain, $(1-\tau\alpha)-\pi p\tau(1-\alpha)\geq 1-\tau$ and reducing it further, we get

$(\tau-\tau\alpha)\geq \pi p\tau(1-\alpha)$, leading us to the condition

$$p\leq\frac{1}{\pi} \tag{8.21}$$

Proposition 2: *In the N period repeated game, the condition for no evasion in any period is given by* $p^* > 1/\pi$.

The condition provides a new result as compared to the earlier game. In a repeated version, if $p > 1/\pi$ the taxpayer has no incentive to evade. The results also establish the original mixed-strategy equilibrium approach (p^*, q^*) where the best strategy for the taxpayer for $p < 1/\pi$ is not to engage in evasion. However, the result is qualified on two counts, namely that (i) penalties are not levied on past accumulated undisclosed income, and (ii) risk preferences of the taxpayer. In specific cases, the result on level of penalty is consistent with the provisions on tax penalties. For instance, under Indian income tax law, the maximum penalty in most cases is up to the amount of evaded tax. In some cases the penalty exceeds 100 per cent, but is at the discretion of the authorities. Thus, in most cases, tax authorities can only recover maximum penalties equal to the amount of evaded tax. If we assume that audits are conducted to revel only the current period evasion, the result provides some intuitive understanding of tax evasion over time. The threat of a regular or an every-period audit is a key deterrent to enforce compliance on the part of the taxpayer.

8.3.4 Rationality, patience, and future payoffs

In the previous model, the future payoffs were not discounted. The formulation assumes that the players are patient throughout such that they do not differentiate between payoffs in different time periods. Therefore, their payoffs in the repeated game can be represented by the sum of utilities in the basic games. In this particular case, the discounting factor is $\beta=\left(\dfrac{1}{1+r}\right)$, where r is a representative interest rate. Applying the discounting to the payoff series would imply discounting the evasion and non-evasion payoffs, leading up to the inequality where the taxpayer compares the two payoffs.

The solution is dealt with in two parts. First, using the payoff stream (see Figure 8.2) for period $t = 1$, the discounted payoff can be written as; $p[ve + \beta Vne + \beta^2 Vne + \cdots + \beta^{N-1} Vne] + (1 - p)Ve$, which sums and simplifies to

$$p\left[V_e + \beta V_{ne}\left(\frac{1-\beta^{N-1}}{1-\beta}\right)\right] + (1-p)V_e \tag{8.22}$$

Using the same sequence, for $t = N$ periods, the general expression is

$$(1-p)^{N-1}\left[p\left(\beta^{N-1}V_e + \beta^N V_{ne}\left(\frac{1-\beta^{N-N}}{1-\beta}\right)\right) + (1-p)\beta^{N-1}V_e\right] \tag{8.23}$$

Second, in case of no evasion for all periods, which is the right-hand side of inequality (8.18), the future payoffs would be discounted as $Vne + \beta Vne + \cdots + \beta^{N-1} Vne$, which can be written as

$$V_{ne}(1+\beta+\cdots+\beta N-1) \text{ or } V_{ne}\left(\frac{1-\beta^N}{1-\beta}\right) \tag{8.24}$$

Combining the two parts gives the comparison that the taxpayer makes between evading and being caught in any period, versus not evading in any period. Reducing both expressions and rearranging the inequality gives the comparison

$$\left[\frac{1-(1-p)\beta^N}{1-(1-p)\beta^N}\right](pV_c + (1-p)V_e) \geq \frac{V_{ne}}{1-\beta}(1-\beta)\left[\frac{1-(1-p)\beta^N}{1-(1-p)\beta^N}\right] \tag{8.25}$$

Cancelling out the common terms on both sides leads us back to the original inequality (8.18), and after substituting the values of the payoffs we obtain the same condition as in (8.23), that is, $(pVc + (1-p)Ve) \geq Vne$ and $p > 1/\pi$. There are, however, few alternatives in the case of infinitely repeated games. First, we may not assume that agents discount future payoffs and instead believe that repeated interactions will continue in the future, that is, from one round to another with some constant probability, say q. Thus, if the probability of moving from one round to another is independent of the previous round, the probability that the game is still being played N rounds from the current round is $q^{N.}$ Therefore, the present value of a future payoff V of every round is simply $V[q + q^2 + \cdots]$ or $V[q/(1 - q)]$, which is similar to the discounting stream, if $q = \beta$. The intuition in this case explains the role of patience and the value that agents put on the future. For instance, if the taxpayer puts a sufficiently high weight on the future, then a reward and punishment mechanism works towards cooperation or non-defection. The trade-off in a one-step-deviation set-up is an immediate gain versus future payoffs, wherein the loss from defection will eventually more than offset the immediate gains. Thus, patience in a repeated setting, that is, $(\beta \rightarrow 1)$, leads to agents continuing on their equilibrium path and not deviating.

The second alternative is to consider the limit of means of payoffs which leads to the proposition that $U_i = lim\ inf_{N \to \infty} \frac{1}{N} \sum_{n=0}^{N} u_i(v_n)t$, where U is the utility associated with the payoff. However, the concept is considered unrealistic and also does not guarantee a subgame perfect Nash equilibrium (SPNE) (see for instance Radner et al. (1986), Aumann (1997) for discussion). Equilibrium strategies in such games, particularly in the one-shot stage game, also depend critically on the assumption of rationality of individual agents. The assumption implies that agents act in their best interest, choose the best actions to achieve their objective, have perfect foresight, and act after using all available information. The difficulty arises particularly in the case of repeated games, as assumptions of perfect foresight imply that agents can contemplate outcomes from the beginning of the interaction. Extensions in areas of evolutionary mechanisms solve such difficulties by taking away the element of foresight, but only mechanically (see Guth et al. (1982), Binnmore (1985), and Aumann (1997)). The results from the infinite game can now be summarized in a few key outcomes.

- Equilibrium strategies in an infinite setting can be taken as 'rules of thumb' (i.e. such strategies tell the player what to do in a long, repetitive engagement).
- As players would continue to have repetitive interactions, the engagement can extend to a long period, without specifying *how* long.
- The limit of means or the average payoff in the repeated game tells the player *how much* to expect gains, whereas the un-discounted version tells the player *how to play* in a long-term engagement.

8.3.4.1 Beyond Payoffs and the Role of Social Preferences

One important insight from the literature has been that the penalty structure and efforts of the tax administration can act as substitutes to each other. Both the penalty rate and audits serve to act as deterrents to tax evasion, in the sense that higher penalty rates may lead to lower frequency of audits and vice versa. It also suggests that while the probability of audit may be dependent on the subjective beliefs of tax authorities on levels of evasion, higher penalty rates do act as a deterrent to tax evasion. Two perspectives emerge from the association between audits and penalty rates. First is the cost of the audit. At the extreme, taxpayers may perceive that tax audits are costless. However, tax audits can prove to be expensive and may entail significant costs, even when the taxpayer has reported the true income. From the tax authorities' perspective, audit costs play a significant in decisions on whether or not to conduct audits based on their subjective beliefs (or sources of information) of tax evasion. Unless the expected benefits of audits are considerably higher (in cases where the reported fraction of income is lower), tax authorities do not have sufficient incentives to increase the number of audits of taxpayers. The belief structure also translates into the fact that taxpayers may also perceive fewer audits if they believe that the cost of audits is significantly high for the tax authorities. Second, the objectives of conducting tax audits by authorities are generally unknown. One can broaden the scope of audits to consider that authorities may be interested in unearthing larger undisclosed incomes, instead of collecting taxes or penalties. This situation is clearly plausible as, given the limits of imposing penalties, it is in the interest of tax authorities to detect more undisclosed incomes.

The analysis on tax evasion in general limits the taxpayer's decision only to maximize gains from evasion. However, the scope of analysis can be extended in several areas, such as social interactions and network effects, reputation, or other dimensions such as predictive auditing strategies. Broadly, going beyond payoffs requires understanding and integrating the role of social preferences, which among others can be narrowed down to at least three dimensions:

- Fairness or fair play: people receive utility from being fair to others.
- Altruistic: people receive utility from being generous and helpful to others.
- Vindictive: people like to punish those deviating from accepted norms of behaviour.

Social preferences also convey a means to understanding compliance behaviour. For instance, work of Hashimzade et al. (2016) has shown the use of networks with heterogeneity in risk preferences, beliefs, attitude towards compliance, and self-selection into different occupational groups can effectively lead to predictive audit strategies. Such preferences can allow tax authorities to have more decision-making variables other than maximizing revenue collections or choosing income thresholds for audits.

8.4 Conclusion

This chapter has taken a renewed approach to analysing the problem of tax evasion by incorporating a simple game-theoretic framework wherein an individual is confronted with the choice of declaring income for taxation or not. The model is a reformulation of the Allingham and Sandmo (1972) and Srinivasan (1973) original single-period decision-making problem of an individual deciding whether or not to under-report income for taxation. However, once we conceptualize that the individual has to decide on reporting incomes in more than one period, the problem of tax evasion in its simplest form can be extended to a repeated problem with strategic interactions of a taxpayer and a tax authority.

The literature in this domain has provided several theoretical insights, beginning with the seminal works of Allingham and Sandmo (1972), Srinivasan (1973), and Yitzakhi (1974). Subsequent extensions to modify the basic framework explored alternatives such as joint decisions of evasion avoidance, different probabilities such as civil and criminal, and additional parameters of non-compliance, to analyse the decision of evasion. Extensions on considering income as endogenous brought out the fact that decisions on evasion are linked with leisure–labour decisions, which earlier models did not consider. However, most of these models were limited to a one-period analysis; hence they do not take into account repeated interactions between a taxpayer and tax authorities.

The game version modifies the single-period problem first by incorporating the cost of audits for the tax authorities. The game provides a mix-strategy Nash equilibrium in which a taxpayer's best response is not to evade as long as the probability of audit is higher than $1/\pi$, where π is the penalty rate on evaded tax. In the literature, penalty rate on tax evasion and the probability of audit are considered as substitutes for deterrence. The mixed-strategy equilibrium result supports the finding and shows that the probability of audit is inversely related to the penalty rate.

A repeated version of the game extends the decision-making problem to multiple periods. In this setting, if a taxpayer is caught evading, the authorities audit the individual in every subsequent period (the underlying logic being that once an evader is found, tax authorities are more likely to audit to prevent further evasion). The principle is similar to a one-step-deviation rule, wherein agents choose a pair of strategies and continue with them up until the other agent defects and, post defection, continues to defect *thereafter*.

The repeated version reestablishes the result of the mix-strategy equilibrium, and the un-discounted version provides the insights that (1) agents would continue to have repetitive interactions, hence the engagement can extent to a long period, without specifying *how* long; and (2) the role of patience and the value that agents put on the future is critical, as short gains from a one-time deviation can be more than offset by a low continued payoff in the future. For instance, if the taxpayer puts a sufficiently high weight on the future, then a reward and punishment mechanism works towards cooperation or non-defection; (3) equilibrium strategies in an infinite setting can be taken as 'rules of thumb' (i.e.

such strategies tell the player what to *do* in a long-repetitive engagement), whereas payoffs tell what to *expect* in the long engagement.

Factors such as audit costs of the tax authority clearly influence the decision of the taxpayer; evasion might increase when individuals perceive that audit costs for the tax authorities are significantly high. A related aspect to audit is that the objectives of the tax authorities are generally unknown. Given that there may be limits to imposing penalties, one can broaden the scope of audits to consider that authorities may be interested in unearthing larger undisclosed incomes, instead of collecting taxes or penalties.

References

Allingham, Michael G., and Sandmo, Agnar (1972). 'Income Tax Evasion: A Theoretical Analysis', *Journal of Public Economics*, 1, 323–338.

Aumann, Robert J. (1997). 'Rationality and Bounded Rationality', *Games and Economic Behavior*, 21, 2–14.

Binmore, K., Shaked, A., and Sutton, J. (1985). 'Testing Non-cooperative Bargaining Theory: A Preliminary Study', *American Economic Review*, 75(2),1178–1180.

Chattopadhyay, Saumen, and Das-Gupta, Arindam (2002). *The Compliance Cost of the Personal Income Tax and Its Determinants*. Planning Commission—NIPFP Study, published by the National Institute of Public Finance and Policy (NIPFP), New Delhi.

Christiansen, V. (1980). 'Two Comments on Tax Evasion', *Journal of Public Economics*,13, 363–373.

Cross, R. B., and Shaw, G. K. (1981). 'The Tax Evasion–Avoidance Choice: A Suggested Approach', *National Tax Journal*, 34, 489–491.

Cross, R. B. and Shaw, G. K. (1982). 'The Economics of Tax Aversion', *Public Finance*, 37, 36–47.

Das-Gupta, Arindam (2004). 'Tax Compliance Costs and Non-filing Behavior', *NIPFP Working Paper* (05), February 2004, National Institute of Public Finance and Policy, New Delhi.

Das-Gupta, Arindam, Ghosh, S., and Mookherjee, Dilip (2004). 'Tax Administration Reform and Taxpayer Compliance in India', *International Tax and Public Finance*,11(5), 575–600.

Gordon, J. (1987). 'Modelling Tax Evasion where Honesty May Be the Best Policy'. ESRC Programme on Taxation, Incentives and the Distribution of Income. Discussion paper 102.

Graetz, Michael J., Reinganum, Jennifer F., and Wilde, Louis L. (1986). 'The Tax Compliance Game: Toward an Interactive Theory of Law Enforcement', *Journal of Law, Economics, and Organization*, 2(1), 1–32.

Guth, W., Schmittberger, R., and Schwarze, B. (1982). 'An Experimental Analysis of Ultimatum Bargaining', *Journal of Economic Behavior and Organization*, 3(3), 367–388.

Hashimzade, N., Khodavaisi, H., and Myles, G.D. (2011). 'Country Characteristics and Preferences over Tax Principles', *International Tax and Public Finance*, 18(2), 214–232.

Hashimzade, N., Myles, G. D., and Tran-Nam, B. (2012). 'Applications of behavioral economics to tax evasion', *Journal of Economic Surveys*, 27(5), 941–977.

Hashimzade, N., Myles, G. D., Page, F., and Rablen, M. (2014). 'Social Networks and Occupational Choice: The Endogenous Formation of Attitudes and Beliefs about Tax Compliance', *Journal of Economic Psychology*, 40, 134–146.

Hashimzade, N., Myles, G. D., Page, F., and Rablen, M.D. (2015). 'The Use of Agent-Based Modeling to Investigate Tax Compliance', *Economics of Governance*, 16(2),143–164.

Hashimzade, N., Myles, G. D., and Rablen, M. D. (2016). 'Predictive Analytics and the Targeting of Audits', *Journal of Economic Behavior and Organization*, 124, 130–145.

Hashimzade, N., and Myles, G. (2017). 'Risk-based Audits in a Behavioral Model', *Public Finance Review*, 45(1), 140–165.

Lui, Francis T. (1986). 'A Dynamic Model of Corruption Deterrence', *Journal of Public Economics*, 31(2), November, 215–236.

Mirrlees, James A. (1971). *Notes on Some Special Cases of The taxation of Risk-Taking*, mimeographed, unpublished.

Mittone, Luigi (2006). 'Dynamic Behaviour in Tax Evasion: An Experimental Approach', *The Journal of Socio-Economics*, 35, 813–835.

Mookherjee, Dilip, and Png, Ivan (1989). 'Optimal Auditing, Insurance, and Redistribution', *The Quarterly Journal of Economics*, 104, (2), 399–415.

Mookherjee, Dilip (1990). 'Enforcement Costs and the Optimal Progressivity of Income Taxes', *Journal of Law, Economics and Organization*, 6(2), 410–31.

Mookherjee, Dilip (2004). 'Tax Administration Reform and Taxpayer Compliance in India', *International Tax and Public Finance*, 11(5), 575–600.

Mookherjee, Dilip (2008). 'Income Tax Compliance in India: An Empirical Analysis', *World Development*, 1995, 23(12), 2051–2064.

Mookherjee, Dilip (2008). *Market Institutions, Governance, and Development: Collected Essays*, Oxford University Press: New Delhi.

Mossin, J. (1968). 'Taxation and Risk-taking: An Expected Utility Approach', *Economica*, 35, 74–82.

Pencavel, J. H. (1979). 'A Note on Income Tax Evasion, Labor Supply and Non-linear Tax Schedules', *Journal of Public Economics*, 12, 115–124.

Pestieau, Pierre, Possen, Uri, and Slutsky, Steve (1994). 'Optimal Differential Taxes and Penalties', *Public Finance*, 49 (supplement), 15–27.

Radner, R., Myerson, R., and Maskin, E.(1986). 'An Example of a Repeated Partnership Game with Discounting and with Uniformly Inefficiency Equilibria', *Review of Economic Studies*, 53(1), 59–69.

Rao, Kavita R., and Tandon, Suranjali (2016). 'Revisiting the Tax Compliance Problem Using Prospect Theory'. NIPFP Working Paper No. 169, April, National Institute of Public Finance and Policy, New Delhi.

Sandmo, A. (2005). 'The theory of Tax Evasion: A Retrospective View', *National Tax Journal*, 58(1), 643–663.

Sharon, Emanuel (1967). 'Income Tax Evasion as Rational Behavior under Risk'. Working Paper 217, Center for Research in Management Science, University of California, Berkeley.

Srinivasan, T. N. (1973). 'Tax Evasion: A Model', *Journal of Public Economics*, 2(4), 339–346.

Stiglitz, Joseph E. (1969). 'The Effects of Income, Wealth and Capital Gains Taxation on Risk-taking', *Quarterly Journal of Economics*, 83, 263–283.

Tirole, Jean (1996). 'A Theory of Collective Reputations (with Applications to the Persistence of Corruption and to Firm Quality)', *Review of Economic Studies*, 63(1), 1–22.

Witte, A. D., and Woodbury, D. F. (1985), 'The Effect of Tax Laws and Tax Administration on Tax Compliance: The Case of the US Individual Income Tax', *National Tax Journal*, 38(1), 1–13.

Yitzhaki, S. (1974). 'A Note on Income Tax Evasion: A Theoretical Analysis', *Journal of Public Economics* 3(2), 201–202.

III
FISCAL FEDERALISM

9

Fiscal Transfers in India

Equalization in Theory and Practice

C. Rangarajan and D. K. Srivastava

9.1 Introduction

According to the Forum of Federations, there are 25 major federal countries in the world, including large and complex democracies such as India, the United States, Brazil, Canada, Australia, and Germany. In federal arrangements, there is a multi-tier structure of governments. In most federal countries, this structure consists of three tiers, relating to a central government at the apex, a set of local governments which are the closest to the citizens, and an intermediate tier consisting of state or provincial governments. While this may be a political and administrative arrangement, governments at all tiers are tasked with providing goods and services—which may be public goods, private goods that are considered as merit goods, and other private goods that require lumpy investment such as infrastructure—to its citizens in an efficient and equitable manner. For this purpose, the powers to collect taxes as well as fees and user charges and the power to undertake public expenditures are constitutionally delineated amongst the different government tiers. These constitutional fiscal arrangements constitute the essence of fiscal federalism. It is considered efficient to give relatively more taxation powers to the higher-tier governments, so as to ensure common tax laws and tax rates across the country and to build a large, country-wide common market. Apart from economies of scale in the collection of taxes, such an arrangement encourages location of industries in such places within the country as would maximize their locational economic advantages. At the same time, responsibilities are assigned relatively

C. Rangarajan and D. K. Srivastava, *Fiscal Transfers in India* In: *Fiscal Policy and Public Financial Management.* Edited by: Pinaki Chakraborty and K R Shanmugam, Oxford University Press. © Oxford University Press 2024. DOI: 10.1093/9780198930464.003.0009 more to the lower tiers of government, who understand better the preferences of citizens regarding publicly provided goods which may be public or merit in nature. This asymmetry in collection and spending powers, such that the central government has larger resources and the subnational governments have the larger responsibilities, leads to vertical imbalance. This necessitates transfer of resources from the higher to the lower tiers of government. These fiscal transfers are best guided by principles of equity and efficiency. Both of these objectives can be served well by determining transfers that are consistent with the equalization principle, which some of the well-known federal countries have been following for a long time.

In this chapter, which is divided into eight sections, we consider fiscal transfers as guided by the equalization principle in both theory and practice. Our illustrations are drawn from major federal countries such as Australia and Canada. In following the equalization principle in India, we have to consider how this can be done by using the two main vehicles of transfers, namely, sharing of central taxes and grants. These transfer vehicles are consistent with the constitutional provisions, and these have evolved over time by the changing schemes and weights used by the different Finance Commissions (FCs). Following this section, Section 9.2 provides the definition of the equalization principle as applied in countries such as Australia and Canada. In Section 8.3, we discuss the Canadian case as an illustration of fiscal capacity equalization, which we have referred to as one-sided equalization. In Section 8.4, we consider the Australian case, where capacity equalization is supplemented by expenditure-side considerations. We refer to this case as an illustration of two-sided equalization. Section 8.5 discusses the empirical situation regarding the way tax devolution and grants have evolved in India, where tax devolution has emerged as the main vehicle of fiscal transfers. This also implies that it is important to incorporate the equalization principle in the determination of states' share in central taxes. Section 8.6 argues the case for further reforming the tax devolution criteria to strengthen its equalization content. It picks up the area criterion for illustrating this further. Section 8.7 illustrates how equalization through tax devolution can be further supplemented by modifications in the methodology of determining grants. Section 8.8 provides concluding observations.

9.2 Defining Equalization

Equalization is meant to serve as a guiding principle to build a system of fiscal transfers that may be characterized by both equity and efficiency. There are two major formats in which the equalization principle has been translated into practice. These may be referred to as 'one-sided' and 'two-sided' equalization approaches. Canada provides an example of one-sided equalization, whereas Australia provides a comprehensive illustration of a two-sided equalization approach. These two approaches are defined below.

Equalization payments in the Canadian Constitution are defined as:

> Parliament and the government of Canada are committed to the principle of making equalization payments to ensure that provincial governments have sufficient revenues to provide reasonably comparable levels of public services at reasonably comparable levels of taxation. (Subsection 36(2) of the Constitution Act, 1982)

In this approach, the focus is on fiscal capacity equalization. Here, transfers make up for the deficiency in fiscal capacity but not that in revenue effort. This is consistent with equity as the equalized fiscal capacities lead to equitable standards of publicly provided public goods such as defence, and government administration, and merit goods such as health and education. Merit goods, that are essentially private in nature, are characterized by significant positive externalities implying that the benefits to the society at large from the provision of merit goods is more than the sum of individual benefits. Such goods are likely to be underprovided if their provision is left entirely to market forces. Equitable provision of public and merit goods across regions ensures that undue migration of people from one region to another in the pursuit of higher standards of such goods does not take place. In this sense, even the one-sided equalization is characterized by efficiency. Efficiency is also ensured in another sense. If citizens of a region prefer a lower size of government, implying that they are willing to make a lower tax contribution, then the equalization principle ensures that such a preference does not lead to higher transfers. Thus, one-sided equalization aims at equalizing fiscal capacity subject to comparable tax effort.

On the other hand, the two-sided equalization takes into account need and cost disabilities in providing public and merit goods and services in addition to fiscal capacity equalization. The principle of horizontal fiscal equalization in Australia is defined as follows.

> State governments should receive funding from the pool of goods and services tax [can apply to any relevant sharable pool] such that, after allowing for material factors affecting revenues and expenditures, each would have the fiscal capacity to provide services and the associated infrastructure at the same standard, if each made the same effort to raise revenue from its own sources and operated at the same level of efficiency. (2015 Review, Commonwealth Grants Commission, Australia)

In this Australian definition, reference is also made to infrastructure, which requires capital expenditures. Further, there is a stipulation regarding incurring expenditures at comparable levels of efficiency. This approach requires that there should be not only a framework for measuring relative expenditure efficiency, but also suitable recognition of difference in conditions affecting unit costs and relative needs across the subnational governments.

In order to translate these guiding principles for fiscal transfers, it is also important to recognize the main instruments of fiscal transfers which may be constitutionally provided for in a federal country. Institutionally, depending on different preferences for such instruments of fiscal transfers, the methodology by which equalization may be achieved may also differ across countries. India is a good example of the differential preference for tax devolution vis-à-vis grants as instruments of transfers. Equalization may still be delivered in India and both aspects of equalization—namely capacity equalization and cost and need disabilities—can be incorporated through tax devolution and general-purpose grants. For a practical implementation of the equalization principle, it is useful to recognize the differential characteristics of these instruments of transfers.

The key features of revenue sharing are summarized below.

1. In this mode of fiscal transfers, only the share of subnational governments in a defined divisible pool which may consist of some or all taxes of the national government is specified.

2. The actual amount of transfer would depend on the revenue raised by the taxes in the divisible pool.
3. If the performance is buoyant in a year, higher revenues will flow to the subnational governments for the same share and vice versa.
4. The relative shares of the subnational governments are usually determined on the basis of a combination of broad criteria such as population, distance of per-capita income from a benchmark, tax effort, index of cost, etc.
5. As such, amounts flowing under revenue sharing can only be broadly targeted for achieving a given purpose.
6. Revenue sharing is generally used for supplementing incomes of the subnational governments, and these constitute examples of unconditional transfers.

Grants, on the other hand:

(1) are specified in nominal amounts and thus do not go up or down when the central tax revenue performance improves/deteriorates;
(2) can be both conditional and unconditional;
(3) can be fine-tuned to serve a given purpose;
(4) can generate both income and substitution effects;
(5) can be designed to affect the decisions or preferences of the subnational governments.

Another important consideration in the delivery of equalization through fiscal transfers is to acknowledge the differences in the initial conditions relating to the state/subnational governments. Thus, in India, the organization of states has been such that there are large differences in the demographic and geographical features across states as well as resource endowments which lead to large initial differences in cost and need conditions. In such a situation, relatively high per-capita transfers may be required for achieving equalization. Since fiscal transfers almost always translate into redistribution of resources from one region to another, large per-capita transfers are often resisted. This leads to recognizing the importance of providing a dynamic perspective to fiscal transfers so that equalization is achieved over time rather than in one step. Some idea as to the differences in the cost and need disabilities in India are illustrated

Table 9.1 Horizontal imbalances in India.

	Area (thousand square km)	**Average nominal per capita GSDP (2017–18 to 2019–20) .3Rs**	**Population (average 2017–18 to 2019–20) in Rs crores**
Maximum	Rajasthan 342	Goa 4,68,764	Uttar Pradesh 22.4
Next highest	–	Sikkim 4,29,784	–
Minimum	Goa 4	Bihar 44,596	Sikkim 0.07
Max. to min. ratio	**92.4**	**10.5**	**339.6**
Max. to min. ratio (next highest)	–	**9.6**	–

Source (basic data): Indian Public Finance statistics, MoSPI, and RBI.

through Table 9.1. In terms of area, the largest state, namely Rajasthan, is 92.4 times bigger than the smallest, namely Goa. In terms of population, the largest state, Uttar Pradesh, has almost 340 times the inhabitants of the smallest, Sikkim. In terms of nominal per-capita GSDP, which can be considered as a proxy for fiscal capacity, the highest per-capita income state, Goa, is 10.5 times as large as the lowest per-capita income state, Bihar.

9.3 One-sided Equalization: Canadian example

The Canadian federal government provides transfers to its 11 provinces and three special territories through three main channels: (1) Canada health transfer, (2) Canada social transfer, and (3) Canada equalization transfers. In the residual category of other transfers, the following are included: (1) Offshore offsets, (2) Territorial formula financing, (3) Total transfer protection.

The relative shares of these different types of federal transfers in total transfers in recent years is given in Table 9.2. The largest share is that of health transfers, followed by equalization transfers and social transfers.

Table 9.2 Relative shares of different types of federal transfers (per cent, selected years).

Major transfers	2013–14	2015–16	2017–18	2018–19	2019–20	2020–21	2021–22	2022–23
Canada Health Transfer	48.6	50.0	51.0	51.2	51.3	51.2	51.4	51.6
Canada Social Transfer	19.6	19.1	18.9	18.8	18.5	18.4	18.4	18.2
Equalization	25.9	25.5	25.1	25.1	25.2	25.2	24.9	25.0
Offshore offsets	0.6	0.2	0.0	–0.1	0.0	0.1	0.1	0.1
Territorial formula Financing	5.3	5.2	5.1	5.0	5.0	5.1	5.2	5.2

Source (basic data): Department of Finance, Canada.

While the shares of the first two have increased over the years, the share of social transfers indicates a decline during 2013–14 to 2022–23.

All the Canadian provinces receive health and social transfers but only a subset of provinces receive equalization transfers. In particular, Newfoundland and Labrador, Saskatchewan, Alberta, and British Columbia did not get any equalization transfers during 2013–14 to 2022–23.

9.3.1 Calculus of equalization in Canada

Equalization is the Government of Canada's transfer programme for addressing fiscal disparities among provinces. It enables less prosperous provincial governments to provide their residents with public services that are reasonably comparable to those in other provinces, at reasonably comparable levels of taxation. The equalization transfer to a province in absolute amount is determined by applying the average revenue effort to the difference between standard base and the actual base for that province with respect to the various revenue sources. This system is often referred to as the representative tax system (RTS). This produces an estimate of revenue which is higher than the actual revenue for provinces that have 'below-average' capacity. This exercise is done for five broad revenue categories, namely personal income taxes, business taxes, consumption taxes, property taxes, and natural resource revenues.

For natural resources, consistent with the 2006 Expert Panel's recommendation, fiscal capacity is assessed based on partial inclusion of actual revenue collected by the province. However, a province's equalization payment cannot raise its fiscal capacity above that of a non-receiving province when all resource revenues are taken into account. Equalization payments are calculated on a per-capita basis, and then adjusted for provincial population. To enhance the stability and predictability of equalization payments, fiscal capacity is estimated based on a weighted three-year moving average, lagged by two years. For example, payments in 2021–22 reflect data for fiscal years 2019–20 (50 per cent weight), 2018–19 (25 per cent weight), and 2017–18 (25 per cent weight). The overall equalization envelope is adjusted to keep the total programme payout growing in line with the economy. The growth track is based on a three-year moving average of national nominal GDP growth.

The equalization grants are supplemented by health and social sector transfers that are equally important in volume and are also of an equalizing nature. Further, territorial formula financing payments enable territorial governments to provide programmes and services that are reasonably comparable to those offered by the provincial governments, at reasonably comparable levels of taxation. They take into account the higher cost of providing services in the North, including the challenges of providing services to a large number of small, isolated communities. Each territory's grant is based on the difference between a proxy of its expenditure needs and 70 per cent of its capacity to generate revenues. The remaining 30 per cent of revenue capacity is excluded from the calculation as an incentive for the territories to increase their own revenues and develop their economies. However, in the Canadian system, there is no direct reference to cost differentials and the provinces are free to use their equalized capacities in providing any mix of public and merit goods.

In mathematical terms, the one-sided equalization framework as followed in Canada is explained below. Considering the overall tax base of a state/province as determined by per-capita GSDP at current prices (y_i)

with the average tax:GSDP ratio as α, the per-capita tax revenue of state/province i is determined normatively by:

$$r_i^* = \alpha * y_i \tag{9.1}$$

where α is the average or benchmark tax:GSDP ratio, a proxy for average tax effort.

As compared to this, the actual tax revenue is given by:

$$r_i = \alpha_i * y_i \tag{9.2}$$

Where the tax:GSDP ratio of the state/province i is denoted by α_i.

In this context, fiscal capacity equalization implies

$$t_i = \alpha(y_s - y_i) \tag{9.3}$$

where per-capita transfer is denoted by t_i, the average tax effort is represented by α, and the benchmark fiscal capacity by y_s. The benchmark may be set up at the mean income across states/provinces or the mean income of a selected set of states.

Since, in the determination of the normative per-capita revenue, average tax effort is used, equalization transfers do not make up for the deficiency in tax effort but provide for the deficiency in fiscal capacity. Thus, it is consistent with the principles of both equity and efficiency. For revenue side equalization, GSDP can be augmented by other determinants of the state-level tax base such as per-capita consumption, per-capita remittances, non-agricultural GSDP, etc.

9.4 Two-sided Equalization: Australian Example

The Australian equalization approach differs from the Canadian one due to the reference to efficiency and standard of services (refer to definitions in Section 9.2). The Canadian system makes reference only to equalization in fiscal capacity. In Australia, fiscal equalization looks at both the revenue and expenditure sides.

Australia is a federation of six states and two self-governing territories, with populations ranging from 246,000 (Northern Territory) to 8.2 million (New South Wales). Australia's states and territories have large spending responsibilities but limited revenue-raising capacity. Commonwealth Government transfers finance 45 per cent of state spending, although this percentage varies significantly across states.

The evolution of the extent and shape of vertical transfers in Australia in more recent years can be seen in terms of four distinct phases: (1) prior to 1976, when general revenue assistance was given to states; (2) 1976–85, when revenue sharing arrangements were put in place; (3) 1986–97, when the system of financial assistance grants was reintroduced; and (4) the intergovernmental agreement in 2000, which provided for the sharing of the GST revenues.

Currently, equalization involves the distribution of GST receipts, along with pool 'top-ups' from the Commonwealth Government. The Treasurer determines the distribution of the GST pool to the states, drawing on the recommendations of the Commonwealth Grants Commission (CGC), an independent agency. The CGC considers the revenue-raising ability and spending needs of each state.

The CGC makes reference to 'three pillars' supporting and guiding the application of equalization. These are capacity equalization, internal service standards, and policy neutrality. Policy neutrality refers to the consideration that state's own policies or choices about services should not directly influence the level of grants it receives. The CGC's calculations are based on all-state averages so that these may reflect average efficiency. These are also treated as ensuring policy neutrality, being the result of policy decisions of all states. There is a comprehensive coverage of the services provided by the states and the revenues raised by them.

The CGC recognizes that since states have differential fiscal capacities and different demographic, economic, and physical circumstances, there aree differences in their revenue-raising capacities and relative costs of providing services. Relative differences that are beyond the control of individual state governments are called 'disabilities'. Standards of services as well as the disabilities are measured relative to the all-state position.

The first step in the equalization exercise is the preparation of the standard budget. The standards are equal to all-state averages in expenditures as well as revenues. The Commission does not consider any exogenous targets or norms. Any departure from the average per-capita expenditure needs is to be justified on account of cost disabilities. The equalization budget brings together all expense and revenue categories of state budgets. The per-capita expense for each service that the state would incur if it were to provide the Australian average standard of service is calculated.

On the revenue side, the per-capita revenue each state would raise if it applied the average revenue effort to its revenue base is calculated (RTS). Expenditure assessment adjusts the standard expenses to allow for the effects of disabilities. Disabilities are broadly classified as use disabilities and cost disabilities, according to whether they affect the rate of use or the cost of each unit of service. Use disabilities reflect differences between states in the use of services as a result of factors such as population characteristics and the availability of private services. Cost disabilities are influences that affect the cost per unit of service provided to particular groups or places, contrasting examples being large cities and remote areas. Cultural and communication factors can increase the costs of providing some services to people from culturally and linguistically diverse backgrounds. Some cost disabilities arise due to variation in inter-state prices as also due to diseconomies of scale. Table 9.3 gives some of the major revenue- and expenditure-side factors that are taken into account in the assessment of disabilities.

The main revenue categories analysed are: payroll tax, land revenue, stamp duty on conveyances, financial transactions taxes, stamp duties on shares and marketable securities, gambling taxation, insurance taxation, heavy vehicle registration fees and taxes, light vehicle registration fees and taxes, stamp duty on motor vehicle registrations and transfers, other tax revenue, mining revenue, and contributions by trading enterprises. For each category, the relevant revenue base for each state is taken up. The actual revenues from all states are added up. Dividing these revenues by the aggregate revenue base of all states gives the average tax rate.

On the expenditure side also, assessment is undertaken in a disaggregated way. Techniques of expenditure assessment are recognized to be the unique part of the CGC methodology of determination of relativities. The overall methodology can be seen in three steps. Aggregate expenditures are the sum of category expenditures. Each category of expenditure consists of a weighted sum of components. Each component is a

Table 9.3 Main factors affecting revenue and cost disabilities.

Revenue bases	Factors affecting expenditures
GSP per capita	Share of Australian population
Payrolls of large businesses	Proportion of population aged 65 years or over
Sales of real estate	Proportion of population who are indigenous
Value of commercial/ industrial land	Proportion of population resident in centres of 50,000 or more
Value of mining production	Proportion of population resident in remote areas
	Proportion of population enrolled in government schools
	Proportion of population with low income
	Relative average weekly earnings
	Relative length of arterial roads

Source (basic data): Rangarajan and Srivastava (2004).

function of one or more disability factors (i.e. variables relating to which disabilities are associated). The main expenditure categories that are separately assessed relate to education; health and community services; law, order, and public safety; culture and recreation; and economic activities. Expenditures are considered net of user charges. The expenditure relativity therefore gives a weighted average of the relativities of the individual expenditure categories. Many of the disability factors, like wages, administrative scale, and socio-demographic compositions, are common for several components in different categories of expenditures, and general methodologies have been developed for treating these disabilities.

Table 9.4 shows each state's GST relativity and share of the GST pool, and its estimated amount of GST for 2021–22 and 2022–23. In this period, the pandemic had an impact. Other important changes were also taken into account in distributing the GST revenues, including an increase in the value of iron ore production; shifting patterns of population growth, wage growth, and the value of properties transferred; and changes in states' shares of Commonwealth payments. In 2018, a floor of 0.7 was set for GST relativity, becoming operative for the first time. This implied that if a state's share in GST relativity turned out to be less than 0.7, it would be fixed at 0.7 and the shares of other states would be adjusted accordingly.

Table 9.4 Change in distribution of GST from 2021–22 to 2022–23, excluding no worse-off payments.

States	GST relativities		GST shares		GST distribution	
	2021–22	2022–23	2021–22	2022–23	2021–22	2022–23
			Per cent	Per cent	AU$ m	AU$ m
New South Wales	0.95617	0.95065	30.3	30	22107	23218
Victoria	0.92335	0.85861	23.8	22.2	17411	17167
Queensland	1.05918	1.03377	21.5	21.2	15739	16384
Western Australia	0.41967	0.70000	4.4	7.3	3199	5682
South Australia	1.34719	1.28411	9.3	8.9	6785	6865
Tasmania	1.96067	1.85360	4.1	3.9	3024	3035
Australian Capital Territory	1.16266	1.09250	2	1.8	1426	1421
Northern Territory	4.79985	4.86988	4.6	4.7	3379	3644
Total	**1.00000**	**1.00000**	100	100	73070	77416

Source (basic data): GST Sharing Relativities: 2022 Update (March 2022), Australian Commonwealth Grants Commission.

Apart from the sharing of GST revenues, there are specific purpose payments (SPPs)—grants from the Commonwealth to the states for specified services, such as health, education, roads, and the environment. Section 96 of the Constitution provides the legal basis for SPPs and other Commonwealth grants. It stipulates that 'the (Commonwealth) Parliament may grant financial assistance to any state on such terms and conditions as the parliament thinks fit'.

9.5 Relative Role of Grants and Tax Devolution in India

In developing an equalization approach for India, we need to recognize that inter-state differences in per-capita GSDPs or per-capita fiscal capacities tend to be rather large. Further, there are also large differences in per-capita costs of providing public and merit services due to differences in terrain, size of states, demographic features, forest and coastal area, etc. Some of these considerations can be incorporated in the tax-devolution methodology by modifying the main criteria used in tax devolution by the FCs.

In India's case, there has been a heavy dependence on devolution of taxes as the principal vehicle of fiscal transfers, while grants, particularly unconditional grants, played only a supplementary role. In Table 9.5, we highlight the relative share of devolution vis-à-vis grants in total FC transfers. Historically, states in India have shown preference for revenue sharing as the more acceptable mode of fiscal transfers. This is brought out by the relative weight given to tax devolution vis-à-vis grants by some of the recent Commissions.

The heavy dependence on sharing of central taxes constrains the delivery of equalization in India since tax devolution has used only broad indicators which are not suitable for finer targeting. Different criteria used in determining state-wise shares in central taxes were characterized by considerable ad hocism in the determination of weights attached to different formulae. Also, different formulae reflected different considerations, which did not add to delivering a meaningful content of equalization through devolution. Some of the formulae contained artificial adjustments as in the case of the area criterion where the concept of ad hoc floors and ceilings was used by some of the commissions. The determination of magnitude of grants has also been characterized by a number of deficiencies. In particular, normative considerations were attempted from time to time, but their scope had remained limited. On the whole, it was the actual history of revenues and expenditures which provided the base for the forecasts submitted by the state governments to the FCs for the relevant period of their award. The FCs utilized these state-level submissions with certain ad hoc adjustments to determine the grants under Article 275 (1). As analysed by many researchers, the determination of grants in India has remained characterized by the so-called gap-filling approach (see Bhatt and Scaramozzino (2015), RBI (2010–11), Economic Survey 2015–16, and Srivastava and Bhujanga Rao (2009)).

Table 9.5 Relative share of tax devolution and grants in total recommended transfer.

Finance commission	Share in taxes	Revenue deficit grants	Disaster relief	Local body grants	Other grants	Total grants	Total transfers
Recommended amounts (Rs crore)							
FC 12	6,05,670	44,502*	15,656	24,681	44,362	1,29,201	7,34,871
FC 13	14,27,913	35,863*	25,495	86,468	90,498	2,38,324	16,66,237
FC 14	38,89,408	1,35,155*	53,829	2,82,667	0	4,71,650	43,61,058
FC 15 (1)	8,55,176	74,340	22,184	90,000	14,499†	2,01,023	10,56,199
FC 15 (2)	42,24,760	2,94,514	1,22,601	4,27,911	1,71,636†	10,16,662	52,41,422
Shares (per cent)							
FC 12	**82.4**	6.1	2.1	3.4	6	**17.6**	100
FC 13	**85.7**	2.2	1.5	5.2	5.4	**14.3**	100
FC 14	**89.2**	3.1	1.2	6.5	0	**10.8**	100
FC 15 (1)	**81**	7	2.1	8.5	1.4	**19**	100
FC 15 (2)	**80.6**	5.6	2.3	8.2	3.3	**19.4**	100

Source: Reports of FC 12 to FC 15.

Note: * Excludes revenue gap grants to Jammu and Kashmir, † For FC 15 (1) and FC 15 (2), some of the grants listed here under other grants are still under the consideration of the central government. These have not been accepted so far

9.6 Need for Reforming Tax-Devolution Criteria: Case of Area Criterion

With a view to reforming India's fiscal transfer system, it is useful to recognize the acceptability by the state governments of the relatively larger importance given to the sharing of central taxes. The first attempt, therefore, should be to improve the equalization content of the tax-devolution formulae. This should then be supplemented by utilizing the scope of fine targeting through the mechanism of grants. Here again, one has to recognize that the central government has shown considerable reluctance to accept FC recommendations regarding sectoral grants, which have been conditional grants, in recent years. This has happened because of the inordinate increase in the share of tax devolution for the states, which was raised from 32 per cent to 42 per cent in one go by the 14th FC. While the central government still accepts the unconditional grants under Article 275 (1), often termed 'revenue deficit grants', there is no certainty regarding the acceptability of sectoral grants, which may have a larger equalization content. Thus, the reform of the fiscal transfer system has to focus on the tax-devolution mechanism and the unconditional grant mechanism as the two main vehicles for improving the equalization content of fiscal transfers.

As shown in Rangarajan and Srivastava (2011), the standard 'distance criterion' serves as an instrument for delivering fiscal capacity equalization under certain assumptions, including the use of a specified per-capita GSDP benchmark. It is possible to modify other main tax-devolution criteria by incorporating factors that may reflect cost or need disabilities and thereby strengthen their equalization content. Here, we illustrate this in the context of the area criterion. The FC10 implemented the area criterion for the first time. It was introduced with exogenously defined floors and ceilings, set at 2 per cent and 10 per cent respectively. States with area less than 2 per cent were given the floor share. States with area higher than 10 per cent were given the ceiling share. The area shares of other states were adjusted so as to keep the total area intact. FC11 continued this practice. FC12 to FC15 retained only the floor of 2 per cent while dropping the ceiling of 10 per cent. We can make a comparison of the pure version of the area criterion with the applied version that uses 2 per cent as the floor. Since there are twelve states which have an area share of less than 2 per cent, 24 per cent of the total area gets earmarked for these states, leaving 76 per cent to be distributed amongst the other states. Thus, almost a quarter of the devolution under the area criterion becomes quite ad hoc. Instead, it would be more useful to directly incorporate those aspects of area of a state which reflect cost or need disabilities. Relevant factors reflecting cost disabilities include a state's share in area under forest, area under hilly terrain, area reflecting international borders, area under glaciers, and coastal areas, in its total area. These factors may be incorporated in the area criterion by assigning to these differential and higher weights as compared to the general weight for area.

In the illustration given below, the area criterion has been modified by giving higher weights to (a) share of hilly area in total area and (b) share of forest area in total area. We may write total area of a state $A_i = H_i + NH_i$ s, where H_i is the hilly area and NH_i is the non-hilly area of the ith state. In determining the share of the ith state, we can give a higher weight to H_i. Thus, the share of ith state can be written as:

$$\psi_i^h = \frac{wH_i + NH_i}{\Sigma\left(wH_i + NH_i\right)} \tag{9.4}$$

For illustrative purposes, we have used $w = 4$ for hilly area.

In Figure 9.1, we show the per-capita transfers using three versions of the area criterion. The pure version gives the share of a state by using the actual state-wise areas (see also this chapter's Appendix, Table 9.6). The applied version shows the share of states where a floor of 2 per cent has been used for states with less than 2 per cent area. In the modified version, a state's total area is first divided into hilly and non-hilly areas. The share of hilly area is given a higher weight of 4 (as shown in equation 9.4), reflecting the related cost disabilities.

Under the modified version, the volatility in per-capita transfers is lower when compared to the applied version. Arunachal Pradesh is the only state which has hilly area covering the entire state. This results in a significantly higher per-capita transfer for this state under the modified criterion.

It is possible to modify other major tax-devolution criteria, such as those regarding population and income distance, to strengthen their equalization content and use these for better targeting of transfers.[1]

[1] See for example Srivastava et al. (2019).

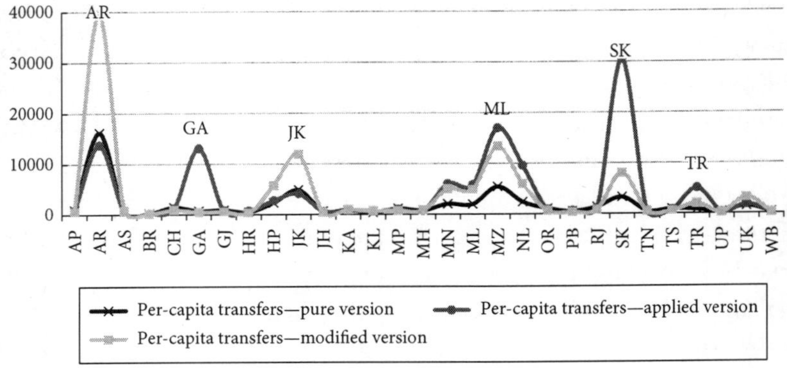

Figure 9.1 Per-capita transfers under area criterion (various versions).
Source (basic data): Census, MoSPI, Report of the FC14.

9.7 Complementing Equalization by Unconditional Grants

One key deficiency in the determination of unconditional grants in India has been the continued reliance on the so-called gap-filling approach. Though there have been a number of efforts by recent FCs to replace gap-filling with a normative approach, these have not proved to be effective. Attempts have been made to introduce service-specific equalization by determining separate grants such as those pertaining to health and education (FC11, FC12); environmental considerations (FC13; for protection of forests, renewable energy and water-sector management); and health, higher education, and certain other sectors (FC15). In the case of FC15, none of these specific-purpose grants, considered as containing equalization elements, have been accepted by the central government. The only grant that they accepted related to the revenue-deficit grants which have essentially remained of a gap-filling nature. The main reason for this is that the central government argues that the share of states in tax devolution was already increased to 42 per cent by FC14, leaving little scope for additional sector-specific grants. This means that the unconditional grants should be used for equalization by reforming their gap-filling nature and modifying these using norm-based estimation. Such an exercise should be designed in such a manner that it plays a complementary role to equalization delivered through the tax-devolution mechanism.

Disparity in per-capita expenditures of states on critical services such as education and health may exist due to several factors. A state's per-capita expenditure may be below the level required because of lower-than-average service standard and state-specific cost and need disabilities. With reference to need disabilities, the average per-capita expenditure for all states may require to be increased based on desirable norms. Further, state-specific per-capita expenditure on a service may be lower than all-state mean per-capita expenditure due to lower-than-average preference or lower-than-average per-capita fiscal capacity. If a state shows lower-than-average preference for a service, it would not merit equalization transfers on this account. Also, since capacity equalization has already been incorporated in the equalization scheme, this need not be considered again. Thus, expenditure-side equalization may deliver two objectives: uplifting overall service standard and meeting state-specific cost and need disabilities (Srivastava, 2006). An illustration of application of this methodology is given in Srivastava et al. (2019).

9.8 Concluding Observations

In this chapter, it has been argued that, in line with the approaches to fiscal transfers followed by federations such as Canada and Australia, India should also be guided by the principle of equalization in determining fiscal transfers. There are two dimensions to the consideration of equalizing transfers. One relates to fiscal capacity equalization while the other relates to expenditure-side equalization.Here we have provided the definitions of equalization transfers under the two approaches as illustrated by the Canadian and Australian examples. When these two approaches are combined a suitable approach for India can be developed, which is consistent with the objectives of equity and efficiency in fiscal transfers while taking into account differential cost and need requirements across states. In implementing this approach, it is useful to recognize that the central government has shown inclination for mainly accepting the transfers recommended by FCs relating to sharing of central taxes and the so-called revenue deficit grants given under Article 275(1). In addition, the central government accepts grants for local bodies and for natural disasters. Other grants, including special purpose grants, were not accepted, especially with reference to sector-specific and state-specific grants recommended by FC15. This has become the approach of the central government after FC14 uplifted the share of states from 32 per cent to 42 per cent. This implies that the role of grants in determining equalization transfers has become limited and the principle of equalization should be endogenized mainly within the methodology of determining tax devolution. In this chapter, ways have been discussed as to how to increase the equalization content of the existing formula of tax devolution by taking as an illustration the area criterion. It is further argued that the equalization content should be further supplemented by the revenue gap grants, determining these with reference to suitable norms rather than based on projections of revenue deficits.

References

Bhatt, A., and Scaramozzino, P. (2015). 'Federal Transfers and Fiscal Discipline in India: An Empirical Evaluation', *Public Finance Review*, 43(1), 53–81.

Courchene, T. J. (1984). *Equalization Payments: Past, Present, and Future.* Toronto, Economic Council.

Dahlby, Bev, et al. (2014). Four New Studies of the Canadian Equalization System. *School of Public Policy Publications*, 6(6), 1–9. University of Calgary, Alberta.

Economic Survey (2015–16). The Fourteenth Finance Commission (FFC)—Implications for Fiscal Federalism in India?, Ministry of Finance, Government of India, 129–137. https://www.indiabudget.gov.in/budget2015-2016/es2014-15/echapvol1-10.pdf.

Mathews, R. W. (1980). 'Mechanism for Fiscal Equalization', in B. S. Grewal, G. Brennan, and R. W. Mathews (eds), *The Economics of Federalism* (Canberra: Australian National University Press).

Rangarajan, C., and Srivastava, D. K. (2011). *Federalism and Fiscal Transfers in India.* Oxford University Press Catalogue.

Rangarajan, C. and Srivastava, D. K. (2004). 'Fiscal Transfers in Australia: Review and Relevance to India', *Economic and Political Weekly*, 39(33), 14 August, 3709–3722.

Rangarajan, C. and Srivastava, D. K. (2004). 'Fiscal Transfers in Canada: Drawing Comparisons and Lessons', *Economic and Political Weekly*, 39(19), 8 May, 1897–1909.

Rangarajan, C., and Srivastava, D. K. (2008). 'Reforming India's Fiscal Transfer System: Resolving Vertical and Horizontal Imbalances', *Economic and Political Weekly*, 43(23), 47–60.

Srivastava, D. K. (2006). Equalizing Health And Education: Approach of the Twelfth Finance Commission. Working Paper 8, Madras School of Economics, Chennai.

Srivastava, D. K., and Aggarwal, Pawan K. (1995). Revenue Sharing in Developing Countries: Role of Population in Criteria-Based Transfers. . NIPFP working Papers no. 95/3, National Institute of Public Finance and Policy, New Delhi.

Srivastava, D. K., Bharadwaj, M., Trehan, R., et al. (2019). 'Designing and Implementing Equalization in India', presented at EY–MSE roundtable on 'Fiscal Federalism in India: Contemporary Perspectives', organized at Madras School of Economics, Chennai, February 2019.

Srivastava, D. K., and Bhujanga Rao, C. (2009). 'Review of Trends in Fiscal Transfers in India', at http://fincomindia.nic.in/writereaddata/html_en_files/report02.pdf.

Srivastava, D. K. et al., (2019). Designing and Implementing Equalization Transfers in India (2019). Presented at the EY–MSE Roundtable on 'Fiscal Federalism in India: Contemporary Perspectives', 22–23 February.

Reserve Bank of India (2011). State Finances: A Study of Budgets of 2010–11. https://www.rbi.org.in/Scripts/AnnualPublications.aspx?head=State+Finances+%3a+A+Study+of+Budgets.

Appendix

Table 9.6 State-wise share in area.

State	Share in area (pure version)	Share in area as per FC 14 (applied version)*	Gain (percentage points)	Loss (percentage points)	Share in hilly area (modified version)
(1)	(2)	(3)	(4) = (3) - (2)	(5) = (3) - (2)	(6)
Andhra Pradesh	4.89	4.16		−0.734	2.98
Arunachal Pradesh	2.56	2.17		−0.384	6.23
Assam	2.39	2.03		−0.360	2.53
Bihar	2.87	2.44		−0.43	1.75
Chhattisgarh	4.13	3.51		−0.62	2.51
Goa	0.11	2.00	1.89		0.07
Gujarat	5.99	5.09		−0.90	3.65
Haryana	1.35	2.00	0.65		0.82
Himachal Pradesh	1.70	2.00	0.30		4.14
Jammu & Kashmir	6.78	5.76		−1.02	16.53
Jharkhand	2.43	2.07		−0.36	1.48
Karnataka	5.85	4.97		−0.88	6.25
Kerala	1.19	2.00	0.81		2.37
Madhya Pradesh	9.41	8.00		−1.41	5.73
Maharashtra	9.39	7.98		−1.41	9.62
Manipur	0.68	2.00	1.32		1.66
Meghalaya	0.68	2.00	1.32		1.67
Mizoram	0.64	2.00	1.36		1.57
Nagaland	0.51	2.00	1.49		1.23
Odisha	4.75	4.04		−0.71	2.90
Punjab	1.54	2.00	0.46		0.94
Rajasthan	10.45	8.88		−1.57	6.36
Sikkim	0.22	2.00	1.78		0.53

Table 9.6 Continued

State	Share in area (pure version)	Share in area as per FC 14 (applied version)*	Gain (percentage points)	Loss (percentage points)	Share in hilly area (modified version)
Tamil Nadu	3.97	3.37		−0.60	3.69
Telangana	3.50	2.98		−0.53	2.14
Tripura	0.32	2.00	1.68		0.78
Uttar Pradesh	7.35	6.25		−1.10	4.48
Uttarakhand	1.63	2.00	0.37		3.56
West Bengal	2.71	2.30		−0.41	1.83

Source (basic data): Report of FC14; planning commission.

Note: * applied version using a 2 per cent floor.

10
Indian Fiscal Federalism in Practice

M. Govinda Rao

10.1 Introduction

Indian fiscal federalism has evolved over the last seven-and-a-half decades, oscillating between harmony and conflict; trust and suspicion; and cooperation, coercion, and competition.[1] It has served to help the country hold together; provided identity and scope for various religious, ethnic, and linguistic groups; and provided an institutional framework for the functioning of the multilevel fiscal system. At the same time, it would be erroneous to conclude that the system has worked to the satisfaction of all the groups. In spite of amending the Constitution 105 times, areas of overlap and conflict continue. The heavy centripetal bias forced centralized decisions in a diverse social, economic, and political milieu. In effect, despite the Constitutional amendments, the decentralization process has not descended below the state level. Thus, there have been both appreciable achievements and glaring shortcomings, and it is important to underline these in order to identify necessary reform areas in policies and institutions.

A number of factors have helped in evolving India as a democratic federal polity. It has provided enough space and scope for diverse groups by listing fundamental rights. Over time, with regular and periodic elections, democratic values have taken deeper roots.[2] The independent

[1] Forty years ago, I had the honour of writing a monograph with Dr Raja Chelliah on *Fiscal Federalism in India* (Rao and Chelliah, 1996) commissioned by the Indian Council of Social Science Research (ICSSR). In subsequent years, we revisited the issues relating to Indian fiscal federalism on a number of occasions, both academically and at policy levels. The academic journey with him on matters relating to fiscal federalism for over four-and-a-half decades has been rewarding to me and this chapter is a tribute to his patience and perseverance in acting as my mentor.

[2] In 1976, Mrs Indira Gandhi invoked Article 352 in order to take power, after the Allahabad High Court had set aside her election to Parliament. However, she and the Congress Party were defeated with overwhelming majority in the elections she called in 1977.

M. Govinda Rao, *Indian Fiscal Federalism in Practice* In: *Fiscal Policy and Public Financial Management.*
Edited by: Pinaki Chakraborty and K R Shanmugam, Oxford University Press. © Oxford University Press 2024.
DOI: 10.1093/9780198930464.003.0010

judiciary has been a great strength in safeguarding the true federal spirit. The free press in the country has been a major factor in providing checks and balances and inculcating democratic values. The All-India services too have played a part in cementing the relationship between the union and the states.

Despite these achievements, there is considerable dissatisfaction at both union and state levels. The centripetal bias, combined with the legacy of the planned development strategy, has considerably undermined the advantages of a decentralized fiscal system and has hindered the creation of a common market. While the state governments were expected to impart dynamism to the economy, they were constrained by the legacy of central planning in resources. For their part, the states have often indulged in the exploitation of fiscal commons and adoption of protectionist and populist policies. Regional disparities in development have shown a steady increase over the years. Despite the amendments to the Constitution to empower the rural and urban local governments, they remain disempowered and the objective of providing efficient levels of public services at local level remains elusive. The country has ceased to be a customs union, as impediments to trade and mobility between the regions continue to deny the benefits of a large common market. On the political front, the regional aspirations and search for identities by different groups continue to raise their heads from time to time. There are many contentious issues—both inter-state and centre–state—that remain unresolved, and there are no satisfactory systems and institutions to negotiate, coordinate, and bargain to deal with externalities and settle disputes.

This chapter presents an overview of Indian fiscal federalism in terms of fulfilling the broad objectives of ensuring stable and secure macroeconomic management, providing public services according to diversified preferences, ensuring a nationwide market, ensuring greater accountability, and promoting and regulating markets to accelerate growth and ensuing equity. In the next section, we provide a brief account of the evolution of Indian fiscal federalism. The salient features of Indian fiscal federalism and its actual functioning are summarized in Section 10.3. Section 10.4 critically analyses general- and specific-purpose transfers in India, including analysis of the performance of Finance Commissions and the problems with the centrally sponsored schemes. Concluding remarks are presented in the section 10.5.

10.2 Evolution of Indian Fiscal Federalism

10.2.1 Historical Factors

The strong centripetal bias in the Constitution has made many astute observers consider India as 'quasi-federal'. The Constitution of India characterizes India as a 'Union of States', and the word federalism does not appear at all in it. Nevertheless, India passes Breton's test of having sufficient checks and balances to prevent extinction or even curtailment of the powers of the states, and therefore qualifies for being labelled as federal. Nevertheless, the extent of centralization inherent in the Constitutional division of powers and the way in which the intergovernmental relationships have evolved over the years shows very high centripetal bias.

The Seventh Schedule of the Indian Constitution demarcates the legislative powers in terms of union, state, and concurrent lists. However, unlike a classical federation—in which confederating units join to form a common market, evolving into an economic and political union—the Indian federation was formed mainly to hold together by unifying the principalities in British India, and accession of the remaining princely states to the union. The 1.4 billion people in the country are spread over 28 states and eight centrally administered territories (two with their own elected governments). Separate legislative, executive, and judicial arms of government are constituted at both union and state level. The upper house, or *Rajya Sabha*, in the Parliament is the House of States, to which members are elected by an electoral college from each of the states. The Constitution also requires the President of India to appoint the Finance Commission every five years (or earlier) to review the finances of the union and the states and recommend devolution of taxes and grants-in-aid for the ensuing five years.

Historical factors have played an important part in the adoption in India of a federal Constitution with strong unitary features. During British rule, administrative and fiscal centralization was a colonial imperative. Although there were strong arguments for decentralization before independence, and even though the Cabinet Mission sent by the imperial government envisaged limited powers for the union in a three-tiered federal structure, the Constitution that was eventually adopted by the Indian Republic closely followed the Government of India Act, 1935, with pronounced 'quasi-federal' features. The shift probably occurred for two reasons: First, once the Muslim-majority areas opted out of India to form a separate country; and second, a strong centre was found to be desirable to safeguard against fissiparous tendencies among constituent units (Government of India, 1968; Chelliah, 1991). The framework provided by the founding fathers of the Indian Constitution was an effort retain central control, but with significant federal features to accommodate the needs of a large and diverse economic, cultural, social, and linguistic country.

The Indian Constitution promulgated in 1950 was adopted on the foundation provided by the Government of India Act 1935. The heavy reliance on the 1935 Act was justified on the grounds of 'continuity and harmony' (Chanda, 1965). Consequently, many important features of the act including its strong centripetal bias, and administrative and judicial arrangements enacted for the colonial administration were formally incorporated into the Constitution. Thus, instead of conceiving federalism as autonomous states coming together, it was an arrangement for 'holding' together—a continuation of the unitary form of government with greater devolution. Thus, the legislative, administrative, and fiscal relationships designed in the new set-up were merely an extension of the existing arrangements.

The Constitution of the Indian Republic, like the 1935 Act, provided the three-fold distribution of powers (Article 246). It transferred a few minor items from the central list to the provincial list, and vested greater powers to the central government in certain other spheres like national highways, inter-state trade, and commerce, to foster national economic unity and promote a common market. Although not explicit, the matters of national importance were assigned to the National Parliament or the Union List (List I) and those of regional importance were assigned to State Legislature and placed in the State List (List II). Those matters relevant to both the Parliament and Legislatures were listed in the Concurrent List (List III). While the attempt was to assign the functions to the two levels based on their comparative advantage, the residuary powers were reserved for the union government.

10.2.2 Centralization in Indian Federalism

10.2.2.1 Constitutional Assignments

The constitutional division of legislative powers between the union and the states has been a subject of considerable debate. Besides the official reports of the Finance Commissions, Administrative Reforms Commission (Government of India, 1968), the study team report on Centre–state relations appointed by the Government of Tamil Nadu (Rajmannar Commission, 1969) and the Commission on Centre–State relations (Government of India, Sarkaria Commission, 1988), a number of scholars have discussed various aspects of the assignment system in the Constitution, notably the intrusion on the powers of the states by the centre over the years.[3]

India evolved as a two-tier federation until the 73rd and 74th amendments to the Constitution recognized local bodies below the state level in rural and urban areas. The Seventh Schedule to the Constitution assigned the legislative domains including the functions and fiscal instruments to carry out the functions of the union and state governments. The Constitution recognizes that there would be fiscal imbalances between the central and state governments and provides for the setting up of the Finance Commission every five years or less to make recommendations on the share of the states in the divisible pool of central taxes and the principles for the distribution among the states *inter se*. The divisible pool consists of total revenue from central taxes, excluding the cost of tax collection and revenues from cesses and surcharges. In addition to the tax devolution, the Finance Commissions are required to make recommendations on the grants-in-aid to be given to each state, measures to augment the consolidated funds of the states to assist the rural and urban local bodies consequent to the 73rd and 74th Constitutional amendments, based on the recommendations of the State Finance Commissions and on any other matter entrusted to the Commission by the President of India in the interests of sound finance.

[3] There is a large body of literature on Centre–state relations, mostly descriptive on this issue. See Rao and Chelliah (1996), George and Gulati (1985), Vithal and Sastry (2001), and Chelliah (1991).

Consequent to the 73rd and 74th Constitutional amendments, two separate schedules were inserted into the Constitution listing the functions to be assigned to rural and urban local bodies. With this, separate Schedules—the 11th and 12th, listing the 29 and 18 functions, respectively, for rural and urban local bodies—are listed and the functions are to be devolved to them. These functions are to be undertaken by the rural and urban local governments concurrently with the state governments, and the extent of devolution of functions would be determined by the states at their discretion. The states are also required to appoint State Finance Commissions every five years to assess the requirements of the rural and urban local bodies and recommend transfers to them. The Union Finance Commission has been assigned the task of recommending measures to augment the consolidated funds of the states based on the recommendations of the State Finance Commissions. However, the responsibility for the local governments is assigned to the states (Entry 5 in the State List), which implies that the extent of devolution of functions, functionaries, and finances essentially is determined at the discretion of the state governments.

10.2.2.2 Centripetal Bias in the Constitution

There are several pronounced unitary features in the Indian Constitution that limit the role of subnational governments in Indian federal polity. Some of the features are: (1) Article 3 of the Constitution allows the union to alter the geographical boundaries of the states, change their names, carve out new ones by combining parts of one or more states after merely referring the bill providing for such changes to the legislature of the states concerned for expressing their views. (2) Article 249 empowers the Rajya Sabha (Council of States) to transfer any item contained in the State List of the 7th Schedule to the Union List with two-thirds of the members present and voting, if it is thought to be expedient in the national interest. (3) Article 250 empowers the Parliament 'to make laws for the whole or any part of the territory of India with respect to any matters enumerated in the State List' when emergency is proclaimed.[4] Also, the

[4] Article 352 provides that if the President is satisfied that there is a grave danger for security of India or in any part of the country is threatened by external aggression or internal disturbance, he can proclaim emergency. When emergency is proclaimed, the fundamental rights under Article 19 remain suspended.

President can, under Article 354, suspend the provisions of Articles 268 to 279 which deal with the distribution of revenues between the union and the states while the proclamation of emergency is in operation. The Constitution also envisages the possibility of financial emergency in the states and, in such circumstances, restricts the financial authority of the states. (4) Although Article 301 guarantees freedom of trade and commerce throughout the country, Articles 302 and 303 read together empower the Parliament to impose restrictions on internal trade if it is required in the 'public interest' and is non-discriminatory. (5) The assignment system has a large concurrent list covering wide areas such as 'economic and social planning', with residuary powers assigned to the centre. (6) The Constitution lays down the primacy of central laws in the event of a conflict between a state legislation and a parliamentary law. (7) Article 201 requires the State Governor's assent for laws passed by state assemblies and the President's assent for state enactments in certain matters. (8) The most serious violation of federal principle is in Article 356, which empowers the President to dismiss the elected government of the state.

10.2.3 Centralizing Trends in the Functioning of Fiscal Federalism

The centralization inherent in the constitutional assignments was accentuated by the working of Indian federalism over the years. The item 'social and economic planning' in the Concurrent List provided tremendous scope for centralization of economic powers and the adoption of planned development strategy with the Central government deciding the resource allocation in the country. As Chelliah (1991) states, 'Centralised planning is the negation of federalism', and the planning process enormously curtailed the powers of the subnational governments.

Allocating resources according to plan priorities called for the introduction of several controls and regulations on both financial and real sectors of the economy with regional allocation implications. These include controls on prices and outputs, industrial licensing to ensure allocation according to plan priorities, legal and regulatory restrictions to control monopoly trade practices, and extortionary tax policy ostensibly to reduce inequalities. Even after market-based reforms were introduced in 1991, the vestiges of the control regime implicit in the planned strategy and inherent centralization have continued.

The most important development that led to significant centralization—almost to the extent that the planning process did—was the nationalization of financial institutions and commercial banks. The nationalization of the Imperial Bank of India to create the State Bank of India in 1947 and the Life Insurance Corporation of India in 1956 was carried out to ensure the allocation of resources according to plan priorities. The subsequent nationalization of commercial banks in 1969, though for the ostensible reason of financial inclusion, completely centralized the financial system, giving overall control to the central government. Other methods of centralization include transferring the subjects included in the State List to the Concurrent List (e.g. education and forestry), creating 'institutions of national importance' to intrude into the areas in the State List, and influencing the pattern of spending on items in the State List through central sector and centrally sponsored schemes (which are specific-purpose conditional transfers).

10.3 Indian Fiscal Federalism: Salient Features

10.3.1 Preserving the Common Market

As discussed in Section 10.2, both MPF and competitive federalism formulations of fiscal federalism underline the importance of ensuring the unfettered movement of factors and products across jurisdictions. In India though, although the Constitution recognizes the need to ensure a common market as stated in Article 301, it allows Parliament to place restrictions under Article 302 in the 'public interest'. This is not surprising due to general scarcity conditions that prevailed at the time the Constitution was framed, and centralized planning introduced a number of other restrictions. The Essential Commodities Act is a case in point. There were several checkposts introduced for tax collection, and with the implementation of GST many impediments have been eased. Labour mobility is considerably hindered by linguistic barriers, and with rising unemployment conditions the states have started reserving employment to the local population.

In addition to the fiscal factors, there are several regulatory policies violating the principles of a common market. These are the vestiges of the past created either as a part of supply management to meet scarcity conditions or as a part of development strategy. While many of the regulations restricting the free flow of goods and factors of production have been removed, the consequences of the past policies continue to distort resources as the investment decisions once made cannot be reversed. The provisions of the Essential Commodities Act are invoked from time to time to prevent the free movement of goods across the country to meet scarcity conditions. The policy of freight equalization was implemented right from 1947 to 1992—the freight charges of transporting raw materials like coal and steel were subsidized to ensure uniformity in prices of these raw materials throughout the country, and this led to serious distortions in the location of investments, besides causing a burden on the taxpayer. In more recent years, with area-based tax exemptions or refunds given to 'backward areas', which include the plains in Uttarakhand and Himachal Pradesh, the problem of migration of industries from the neighbouring states and resource distortions arising from them has become even more acute. These policies and regulations have created several tariff zones within the country to alter resource allocation in unintended and inefficient ways.

Some of the state-level policies ostensibly taken to protect the interest of the disadvantaged sections in urban areas have harmed their interest. Classic examples are the Rent Control Act and the Urban Land Ceiling Act. Both policies have reduced investments in the housing sector and availability of rental housing at reasonable rents in urban areas. Poor urban infrastructure, particularly water supply and sanitation facilities, is a major hindrance in the mobility of the rural population to urban areas.

10.3.2 Institutional Vacuum

In a large and diverse fiscal federalism like that of India, there can be several sources of friction between the centre and the states, and among the states *inter se*. In economic spheres, there can be several issues and frictions requiring resolutions, arising from factors such as spillovers in public service delivery, mobility of people and resources, inter-state tax competition and tax exportation, incentives causing competition for investments, ownership rights relating to minerals, and inter-state river water disputes. An important prerequisite for efficient working of fiscal federalism is to promote cooperation in feasible areas, and to regulate and prevent predatory competition. This would be greatly facilitated by having institutions for intergovernmental bargaining and conflict resolution.

Unfortunately, in the initial years after independence, with the same political party in power in both the union and the states, intergovernmental bargaining and settlement were conducted in an environment of informality. However, with different political parties gaining power at central and state levels, not always in harmony with one another, the coercive cooperation that once existed no longer does, and an institution for bargaining and conflict resolution has become necessary. The Sarkaria Commission went into this question and recommended the appointment of the Inter-State Council. However, the Council has ceased to be independent and is ineffective as it is placed within the Union Home Ministry.

Another institution that was created to facilitate and coordinate the planning process in the country is the National Development Council (NDC). The Council is chaired by the Prime Minister and its members include the cabinet Ministers of the Centre, State Chief Ministers, the Deputy Chairman, and members of the Planning Commission. One can view this as an institution with the purpose not only to foster both vertical and horizontal cooperation but also to resolve all outstanding issues between the centre and states and among the states *inter se*. Unfortunately, the NDC has not evolved itself into taking such a role. NDC meetings are far too infrequent to enable it to undertake the above task. With the Planning Commission, it is not clear what its composition is.

In a democratic polity, the parliament remains the primary forum for raising concerns about centre–state issues. Surely, the Rajya Sabha (Council of States) should safeguard the states' interests. In countries like the United States, the Senate has been playing a constructive role in safeguarding the interest of the states. However, when the choice of the candidates to be nominated to the Rajya Sabha by every political party is based on political considerations rather than representing the states they are nominated from, the institution fails to safeguard the interest of the states.

In this context The GST (Goods and Services Tax) Council was established, providing the important innovation of a joint forum for reforming domestic trade taxes in the country. After years of discussion, the consensus was reached to replace the existing domestic indirect taxes levied by the centre and states with the Goods and Services Tax (GST)—a value-added tax on the supply of goods and services—from July 2017. The tax is collected simultaneously by the centre and the states. The GST Council is a body comprising the centre and the states and the decisions are taken on a majority basis. The centre has one-third weight, the states the remaining two-thirds, with each state having equal weight. Although the Supreme Court judgment in the case of *Union of India versus M/S Mohit Minerals Pvt Ltd* clarifies that that the role of the Council is merely advisory, the Council is considered to be an important cooperative institution to facilitate bargaining and help in taking decisions regarding GST structure and operations in the country. This, in fact, has been cited as a unique experiment in 'cooperative federalism'.

10.3.3 Sharing of Water Resources

10.3.3.1 Overlapping Domains and Settlement Procedure

The institutional vacuum for bargaining and conflict resolution is one of the most important and emotional issues in the Indian federation.[5] It is therefore not surprising that the Commission on Centre–State Relations (Government of India, 1988) devoted an entire chapter on the subject and made a series of recommendations.

The issues relating to water are included in Entry 17 in the State List of the Seventh Schedule, but legislative power relating to the regulation and development of inter-state rivers is assigned in Entry 56 of the Union List. Besides, Article 262 of the Constitution specifically states that the adjudication of inter-state river waters is to be carried out by the Parliament and excludes any jurisdiction on the issue to the judiciary. As documented by Iyer (1994), Parliament has not made much use of Entry 56. Various river authorities have been proposed, but these have not been legislated or

[5] This section has been taken from the joint work with Nirvikar Singh (Rao and Singh, 2005).

established as bodies vested with powers of management. Instead, river boards with only advisory powers have been created.

Thus, so far, the resolution of inter-state river-water disputes has proved elusive. The tribunal established under the River Water Dispute Act 1956 has failed, and the states have frequently refused to accept the decisions of tribunals. Often the centre has intervened directly, but in most cases—such as the sharing of the Ravi-Beas waters among Haryana, Jammu and Kashmir, Rajasthan, and Punjab, and Cauvery waters between Karnataka and Tamil Nadu—central interventions have been unsuccessful. An effective institutional mechanism for settling inter-state water disputes simply does not exist.

10.3.4 State–Local Relations

An important part of making Indian fiscal federalism competitive is the reform of fiscal relationships between the states and local governments. There is much that is wrong with sub-state fiscal decentralization. While in China the local governments have proved to be catalysts in the developmental process (intergovernmental competition in particular has been a major factor in innovation, accelerating growth, and expanding exports), in India they have not matched their potential in the developmental process. The problem begins with ambiguity and overlap in the assignment system. The areas earmarked to rural and urban local governments in Schedules 11 and 12 of the Constitution have to be concurrently carried out by them with the states, and the nature and extent of functional devolution is determined at the state's discretion. At the initiative of the Ministry of Panchayati Raj, many states undertook activity mapping, but this became a ritualistic exercise and the ambiguity in assignments has continued.

The design of decentralization is just not in keeping with the implementable rules of fiscal decentralization (Bahl, 2002). The assignment system is unclear. Local governments do not have revenue handles to vary public services according to their residents' preferences. Obviously, there is no way to match revenue–expenditure decisions even at the margin to ensure incentives and accountability. There is no system of devolving functions, finances, and functionaries in a coordinated manner. The transfer system is unstable and ad hoc and is not based on the requirements of the local governments to enable them to provide the public services devolved to them. There is virtually no reliable information system to enable proper planning and implementation of public service delivery.

Ironically, the local governments have not been able to undertake the functions assigned to them. As mentioned, they do not have adequate revenue handles to finance the public services they are required to provide. Further, they are unable to raise revenues even from the revenue handles assigned to them due to poor revenue-collection capacity. Nor is there any satisfactory system of providing systematic and regular grants to them. The states have been irregular in appointing State Finance Commissions. In many cases, the Commissions do not have the capacity to undertake the task of assessing the requirements of the local governments in any systematic manner. The recommendations made by the Commissions are often not implemented. On the whole, the issue of assessing the expenditure requirements of the local governments for the functions devolved to them is not done in any systematic manner. The grants given by the state governments are ad hoc, often scheme based, and even when block grants are given, deduction of electricity bills at the source takes away a significant proportion of the grants given. The consequence of all these shortcomings is that the standards of local public services delivered is abysmal. So reform of the local government fiscal system is another important component of the reform of Indian fiscal federalism.

10.4 Intergovernmental Transfers in India

As discussed in Section 10.2, assignment according to comparative advantage results in vertical imbalance. Similarly, variations in taxable capacity and expenditure needs of the constituent units result in horizontal imbalances. Furthermore, transfers are necessary when there are inter-jurisdictional spillovers, or minimum standards of services have to be provided across the country for merit-good reasons. General-purpose transfers are given to resolve horizontal and vertical imbalances by designing them to *enable* the states to provide a comparable level of public services at comparable tax effort. Specific-purpose transfers with matching requirements are necessary to *ensure* minimum standards of selected services to deal with inter-state spillovers or for merit-good reasons.

In India, both vertical and horizontal imbalances are large, and resolutions of these are important not merely to ensure balanced development of the regions but also to the larger context of securing the economic and political stability of the federation. The founding fathers of the Constitution were aware of the problem and provided for the sharing of the taxes levied by the union government with the states and the giving of grants to the states from the consolidated fund of the union government. To determine the transfer system in an objective manner, they provided for the appointment of the Finance Commission by the President every five years. The task of the Commission includes making recommendations to the President on the devolution of taxes collected by the union with the states and to recommend grants-in-aid of revenues to them.

There is considerable variation among the states on their fiscal dependence on the union government. There are 17 relatively homogeneous general-category states, but even these have wide differences in size, revenue-raising capacities and efforts, per-capita developmental and total expenditure levels, and fiscal dependence on the union government (see Table 10.1. Per-capita own revenues of the states closely follow variations in per-capita GSDP, with the correlation coefficient of 0.951 broadly reflecting their revenue capacities. Per-capita expenditures of the States—both developmental expenditures (expenditures on social and economic services) and per-capita total expenditures—also have a positive and significant correlation with per-capita GSDP (0. 910 and 0.880). This shows that even after the central transfers, the low-income states with low revenue capacity spend significantly lower per-capita expenditures on social and economic services.

Some important features of the state finances are summarized here. First, inter-state disparities in per-capita incomes (GSDP) are very high. In 2018–19, for example, among the general category states, at Rs 2,26,409, Haryana state had the highest per-capita income (leaving out the small state of Goa). This was 5.6 times the per-capita income of Bihar, the lowest-income state. The coefficient of variation (CV) in per-capita incomes in the states steadily increased from 0.30 in 1981–82 to 0.35 in

Table 10.1 Differences in per-capita income and fiscal variables among states (2021–22).

States	Per-capita GSDP	Per-capita own-tax revenue	Tax:GSDP ratio	Per-capita general-purpose transfers	Per-capita specific-purpose transfers	Per-capita total transfers	Per-capita total expenditure	Per-capita dev. expenditure
	Rs	Rs	Rs	Rs	Rs	Rs	Rs	Rs
Andhra Pradesh	195275	11030	7.24	6602	2421	9023	26291	19067
Bihar	47983	2698	6.63	5932	1533	7465	11368	8129
Chhattisgarh	117615	9449	9.62	7657	3309	10966	22443	17644
Goa	486851	45672	10.78	17373	4399	21772	78112	52701
Gujarat	238716	12476	6.32	3486	2075	5560	21466	15051
Haryana	261454	16290	7.19	3008	1862	4870	29867	20574
Jharkhand	78620	5677	7.53	6160	2017	8177	15408	10912
Karnataka	259804	14469	7.06	5349	3067	8415	27467	21435
Kerala	228364	16367	7.97	5293	2539	7832	28973	15671
Madhya Pradesh	116169	8743	9.45	6299	3158	9458	18298	14040
Maharashtra	218753	14811	7.92	3322	2104	5427	20565	14303
Odisha	116933	9160	9.08	7584	3389	10973	21974	16951
Punjab	169457	11527	7.69	3655	3040	6694	22507	11640
Rajasthan	128495	8064	7.47	4840	2319	7159	21949	15517
Tamil Nadu	237131	14348	7.38	4024	2344	6367	25410	16656
Telangana	255804	18367	8.75	4903	1551	6455	31431	22879
Uttar Pradesh	71324	6026	9.66	5651	1327	6978	14124	8824

(*continued*)

Table 10.1 Continued

States	Per-capita GSDP	Per-capita own-tax revenue	Tax:GSDP ratio	Per-capita general-purpose transfers	Per-capita specific-purpose transfers	Per-capita total transfers	Per-capita total expenditure	Per-capita dev. expenditure
	Rs	Rs	Rs	Rs	Rs	Rs	Rs	Rs
West Bengal	152846	11061	5.94	9954	3639	13594	30480	20719
All general-category states	149943	10448	7.74	5421	2226	7647	20653	14291
Special-category states								
Arunachal Pradesh	204935	11525	7.43	62628	24996	87624	111282	81343
Assam	97509	6455	7.97	6720	3454	10174	17810	12171
Himachal Pradesh	212469	12410	7.03	16753	7383	24136	40704	26925
Manipur	97061	3546	4.81	12381	5666	18047	28198	18357
Meghalaya	95433	5954	7.20	18107	907	19014	28028	20833
Mizoram	149050	9358	5.68	45484	13102	58586	90583	49709
Nagaland	138439	4841	4.43	31816	10423	42239	37526	29157
Sikkim	472512	21248	5.65	37958	19131	57090	128021	59074
Tripura	134324	5067	4.48	13438	8783	22221	49688	17979
Uttarakhand	206821	12656	6.80	6741	5838	12580	98696	18695
All special-category states	137255	8197	5.10	12756	5565	18321	30482	19953
All states	149266	10292	7.71	11822	2449	14270	21310	14669

Source: Finance accounts of the state governments, Comptroller and Auditor General, Government of India.

1991–92, and further to 0.40 in 2014–15 (Panagariya, Chakraborty, and Rao, 2015).

In 2018–29, the CV is estimated at 0.675 for the general category states, even after excluding the small state of Goa. Second, and not surprisingly, per-capita revenues vary with per-capita incomes predominantly due to variations in revenue capacity. The tax:GSDP ratios do not show a clear trend, and therefore the variations in tax:GSDP ratios are due to variations in both taxable capacity and effort. Third, although per-capita transfers are higher in the states with lower per-capita incomes, it fails to offset the revenue disabilities of the poorer states fully, and more affluent states end up spending significantly higher per-capita expenditures than their poorer counterparts. It is not surprising that the low-income states with poorer infrastructure deficits are unable to catch up with their more affluent neighbours.

10.4.1 General-Purpose Transfers

As mentioned, Article 280 of the Constitution requires the President to appoint the Finance Commission every five years. The Commission has a chairman, and four other members whose qualification for appointment is laid down in the Finance Commissions (Miscellaneous Provisions) Act 1951. The terms of reference (TOR) of the Commission are (1) the distribution of the net proceeds of union taxes between the union and states and among the States *inter-se*; (2) grant-in-aid of revenues to be given to the states; (3) measures to augment the consolidated funds of the states to supplement the resources of rural and urban local governments in the states based on the recommendations of the State Finance Commissions; and (4) any other matter referred to the Commission by the President in the interest of sound finance. Under the last item, a number of tasks have been assigned to the Commission, such as setting the fiscal rules and targets for the union and states, measures to be taken for sustainable development and the protection of ecology and the environment, rescheduling and writing off of states' loans, examination of public expenditure management systems, review of disaster-management systems, strategic approach to public enterprise reform, and incentivizing the states to undertake tax reforms.

However, with the appointment of the Planning Commission under a Cabinet Resolution, the role of the Finance Commission was restricted to recommend tax devolution and grants only to meet non-plan requirements of the states, the plan requirements being determined by the Planning Commission. Initially, the plan assistance comprised both loans and grants, but after the 12th Finance Commission recommended that the centre should stop intermediating the loans for the states, from 2004–05 the plan assistance consisted only of grants. After the abolition of the Planning Commission, however, the plan grants were discontinued and the Finance Commission's role in recommending assistance to meet both plan and non-plan requirements was restored.

10.4.2 Specific-Purpose Transfers

In addition to the tax devolution and grants given to the states based on the recommendations of the Finance Commissions, the central government gives specific-purpose grants for various purposes through the respective ministries. The objective of specific-purpose grants, as mentioned earlier, is to *ensure* minimum standards of services in respect of those services that are considered meritorious or as having significant inter-state spillovers. However, in the Indian context, this has been used as a patronizing instrument to serve the political objectives of the ruling parties at the centre, to woo the states and the electorate by expanding its reach to spend on the state subjects.

In 2012, there were 147 schemes initiated by various central ministries. In 2013, these schemes were consolidated into 66, and in 2014, based on the recommendation of the Expert Committee on Efficient Management of Public Expenditure, the central government channeled all the grants through the state governments (Government of India, 2011). After the 14th Finance Commission made the recommendation to increase the tax devolution to 42 per cent of the divisible pool, the central government appointed a committee of selected Chief Ministers of the States, with the Chief Minister of Madhya Pradesh as the Convener to further consolidate and rationalize the schemes. The Committee consolidated the schemes into 28 and classified them into 'core of the core', 'core', and 'optional', with matching requirements from the states stipulated at 30, 40, and 50 per cent respectively.

There are six 'core of the core' schemes including the Mahatma Gandhi National Rural Employment Guarantee Act (MGNREGA), and 22 'core' schemes. In addition to these, there are 45 central sector schemes implemented in states for specified purposes. The total amount of funds spent on all central sector and centrally sponsored schemes in 2016–17 amounted to 1.8 per cent of GDP, constituting about 28 per cent of total transfers. Of these, only five schemes—National Rural Employment Guarantee, National Health Mission, Elementary Education, Rural Roads, and Housing schemes—constituted 66 per cent of specific-purpose transfers.

The analysis of the various components of transfers shows that the general-purpose transfers are most equalizing, with an elasticity coefficient of (–) 0. 452 (significant at 1 per cent level), and the specific-purpose transfers are the least equalizing, with an elasticity coefficient of 0.162, which is not significant. The overall transfer system is equalizing, with an elasticity coefficient of (–) 0.267. This is shown in Figure 10.1.

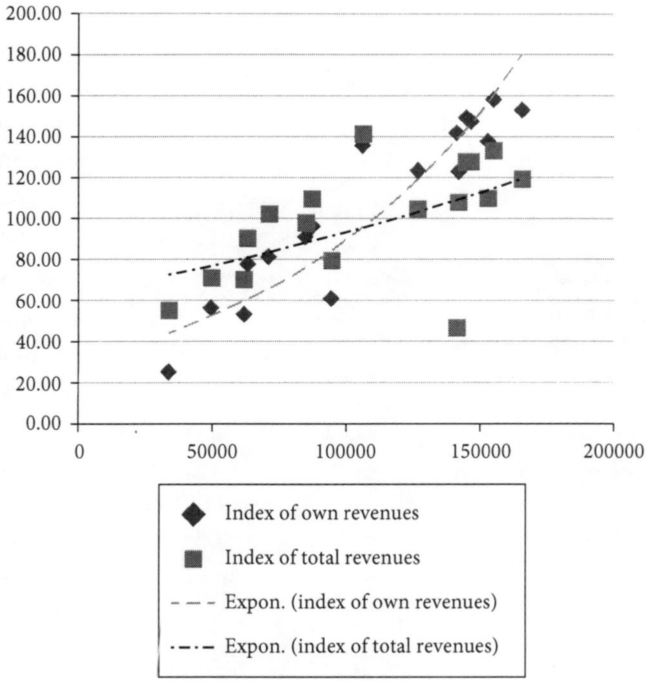

Figure 10.1 Progressivity of the transfer system.

Note: The vertical axis represents the index of own revenues and total revenues, with the states' average set at 100. The differences in the slopes represent the extent of equalization.

Source: Author's estimate.

The index of own revenues of the states (with all-state average specified at 100) increases steeply with per-capita incomes. The index of total revenues (including transfers) too shows a positive slope with per-capita incomes, but is flatter than the former, reflecting the extent of equalization. Thus, it is seen that (1) the Finance Commission transfers are equalizing but offset the fiscal disabilities of the states only partially; (2) the central schemes are not equalizing at all, and (3) even after the fiscal transfers are considered, per-capita revenues accruing to the states are positively correlated with per-capita incomes of the states. The resources in low-income states enable them to incur much lower levels of spending than their richer counterparts.

The lower levels of per-capita expenditures in states with lower per-capita incomes is clearly brought out in Table 10.2, where per-capita

Table 10.2 Elasticities of per-capita expenditures with respect to per-capita incomes in the states.

Expenditure category	Constant(*a*)	Regression coefficient (*b*)	Adjusted R^2
1. Revenue expenditure	1.5486 (1.2189)	0.6906 (6.2535)*	0.70
2. Capital expenditure	2.6142 (0.8169)	0.4248 (1.5202)	0.077
3. Expenditure on economic and social services	2.9471 (2.0104)	0.5488 (4.3063)*	0.52
4. Expenditure on social services	1.1281 (0.8551)	0.6511 (5.6781)*	0.66
5. Expenditure on economic services	3.5793 (1.8422)	0.4274 (2.5307)*	0.25
6. Expenditure on education	0.4324 (0.2499	0.6420 4.2681)*	0.52
7. Expenditure on public health	−1.6654 −(1.0743)	0.7185 (5.3322)*	0.63
8. Total expenditure	2.0866 (1.6440)	0.6562 (5.9465)*	0.68

Note: Estimated equation is: per-capita expenditure = log a + b log per-capita income + $\in$.
* denotes significant at 1 per cent level.

Source: Author's estimate.

expenditures under various categories are regressed on per-capita incomes in the states for the year 2014–15 in a double-log function. It is seen that total as well as almost all expenditure categories except capital expenditures show a positive and significant relationship. In the case of total state expenditures, per-capita expenditures are higher by 0.65 per cent when per-capita incomes are higher by 1 per cent. The relevant elasticity is 0.69 in the case of current expenditures, 0.65 in the case of expenditures on social services, and 0.43 in the case of economic services. Within social services, the elasticity is 0.64 in the case of education and 0.72 in the case of healthcare. The analysis shows that despite equalizing transfers, public expenditures are significantly higher in more-developed states. This trend leads to increasing inequalities in infrastructure levels and human development, causing divergence of incomes across Indian states. The matter is particularly concerning in the case of education and healthcare, where the requirements are high as a greater proportion of the school-age population lives there. The requirement for public spending in these states is much higher, but these states continue to spend lower per-capita expenditures due to their lower taxable capacity and the inability of the transfer system to offset their fiscal disabilities.

Considering the wide variations in per-capita GSDP among the states, with the richest state having more than five times the per-capita GSDP of the poorest, completely offsetting the fiscal disabilities to enable the low-income states to equalize their per-capita expenditures may simply not be politically feasible in India. First, presently the union government does not have fiscal space to meet its own obligations and cannot be expected to make any significant increase in the transfers. Second, there are significant deficiencies in the standards of physical and social infrastructures provided even in high-income states, and they too need to spend large amounts on the developmental heads. Therefore, the general-purpose transfers, which are supposed to enable all the states to provide comparable levels of public services at a comparable tax effort, can do so only to a limited extent.

It is in this context that the role of specific-purpose transfers becomes critical. In particular, equalization in specific meritorious services such as education, healthcare, rural roads, and anti-poverty interventions can help in augmenting the services in these areas. However, as pointed out, in the Indian context the central government has adopted 28 schemes under centrally sponsored schemes and another 45 central sector schemes competing for assistance. With too many schemes for equalization and with limited fiscal space available for giving grants, this has meant a thin spread of resources without much impact on service levels. Of course, specific-purpose grants should be given to augment services with a high degree of inter-state externalities or those which are considered highly meritorious, but these will have to be few and well targeted to make a difference to service levels. A detailed study (Rao, 2017) of schemes for rural employment, elementary education, and healthcare brings out the following shortcomings:

1. There are too many schemes, and within each scheme, too many sub-schemes with different objectives to be financed. This results in the thin spread of resources, and it is not possible to clearly specify the target in terms of minimum standards of services to be achieved.
2. The grants for the schemes are not determined on the basis of the shortfall in the prescribed standard of services. Both the total and individual state allocations are based on incremental plans prepared by the respective state governments and approved by the Committee. The inability to link the transfers with service levels makes it difficult to judge them based on achieving minimum standards. The focus is on spending money rather than ensuring services.
3. Designing the grants not linked to meet the shortfall in services from the prescribed standard causes significant misallocation of resources. It is not necessarily the educationally backward state or the states with poor health indicators that get more education or health grants. The telling case is of rural employment guarantee. The volume of grants depends on the ability of the bureaucracy in preparing the plans and fulfilling the formalities including the furnishing of the utilization certificate.
4. The uniform matching ratio across states makes it difficult for the low-income states to utilize the grants allocated to them fully. In a situation in which the general-purpose transfers are not able to offset the fiscal disabilities of the low-income states fully, they

are constrained to provide matching requirements. In the event, Kerala, one of the most advanced states in elementary education and healthcare comparable to many advanced economies, also avails the grant by making the same matching contribution, while Bihar, which is educationally the most backward state, does not get adequate grants as it finds it hard to contribute the same matching ratio. Introduction of varying matching ratios depending on the shortfall in services levels could improve the design of the grant system.

5. There is a considerable difference between the approved allocation and actual grants given. In 2014–15, for example, only 71 per cent of the allocated funds were disbursed in the case of rural employment guarantee scheme and the extent of difference varied between 38 per cent in Bihar, the poorest state, and 91 per cent in West Bengal, a middle-income state. This creates uncertainty in implementing schemes and invariably the states with greater shortfall in services levels suffer the most. A careful analysis shows that the shortfall from the approved is generally higher in the states with lower incomes.
6. The analysis of health grants shows that the states are able to substitute grants to their own spending so that the incremental spending on the services is much less than the grant amount. In the case of healthcare, for example, econometric analysis relating to changes in health expenditures with changes in own revenues, general-purpose transfers, and specific purpose transfers shows a significant substitution of expenditures on account of specific-purpose grants (Rao and Choudhury, 2012).

10.5 Concluding Remarks

Considering the high degree of vertical and horizontal imbalances in India, fiscal transfers from the union to the states are critical. Unlike in many developed federations when the tax base differentials are not very significant, India has large and growing horizontal fiscal imbalances besides a high degree of vertical imbalances arising from the assignment of tax powers and expenditure responsibilities in the Constitution.

Therefore, the design and implementation of general- and specific-purpose transfers are critical in the Indian federation from the viewpoint of ensuring horizontal equity, balanced regional development, and overall stability and integrity of the federation. This becomes even more important as there are significant hindrances to mobility of the population, it being necessary to take capital to the people and not wait for the people to move in search of capital.

Analytically, general-purpose transfers are given to offset fiscal disabilities of the states so that all the states are enabled to provide comparable levels of public services at comparable tax rates. However, given the large variations in fiscal disabilities in Indian states, with per-capita income in the highest-income state is five times that in the lowest-income state, it becomes difficult to design general-purpose transfers that can fully offset the revenue and cost disabilities. Even the richest state suffers from physical and social infrastructure deficits, and therefore seeks transfers, and posing constraints on the extent of targeting and equalization through instruments like tax devolution. This brings in the importance of specific-purpose transfers to ensure minimum standards of services considered meritorious or those with significant inter-state externalities.

The analysis of intergovernmental transfers shows that that the tax devolution and grants given on the recommendations of the Finance Commission have a strong equalizing element, whereas those given by various central ministries do not. Even the former is only partially able to offset the revenue disabilities of low-income states. The consequence of this is that the higher-income states are able to incur significantly lager per-capita expenditures on all major social and economic services as well as in the aggregate. This tends to accentuate inequalities in social and economic infrastructures among the states, leading to increasing divergence in developmental outcomes.

There are a number of problems with the design and implementation of specific-purpose transfers. First, there are too many schemes, each often with multiple objectives, resulting in the thin spread of resources, leading to minimal impact on service levels. Second, these are not linked to service-level outcomes but tend to be incremental; thus, the transfers are not designed to achieve the basic purpose of ensuring minimum standards of services. Third, the grants are not linked to improving service levels and it is not necessarily the states with larger shortfall in services receiving higher grants. Thus, educationally backward states do not get larger grants for education and the states with the lowest health standards do not get higher per-capita grants for health. The analysis shows that the states with a higher concentration of the rural poor get lower per-capita grants for rural employment. Fourth, there is a considerable difference between the originally approved allocation and the final release of funds under various schemes. In the case of rural employment, the shortfall was 20 per cent in 2014–15. The variation between allocation and release is different in different states, and generally the difference is larger in the case of low-income states. The inability of the centre to provide the funds allocated in the beginning of the year creates considerable uncertainty in the use of funds. Fifth, a part of the reason for the greater shortfall in low-income states is perhaps the uniform matching requirements. The low fiscal space available in these states makes it difficult to provide the matching contributions to fully utilize the funds allocated to them. Sixth, the requirement to seek grants under several different interventions within a scheme results in lack of flexibility to the recipient in the use of funds. Finally, in some schemes like healthcare the states were able to substitute grants for their own spending, with the result that there has not been a commensurate increase in spending on healthcare after the grants are received.

The central government may not be able to influence much as far as the Finance Commission's recommendations are concerned, as the latter is an independent body making assessments of union and state finances and recommending tax devolution and grants. However, while providing guidelines to the Commission in the Terms of Reference, the government can specify the need to design the devolution system to incentivize tax effort and expenditure efficiency in its recommendations. However, the centre can certainly do well to rationalize the centrally sponsored schemes. In the case of specific-purpose transfers, the centre has to determine the design itself. Here, it is important to limit the number of schemes and fund them adequately to make a difference to service levels. It is important to link them to the shortfall in specified services so that the overall objective of ensuring minimum standards is achieved. The design should result in increased outlay on the aided services. There is certainly a case for having differential matching requirements, with the states' contribution increasing as the shortfall in services reduces. The 14th Finance

Commission has made the recommendation that the number of transfers should be reduced and the design and implementation mechanism for each scheme should be decided by a committee comprising union and state government representatives and domain experts.

References

Bahl, R.W. (2002). 'Fiscal Decentralization, Revenue Assignment and the Case for the Property Tax', in Michael Bell and John Bowman (eds), *South Africa: Challenges in the Post-Apartheid Era*. Lincoln Institute of Land Policy, Cambridge, MA.

Besley, T., and Coate, S. (2003). 'Centralized versus Decentralized Provision of Public Goods: A Political Economy Approach', *Journal of Public Economics*, 87, 2611–2637.

Bird, Richard M. (2000). 'Fiscal Decentralization and Competitive Governments', in Galeotti, Gianluigi, Pierre Salmon and Ronald Wintrobe (eds), *Competition and Structure: The Political Economy of Collective Decisions* (Essays in honor of Albert Breton). Cambridge University Press, Cambridge, 129–149.

Boadway, R. W., and Flatters, Frank (1982). 'Equalization in a Federal State: An Economic Analysis', Economic Council of Canada, Canadian Government Publishing Centre, Ottawa.

Brennan, Geoffrey, and Buchanan, James (1980). *The Power to Tax: Analytical Foundations of a Fiscal Constitution*, Cambridge University Press, Cambridge.

Breton, Albert (1965). 'A Theory of Government Grants', *Canadian Journal of Economics and Political Science*, 31(2), 175–187.

Breton, Albert (1981). 'Federalism versus Centralism in Regional Growth', in *Public Finance and Economic Growth*: Proceedings of the 37th Congress of the International Institute of Public Finance, Tokyo. Wayne State University Press, Detroit, MI, 252–263.

Breton, Albert (1987). 'Towards a Theory of Competitive Federalism', *European Journal of Political Economy*, 2(1–2), 263–329.

Breton, Albert (1995). *Competitive Governments*, Cambridge University Press, Cambridge.

Breton, Albert (2000). 'Federalism and Decentralization: Ownership Rights and the Superiority of Federalism', *Publius: The Journal of Federalism*, 30(2), 1–15.

Breton, Albert (2006). 'Modeling Vertical Competition', in Ehtisham Ahmad and Georgio Brosio (eds), *Handbook of Fiscal Federalism*, Edward Elgar, Cheltenham, 86–105.

Buchanan, J. M. (1950). 'Federalism and Fiscal Equity', *American Economic Review*, 40(4), 421–432.

Chanda, Ashok (1965). *Federalism in India*, George Allen and Unwin, Ltd.

Chelliah, Raja (1991). 'Towards a Decentralized Polity', L. K. Jha Memorial Lecture, Fiscal Research Foundation, New Delhi.

Coase, Ronald (1960). 'The Problem of Social Cost', *Journal of Law and Economics*, 3, 1–44.

Feldstein, Martin S. (1975). 'Wealth Neutrality and Local Choice in Public Education', *American Economic Review*, 65, 75–89.

George, K. K., and Gulati, I. S. (1985). 'Centre–State Resource Transfers, 1951–84: An Appraisal', *Economic and Political Weekly*, 20(7), 287–295.

Government of India (1968). Report of the Administrate Reforms Commission.

Government of India (1988). Report of the Sarkaria Commission, https://interstatecouncil.gov.in/report-of-the-sarkaria-commission/.

Government of India (2011). Expert Committee Report on Efficient Management of Public Expenditures, (Chairman: C. Rangarajan), Planning Commission, Government of India.

Inman, Robert P., and Rubinfeld, Daniel (1997a). 'Rethinking Federalism', *Journal of Economic Perspectives*, 11, 43–64.

Inman, Robert P., and Rubinfeld, Daniel (1997b). 'Political Economy of Federalism', in Dennis Mueller (ed.), *Perspectives in Public Choice: A Handbook*, Cambridge University Press, Cambridge, 73–105.

Iyer, R. R. (1994). 'Federalism and Water Resources', *Economic and Political Weekly*, 29(13), 733–738.

Kornai, Janos (1986). 'The Soft Budget Constraint', *Kyklos*, 39(1), 3–30.

Levaggi, R. (2002). 'Decentralized Budgeting Procedures for Public Expenditures', *Public Finance Review*, 30, 273–295.

McKinnon, Ronald L. (1997). 'Market Preserving Fiscal Federalism in the American Monetary Union', in Mario Blejer and Teresa Ter-Minassian (eds), *Macroeconomic Dimensions of Public Finance: Essays in Honor of Vito Tanzi*, Routledge, London and New York, 73–93.

Oates, W. E. (1972). *Fiscal Federalism*, Harcourt, Brace and Jovanovich, New York.

Oates, W. E. (1977). 'An Economist's Perspective on Fiscal Federalism', in W. Pates (ed.), *The Political Economy of Fiscal Federalism* , Lexington, MA, 3–20.

Oates, W. E. (1999). 'An Essay on Fiscal Federalism', *Journal of Economic Literature*, 37 (September), 1120–1149.

Oates, W. E. (2005). 'Toward a Second Generation Theory of Fiscal Federalism', International Tax and Public Finance, 12, 349–373.

Olson, Mancur (1965). 'The Principle of Fiscal Equivalence', *American Economic Review*, 59(2), 479–487.

Panagariya, A., Pinkai, C., and Govinda Rao, M. (2015). *Growth and Development of States in India,* Oxford University Press, New York.

Prud'homme, Rémy (1996). 'The Dangers of Decentralization', *World Bank Research Observer*, 10, 201–220.

Qian, Yingyi, and Weinghast, Barry (1997). 'Federalism as a Commitment to Preserving Market Incentives', *Journal of Economic Perspectives*, 11, 83–92.

Rao, M. Govinda (2006). 'Fiscal Federalism in Planned Economies, in Ehtisham Ahmad and Georgio Brosio (eds), *Handbook of Fiscal Federalism*, Edward Elgar, Cheltenham, 224–239.

Rao, M. Govinda (2017). Central Transfers to States in India: Rewarding Performance While Ensuring Equity. Final Report of a Study Submitted to NITI Aayog. https://www.niti.gov.in/sites/default/files/2019-01/Report%20on%20CENTRAL%20TRANSFERS%20TO%20STATES%20IN%20INDIA.pdf.

Rao, M. Govinda, and Chaudhury, Mita (2012). 'Healthcare Financing Reforms in India', NIPFP working paper, 100.

Rao, M. Govinda, and Chelliah, Raja (1996). *Fiscal Federalism in India*, India Council of Social Science Research.

Rao, M. Govinda, and Singh, Nirvikar (2005). *Political Economy of Federalism in India*, Oxford University Press, New Delhi.

Salmon, Pierre (2006). 'Horizontal Competition among Governments, in Ehtisham Ahmad and Georgio Brosio (eds) *Handbook of Fiscal Federalism*, Edward Elgar, Cheltenham, 61–85.

Seabright, P. (1996). 'Accountability and Decentralization in Government: An Incomplete Contracts Model', *European Economic Review*, 40, 61–89.

Tommasi, M. (2003). 'Centralization versus Decentralization: A Principal Agent Analysis', unpublished paper.

Tiebout, Charles M. (1956). 'A Pure Theory of Local Expenditures', *Journal of Political Economy*, 64, 416–424.

Vithal, B. P. R., and Sastry, M. L. (2001). *Fiscal Federalism in India.* Oxford University Press.

Wheare, Kenneth (1964). *Federal Government* (fourth edition), Oxford University Press, London.

Weingast, Barry R. (1995). 'The Economic Role of Political Institutions: Market Preserving Federalism and Economic Development', *Journal of Law, Economics and Organization*, 11, 1–31.

Weingast, Barry R. (2009). 'Second Generation Fiscal Federalism: The Implications of Fiscal Incentives', *Journal of Urban Economics*, 65, 279–293.

11

Environmental Federalism in an Emerging Economy

An Empirical Analysis

Lekha Chakraborty, Amandeep Kaur, Ranjan Kumar Mohanty, Divy Rangan, and Sanjana Das

11.1 Introduction

Fiscal policy stance is a key policy instrument to ensure sustainable development, which rests on the fact that the functioning of the market cannot, by itself, activate the signalling, response, and mobility of economic agents to achieve efficiency in both static (allocative efficiency) and dynamic (shift in the production frontier) terms.[1] The role of fiscal policy stance in sustainable development proceeds from market failures of one kind or another. The emerging literature on *environmental federalism* deals with the fiscally decentralized determination of environmental quality and the dangers of the 'race to the bottom'. The 'race to the bottom' happens due to inter-jurisdictional competitiveness to attract the mobile capital (mobile firms) by allowing excessively lax environmental standards. This chapter aims to examine the link between fiscally decentralized public policy stance and environmental quality.

Existing theoretical and empirical literature on environmental federalism is heavily skewed towards the discussion on environmental regulations, and ignores the fiscal policy content in it to a great extent. This

[1] This is an updated version of the paper presented at the International Institute of Public Finance meetings at Linz, Austria. The authors are grateful for the valuable comments and suggestions of the participants at the IIPF meetings.

Lekha Chakraborty, Amandeep Kaur, Ranjan Kumar Mohanty, Divy Rangan, and Sanjana Das, *Environmental Federalism in an Emerging Economy* In: *Fiscal Policy and Public Financial Management*. Edited by: Pinaki Chakraborty and K R Shanmugam, Oxford University Press. © Oxford University Press 2024.
DOI: 10.1093/9780198930464.003.0011

is a nascent attempt to empirically capture the impact of fiscal policy in a federal economy on the environmental quality using Kuznets' U specification. This chapter does not refute the widely explored Kuznets U connection between economic growth and environmental quality, but emphasizes that this occurs substantially through conscious public policies at the subnational level of government, incorporating fiscal policy variables. The crucial question thus is whether fiscal policy stance has an impact on environmental quality.

The chapter is divided into seven sections. Following this introduction, Section 11.2 deals with the theoretical framework of environmental federalism, while Section 11.3 discusses empirical issues related to fiscal policy stance and environmental quality. The data and methodology are discussed in Section 11.4. Section 11.5 interprets the data and Section 11.6 deals with the specification of the model and econometric estimation. Section 11.7 draws conclusions.

11.2 The Analytical Framework

In a fiscal federal set-up, Oates (2001) envisions *three standard-setting functions* of environmental quality within the intergovernmental hierarchy. The first case considers environmental quality as a *pure public good* for the nation as a whole; the second prototypical case considers environmental quality as a *pure local public good*; the third case deals with the effects of inter-jurisdictional externalities and Coasian-type negotiations. Oates (2001) narrated the three functions as follows.

11.2.1 Environmental Quality Is a Pure Public Good: Centrally Determined Standard-Setting Function

This benchmark case considers that the vector of environmental quality (Q_i) is a function of aggregate level of emissions from all sources in the nation (E).

$$Q_i = f\{E\} \tag{11.1}$$

Global warming and depletion of the ozone layer falls under this category. For these matters, environmental quality is an international *public good*.

11.2.2 Environmental Quality is a Pure Local Public Good: Decentralized Determination of Standard-Setting Function

This prototypical case considers the level of environmental quality in the *i*th jurisdiction as a function of level of activities in that jurisdiction alone.

$$Q_i = f\{e_i\} \tag{11.2}$$

The 'principle of subsidiarity' is directly applicable to this case, envisioning a decentralized determination of environmental quality. Each jurisdiction is expected to set its own appropriate standard for environmental quality—for instance, the protected area or net forest cover.

However, the empirical evidence suggests that in decentralized determination of environmental quality, there are dangers of a 'race to the bottom', which can emerge due to inter-jurisdictional competitiveness to attract mobile capital by permitting excessively lax environmental standards. This can result in suboptimal outputs of local public goods, including environmental quality.

11.2.3 Environmental Quality as a Function of Inter-Jurisdictional Spill-Over Effects

This most recurring case considers environmental quality as a function of activities that flow across boundaries from other jurisdictions.

$$Q_I = f\{e_i, e_{2,} \ldots e_n\} \tag{11.3}$$

For instance, both air and water pollution flow across jurisdictions. In this case, one solution is to invoke central intervention, though the centrally determined uniform ambient national standards for environmental quality are not an optimal solution.

A Coasian sort of resolution of jurisdictional spill-over effects can occur through regional cooperation. But such cooperation is not easy to come as the cases of spill-over effects across jurisdictions support a complex set of policy alternatives. It is also to be noted that there exists a dichotomy in the nature of inter-jurisdictional externalities, depending on whether emission of pollution flows is unidirectional or bidirectional.

11.3 Empirical Literature

There has been a continuous debate on the relationship between economic growth and environmental quality. In the initial phases of the debate, the idea was that economic growth is followed by increased economic activity and hence results in degradation of the environment (Ardndt, 1998; Meadows et al., 1972). However, proponents of industrial growth were of the view that only by increasing economic activity can the problem of environmental degradation be dealt with. Hence, the arrival of the synthesis argument, with the introduction of the environmental Kuznets curve (EKC) concept in the early 1990s, termed thus as similar to that by Kuznets (1955) that claimed an inverse relationship between economic development and income inequality. By definition, the EKC depicts a hypothezised nonlinear relationship between income (proxied for economic activity) and environmental degradation. The curve is an inverted U shape, implying that although as an economy grows the environmental degradation increases, when the economy reaches certain level of income per capita, the degradation starts to decline and the trend reverses (Stern, 2004). When countries are beginning to industrialize, pollution increases because people are more concerned for jobs and income than clean water and air; this trend reverses when the people are able to afford abatement and value the environment (Dasgupta et al., 2002). The concept came through the study by Grossman and Krueger (1991) on the impact of the North American Free Trade Agreement, and was subsequently introduced in the report on World Development (1992).

Soon, with the availability of data for a larger number of countries, the concept was empirically tested by Shafik and Bandyopadhyay 1992, Stern et al. (1996), and many others. Over the period, a large volume of work has been published that empirically examines the EKC curve (pollution–income–growth relationship). Shafik (1994) mentions four possible indicators of environmental quality for any given country. These are: endowment (climate- and location-specific characteristics), income (per capita), technology (proxied by time-trend), and policy (regulatory framework for emissions, energy taxation, investments, trade regimes). But she essentially examines the pollution–growth–income relationship through various indicators based on endowment. Stern (2004) in his review on the EKC explains that much of the studies tried to test the theory for local and global pollutants where local pollutants displayed the inverted U relationship (Shafik,1994; Lopez, 1994; Stern et al., 1996; Seldon and Song,1994), while for the global pollutants, environmental impact increases with income or has a high turning point with large standard errors (Cole et al., 1997. Once the economy crosses the desired level of income per capita, with increased resources, the country then tries to invest in abatement technology, confirming the EKC curve by implying 'grow first and then clean up'. At higher levels of development come structural changes in the information-intensive industrial services, environmental awareness, increased environmental expenditures, etc. (Dinda, 2004). Since regulation plays an imperative role in reducing emissions, many countries have liberalized economies by lowering subsidies, reducing barriers to trade and investments, privatizing firms, and ceasing price controls. It is therefore critical to know the relationship between environmental policy regimes and economic development. Dinda (2004) emphasizes in his paper that the availability of public goods is a state concern because people can't afford abatement technology. This implies that environmental policy is subject to societal preferences, and hence demands for environmental protection come from the local level but get framed at the national level, as generally happens. However, empirical studies have mostly used absolute measures of pollutants to derive this relationship. Additionally, there is some literature that examines the relationship between environmental quality, economic development, and human health. Air pollution leads to considerable health deterioration (Zhao et al., 2016), reduces human capital (Schmidt, 2019), and affects quality of life (Porreca, 2020). The paper by Porreca (2020) claims that a positive relationship exists between carbon emissions and the quality of life in the developing countries but that this disappears once the country has achieved a certain level of economic development.

Only a handful of research exists on how the government expenditures impact the level of environmental quality (Lopez et al., 2011; Halkos and Paizanos, 2013; Galinato and Islam, 2017). In the paper by Halkos and Paizanos (2013), government expenditures can have both direct and indirect impacts on an economy's pollution level. The paper examines 77 countries for the period 1970–2008 to analyse the relationship between government size and income on pollution, suggesting the long-term impact of government expenditures on the level of pollutants. The indirect impact of government spending through income implies that reduced government size reduces environmental quality. In contrast, for the countries with higher income levels, *increases* in government size tend to reduce environmental quality because such countries are at the decreasing end of the EKC and already have an established regulatory framework in place. This means that any further increase in the government size will decrease the marginal utility and witness diminishing returns.

Another study, by Galinato and Islam (2017), reveals that a higher government expenditure on public goods raises income and so there is increased consumption and higher pollution levels as well. However, this is counteracted by strict regulatory measures and hence the pollution levels are kept in check. This is true for democratic nations where higher regulatory measures reduce the levels of pollution considerably.

Adding another perspective to the government spending, non-market-based environmental policy instruments showed statistically insignificant results in the study by Badunenko et al. (2021), while the market-based policy instruments have a greater impact. As the environmental policy indicators rise by 1 per cent, emissions growth falls by 20 per cent. This reaffirms the idea that government spending plays an essential role in improving the environmental quality of the country.

Quoting Dasgupta et al. (2002), a correlation between a productive public policy and economic development appears to exist, but there is considerable variation in the way this relationship is studied. In this chapter, we seek to examine the impact of government spending on the environment in the context of India, and to check whether fiscal spending affects environmental quality or not. Primarily, we shall also examine the role of transfers in improving forest cover (proxied for environmental quality).

11.4 The Data and Methodology

We use panel regression (fixed-/random-effect) models for the empirical analysis. The variable of our interest is gross state domestic product (GSDP) and its square term (Table 11.1). The study has also included other control variables including population and fiscal transfers (Table 11.2).

Table 11.1 Description of the variables.

Variables	Description	Source
VDFC	Very dense forest cover	India State of Forest Reports
POPL	Population	Report of the Technical Group on Population Projection by the National Commission on Population
TRNS	Total transfers (grants + share in taxes)	State budget documents
GSDP	Gross state domestic product	Economic and Political Weekly Research Foundation

Source: Authors' compilation.

Table 11.2 Descriptive statistics of the selected variables.

Statistic/variable	VDFC	POPL	TRNS	GSDP	GSDPSQ
Mean	2662.86	4.30e + 07	2137247	3.46e + 07	3.29e + 15
Maximum	21095	2.28e + 08	2.25e + 07	2.82e + 08	7.94e + 16
Minimum	2	559000	18814.22	194552	3.79e + 10
Standard deviation	4028.027	4.62e + 07	2823369	4.58e + 07	8.75e + 15
Observations	486	486	486	486	486

Source: Authors' estimation.

We used the following regression models as follows.

$$F_{it} = \beta_i + \beta_1 G_{it} + \beta_2 T_{it} + \beta_3 P_{it} + \lambda_i + \varepsilon_{it} \quad (11.4)$$

Where, 'i' represents States and 't' refers to the time period. F_{it} represents very dense forest cover (VDFC), G_{it} relates to GSDP, T_{it} refers to fiscal transfers, and P_{it} refers to population. β_i represents intercept or constant. λ_i shows the effects of excluded variables in the model which are invariant overtime. ε_{it} is an error term, often called the idiosyncratic error or time-varying error because it represents unobserved factors that change over time and affect F_{it}.

11.5 Interpreting Data

Figures 11.1 to 11.3 illustrate the share of ecological fiscal transfers in the 14th and 15th Finance Commissions (FCs) to states in India. Notably, Uttar Pradesh receives the highest devolution share, while Sikkim has the lowest, as per the 14th FC recommendations (Figure 11.1). Given the retention of the ecology-based criterion by the 15th FC, Figure 11.2 displays the interim devolution share. Figure 11.3 portrays the final devolution according to the 14th FC recommendations unveiled in the 15th FC report of 2021. In this final devolution, Goa received the lowest share, followed by Sikkim.

The point to be noted here is that the consistency of finance commissions in integrating climate change variables in tax devolution has led to an increase in forest cover in India. The bivariate scatter plots reveal that the link between ecological fiscal transfer share and the very dense forest cover is positive.[2]

The rationale of 15th FC (both in interim and final reports) to retain the forest and ecology criterion with a higher weight of 10 per cent was based on their 'impact on the revenue disabilities and expenditure needs of States, and also on the huge ecological benefits to the nation and for meeting our international commitments'. However, forest sector variables are not the only climate change-related variables. Future finance commissions may consider other crucial ecological variables, based on a composite ecological fiscal transfer index.

Three questions are crucial here. What is the effect of ecological fiscal transfers on state-level spending on ecology? Are there any flypaper effects—evidence of the impact of intergovernmental transfers on local spending other than own income? Jonah Busch et al. (2020) found that introduction of ecological fiscal transfers (EFTs) has not yet led states to increase their forestry budgets. Kaur et al. (2021), however, found evidence of the impact of intergovernmental fiscal transfers on ecological budgets other than just own income. The existence of flypaper effects in the context of ecological fiscal space is thus reiterated. Having established the evidence for the impact of ecological fiscal transfers on state-level spending decisions on ecology (Kaur et al., 2021), it is inevitable to

[2] The details of the scatterplot can be made available upon request from the authors.

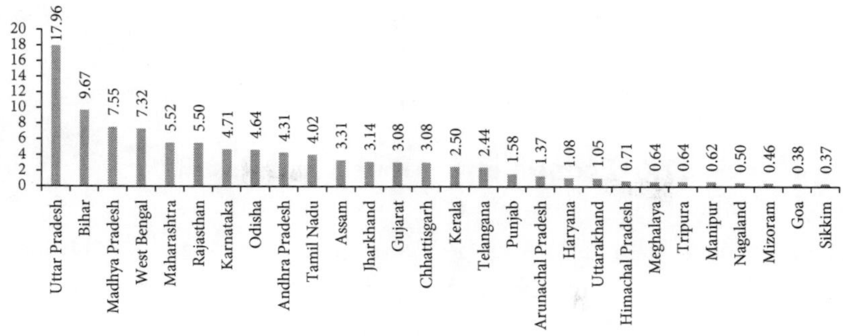

Figure 11.1 Inter-se share of states including ecological fiscal transfer in 14th Finance Commission.

Source: Authors' compilation from 14th Finance Commission report (2014).

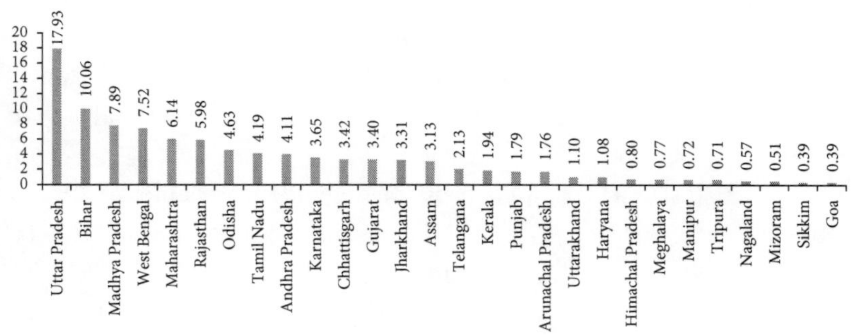

Figure 11.2 Inter-se share of states including ecological fiscal transfer in 15th Finance Commission interim devolution.

Source: Authors' compilation from 15th Finance Commission Report (Interim) (2020).

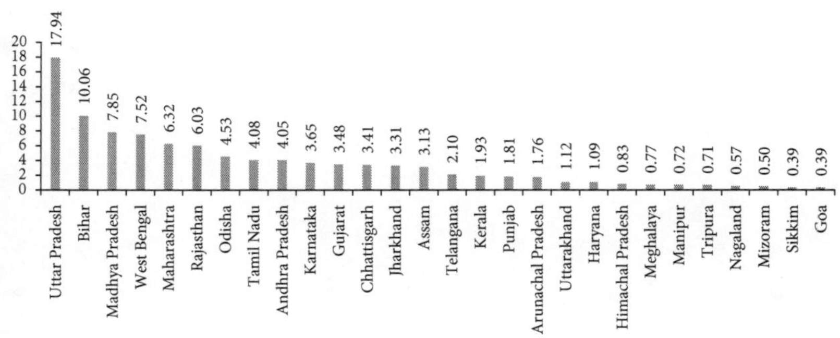

Figure 11.3 Inter-se share of states including ecological fiscal transfer in 15th Finance Commission final report.

Source: Authors' compilation from 15th Finance Commission Report (Final) (2021).

examine the degree to which the fiscal transfer is translated into better forest cover.

11.6 Econometric Models and Results

In order to test the relationship between intergovernmental fiscal transfers (IGFT) and net forest cover, we used the panel dataset for 27 states in India for the period 2003–2020. The states not under the analysis include Telangana and the state of Jammu and Kashmir. The reason for dropping Telangana is that the state became independent in 2014 (formerly being part of Andhra Pradesh). With the resolution passed to repeal section 370 of the Indian Constitution in August 2019 came the reconstitution of Jammu and Kashmir and Ladakh as two separate Union territories. Such reorganization implies reorganization in the resource devolution framework. Hence, to maintain consistency with the data, these two states were dropped.

In the analysis, net forest cover is the dependent variable. The independent variables include GSDP, GSDP squared, population, and IGFTs. The econometric results are presented in Table 11.3. In the models, we try to examine the relationship between forest cover and total IGFT, controlling for GSDP and population. Primarily, the purpose is to examine whether there is positive relationship between the forest cover and the total fiscal transfers to the states by the union government. Furthermore, we need to test the existence of the EKC for India. The results reveal that there is a significant positive relationship between IGFT and net forest cover. Taking population as an independent variable, we see there is an inverse and significant relationship between population and net forest cover.

Table 11.3 Econometric results.

Variables	Model (1)	Model (2)
	NFC	NFC
GSDP	0.0000164*** (4.52e-06)	0.0000164*** (4.52e-06)
GSDP squared	−5.64e-14*** (1.57e-14)	−5.71e-14*** (1.57e-14)
Total transfers	0.000115*** (0.0000391)	0.0000862*** (0.0000354)
POP	−.0000154* (8.83e-06)	
Cons	2694.587*** (805.5464)	2097.434*** (772.7207)
No. of observations	486	486
No. of groups	27	27

Source: Authors' estimations.

Notes: ***, **, and * denote the significance level at 1 per cent , 5 per cent, and 10 per cent, respectively. Figures in the brackets denote standard errors.

11.7 Conclusions

This chapter has explored the fiscal policy imperatives for integrating ecological criteria in the intergovernmental fiscal transfers in India. Translating three setting functions of climate change commitments—as an international public good, along with the plausibility of inter-jurisdictional spill-overs, and localized public good characteristics—into three components of a tax-transfer formula encounters measurement issues, as well as the methodological challenges encountered in constructing a composite ecological intergovernmental fiscal transfers (IGFT) index. Given that the global public good characteristics is outside the purview of IGFTs, a simple indicator capturing the local ecological public good can be a criterion of tax transfers. From that perspective, the 14th Finance Commission of India designed the world's first-ever and largest ecological fiscal transfers, and the 15th FC has retained the ecological criterion. To keep the ecological criteria simple and practical, the FCs have used a single-indicator approach and use only net forest cover as the criteria for tax transfers, along with the other non-ecological variables, including population, area, and income distance. The empirical evidence suggests that the consistency of the ecological criterion in IGFTs in India has helped to increase the net forest cover—the econometric results reveal a positive and significant relationship between IGFT and net forest cover. This has policy implications for India's 16th FC.

References

Ardndt, Heinz W. (1998). 'Market Failure and Underdevelopment', *World Development*, 16(2), 219–229.

Badunenko, O., Galeotti, M., and Hunt, L. C. (2021). 'Better to Grow o Better to Improve? Measuring Environmental Efficiency in OECD Countries with a Stochastic Environmental Kuznets Frontier', FEEM Working Papers 316226, Foundazione Eni Enrico Mattei, Milan.

Cole, M. A., Rayner, A. J., and Bates, J. M. (1997). 'The Environmental Kuznets Curve: An Empirical Analysis'. *Environment and Development Economics*, 2(4), 401–416.

Dasgupta, S., Laplante, B., Wang, H., and Wheeler, D. (2002). 'Confronting the Environmental Kuznets Curve', *Journal Of Economic Perspectives*, 16(1), 147–168.

Dinda, S. (2004). 'Environmental Kuznets Curve Hypothesis: A Survey', *Ecological Economics*, 49(4), 431–455.

Finance Commission, 2019. *Fifteenth Finance Commission Interim Report*, New Delhi.

Finance Commission, 2020. *Fifteenth Finance Commission Final Report*, New Delhi.

Finance Commission, 2013. *Fourteenth Finance Commission Report*, New Delhi.

Galinato, G. I., and Islam, A. (2017). 'The Challenge of Addressing Consumption Pollutants with Fiscal Policy', *Environment and Development Economics*, 22(5), 624–647.

Grossman, G. M., and Krueger, A. B. (1991). *Environmental Impacts of a North American Free Trade Agreement*, NBER Working Papers 3914, National Bureau of Economic Research, Cambridge, MA.

Halkos, G. E., and Paizanos, E. A. (2013). 'The Effect of Government Expenditure on the Environment: An Empirical Investigation', *Ecological Economics*, 91, 48–56.

Jonah Busch et al. (2020). 'Did India's Ecological Fiscal Transfers Incentivize State Governments to Increase Their Forestry Budgets?', *Environmental Research Communications*, 2(3). 1–8.

Kaur, A., Mohanty, R. K., Chakraborty, L., et al. (2021). 'Ecological Fiscal Transfers and State-level Budgetary Spending in India: Analyzing the Flypaper Effects', *Levy Economics Institute*, Working Paper no. 990, July, New York.

Kuznets, S. (1955). 'American Economic Association', *The American Economic Review*, 45(1), 1–28.

Lopez, R. (1994). 'The Environment as a Factor of Production: The effects of Economic Growth and Trade Liberalization', *Journal of Environmental Economics and Management*, 27, 163–184.

López, R., Galinato, G. I., and Islam, A. (2011). 'Fiscal Spending and the Environment: Theory and Empirics', *Journal of Environmental Economics and Management*, 62(2), 180–198.

Meadows, D. H., Meadows, D. L., Randers, J., et al. (1972). *The Limits to Growth.* Universe Books, New York.

Oates, Wallace, (2001). 'A Reconsideration of Environmental Federalism'. Discussion Papers (dp-01-54), Resources for the Future.

Porreca, Z. (2020). 'Environmental Sustainability and Human Capital Development', *Consilience*, (22), 48–57, doi:10.7916/consilience.vi22.6746.

Schmidt, S. (2019). 'Brain Fog: Does Air Pollution Make Us Less Productive?', *Environmental Health Perspectives*, 127(5), 052001.

Selden, T. M., and Song, D. (1994). 'Environmental Quality and Development: Is there a Kuznets Curve for Air Pollution?', *Journal of Environmental Economics and Management*, 27, 147–162.

Shafik, N. (1994). 'Economic Development and Environmental Quality: An Econometric Analysis', *Oxford Economic Papers*, 46, 757–773.

Shafik, N., and Bandyopadhyay, S. (1992). 'Economic Growth and Environmental Quality: Time Series and Crosscountry evidence'. Background Paper for the World Development Report 1992, World Bank, Washington, DC.

Stern, D. I. (2004). 'The Rise and Fall of the Environmental Kuznets Curve', *World Development*, 32(8), 1419–1439.

Stern, D. I., Common, M. S., and Barbier, E. B. (1996). 'Economic Growth and Environmental Degradation: The Environmental Kuznets Curve and Sustainable Development', *World Development*, 24, 1151–1160.

Zhao, X., Yu, X., Wang, Y., and Fan, C. (2016). 'Economic Evaluation of Health Losses from Air Pollution in Beijing, China', *Environmental Science and Pollution Research*, 23(12), 11716–11728.

12

Fiscal Federalism in India

A Case for Reassigning of Tax Powers

R. Srinivasan and S. Raja Sethu Durai

12.1 Introduction

The distribution of spending and revenue powers between two tiers of the government is based on the idea of reaping welfare gains by taking the public expenditure decision-making authorities closer to the people while achieving economies of scale in revenue collection. The assignment of a greater amount of public expenditure responsibilities to the regional governments and retaining revenue-raising powers with the federal government are evident in the fiscal structure of several federal governments (Eyraud and Lusinyan, 2013). The endowment of the revenue base and costs of public services differ between regional governments; hence, the variation in fiscal imbalance across regional governments. The financial transfers from centre to subcentral governments address two issues—the vertical fiscal imbalance (VFI) and the horizontal fiscal imbalance (HFI). Improper financial transfer itself may exasperate the fiscal imbalances of regional governments (Eyraud and Lusinyan, 2013; Koley and Kumarjit, 2019).

Theoretical developments influenced the evolution of fiscal federalism in India. The centralization of revenue powers to reap benefits of economies of scale in revenue collection and decentralization of public expenditure to improve welfare through the provision of regional specific public goods and a constitutional finance commission to decide financial transfers broadly reflect the conclusions of the first-generation theories of fiscal federalism like allocation of functions in federal set-up and neutrality in transfers including formula-based transfers (Oates, 1972; Musgrave and Musgrave, 1984). Since 2000, we have seen enforcement

R. Srinivasan and S. Raja Sethu Durai, *Fiscal Federalism in India* In: *Fiscal Policy and Public Financial Management.* Edited by: Pinaki Chakraborty and K R Shanmugam, Oxford University Press. © Oxford University Press 2024.
DOI: 10.1093/9780198930464.003.0012

of fiscal discipline, a legal constraint on borrowings, rationalization of commodity taxation, and pooling all union taxes into the divisible pool. These aspects broadly reflect the elements of market-friendly federalism that the second-generation theories prescribe (Oates, 2005).

However, there are unresolved issues in Indian fiscal federalism. The VFI could be corrected through assignment of revenue powers to match the expenditure responsibilities of the governments (Oates, 2006; IMF, 2009), and the HFI should be corrected through equalization transfers. Therefore, correction in the assignment of revenue powers and expenditure responsibilities is a continuous process in federal countries like India. This chapter engages two important issues of fiscal federalism in India. One, whether the VFI can be corrected with the reassignment of tax powers. Two, if the VFI is corrected through tax reassignment, would there be a need only for equalization transfers?

This chapter is organized as follows: Section 12.2 describes the vertical fiscal imbalance in India; Section 12.3 discusses the possibility of tax reassignment to correct the VFI in India; Section 12.4 assesses the effects of reassignment on horizontal fiscal imbalance and the need for equalization transfers, and the final section (12.5) concludes with policy implications.

12.2 Vertical Fiscal Imbalance in India

The VFI is the fiscal gap in the subnational governments due to improper decentralization of public revenue and expenditure. The asymmetry in revenue and expenditure decentralization is called vertical fiscal asymmetry (VFA). The VFI arising out of VFA is corrected through financial transfers, and such transfers should not create any other fiscal effects in the states.

The literature points out that financial transfers can create two types of fiscal effects. First is the soft budget constraint. The state's expenditure is partially financed by federal financial transfers, so they may not be fiscally prudent (Rodden, 2003). Second is the common resources problem. If the assured federal financial transfers are forthcoming without much effort, the states are enthused to overspend, thus drawing from the common financial resources perpetually (Velasco, 2000). The solution to these two problems lies in the reassignment of revenue and expenditure functions between the tiers of the federal government. If the VFA is considered undesirable, then reducing VFA is the solution to the problem of VFI. An optimal VFA still leaves some amount of VFA because the federal government may consider ensuring a minimum standard of public services across the country through federal transfers, particularly to address fiscal externalities, income redistribution, and fiscal constraints to maintain macroeconomic stability.

If each government has enough revenue powers to finance its autonomous expenditure, then the vertical fiscal gap (VFG) is negligible. Such fiscal decentralization makes a government fiscally accountable to its citizens, and the optimal size of government is achievable. VFI arises out of VFA, and VFG arises despite optimal VFA. VFI is solved through reassignment of revenue powers and expenditure responsibilities, and VFG is filled by federal transfers (Sharma, 2012).

The VFI is usually measured as the ratio of the state's own revenue to its own expenditure. If this ratio is less than one, the adverse VFI is noted and transfers flow to states. There are several alternative measures of VFI, and equally, there are measures of fiscal decentralization, that is, VFA, that can possibly explain the extent of VFI (Sharma, 2012).

The fact that the constitutionally mandated Finance Commission should recommend the states' share in union government tax revenue is an acknowledgment of VFI in the Indian federation (Rao and Nirvikar Singh, 2004). Rao and Singh (2004) calculated that the states' own current revenue as a ratio to the country's total current revenue was in the range of 35–40 per cent in the period 1955–56 to 1997–98. During the same period, the ratio of the state's current expenditure to the country's current expenditure was in the range of 55–60 per cent, thus clearly establishing the VFI in Indian federation. Rao (2000) and Rangarajan and Srivastava (2008) have shown that the states have incurred a disproportionately larger amount of current expenditure than their own revenues. Suppose we take the current revenues and expenditures of the union and state governments in the period 2019–22. The current revenues of the states are only 51 per cent of the net current revenue of the union government, while the current expenditure of the states is 115 per cent of the current expenditure of the union government.[1] The share in union tax revenue and grants from the union government partially fill the fiscal gap of the states (Rao and Srivastava, 2014).

One of the more recent and comprehensive studies on VFI in India was that of Koley and Mandal (2019). This paper directly takes the methodology developed by Eyraud and Lusinyan (2013). While Eyraud and Lusinyan aimed to compare fiscal decentralization and its impact on the fiscal performance of federal countries, their study did not include the impact of VFI in subcentral governments in each federation; whereas Koley and Mandal studied the trend in VFI in India over two-and-a-half a decades and its impact on the fiscal performance of states in India. Koley and Mandal used the ratio of the state's own revenue to the state's own expenditure as a measure of VFI and calculated this value for 25 years from 1990–91 to 2015–16. The VFI was as low as 32.69 per cent in Haryana, and as high as 92.78 per cent in Nagaland, but the state average was 62.83 per cent. The difference in fiscal gaps between states reflects the HFI in India. The average VFI for all states remained stable at around 50 per cent for non-special-category states and 80 per cent for special-category states. The impact of VFI is seen to be positively correlated with the fiscal deficit of states. However, both VFI and HFI together explain the state's primary deficit.

12.2.1 Measuring VFI

There are several quantitative measurements of VFI (Kowalik, 2016). Conceptually the revenue not under the control of the state (aggregate financial transfers from the union to states) reflects the extent of fiscal dependence of states on the union government. Including the net borrowings of state government is another option, as the quantum of state borrowings is controlled by the union government. Therefore, these two definitions of the 'revenue not under the control of the state governments' give two different measures of VFI.

[1] The financial accounts 2019–20 (actual), 2020–21 (revised estimate), and 2021–22 (budget estimate) were used for the calculation. The net revenue of the union government is used in this study which is net of states' share in union taxes from the gross revenue of the union.

Further, the state expenditure shall be defined as the total or only a part of the expenditure that the state government autonomously decides. To arrive at the autonomous expenditure, we should exclude tied grants-induced expenditure from the total expenditure, whereas the debt-financed expenditure may be retained. Therefore, a range of VFI measurements is plausible. However, we take the ratio of own revenue to own expenditure of state governments as the conceptual measure of VFI. Here, we use the two ratios from Eyraud and Lusinyan (2013). The first is:

$$\text{VFI}(1) = 1 - \frac{\text{States' own revenue}}{\text{States' own expenditure}}$$

Here the states' own revenue is the aggregate revenue of all the states, excluding share in central taxes, grants, and borrowings; the states' own expenditure excludes the expenditure met from the union government's grants. The state's own revenue includes major revenue sources such as state excise, motor vehicle tax, stamp duty and registration, and state goods and services tax (SGST), and the compensation for implementation of GST at the state level. Here we consider the GST compensation as the legitimate own revenue of the states in lieu of surrendering state autonomy in commodity taxation.[2] States' own revenue includes non-tax revenue in the revenue account and non-debt capital receipts.

The share in central taxes is to fill the VFI. The grants are tied transfers to induce states to spend on specific public projects. Here the states also have to commit their own revenue for a part of the expenditure on such projects. However, the expenditure equivalent to grants alone is netted out. The borrowings are also tied to the implementation of fiscal policies in order to reduce the deficit, curtail expenditure, and raise non-tax revenue. Though borrowings are excluded from states' own revenue, interest payment and debt servicing are not excluded from states' own expenditures as they are contractual payments of the states.

[2] The states were assured to get compensation if the SGST collection fails to increase by 14 per cent every year from July 2017 to June 2022. This compensation is estimated based on the revenue collected by states in 2016–17 from those taxes that were replaced by GST since June 2017.

In the second ratio, we bring a slight change to conceive a VFI that reflects the states' own revenue and expenditure autonomously decided by the states. First, the own revenue excludes the state GST (SGST), including compensation. The GST Council decides the SGST and compensation; hence, the states have lost the autonomy to determine this tax base and tax rates.[3] In the case of states' own expenditure, we exclude 130 per cent of grants as expenditure induced by the union government because the union government mostly implements programmes with the allocation of grants to states while emphasizing a matching revenue commitment on those projects by the states. Therefore, through the allocation of grants, the expenditure autonomy of states is taken away by more than 100 per cent of the grants.

$$\text{VFI}(2) = 1 - \frac{\text{States' own revenue} - \text{SGST including compensation}}{\text{States' own expenditure} - \text{grant induced expenditure}}$$

In Table 12.1, we give both VFI(1) and VFI(2) over the period from 2005–06 to 2021–22. We divide this period into three phases. The first phase is the 13th Finance Commission period from 2005–06 to 2010–11. During this period, all taxes of the union government were brought into the divisible pool. Further, the states were compelled to implement fiscal responsibility legislation to curtail the fiscal deficit ratio to 3 per cent within a specific period to avail grants-in-aid. The second phase is the 14th Finance Commission period from 2011–12 to 2015–16. During this period, the states were asked to continue with fiscal consolidation.

Two important changes happened during the third phase, the 15th Finance Commission period of 2016–17 to 2020–21: First, GST was introduced in June 2017, and second, plan grants and loans were stopped since the planning commission was dissolved in 2015.[4] We have noted

[3] The GST in India is divided into Central GST (50 per cent) and State GST (50 per cent). A state realizes the SGST revenue when the final destination of retail trade takes place in the states. The tax base and the tax rates are decided by the GST council in which the union government enjoys 33 per cent vote share. But the decision should be passed with 75 per cent of votes. This gives a lopsided veto for the union government, and consequently the states have lost their autonomy in regard to the levy of SGST.

[4] VFI existed during the Planning Commission period as well, but the significant rise in the imbalance was effected due to the implementation of GST.

Table 12.1 Measures of vertical fiscal imbalance in India: 2005–06 to 2020–21.

Phases	SOR (Rs in million crore)	SOR – (SGST + compensation) (Rs in million crore)	SOE (Rs in million crore)	SOE – grant-induced expenditure (Rs in million crore)	VFI(1)	VFI(2)
I (2005–2010)	2.35 (9.58)	–	4.54 (18.51)	3.60 (14.67)	0.483	0.347
II (2010–2015)	4.20 (8.49)	–	8.06 (16.30)	6.45 (13.05)	0.479	0.350
III (2015–2021)	6.76 (7.61)	4.54 (5.11)	14.40 (16.19)	11.17 (12.56)	0.530	0.594

Note: Figures in parentheses are percentages of GDP. Calculated based on data from State Finance Statistics, RBI.

the change in VFIs in terms of the two measurements and understand such changes due to alterations in the revenue and expenditure decentralization during these three phases. These two VFIs reflect the level of fiscal dependence of states on the union government.

Both the measures of VFIs have marginally declined in phase 2, only to increase sharply in phase 3. The marginal decline in VFIs in phase 2 despite a steep fall in own-tax revenue:GDP ratio was mainly due to a steeper fall in own-expenditure:GDP ratio of the states. A further decline in the own-revenue:GDP ratio in the third phase further increased states' fiscal dependence though the own-expenditure:GDP ratio also declined marginally in this period.

If we compare the difference between VFI(1) and VFI(2), where VFI(2) represents the greater degree of fiscal autonomy, in the first two phases, VFI(2) is less than VFI(1). The decline in the fiscal dependence of states by the measure VFI(2) indicates the autonomous expenditure of states is reduced by the grant-induced expenditure of states. The VFIs of phase three should be analysed differently because the VFI(2) has changed in both numerator and denominator. The VFI(2) is greater than VFI(1) in phase 3 mainly because the revenue autonomy of states is reduced by

SGST and its compensation. However, the fiscal dependence of states increased over these three phases, particularly in the last phase, mainly due to the introduction of GST.

12.2.2 An Alternative Measure of VFI

An alternative formula to measure VFI given by Eyraud and Lusinyan (2013) is:

$$\text{VFI}(3) = 1 - \frac{\text{Revenue decentralization}}{\text{Expenditure decentralization}} \times (1 - \text{centre's deficit})$$

$$\text{Revenue decentralization} = \frac{\text{State's own revenue}}{\text{Centre's revenue}}$$

$$\text{Expenditure decentralization} = \frac{\text{State's own expenditure}}{\text{Centre's expenditure}}$$

$$\text{Centre's deficit} = \frac{\text{Centre's expenditure} - \text{Centre's revenue}}{\text{Centre's expenditure}}$$

This measure helps evaluate the impact of revenue and expenditure decentralization on VFI. However, this formula will also give the same measure of VFI as in the previous formula. In VFI(3), the state's own revenue and expenditure are defined as they are defined in VFI(1). Similarly, we have defined the own revenue by excluding SGST and compensation and own expenditure by reducing 130 per cent of grant-induced expenditure. Using these adjusted measures, we constructed VFI(4).

The measures of VFI as per VFI(3) and VFI(4) over the three phases are given in Tables 12.2 and 12.3. The values of VFI(3) and VFI(4) are the same as those of VFI(1) and VFI(2). In both tables, we can find that the indices of expenditure decentralization are higher than the indices of revenue decentralization. This gives rise to a higher level of VFI in the 15th FC period compared to the 14th FC period. Further, there was a

Table 12.2 Alternative measure of vertical fiscal imbalance (VFI-3) in India: 2005–06 to 2020–21.

Phases	SOE (Rs million crore)	SOR (Rs million crore)	Union expenditure (Rs million crore)	Union revenue (Rs million crore)	Union govt deficit	Expenditure decentralization	Revenue decentralization	VFI(3)
1 (2005–2010)	4.53	2.35	4.91	4.90	0.001	0.925	0.479	0.483
2 (2010–2015)	8.06	4.20	7.73	7.72	0.001	1.043	0.543	0.479
3 (2015–2021)	14.40	6.76	12.57	12.59	0.001	1.146	0.537	0.530

Source: Author's calculation based on data from State Finance Statistics, RBI.

Table 12.3 Alternative measure of vertical fiscal imbalance (VFI(4)) in India: 2005–06 to 2020–21.

Phases	SOE – 130 per cent grant (Rs million crore)	SOR – (SGST + compensation) (Rs million crore)	Union expenditure (Rs million crore)	Union revenue (Rs million crore)	Union govt deficit	Expenditure decentralization	Revenue decentralization	VFI(4)
1 (2005–2010)	3.60	2.35	4.91	4.90	0.001	0.733	0.479	0.347
2 (2010–2015)	6.45	4.20	7.73	7.72	0.001	0.834	0.543	0.350
3 (2015–2021)	11.17	4.54	12.57	12.59	0.001	0.889	0.361	0.594

Source: Authors' calculation based on data from State Finance Statistics, RBI.

marginal decline in VFI in the 14th FC period compared to the 13th FC period because the relative increase in revenue decentralization is higher than the increase in expenditure between the two periods.

If we compare the values of VFI between Tables 12.2 and 12.3, the values of VFI in Table 12.3 in the first two periods are lower than the corresponding values in Table 12.2. As stated earlier, this is because of the change in the definitions of own expenditure and revenue. However, the VFI in Table 12.3 is higher than in Table 12.2 for the third period because a major part of commodity taxation has been brought under GST, and that part is not recognized as the state's own revenue. Obviously, the revenue decentralization measure in this period is far less than in the previous two periods in Table 12.3. It has been noted by almost all scholars since 1950 that the states are burdened with higher expenditure responsibility and endowed with a lower amount of revenue potential and hence the higher level of VFI.

12.3 Reassigning Tax Powers and VFI

One of the possible solutions discussed in the literature to correct fiscal imbalances, particularly the VFI, is an appropriate restructuring of intergovernmental transfers and reassigning tax powers (Ruggeri et al., 1993). Indeed, they argued a case for Canada to bring in fiscal balance in the long run by transferring the personal income tax to the provinces and looked at the issue of VFI in a dynamic setting. They argued that the fiscal imbalance is an outcome of the dynamic interaction between the fiscal institutions of the federal and regional governments, noting that 'VFI involves a comparison of the dynamic properties of the basic structures upon which the fiscal system of different orders of government rest'. Before we analyse this issue, let us explore the possibility of tax reassignment in the Indian federation.

The rationale for assigning tax powers between the federal and regional governments is conceptualized differently in first- and second-generation theories of fiscal federalism. Accepting Musgrave's division of functions in a federation, the regional governments have to take up allocative functions of the state. Therefore, the fiscal policies, including taxation relating to stabilization and redistributive functions, should be with the federal government, and the taxes that align with the allocative function should be with the regional governments. This argument of the first-generation theory of fiscal federalism, if extended to the types of taxes, is broadly that the regional governments should levy only such taxes that could keep the distribution of income intact, and that such taxes have little destabilization effect on the national economy. Benefit taxes, like user charges, satisfy these principles; however, the benefit tax system breaks down without perfect knowledge of peoples' preferences for public goods.

The non-benefit taxes will create an income redistribution effect that has to be compensated for by the federal transfers. Instead, there is little difference between non-benefit tax and untied federal grants as sources of revenue to the regional governments if they are committed to welfare-maximizing public spending. Therefore the first-generation theories (FGT) have little to offer for designing tax assignments in a federal system. The local and historical conditions should guide the tax assignments between governments in a federation.

The second-generation theory (SGT) of fiscal federalism is based on the fundamental premise that the political economy of tax assignment should ensure preference matching and accountability of the regional governments. With democracy, the regional governments shall levy taxes reflecting the preferences of the local population and be accountable to them. Another important aspect of the SGT is that the regional taxes should preserve the functioning of the market. Regional taxes should not distort the market, and regional governments should not indulge in tax exportation. Ensuring a market-preserving tax system amounts to a minimum tax that disciplines excessive abuse of the public sector. Obviously, these principles direct us to consider only taxes with restricted bases in the local region and that harmonizing the tax system across the regional governments is essential to ensure free trade and not to distort the federal market. Therefore, even the SGT gives principles that do not clearly demarcate the tax powers between the federal and regional governments. But the principles of localized and harmonized taxes that do not distort markets automatically ensure minimum government. Therefore the tax assignment as per both the FGT and SGT allows experimentation that suits the specific federations as long as such experiments are aimed at attaining the market-preserving minimum government.

Given these theoretical considerations, we argue that all commodity taxation, except customs duty, should be assigned to the states. This is based on the fact that the commodity tax base is already taxed by both government levels. The union government has exclusive power to levy excise duty on petroleum products, and the states have exclusive power to levy excise duty and sales tax on liquor. All other commodities suffer the harmonized GST, which is concurrently levied by both government levels equally. The entire commodity tax base, except liquor, is concurrently exploited by the union and state governments; reassignment of all commodity taxation, including excise on petroleum products and CGST to states, will not adversely affect the market. At the same time, it will ensure enough own revenue for the states to meet their assigned expenditure responsibilities and make the states accountable to the local population.

This reassignment should be conceived as follows. One, we should bring all commodities, including petroleum products, under the GST. Two, the union government should continue to collect IGST only to settle revenue on destination basis. This will ensure smooth harmonization of GST across states as well as zero-rating GST on inter-state trade. The GST shall continue as a tax determined by the GST Council. However, the veto power of the union government should be removed. Then the GST Council shall truly become a tax decided by the states themselves, with the union government facilitating the arrival of consensus among the states on tax issues. This may once again require some constitutional amendments. The commodity taxation in its entirety should be moved to the State List III of the Seventh Schedule of the Constitution of India, with a rider that harmonization of commodity taxation should be maintained.

Moreover, the assignment of excise duty to states will hasten the process of integrating taxes on petroleum products into the GST. Since the tax proceeds will be distributed based on states' consumption, the efficiency of tax collection and the structure and size of the economy will decide the tax collection in each state. Thus there can be little disagreement on this reassignment of commodity taxes to states. The gross tax revenue after the integration of excise duty on petroleum products will be less than what is being collected now because the cesses and surcharges of the union government will be removed. The positive aspect of this reassignment of tax shall be the increase in own-tax revenue of the states. This will also improve the accountability of states to their people on fiscal matters. However, the ultimate differences in the revenue distribution between the states will largely be between the existing tax-assignment scheme and the reassignment, as suggested.

In addition to reassigning all the commodity taxation power to the states, we suggest another simple rule for an effective equalization transfer that simultaneously addresses the problems of VFI and HFI. A proportion of the revenue surplus[5] of the union government after reassignment as equalization transfer can be shared with the states equivalent to their contribution to the national income, bringing in a significant reduction in VFI and HFI. It also acts as an effective mechanism for the states to increase their gross state domestic product (GSDP).

12.3.1 Impact of Reassignment of Commodity Taxes to States

The impact of the proposal mentioned above on the dynamic vertical fiscal imbalance is now examined. We conceive the impact of reassignment of commodity taxes to states on the revenues and expenditures of union and state governments, as given below.

1. Revenue of union government after reassignment = gross tax revenue of union government – excise duty with cess and surcharges – CGST – IGST.

   After reassigning all commodity taxes to states, we assume that the states have no claim on share in central taxes because the tax powers are adequate to meet their expenditure responsibilities. Therefore, we consider gross tax revenue net of excise duty with cess and surcharges, CGST, and IGST.
2. Expenditure of union government after reassignment = total expenditure – untied and tied grants to states.

   The union has no obligation to make transfers to all states as the vertical fiscal imbalances are corrected through the reassignment

[5] The proportion can be determined dynamically by the union government to bring a balance in the state budgets every year considering their revenue requirements. For calculations we used 75 per cent.

of taxes. Therefore, we start with the ideal situation where no effective grants exist for all states. However, there is still a need for equalization grants, which can be separately considered.

3. Own revenue of state governments = own revenue of states + excise duty of union government net of cess and surcharges + CGST + IGST.
   The own revenue of state governments is the aggregation of existing own revenue plus excise duty net of cess and charge because we expect the petroleum products to be brought under GST.
4. Expenditure of state government = expenditures of states – 130 per cent of grants.
   Since, in principle, all the state governments are not expected to receive any grants, and because of matching grants received till now, we deduct 130 per cent of expenditures induced by grants.

Table 12.4 gives the VFI after the suggested proposal of reassignment of commodity taxation to states. The table shows that both the union and the the state governments have a revenue surplus, and VFI is close to zero. Comparing it to the existing system and the VFI reported in Tables 12.2 and 12.3, the proposed tax-reassignment scheme suggested in this study shows a revenue surplus for both the union and the state governments and a drastic fall in the VFI.

Coming back to the arrangement of Ruggeri et al. (1993) about the dynamic aspects of fiscal federalism, we derive the aggregate revenue and expenditure elasticity for union and state governments.[6] The difference in these elasticities is called structural imbalance in a government, and the difference in the structural imbalances between union and state governments is defined as a dynamic vertical fiscal imbalance. The focus here is to compare the structural imbalances measured as the difference between the income elasticities of revenue and expenditure of two tiers of government in the federal system. The dynamism in the structural imbalance of each level of the government is the most suitable approach to understand the evolving VFI in the Indian federation, given the political dynamics

[6] Estimated as β coefficient from the regression of the form $\log Y = \alpha + \beta \log X + e$, where Y is revenue or expenditure of the union or the state government and X is the national GDP. The estimation is carried out for the data from 2005–06 to 2020–21.

Table 12.4 Vertical fiscal imbalance after reassignment: 2005–06 to 2020–21.

Phases	SOE (Rs million crore)	SOR (Rs million crore)	Union expenditure (Rs million crore)	Union revenue (Rs million crore)	Union govt deficit	Expenditure decentralization	Revenue decentralization	VFI
1 (2005–2010)	3.60	3.8	4.18	4.52	−0.081	0.861	0.841	0.026
2 (2010–2015)	6.45	6.71	6.49	7.12	−0.097	0.994	0.942	0.057
3 (2015–2021)	11.17	12.33	10.08	11.18	−0.109	1.108	1.103	0.005

Source: Authors' calculation based on data from State Finance Statistics, *Handbook of Statistics on Indian Economy*, RBI.

in India. Notably, the interaction between the fiscal policies, and the resultant fiscal behavioural changes of the union and state governments, are important determinants of the dynamic VFI. An ideal reassignment should bring the structural imbalance closer to zero for both governments.

Table 12.5 shows the elasticities and structural imbalances in the existing system as well as after the reassignment, as suggested. As per the estimates in the present system, the union and the state governments have a negative structural imbalance indicating deficits and a dynamic vertical imbalance value at 0.067. These deficits can be reduced by rationalizing the expenditures of both the governments by removing the grants to the states from the union expenditure, and an equivalent of 130 per cent of that is excluded from the states' expenditure. In this arrangement, the union government's expenditure elasticity (0.931) improves the structural imbalance and becomes a positive value. Still, the states governmentss expenditure elasticity (1.101) provides an improvement in the structural imbalance but not to the extent of a positive value.

Further rationalizing state expenditure must bring its structural imbalance to zero or a positive value. This can be achieved in two ways. First, the statutory grants from the union government are generally aimed at filling the fiscal gap of the states, thus incentivizing the states to sustain the fiscal gap, so in the absence of a gap-filling grant, this

Table 12.5 Vertical fiscal imbalance before and after reassignment.

Description	Estimates in the present system	Estimates after suggested reassignment
Union government		
Aggregate revenue elasticity	0.964	0.951
Aggregate expenditure elasticity	0.972	0.931
Structural imbalance	−0.008	0.020
State government		
Aggregate revenue elasticity	1.042	1.112
Aggregate expenditure elasticity	1.117	1.101
Structural imbalance	−0.075	0.011
Dynamic vertical fiscal imbalance	**0.067**	**0.009**

Source: Authors' calculation.

fiscal gap will be vastly reduced. Second, if the reassignment of taxes improves the states' revenue capacity, they are accountable for their fiscal prolificacy. So there will be an intention to reduce the structural imbalance. The reassignment of entire commodity taxes to states and a proportion of the union government's revenue surplus distributed as per the shares of each state to national income can bring structural balance to a positive value and the dynamic vertical fiscal imbalance close to zero.

12.4 Effects of Reassignment on Horizontal Fiscal Imbalance

Reassignment of commodity taxes to states might impact the horizontal fiscal imbalance (HFI), which measures the disparity in fiscal capacity and effort across the states. This is measured by the coefficient of variation in own revenue as a percentage of GSDP of the states for 2019–20. Table 12.6 provides the change in HFI before and after reassignment. The coefficient of variation of own-tax:GSDP ratios is reduced from 0.27 in the present system to 0.19 after the suggested reassignment.

Let us look at the disaggregated data of states' own-tax:GDP ratios before and after the tax reassignment in Table 12.6. All the smaller states, which are essentially not exporting states, have shown a substantial increase in their own-tax:GSDP ratio compared to larger, industrialized, and exporting states. Therefore, it is clear that the reassignment of consumption-based commodity taxation to states brings in greater equity in states' own revenue mobilization if the larger states improve their tax efforts. Therefore, there will be little need for grants to equalize the own-revenue capacity of states.

We know the fact that indicators of literacy, public health, and infrastructure facilities vary even among states that are otherwise equal in terms of the level of development measured by GDP—this has been amply documented in various human development reports in India and state human development reports. Therefore, to ensure minimum standards of delivery of public utilities across all states, some amount of tied grants for specific purposes will still be essential.

Table 12.6 Horizontal fiscal imbalance before and after reassignment: 2019–20.

State	Own revenue:GSDP (per cent)	Own revenue:GSDP after reassignment (per cent)
Andhra Pradesh	6.3	11.3
Arunachal Pradesh	6.7	21.3
Assam	6.6	12.8
Bihar	5.7	13.3
Chhattisgarh	8.7	14.7
Goa	9.9	15.3
Gujarat	6.0	10.5
Haryana	6.4	10.8
Himachal Pradesh	6.2	11.3
Jammu and Kashmir	8.1	13.5
Jharkhand	7.9	14.2
Karnataka	6.8	11.5
Kerala	7.3	12.1
Madhya Pradesh	7.1	12.9
Maharashtra	7.2	11.7
Manipur	4.2	12.5
Meghalaya	7.0	15.1
Mizoram	5.0	13.0
Nagaland	4.4	12.1
NCT Delhi	4.5	8.6
Odisha	8.6	14.5
Puducherry	10.8	14.9
Punjab	6.8	11.5
Rajasthan	7.5	12.8
Sikkim	5.4	11.9
Tamil Nadu	6.7	11.3
Telangana	7.8	12.5
Tripura	4.2	10.8
Uttar Pradesh	12.1	18.5
Uttarakhand	6.1	11.1
West Bengal	5.3	10.7
Coefficient of Variation	**0.27**	**0.19**

Source: Authors' calculation based on data from State Finance Statistics *and Handbook of Statistics on Indian States*, RBI.

12.5 Summary and Conclusion

The inevitable VFI and HFI exist in the Indian federation, as in most other federations. The instruments of federal transfers in terms of share in central tax revenues and statutory and discretionary grants, which may be tied or untied, have been used to fill the fiscal gap and to incentivize states to expend as per the priorities of the union government. This has to some extent prevented the states from prioritizing their own expenditures. The hard budget constraint-fixing targets for revenue and fiscal deficits through fiscal legislation are also in place. However, correcting the vertical and horizontal fiscal imbalances by matching the own revenues of the states with their own expenditure responsibilities is an ideal approach that every federation would like to achieve. We have traced the increase in VFI in the Indian federation over recent decades through the acknowledged objective measures in the literature. We have also shown that the VFI can be corrected by reassigning the entire commodity taxation to states, that is, transferring excise duty on petroleum products and CGST and IGST from the union government to state governments.

Consequently, the tax reassignment would correct the VFI and avoid distributing shares in central taxes to states. The reassignment of commodity taxes to states would solve the contentious issue of bringing petroleum products under GST. Further, estimates based on historical data show that the reassignment of commodity taxes to states improves the tax:GSDP of smaller states and brings their tax-revenue capacity to more than that of the larger states. However, the need for equalization transfers cannot be wished away, given the differences in the level and structure of development of states. Therefore, equalization transfers should be effected, based on revenue needs to ensure minimum standards of delivering public utilities across states.

References

Eyraud, Luc, and Lusinyan, Lusine (2013). 'Vertical fiscal imbalances and fiscal performance in advanced economies', *Journal of Monetary Economics*, 60, 571–587.

International Monetary Fund (IMF) (2009). Report on Macro Policy Lessons for a Sound Design of Fiscal Decentralization, https://www.imf.org/external/np/pp/eng/2009/072709.pdf.

Koley, M. and Mandal, Kumarjit (2019). 'Vertical Fiscal Imbalances and its Impact on Fiscal Performance: A Case for Indian States', in S. Bandyopadhyay and M. Dutta (eds) Opportunities and Challenges in Development, Springer, Singapore, 243–282.

Kowalik, P. (2016). 'Measurement of Vertical Fiscal Imbalance in Germany', *Argumenta Oeconomica*, 37(2), 131–146.

Musgrave, Richard, A., and Musgrave, Peggy B. (1984). *Public Finance in Theory and Practice.* McGraw-Hill, San Francisco.

Oates, Wallace E. (1972). *Fiscal Federalism.* Harcourt Brace Jovanovich Inc, New York.

Oates, Wallace, E. (2005). 'Towards a Second-generation Theory of Fiscal Federalism', *International Tax and Public Finance*, 12(4), 349–73.

Oates, Wallace, E. (2006). 'On the Theory and Practice of Fiscal Decentralization', IFIR Working Paper 2006, 05.

Rangarajan, C., and Srivastava, D. K. (2008). *Reforming India's Fiscal Transfer System: Resolving Vertical and Horizontal Imbalances*, Madras School of Economics, Working Paper 31/2008.

Rao, C. B., and Srivastava, D. K. (2014). *Dependence of States on Central Transfers: State-wise Analysis.* NIPFP Working Paper 2014-137. National Institute of Public Finance and Policy, New Delhi.

Rao, M. G. (2000). *Fiscal Decentralization in Indian Federalism.* Retrieved from http://www.imf.org/external/pubs/ft/seminar/2000/fiscal/rao.pdf.

Rao, M. Govinda, and Singh, Nirvikar (2004), *The Political Economy of India's Federal System and its Reform*, Economics Department Working Paper 566, University of California, Santa Cruz, CA.

Rodden, Jonathan (2003). 'Federalism and Bailouts in Brazil', in Jonathan Rodden, Gunnar S. Eskeland, and Jennie Litvack (eds), *Fiscal Decentralization and the Challenge of Hard Budget Constraints*, MIT Press, Cambridge, MA, 213–248.

Ruggeri, G. C., Van Wart, D., Robertson, G. K., and Howard, R. (1993). 'Vertical Fiscal Imbalance and the Reallocation of Tax Fields in Canada', *Canadian Public Policy*, 19(2), 194–215.

Sharma, C. K. (2012). 'Beyond Gaps and Imbalances: Restructuring the Debate on Intergovernmental Fiscal Relations, *Public Administration*, 90(1), 99–128.

Velasco, Andres (2000). 'Debts and Deficits with Fragmented Fiscal Policymaking', *Journal of Public Economics*, 76(1), 105–125.

IV

PUBLIC FINANCIAL MANAGEMENT AND ENVIRONMENTAL AND CLIMATE FINANCE

13

Public Financial Management in India

Reforms and Opportunities

Pratap Ranjan Jena

13.1 Public Financial Management: An Introduction

A sound public financial management system (PFM) is based on the principles of fiscal discipline, strategic resource allocation, and result-oriented operational management. PFM has evolved over the years from its traditional focus on expenditure by incorporating management of other facets of public finance. A working PFM system acts as a practical arrangement for better use of fiscal instruments like expenditure, revenue, fiscal deficit, and debt, to enable macroeconomic goals to be achieved, and is attracting increasing attention (Hemming, 2013).

The analytical background for PFM's institutional reforms involves addressing problems of excessive sector demands for resources and accompanying distortions. Theories such as principal–agent relationship between voters (the principals) and politicians (the agents), and the common pool problem of public finances, reflect these tendencies (Hagen, 2007). The political choices to be made in resource allocation to various public budgeting programmes can lead to higher demand for budgetary resources (Folscher, 2007). The transaction costs associated with mapping expenditures to the perceived preferences are also high (Campos and Pradhan, 1996). Intra-agency information asymmetry arising due to the fear of losing out on resources in a competitive environment affects the quality of budgeting decisions. The government usually tries to manage the resources available to suffice and to satisfy

Pratap Ranjan Jena, *Public Financial Management in India* In: *Fiscal Policy and Public Financial Management.* Edited by: Pinaki Chakraborty and K R Shanmugam, Oxford University Press. © Oxford University Press 2024. DOI: 10.1093/9780198930464.003.0013 resource needs, sacrificing value for money in doing so (Wildavsky and Caiden, 1997).[1]

Appropriate designing of institutions to improve decision-making in public finances includes improving the environment of the budgeting system, adopting fiscal rules, and determining resources and expenditure composition through a broad macro framework. Instilling comprehensiveness and transparency, putting in place a hard budget constraint to address populist demands and control aggregate spending level, prioritizing for allocative efficiency, and enhancing capacity and technical efficiency in the government organizations are other features of the PFM reform agenda (Campos and Pradhan, 1996).

The Public Expenditure and Financial Accountability (PEFA) framework for assessing PFM sets out the following as key components of the good PFM system needed for desirable fiscal and budgetary outcomes.[2]

- The budget is credible—it is realistic and is implemented as planned.
- Information on PFM is comprehensive, consistent, and accessible to users.
- There is effective management of assets and liabilities, including identifying fiscal risks and prudent planning of debts and guarantees, ensuring value for money from public investments.
- The fiscal strategy and the budget are prepared with due regard to government fiscal policies, strategic plans, and adequate macroeconomic and fiscal projections.
- The budget is implemented within a system of effective standards, processes, and internal controls, ensuring that resources are obtained and used as intended.
- Accurate and reliable records are maintained, and information is produced and disseminated at appropriate times to meet decision-making, management, and reporting needs.
- Public finances are independently reviewed and there is external follow-up on the implementation of recommendations for improvement by the executive.

[1] Wildavsky and Caiden (1997) termed this way of managing budgetary decisions 'satisficing'.
[2] PEFA (2016) provides a revised framework for assessing public financial management systems.

For a long time, financial management in developing countries has been viewed as a process that enables central agencies like the Ministry/ Department of Finance to keep spending agencies under control through continuous review and specification of inputs, and verification of documents submitted for payment (Premchand, 2005). Subsequent reforms in financial management have concentrated on the use of the government budget as a vehicle to address emerging economic stress in the form of high fiscal deficit and debt burden, assuring accountability of the government to the people, and economic development. The financial management system has generally been slow in adapting to changing requirements and has witnessed a segmented approach to reforms.

13.2 Public Financial Management System and Reform Initiatives in India

The PFM system in India, with established institutional structures like budgeting, accounting, audit, and legislative control systems, has its root in the constitutional provisions (Swarup, 1990). Increasing demand for better accountability, good governance, and improved service delivery has made it imperative to explore more ways to strengthen India's PFM system. The need and scope for improving the efficiency of government spending by strengthening the institutional framework has been acknowledged and recommended by several expert bodies, committees, and statutory bodies. While there have been initiatives to improve the PFM systems and processes over the years, yielding some enduring changes, the discontinuities and indifferent implementation have remained key concerns (Premchand, 2008; Jena, 2016).

Major interventions in recent decades that have influenced PFM reforms in the country are as follows;

- The Second Administrative Reform Commission (2009) emphasized the effectiveness of public spending and suggested several institutional reform measures in the areas of budgeting, internal control and audit, and external audit.
- The recommendations of the Expert Committee on Expenditure Management (2011) played a crucial role in the removal of the

plan/non-plan distinction and strengthening of the Central Plan Scheme Monitoring System (CPSMS), which further evolved into the PFMS platform in later years.

- The Central Finance Commissions, particularly FCs 12, 13, and 14, made recommendations that have far-reaching consequences for institutional development in the PFM system.
- FC 15 compellingly argued for a comprehensive PFM reform strategy for both the union and the states based on policy, regulatory and institutional measures, and leveraging technology to drive these reforms.
- The identification of areas in need for reforms by the PEFA report (2010), through measuring the performance of PFM institutions at the union level, provides another useful reference for reform initiatives.

The contours of PFM institutions in a large country like India have to be seen in the context of its fiscal federal nature and constitutional assignment of large functional responsibilities to the subnational governments. The contemporary challenges faced by the states, judged from the basic objectives of the PFM system, comprise issues related to allocative and operational efficiency. States suffer from issues like the tendency to expand budget size, spreading resources thinly, and inadequacies in designing and implementing the programmes. Several positive developments at the state level have paved the way for improving effectiveness and efficiency of public spending. Post fiscal rules (FRBM Act 2003), the state governments have showed maturity in fiscal management and have improved fiscal consolidation, which has created an enabling environment. Advances made in utilization of information technology, and easy access to data and information, have enhanced capacity to take appropriate decisions.

The reform initiatives undertaken over the decades, elaborated here, reflect opportunities to enhance the PFM architecture. It is becoming increasingly apparent, particularly after the distortions created by COVID-19 pandemic in the public finances, that a PFM system is crucial to improving institutional efficiency in order to implement required polices and achieve the desired results. These reform initiatives are now described.

- **Outcome budget:** To improve the performance orientation in the budgeting system, the Government introduced the outcome budget, a revised form of the already existing performance budget, in 2005. Major features of this system, including framing of performance targets, standardizing unit costs of delivery, and benchmarking the standards/quality of outcomes, continue to be work in progress and their impact on resource-allocation decisions and programme formulation is not discernible.
- **Performance monitoring and evaluation system (PMES):** The government introduced PMES in 2009 to strengthen performance management across departments. Its utility in the presence of outcome budget was not clear and it was given up after a few years.
- **Medium-term perspective in expenditure planning:** The medium-term expenditure framework (MTEF) was introduced in India in 2012 as part of the revision of the FRBM Act. While the preparation of the MTEF was paused due to COVID-19, the need to strengthen this instrument in the budgeting process is unmistakable.
- **Fiscal Responsibility and Budget Management (FRBM) Act 2003:** This fiscal rule was adopted in India in 2003 in response to severe deterioration of public finance at both central and state levels. While the country achieved a significant fiscal correction from 2001–02 to 2007–08 riding on higher growth, this was breached due to a slowing in the national growth rate because of the international financial crisis. The timeline to achieve the target remained elusive and the Act has been amended several times. COVID-19 disrupted the country's public finances and the FRBM Act was further extended until 2025–26.
- **Modified cash management system:** To reduce unevenness in expenditure patterns over the year and the rush of expenditure in the last quarter of the financial year, the government introduced a modified cash management system. The objective of this scheme is to obtain greater evenness in spending during the year, reduce the rush of expenditure during the last quarter, and reduce the tendency to 'park' funds.
- **Efforts to change the budget and accounting classification:** A committee chaired by the Controller General of Accounts has recommended revisions in the existing budget and accounting

classification to address problems in: getting a comprehensive view of central transfers to the states, translating accounting information into plan schemes, showing clarity in functional classification of expenditure, reporting costs incurred by the government in providing services to facilitate preparation of outcome budget, and finding uniform accounting codes for plan schemes across the states.

- **Efforts to adopt accrual accounting:** The Government of India had accepted in principle the recommendations of FC 12 to make a gradual transition to an accrual-based accounting system. The Government Accounting Standards Advisory Board was entrusted with the responsibility to prepare a detailed road map and an operational framework for this.
- **Efforts to modernize internal audit have not materialized:** The internal audit system in India has not been updated to emphasize its role as a management tool and an integral part of both management controls and communication processes. The report of the Task Force constituted to provide a road map to improve the internal audit in 2006 has not yet been adequately considered.
- **External audit:** The external audit by the Comptroller and Auditor General of India has played a crucial role in assisting the parliament in exercising financial control. While external audit has been a strong element of the Indian PFM system, the follow-up process needs improvement to enable the external audit system to play its desired role.
- **Web-based PFM system:** The PFMS is a web-based online software application implemented by the government to facilitate payment and exchequer control, accounting and reporting, and integration with states' financial management systems.
- **Development of integrated financial management information system (IFMIS) by state governments:** State governments in India, aided and encouraged by the central government, have made considerable progress in adopting IT-enabled IFMIS to facilitate improved accounting and budgeting, and manage payment processing, spending, and reporting activities.

These initiatives having been undertaken to strengthen PFM institutions over the decades provides opportunities to further build upon them. India's contemporary PFM system continues to face challenges to maintaining a sustainable fiscal position, undertaking effective allocation of resources, and providing public services effectively. FC 15, acknowledging the need for strong institutional support for the PFM system, suggested policy, regulatory, and institutional measures leveraged by technology to bridge the gap between the existing PFM system and the required changes.[3] As the PFM system is complex by nature and individual processes are interlinked, a framework treating them comprehensively will lead to achieving outcomes from intents. We now discuss two key developments in the PFM innovations, bringing in performance orientation in the budgeting system and taking a medium-term perspective on budgeting to highlight reform processes and opportunities.

13.3 Performance Orientation in Budgeting: The Outcome Budget

13.3.1 The Performance Budget Innovation

The demand for higher accountability and improvement in public service delineates the idea of a performing state associated with economic and social wellbeing of citizens. While countries adopted several reforms influenced by the new public management process, the budgeting system emerged as an important instrument to improve government performance (Curristine and Flynn, 2013). The budget assumes a crucial position in the governance structure as it controls money and provides the methods, authority, and timeline to raise and utilize it. The traditional budget, despite its simplicity, potential for budget control, and financial compliance, was not effective in promoting efficient public planning and nurturing a results-oriented accountability through the spending of public resources (Wildavsky, 2006; Shah and Shen, 2007). Budget reforms have established the necessary linkage between availability of

[3] FC 15 elaborated upon three themes—fiscal rules, the public financial management system, and independent institutional developments like fiscal councils—to bring India's fiscal architecture up to 21st-century international standards.

resources and activities to be carried out by making explicit the results that will be produced.

Since its American debut in 1949, following the report of the Hoover Commission,[4] the performance budget has become integral part of budget reform processes, and many countries have refurbished their budgeting systems by focusing on performance orientation (Curristine and Flynn, 2013). Improving expenditure prioritization, efficient implementation, and effectiveness in achieving results are crucial features of a performance-oriented budget. Practising countries' experiences show that, despite setbacks, budgetary reforms always include performance-based principles in core processes of budgeting (Schick, 2003).

In performance budgeting, information about the outputs, results, and/or impacts of public policies are used systematically to determine the allocation of funds towards those policies (Dowens et al., 2017). The use of such performance information was considered to enhance transparency in programme formulation, service delivery, quality of service, and accountability in public administration (OECD Recommendation on Budgetary Governance, 2015). Comparable indicators of outputs and impact in different sectors with expenditure implications help us understand how to design and cost such programmes efficiently within the available resources. Thus, measurement of performance information for various inputs, outputs with regard to quantity and quality of goods and services, efficiency in determining unit cost of outputs, service quality, and outcomes in the form of progress in achieving programme objectives become essential (McGill, 2001; Wang, 1999).

While it was sought to improve decision-making by providing better quality of information on performance of agencies and programmes, actual practice varies across countries (OECD Report, 2007; Schick, 2014). In some OECD countries, performance information is used for reporting purposes, and in some others it plays an important role for resource-allocation decisions (Shah and Shen, 2007). As compared to the performance-informed budgeting system, determining spending level

[4] In 1949 the Hoover Commission called for alterations in budget classification consonant with the management orientation. It recommended the adoption of a budget based on functions, activities, and projects. A new label, performance budget, came into being in this report. Another term, programme budgeting, was also used in the task force report attached this Commission.

exclusively based on quantified results, implying allocation of resources directly linked to units of performance, is argued to have more chance of success (Robinson, 2007).

13.3.2 Performance and Outcome Budget in India

The performance budget was introduced in India in 1968 following the recommendations of the first Administrative Reform Commission. Achievement of plan programmes was the dominant political concern for adopting this innovation. The objectives were to provide a link between public spending and physical targets and to achieve the development plan objectives. The performance budget was adopted as a supplemental instrument to the main budget and was limited to only planned departmental programmes. It was expected that this supplemental system would evolve into a sophisticated system of programme budgeting (Cutt, 1972).

The experience of the performance budget shows that it did not have any discernible influence on expenditure management by linking the budgeting decisions to performance indicators (Premchand, 2008)—it became a routine exercise, with some historical performance information but without any perceptible influence on budgetary decisions. The performance indicators derived from general objectives of departmental schemes and projects were inadequate in linking the financial budget to the performance budget in terms of physical targets (Toye, 1981). The weakness of the performance budget was acknowledged when the government decided to adopt another version of the performance budget, called the Outcome Budget, in 2005.[5]

The objective of adopting the outcome budget was to bring in changes and make a transition from the traditional line-item system to clearly defined outcomes of all government programmes.[6] The outcome budget

[5] In the Guideline for outcome budget 2006–07, the Ministry of Finance (MOF) elaborated on a need for establishing linkage between the financial budget and the performance budget, improving target-setting, going beyond the intermediate physical 'outputs' to measurable outcomes, which are the end objectives of state intervention.

[6] Outcome budget, Ministry of Finance, 2007–08 described the outcome budget as an endeavour to convert the 'outlays' into 'outcome' by planning the expenditure, fixing appropriate targets, and quantifying the deliverables in each scheme.

involved several features, including defining measurable outcomes, standardizing the unit costs of delivery of services, benchmarking standards, capacity building for attaining the requisite administrative capacity, ensuring necessary funding, effective monitoring and evaluation, and making the system far more inclusive through the participation of the community and the stakeholders (Department of Expenditure, 2007). The outcome budget continued to be supplemental to the main budget being prepared by all the departments separately and presented in the budget session. The objective was to influence the budgetary decisions through use of performance information.

Some of the important features of outcome budget and their implications are described here.

- **Emphasis on quantifiable outcomes:** The objective of achieving outcomes did not match with managerial strategy to build an adequate set of performance indicators for programmes and link them with resource-allocation decisions (Jena, 2016). While outcomes tend to remain beyond the direct control of the managers, difficult to quantify and use as a costing basis, outputs in terms of goods and services produced should not be replicated mindlessly without relating to departmental goals and objectives (Shah and Shen, 2007). The departmental outcome budgets showed considerable ambiguity while presenting outputs and outcomes, and for many programmes general objectives are shown as outcomes.
- **Measuring unit cost of delivery of services:** While preparing the budget, funding requirements are supposed to be calculated as a function of the quantity of services to be delivered using the unit cost of each unit. Despite placing faith in the unit cost approach, the guidelines to the outcome budget did not deliberate upon how to estimate and use unit costs, and alternative costing mechanisms, where it is difficult to estimate.
- **Centrally sponsored schemes (CSS) and performance framework**: Budgeting and monitoring the progress in expenditures and achievements under CSS have remained difficult due to the involvement of various layers of agencies, starting from central departments up to the lower-level implementing agencies in the states. Delays in implementation, utilization of available funds, issues relating to

states' share of funding, accountability arrangements, and information on achievements remained crucial issues in this stretched performance chain, with gaps in information.

- **Monitoring mechanism**: While the outcome budget was intended to effectively monitor and evaluate the results achieved, no credible system was evolved. While a section in the outcome budget was designated to show performance achieved in the past year, given the ambiguity in performance indicators it was not considered to be credible. The performance monitoring and evaluation system (PMES) adopted in 2009 to measure performance across all schemes and projects remained outside the ambit of the outcome budget. While the PMES met its end after a few years of paperwork, it diluted the status of the outcome budget.
- **Supplemental nature:** Political concerns and value judgements involved in resource trade-offs have remained important factors in India. The formulation of result indicators derived from various schemes run by the departments, was an *ex post facto* action and remained disconnected from resource-allocation decisions.
- **Plan/non-plan distinction in budgets**: Over the decades this created complexities in budget planning, with a tendency to inflate the plan size every year. This dichotomy has resulted in a fragmented view of resource allocation to various sectors. The removal of plan/non-plan distinctions with the closure of the Planning Commission, while creating an enabling environment, was not effectively utilized.

The outcome budget could be considered one of the crucial innovations that showed the intent of the government to improve the performance orientation in the budgetary system. The experience in many other countries showed that mere adoption should not be believed to incorporate the principles in the core processes of budgeting (Schick, 2014). The transition from performance budget to outcome budget did not learn from the contribution or problems faced in previous innovations. The government changed the format of the outcome budget again in 2017, opting for a more compact version called the output–outcome framework (OOF). Pursuing one round of reforms followed by another indicates that performance is a compelling idea based on which public resources should be spent.

13.3.3 Output–Outcome Framework for Schemes

The government adopted the output–outcome framework (OOF) from the year 2017–18 to bring the public schemes and projects under a unified framework by discontinuing preparation of ministry-wise outcome budgets. The OOF covers major central sector (CS) schemes and centrally sponsored schemes (CSS), with an outlay of Rs 500 crore or more. The CS/CSS schemes form the primary mode of government service delivery to beneficiaries, covering approximately 40 per cent of the central government's expenditure. It contains financial outlays, outputs, and outcomes of the schemes similar to the outcome budgets. NITI Aayog prepares this document in consultation with the implementing ministries and departments. The office of the Development Monitoring and Evaluation Office (DMEO) of NITI Aayog prepares the Output–Outcome Monitoring Framework (OOMF) containing measurable indicators for achievement of scheme objectives. The DMEO developed an online OOMF dashboard which helps in monitoring of the budgetary outlays, targets, and progress against them. However, use of this dashboard is limited to only government departments.

The OOF has the unique advantage of being a unified document of high-value CS and CSS, unlike the myriad outcome budgets of individual departments. The preparation of OOF by a professional body like the DMEO, in consultation with implementing ministries and departments, is considered to add value to the whole process and reduce subjectivity in targeted outcomes. A unified document makes it easy to refer to result expectations along with the outlays.

While the format of the outcome budget took a consolidated outlook, the basic issues relating to formulation of performance indicators for the schemes, the costing basis, and determining the quality of public services more or less remain. The crucial aspect of any supplemental device lies in its utility to influence spending decisions in the budget. Like its predecessor, the OOF suffers from lack of public scrutiny, and its impact on budget decisions cannot be verified. The achievement of outputs and outcomes, which are supposedly provided in the OOMF framework of the DMEO, are not in the public domain. The commitment and ownership of departments to this document is also not clear, as it does not cover the whole expenditure.

13.4 Building a Medium-Term Perspective in Budget Management: Indian Experience

The medium-term expenditure framework (MTEF) is considered one of the most popular budget innovations in recent times and has many takers in both the developed and the developing world. The medium-term perspective, as compared to the short-range horizon of an annual budget, was the persuasive reason behind the rapid expansion of this instrument. The MTEF reflects two major preoccupations of post-fiscal crisis budget reforms—fiscal consolidation and expenditure prioritization. It is a relevant budgetary institution to facilitate adherence to the fiscal rule targets as it provides a framework for taking budgetary decisions over a three- to five-year period. As the budgeting system complies with the predetermined fiscal targets and consequent expenditure constraints under the fiscal rules, a medium-term expenditure perspective of the policy decisions taken in the budget becomes helpful.

13.5 MTEF: Linking Policy, Planning, and Budgeting

Implementation of the MTEF is known to improve the relationship between policymaking, planning, and budget implementation (World Bank, 1998). The expectation of improved performance from the implementation of the MTEF is due to its impact on budget quality and budget credibility (World Bank, 2013). The MTEF helps to reduce the ever-increasing tendency of expanding annual spending plans based on overestimation of revenues. It counters incrementalism by emphasizing sector priorities based on objectives and policies laid down by the government. It is expected to become instrumental in facilitating efficient resource-allocation decisions and addressing fiscal imbalances emerging from politically induced resource trade-offs. If spending departments adopt a multi-year mode when designing and costing their programmes, this can help increase the predictability of the flow of resources (PEFA, 2016), improving performance.

The shift in focus from controlling the expenditure to pragmatic spending plans and achievement of results commensurate with objectives stems from the following features of MTEF.

- **Top-down resource envelope:** Linking policy, planning, and budgeting is conceptualized by determining the resource envelope available to the government and allocation in line with priorities in a multi-year budgeting framework. The top-down resource envelope is estimated through a macro fiscal framework, which captures comprehensively all resources, internal and external. The resources available to the government become the budget constraint that guides policymaking and establishes resource-allocation trade-offs across sectors in order to achieve sector policy goals.
- **Bottom-up estimate of the current and medium-term costs:** The MTEF involves preparing sector studies consisting of strategies for the sectors and the estimated costs of existing and new programmes. The expenditure implications of the sector policies are estimated using costing techniques.
- **Output budgeting:** The MTEF needs output budgeting to build sector objectives and strategies to achieve them, and to estimate cost implications in the medium term.
- **Resource allocation:** In situations where the needs far exceed the available resources, the MTEF can provide a mechanism for allocation of limited resources between sectors, and between specific activities within sectors, by listing activities according to priority. The MTEF can be used to highlight the opportunity costs of various policies and programmes that need to be foregone if additional resources are to be allocated to a particular programme.

The countries adopting medium-term approaches do not practise a standard form of MTEF. The MTEF is often considered as an umbrella framework with interconnected frameworks or sequences of stages (Castro and Dorotinsky, 2008; World Bank, 2013).

- A medium-term fiscal framework (MTFF) constitutes specifying a top-down aggregate resource envelope and allocation to major categories of expenditure items. It shows the fiscal stance of the government through a set of integrated medium-term macroeconomic and fiscal targets and projections.
- The medium-term budgeting framework (MTBF), the more popular variant of the existing medium-term frameworks, develops

further by including bottom-up resource requirements prepared by the spending departments and reconciling with the resource envelope available with the government. In this framework, budget estimates for individual spending departments are indicated for the medium term, and resource allocation follows strategic priorities.

- The medium-term performance framework (MTPF) takes this process further by shifting the focus from inputs to outputs. This is basically the output–outcome-type budget in which performance indicators can be worked out for each sector's programmes, and through them sector outputs defined.

13.6 Experience of the Spread of the MTEF

The MTEF gained popularity in developing countries during the early nineties, with the World Bank and other donor agencies supporting it in their poverty-eradication programmes. The early experience with the implementation of MTEFs in developing countries, particularly in Africa, showed several weaknesses (Le Houerou and Taliercio, 2002; Homes and Evans, 2003; Brumby, 2008; Schiavo-Campo, 2009). The initial wave of MTEFs in developing countries were ineffective in improving budgetary outcomes due to a neglect of institutional and capacity considerations. The MTEF was found to be ineffective in influencing annual budgets due to lack of political ownership, often resulting in unrealistic projections. The basic objectives of achieving fiscal discipline, setting priorities in resource allocation, predictability in fund flows, and efficiency gain in budgetary operations were not clearly visible.

However, applying a medium-term perspective to annual budgets has persisted since the late nineties, despite initial discouraging experiences. The Australian experience of using the MTEF consistently to plan and finance spending initiatives, as well as positive experiences from other industrial countries, encouraged its acceptance (Brumby and Hemming, 2013). It is considered an effective budgetary instrument to successfully address fiscal policy challenges and modernize the budget planning process. While its impact on efficiency gains has not been conclusive, the cross-country data showed strong evidence of promoting fiscal discipline (World Bank, 2013).

13.7 Emergence of the Medium-Term Perspective and the MTEF in India

13.7.1 The Planning Process and the Medium-Term Perspective

The five-year development planning was conceptually close to the theme of the MTEF as the plan (investment) and non-plan expenditure (spending on existing programmes and recurrent expenditure) was planned based on projected resources (Thimmaiah, 1984). The plan–budget linkage, however, was not smooth, as planned goals, objectives, outputs, and resources allocated to achieve them were not adequately integrated into the annual budgets (Premchand, 1983; Planning Commission, Expert Committee on Expenditure Management, 2011; Jena, 2016). The plan/non-plan distinction led to expanding the plans beyond the resource limits and neglect of existing assets (Ministry of Finance, 2008). The abolition of the Planning Commission in 2014 formally put to rest any misgivings regarding the scope for a perceived multi-year budget planning within the five-year development planning process.

13.7.2 Medium-Term Framework under the Fiscal Rules

The FRBM Act, adopted in 2003 by the union government and by states in 2005, provided an opportunity to establish a medium-term perspective through the stipulated requirement of presenting a medium-term fiscal policy (MTFP). The MTFP contained projections of fiscal variables like revenue deficit, fiscal deficit, and outstanding liabilities relative to GDP as rolling three-year targets. The government also has to present a macroeconomic statement along with the MTFP. While the MTFP was expected to progressively develop into a medium-term framework, it remained limited to the projection of the target fiscal variables, facilitating tracking of macro numbers rather than any expenditure planning.

The MTFP, laid down under the fiscal rules, can be compared to the basic level of the medium-term expenditure framework (MTEF). It does not help in preparing the top-down resource envelope based on a medium-term macro-fiscal framework and to allocating resources to major spending categories. It is not an adequate document to assess future years' fiscal impact of the government policies. FC 13, while suggesting strengthening the MTFP, recommended revising the existing MTFP statement to provide a detailed framework containing three-year estimates of revenues and expenditures, with detailed break-down of major constituent items.

13.7.3 Attempt to Introduce a More Structured MTEF

The Government of India introduced MTEF in 2012 following the recommendations of the FC 13. The MTEF thus adopted was designed keeping broad functional categories of expenditure in consideration. It contained estimates of expenditure commitments in various sectors, namely education, health, rural development, energy, subsidies, pensions etc., and expenditure commitments are shown separately for revenue and capital expenditure. The MTEF projected expenditure indicators for three years in a rolling manner and contained descriptions relating to the assumptions while making the projections. This initial effort, however, fell short of features required in a structured MTEF and had limited impact on budget management. The MTEF introduced in 2012, combined with the already existing MTFP, could be considered as close to what is called a 'forecasting MTEF' (Schiavo-Campo, 2009).

- The assumptions relating to projections did not provide a clear insight into the derivation of the numbers, casting doubts on their utility. It was prescribed that the projections should be made taking into account the expenditure commitments of policy changes, contingent liabilities, and grants given for capital assets. Leaving aside the committed expenditures like salary, pension, and interest payments, where guidance has been given for their estimation and projection, the assumptions behind the projections of spending items were not clear.
- The document did not elaborate on the linkages between spending commitments and policy decisions.

- The projections presented after the budget show a strong annual budget bias, where the spending on development and capital outlay becomes residual after meeting the committed spending.
- The MTEF, structured around aggregate spending variables of the departments, did not look like an outcome of prioritized spending preferences revealed by the departments.

13.7.4 The Revised Version of the MTEF

The Government of India revised the format of the MTEF following the inputs provided by the Expenditure Management Commission (EMC). The MTEF was expanded consistent with the Demand for Grants of the expenditure budget and contained demand-wise projections of revenue and capital expenditure for the two outward years (MTEF Circular, 2016–17).[7] The initial projections were taken from the ministries and departments and a suitable growth factor was used to work out projections. The objective was to use these projected data in the interaction between the departments and the Ministry of Finance.

- The MTEF revision plan showed positive intent. In the revised projection exercise, the role of the administrative departments has been acknowledged and a scope for policy dialogue was opened up using the MTEF.
- This exercise was more suited for expenditure control and served the purposes of complying with fiscal rules. The medium-term projections of line items and an aggregate view taken at the Ministry of Finance level facilitate expenditure control.
- The MTEF continues to be a work in progress. It did not clarify on the role of spending departments preparing a medium-term sector plan, negotiate for resources for the budget based on this plan, or prioritize programmes based on the spending limit.

[7] Demand for Grants of the budget document shows the estimates of expenditure from the Consolidated Fund, included in the annual financial statement and required to be voted upon in the Parliament.

The preparation of the MTEF has been paused since 2019–20. It needs to make a comeback as it has the ability to provide a robust indication of resource allocation to the ministries and departments, to enable them to prioritize their spending plan according to the requirements for on-going and newly initiated programmes. The bottom-up expenditure programmes formulated by the line ministries based on the fiscal space provided through a top-down approach will ensure ownership and facilitate better achievement.

13.8 Looking Ahead to Opportunities from Budget Innovations

13.8.1 Taking Decisions by Utilizing Performance Indicators in Outcome Budget

There is no standard form of performance budget followed by all countries. Some countries have attempted to establish an explicit linkage between resources allocated to performance measures in specific sectors. Most of the OECD countries have followed a budgeting system in which performance indicators along with other information on economic, political, and policy priorities are used to make informed decisions on resource allocation (Curristine and Flynn, 2013). Developed countries like Australia, New Zealand, Sweden, and the United Kingdom have adopted an output or outcome-type budgeting system. Developing countries like Malaysia, Chile, and Thailand have developed performance-informed budgets targeting outputs. The important aspect of these efforts has been to develop realistic performance indicators to make resource-allocation decisions and evaluate performance.

Having come a long way with the performance budget, and reviving its spirit in the form of outcome budget and output–outcome framework, the importance and requirements of a result-oriented budgeting system have been acknowledged. Strengthening the management process geared towards developing a performance information base, appropriate and acceptable indicators are crucial in this context. Although accurately measuring the diversity of the government's activities is complex, it is not impossible. FCs 14 and 15 have given emphasis to developing appropriate performance indicators to improve the outcome budget. Budgetary achievements need measuring performance indicators.

Deriving cost information for provision of services incrementally and using them carefully while developing programmes is another crucial requirement to develop performance indicators. Although the regular budget continues to be managed on departmental lines, the unit of legislative appropriation has been the major function of the spending departments. In addition to developing unit costs for services where standard unit costs can be derived, existing line items can be analysed to develop rough cost data for unit cost analysis.

The crucial factor that would enable the outcome budget to emerge as an effective system in India is the ability to utilize the performance information in budget decisions relating to programme formulation and resource allocation. Performance information, along with financial and other information relating to the programmes, should be used in the budget decisions regarding resource allocation. Poor results can be analysed for likely weaknesses so that measures can be taken to strengthen them.

At the subnational level, the outcome budget has remained a routine exercise. Given their functional responsibilities spanning over a vast expanse of social and economic sectors, there is compelling reason for the states to plan and design public spending programmes efficiently. It is important for the states to put in place practical arrangements and develop capacity to prepare performance indicators in different sectors and utilize them in resource-allocation decisions.

13.8.2 Renewing the MTEF to Widen the Horizon on Spending Decisions

Successful implementation of the MTEF requires credible annual budgets, accurate medium-term macroeconomic and demographic projections, established fiscal objectives and rules, and a comprehensive and unified top-down budget process (Harris et al., 2013). The Ministry of Finance has to prepare a robust estimate of revenue consistent with the macroeconomic outlook and provide expenditure ceilings. The macroeconomic and fiscal management in India has been improving after the disruptions caused by COVID-19 and resultant volatility in the international economic environment. The credibility of the budget, assessed by comparing revenue and expenditure out-turns with budgeted variables, should be strengthened to provide an improved basis for a medium-term perspective. Fiscal rules will also define the stance of the government in the medium term with regard to key variables like deficit, tax, and debt, putting restraint on the fiscal behaviour of the government.

The MTEF should move towards adopting the features of the medium-term budgeting framework (MTBF). The core theme of this should be to improve predictability of flow of funds, reflect the future costs of policy decisions adopted in the annual budget through multi-year revenue and expenditure estimates, and improve service delivery mechanism. Distinction between ongoing and newly initiated programmes and providing higher fiscal space to high-priority programmes in a politically influenced resource trade-off will be crucial in this context. Spending departments have to overcome the conflicting pressures to prepare a sectoral plan and prioritize within the resource limit.

The MTBF can be taken forward using output-type budgeting with performance indicators to prepare what is known as medium-term performance framework (MTPF). This will shift the focus from inputs to outputs and to measuring performance. Although the MTEF does not specifically need a performance budget and can be adopted in a cash-based line item budgeting environment, promoting results and encouraging better performance from the sector programmes are always considered as improvements in the system.

13.9 Concluding Observations

The budgetary innovations in the Indian context continue to be a work in progress and provide opportunities to benefit from the changes. With regard to improving the performance orientation of the budgeting system, significant care needs to be taken to develop credible performance information—result indicators and cost data—and integrate them in the budget decisions. These issues assume significance given the fact that the outcome budget in India has more or less remained outside public scrutiny. The recent changes in the form of output–outcome framework need to be integrated in the scheme of the departments to give an overarching performance-management system.

The medium-term expenditure framework (MTEF) in India needs to shed the mechanical approach to make it an efficient budgetary instrument. The projection of expenditure variables in the existing process does not sufficiently inform the budgetary implications of policy changes. The need for investment and development of human and physical infrastructure often leads governments, both at central and subnational levels, to plan more than they can support. The government needs to strengthen the MTEF process to establish a hard budget constraint, improve the predictability in the flow of resources to ministries and departments, and improve the strategic priorities in resource allocation.

Budgetary institutions play a crucial role in establishing an accountable governance system and guard against fiscal mismanagement. Innovations in the budgeting system should not be treated as isolated activities. The complexity and interrelated nature of public financial management demands improvements in supportive machineries for the success of any initiative. While the fiscal rules provided the initial drive for a MTFF, its effectiveness requires a credible MTBF system. A better coordination and consultative process in the parliamentary system of democracy in India is required in the budget-reform process.

References

Brumby, Jim (2008). 'MTEFs: Does the Walk Match the Talk? From Diagnosis to Action Workshop', World Bank.

Brumby, James, and Hemming, Richard (2013). 'Medium-term Expenditure Frameworks', in Richard Allen, Richard Hemming, and Barry H. Potter (eds), *The International Handbook of public Financial Management*, Palgrave Macmillan, 219–236.

Campos, Ed, and Pradhan, Sanjay (1996). 'Budgetary Institutions and Expenditure Outcomes: Binding Governments to Fiscal Performance'. Policy research working paper 1646, World Bank, Washington, DC.

Castro, I., and Dorotinsky, W. (2008). 'Medium-term Expenditure Frameworks: Demystifying and Unbundling the Concepts', World Bank, Washington, DC.

Curristine, Teresa, and Flynn, Suzanne (2013). 'In Search of Results: Strengthening Public Sector Performance', in Marco Cangiano, Teresa Curristine, and Michel

Lazzre (eds), *Public Financial Management and Its Emerging Architecture*, International Monetary Fund, 238–240.

Cutt, J. A. (1972). 'Programme Budgeting in Developing Countries: Its Application and Relevance in the Context of National Planning', *Public Finance/Finances Publiques*, 27.

Department of Expenditure, Ministry of Finance (2007). Guideline for Preparation of Outcome Budget 2007–08, Government of India.

Downes Ronnie, Moretti, Delphine, and Nicol, Scherie (2017). 'Budgeting and Performance in the European Union: A Review by the OECD in the Context of EU Budget Focused on Results', *OECD Journal on Budgeting*, 1.

Fölscher, Alta (2007). 'Budget Methods and Practices', in Anwar Shah (ed.), *Budgeting and Budgetary Institutions*, World Bank, 109–136.

Hagen, Jürgen von (2007). 'Budgeting Institutions for Better Fiscal Performance', in Anwar Shah (ed.), *Budgeting and Budgetary Institutions*,World Bank, 27–51.

Hemming, Richard (2013). 'The Macroeconomic Framework for Managing Public Finances', in Richard Allen, Richard Hemming, and Barry H. Potter (eds.), *The International Handbook of Public Financial Management*, Palgrave Macmillan, 219–236.

Holmes, Malcolm, and Evans, Alison (2003). 'A Review of Experience in Implementing Medium-term Expenditure Frameworks in a PRSP Context: A Synthesis of Eight Country Studies', Overseas Development Institute, London.

Houerou, Philippe Le, and Taliercio, Robert (2002). 'Medium-term Expenditure Frameworks: From Concept to Practice. Preliminary Lessons from Africa', Africa region working paper series 28, World Bank.

Jena, Pratap Ranjan (2010). 'India: Public Expenditure and Financial Accountability'. Public Financial Management Performance Assessment Report, National Institute of Public Finance and Policy, New Delhi.

Jena, Pratap Ranjan (2016). 'Reform Initiatives in the Budgeting System in India', *Public Budgeting & Finance*, Wiley-Blackwell, 36(1), 106–124.

McGill, Ronald (2001). 'Performance budgeting', *International Journal of Public Sector Management*, 14(5), 376–90.

Ministry of Finance (2008). 'Economic Survey 2007–08', government of India.

Ministry of Finance (2016). Medium-term Expenditure Framework Circular 2016-17. Government of India.

OECD (2007). 'Performance Budgeting in OECD Countries', OECD publishing, Paris.

OECD (2015). Recommendation of the Council on Budgetary Governance, Public Governance and Territorial Development Directorate, OECD Publishing, Paris.

PEFA (2016). Public Financial Management Performance Measurement Framework, PEFA Secretariat, Washington, DC.

Planning Commission (2011). 'Report of the High Level Expert Committee on Efficient Management of Public Expenditure'. Government of India.

Premchand, A. (1983). 'Government Budgeting and Expenditure Controls: Theory and practice', *International Monetary Fund*, Washington DC.

Premchand, A. (2005), *Controlling Government Spending: the Ethos, Ethics, and Economics of Expenditure Management*, Oxford University Press.

Premchand, A. (2008). *Trapped in The Comfort Zone of Denial: 50 Years of Expenditure Management in India*. National Institute of Public Finance and Policy, New Delhi.

Robinson, M. (2007). *Performance Budgeting: Linking Funding and Results*, International Monetary Fund, Palgrave Macmillan.

Schiavo-Campo, Salvatore (2009). 'Potemkin Villages: "The" Medium-term Expenditure Framework in Developing Countries', *Public Budgeting Finance*, Summer.

Schick, Allen (2003). 'The Role of Fiscal Rules in Budgeting', *OECD Journal on Budgeting*, 3(3), 7–34.

Schick, Allen (2014). 'The Metamorphoses of Performance Budgeting', *OECD Journal on Budgeting*, 2013(2), 49–79.

Shah, Anwar, and Shen, Chunli (2007). 'A Primer on Performance Budgeting', in Anwar Shah (ed.), *Budgeting and Budgetary Institutions*, World Bank, Washington, DC, 137–178.

Thimmaiah, G. (1984), 'Budget Innovation in India: An Evaluation', in A. Premchand and Jesse Burkhead (eds), *Comparative International Budgeting and Finance*, Transaction Books, New Brunswick, NJ and London, 159–173.

Toye, John (1981). 'Public Expenditure Reforms in India and Malaysia', *Development and Change*, SAGE, 12(1), 121–144.

Wang, Xiao-Hu (1999). 'Conditions to Implement Outcome-oriented Performance Budgeting: Some Empirical Evidence', *Journal of Public Budgeting, Accounting, and Financial Management*, 11(4), 533–52.

Wildavsky, Aaron (2006). *Budgeting and Governing*, New Brunswick, NJ: Transaction Books.

Wildavsky, Aaron, and Caiden, Naomi (1997). *The New Politics of the Budgetary Process*, Longman.

World Bank (1998). *Public Expenditure Management Handbook*, Washington, DC.

World Bank (2013). *Beyond the Annual Budget: Review of Global Experience with Medium-term Expenditure Frameworks*, Washington, DC.

14

Economic Valuation of Wetland Ecosystem Services

Current Status and the Way Forward

L. Venkatachalam

14.1 Introduction

The United Nations (UN) declared 2021–2030 a *Decade of Ecosystem Restoration* to encourage governments to initiate massive efforts to restore and protect the environment across the globe.[1] The Third UN Environment Assembly passed a key and comprehensive resolution to protect 'water-related' ecosystems, and subsequently developed a Framework for Freshwater Ecosystem Management[2] to help governments manage freshwater ecological systems.[3] Of all water-related ecosystems, wetlands act as the most productive (Ghermandi et al., 2008) but they are subjected to major anthropogenic threats such as pollution, encroachment, environmentally harmful tourism, and over-exploitation (Bassi et al., 2014). India's Wetlands (Conservation and Management) Rules 2017 prescribes various measures that include preparing a 'brief document', determining 'wise-use' and ecological characteristics, preparing a list of activities for regulation and permission, and developing an integrated management plan (IMP). One of the reasons for the sorry state of wetlands is the lack of information about the value of

[1] https://www.iucn.org/theme/nature-based-solutions/initiatives/decade-ecosystem-restoration.

[2] https://www.unep.org/news-and-stories/story/wetlands-and-biodiversity-theme-world-wetlands-day-2020.

[3] https://www.unep.org/resources/publication/framework-freshwater-ecosystem-management?_ga=2.90012828.665537988.1624694456-1775488713.1624694456.

L. Venkatachalam, *Economic Valuation of Wetland Ecosystem Services* In: *Fiscal Policy and Public Financial Management*. Edited by: Pinaki Chakraborty and K R Shanmugam, Oxford University Press.
 DOI: 10.1093/9780198930464.003.0014

their ecosystem services (hereafter, ESs). The Ramsar Strategic Plan 2009–15 states that a key driving force for the continued deterioration and loss of wetlands is the scarcity of information on the economic value of wetlands and their ESs; therefore, 'to ensure wise use of wetlands, it is important that we know the values, both costs and benefits, of our wetlands resources relating to the services provided' (Whiteoak and Binney, 2016: 1). In the absence of such information, we need to deploy scientifically established economic valuation methods to generate *valid* and *reliable* information for policy purposes. In this chapter, we will review the current status of the economic valuation of wetland ecosystems, the issues involved in generating such values, and how to strengthen future valuation so that governments can formulate evidence-based policies for an efficient, equitable, and sustainable management of wetlands.

14.2 Wetland Ecosystem Services

The Ramsar Convention defines wetlands as areas of marsh, fen, peatland, or water, whether natural or artificial, permanent or temporary, with water that is static or flowing, fresh, brackish, or salt, including areas of marine water, the depth of which at low tide does not exceed six metres. They include riparian and coastal zones adjacent to the wetlands, and islands or bodies of marine water deeper than six metres at low tide lying within the wetlands. The Convention classifies wetlands into 42 types, which fall under one of the following three broad categories: (1) inland wetlands, (2) marine/coastal wetlands, and (3) human-made wetlands. Therefore, wetlands broadly include the following types of water bodies: *marine*, which includes coastal wetlands such as coastal lagoons, rocky shores, and coral reefs; *estuarine*, which includes deltas, tidal marshes, and mangrove swamps; *lacustrine*, consisting of wetlands associated with lakes; *riverine*, which includes wetlands along rivers and streams; *palustrine*, consisting of marshes, swamps, and bogs; and *human-made wetlands* such as reservoirs, fish ponds, flooded mineral workings, aquaculture, permanently or temporarily inundated agricultural land (e.g. rice paddies), salt pans, reservoirs, gravel pits, sewage farms, and canals (Russi et al., 2013). Globally, wetlands occupy an area of more than 1,280 million hectares. Across the globe, inland wetlands occupy approximately 9.5 million km^2 (i.e. about 6.5 per cent of the geographical area of the Earth), and coastal wetlands 12.8 million km^2 (Finlayson et al., 1999). However, IPBES (2019) found that around 85 per cent of wetlands across the globe have been lost, mainly due to anthropogenic factors; when wetlands are lost, the species unique to the local environment are also lost. Thus, at the global level, the wetlands as natural capital or as 'term-deposit' are declining over a long period, resulting in continuous loss of welfare to the people.

Wetlands as a non-reproducible natural capital (Barbier, 2011a) generate highly valuable ESs that are utilized in numerous consumption and production activities in the economy. Nature and human wellbeing are inextricably interlinked and the ESs 'represent an instrumental value of nature as a means to enhance human wellbeing' (Schroter et al., 2021: 290). Wetland-based ESs are a variety of goods and services originating from water bodies such as marshes, swamps, bogs, and fens (Mitsch and Gosselink, 2015), which both directly and indirectly contribute to human wellbeing (MEA, 2005). The ESs are classified into: (1) *provisioning services*; (2) *regulating services*; (3) *cultural services*; and (4) *supporting services* (TEEB, 2010).[4]

Most of the wetland ESs are 'non-marketed' in nature (Costanza et al., 1997). Since they are extracted mostly in informal settings, especially in developing countries, the value of the existing ESs extracted as well as the value of the ESs lost due to depletion and degradation are not adequately captured by any formal institutions in the economy. The lack of relevant information on the benefits and costs of the ESs leads to 'policy failure' in the area of wetland protection and management. Addressing such a failure requires generating adequate information about the social benefits and social costs resulting from changes in the non-market ecosystem services at different points in time. As the United Nations World Water Development Report 2021 states, recognizing, quantifying, and expressing the value of water, and incorporating the value into decision-making, are important in achieving sustainable and equitable water management (United Nations, 2021). Thus, the economic valuation

[4] The supporting services provide fundamental support to the first three services. Since supporting services enhance the other three, they are not subjected to economic valuation due to a potential double-counting problem.

exercise helps us generate useful information for various purposes, including policymaking.

14.3 Economic Valuation: Current Status

Economic valuation is a difficult, controversial, and highly challenging task (see Barbier, 2011b). It is difficult because the value assigned should capture the 'true value' of the non-market good being valued. The true value equals the market price of that good in case it was bought and sold in a competitive market. Since we don't have prices from fully developed markets for most non-market goods and services, whether the estimated monetary values reflect the true value or not will have to be validated through different scientific yardsticks—a difficult task. Similarly, economic values estimated especially through the *stated preference methods* are potentially affected by various *biases* and *errors* if the preferences are not elicited scientifically (Venkatachalam, 2004). Economic valuation is also controversial because many critics argue that the valuation exercise tries to put the ecosystem services—which are otherwise invaluable and incommensurable and which cannot be measured in a single monetary unit—into a 'price jacket'. In Section 14.4, we will critically review a limited number of empirical studies dealing with wetland-based ecosystem services so that we can understand the progress made in valuing wetland ESs, analyse some of the pertinent issues of non-market valuation of wetland ecosystem services, and suggest a way forward.

14.4 Empirical Studies

Let us start with some of the global studies. Costanza et al. (1997) pioneered in empirically estimating the economic value of 17 ESa delivered by 16 biomes (including wetlands) using the *benefit-transfer method (BTM)*—a method used to transfer already estimated values through *meta-analysis* (Woodward and Wui, 2001) to another wetland or a group of wetlands for which value estimation is required. The estimated annual global value (1997 value) of these services ranges between US$16 trillion and US$54 trillion, with the average value being US$33 trillion.

Wetland goods and services contributed US$14.9 trillion per year (minimum), which is equivalent to 45 per cent of the value of the then global ESs. This implies that the largest contribution to total global ecosystem values comes from wetlands. Though this is a pioneering study, environmental economists criticized it for not being theoretically and methodologically sound. Later on, Costanza et al. (2014) updated the original values based on additional information on the improved biome area as well as on comprehensive estimates of unit values (per hectare values). The revised global ecosystem values for the year 2011 stood at US$145 trillion/year (assuming only unit values have changed) and US$125 trillion/year (assuming change in both unit value and the area of wetlands) (both estimated in 2007 US$ values). This value is three times greater than the original value, despite a considerable amount of loss of ESs (US$4.3–US$20.2 trillion/year) during the period from 1997 to 2011. It should be noted that along with the benefits, the loss of ESs increased significantly over the same time, posing a challenge to sustainable human wellbeing. The minimum monetary value (2007 US$ values) of natural wetland ESs stood at US$50.7 trillion per year, which is 41 per cent of the global value. The results from these studies highlight the importance of ESs in enhancing human wellbeing when compared to conventional economic factors (Costanza et al., 2017).

Another attempt to assess the economic value of global wetlands using the BTM was by Brander and Schuyt (2010), who obtained relevant information from 89 suitable wetland studies out of a total of 197. From the selected wetland studies, 246 separate observations of wetland values were extracted, based on several variables such as wetland type, income per capita, population density, and wetland size. The values were adjusted for price differentials in different countries using 'purchasing power parity' (PPP), an indicator used to allow for variability in the prices of commodities in a basket of commodities consumed in different regions. Wetlands were also divided into five types: mangroves, unvegetated sediment, salt/brackish marsh, freshwater marsh, and freshwater woodland. Next, a regression analysis was used to obtain the wetland value function which was used to predict the value of wetlands of policy interest with similar characteristics. Finally, the values were transferred to 3,800 wetland sites covering 63 million hectares around the world to estimate the global economic value of wetland benefits. The results revealed that the 'total economic value' (TEV) of 63 million hectares of wetland stood at US$3.4 billion per year. It was also found that with high population density with high demand for wetland goods and services, the wetlands in Asia generate the highest economic value at US$1.8 billion per year. Latin American wetlands generate the lowest value because of low population density. Similarly, sediment wetlands generate the highest values (US$374/hectare/year) followed by freshwater wooded wetlands (US$206/hectare/year) (Schuyt and Brander, 2004). The wetland values appear to be relatively small compared to the previous studies (e.g. Costanza et al., 2014), highlighting the challenge of estimating the 'true value'. Yet the results suggest that the economic valuation of wetlands can help policymakers across the globe to recognize their value as important natural capital, and consequently to make a collective effort towards their sustainable management globally.

In a similar exercise, de Groot et al. (2012) estimated the global ecosystem values of ten major biomes[5] including the values of wetland ecosystems using the BTM. They screened over 320 publications covering over 300 individual case studies conducted across the globe. Out of 1,350 value estimates generated from these case studies, 665 values found to have the required level of information were used for quantifying the global economic values of the selected biomes. As far as wetlands are concerned, the selected studies provided value data points for inland wetlands (25 per cent), coastal wetlands (mangroves) (21 per cent), tropical forests (14 per cent), and coral reefs (14 per cent). The geographic distribution of the valuation data was balanced over all continents: 28 per cent from Asia, 26 per cent from Africa, 14 per cent from Europe, 12 per cent from Latin America and the Caribbean, 12 per cent from North America, and 8 per cent from Oceania. For each biome, 22 ESs were considered for economic valuation. The total global values range between int$490/hectare/year (for open oceans) to almost $350,000/hectare/year (for coral reefs). While coastal wetlands deliver $193,845/hectare/year, the inland wetlands generate benefits worth $25,682/hectare/year. The issue is that this study considered only 22 ESs, whereas in a developing country like India, some of the wetlands generate more than 31 services

[5] The biomes are: open oceans, coral Reefs, coastal systems, coastal wetlands, inland wetlands, lakes, tropical forests, temperate forests, woodlands, and grasslands.

(Venkatachalam, 2022). The values of such locally important ESs are not getting reflected in the global values and, as a result, the values are considered underestimated as far as developing countries are concerned.

Davidson et al. (2019) recalculated the wetland values estimated by Costanza et al. (2014) using more wetland class areas and ESs of the forested wetlands. The recalculated values of the wetlands amounted to \$47.4 trillion/year (approximately \$3 trillion less than the value from Costanza et al., 2014) at 2011 prices, which is 43.5 per cent of the global values (\$109.1 trillion/year) originating from all-natural biomes. Out of \$47.4 trillion, natural coastal wetlands (occupying 15 per cent of the area of all-natural wetlands) delivered values worth \$20.4 trillion/year, which is 43.1 per cent of the global economic value of all-natural and coastal natural wetlands. Of all values from coastal wetlands, coral reefs contributed 49 per cent (i.e. i\$10.0 trillion/year). Inland natural wetlands delivered \$27.0 trillion/year at 2011 values, and the largest contributions (53 per cent) come from vegetated non-forested wetlands (non-forested peatlands, marshes, and swamps), accounting for \$14.5 trillion/year. On the other hand, \$7.1 trillion/year's worth of value (i.e. 27 per cent of inland wetland value) comes from forested wetlands. The lakes and rivers contributed \$5.5 trillion/year (20 per cent of inland wetland value). While the largest contributions from all the wetlands come from those in Asia (33.7 per cent of the regional total), North America (22.3 per cent), and Oceania (18.4 per cent), the largest values for 'inland wetlands' come from those in North America, Asia, and Europe. The authors estimate the value of the annual loss of ecosystem services as equivalent to \$47.8 million, with the largest loss coming from forested peatlands. The relative values of wetlands from different regions will have to be interpreted with caution because the condition of the wetlands, especially in developing countries, is poor. Estimating the maximum potential values that can be obtained when the wetlands are fully restored can not only increase the total contribution but also change the relative contributions of regional wetlands, significantly.

Most of the studies that we have reviewed here happen to use a macroeconomic valuation approach that broadly utilizes the BTM. Different studies have come out with different types of results, indicating that there are issues with the macroeconomic valuation methods. In the following section, we will review the studies from developing countries, with the aim of better understanding the issues involved in estimating the ecosystem values in a completely different context; one where social, economic, institutional, political, and ecological factors play a complex role in explaining the economic values.

14.5 Economic Valuation in the Developing Country Context

Korsgaard and Schou (2010) critically evaluated 27 valuation studies conducted in developing countries dealing with the *direct use values*, *indirect use-values*, and TEV of aquatic ecosystems. They found that the TEV of aquatic ecosystem services was in the range from US$30 to US$3,000/ha/year or US$10 to US$230/capita/year. The values were found to be scattered due to the valuation method used, the context of the study, and the type of ecosystem valued. The authors identify four main premises for the valuation of aquatic ecosystem services, namely acknowledging the assumptions of marginality and substitutability; using the TEV framework which includes both *use* and *non-use values*; defining spatial (geographical extent of the services and location of the beneficiaries), socioeconomic (different value of ESs to different groups of people), and temporal (change in the ESs and their values over a period) scale; and appropriately dealing with *uncertainty* (e.g. the nonlinear impact of ESs). These premises are important for strengthening valuation studies in developing countries. The authors conclude that, though economic valuation methods have some disadvantages, their wise use helps in raising awareness about the roles and values of ESs for decision-making and enhanced human wellbeing.

An empirical study related to coastal wetlands by Tan et al. (2018) demonstrates that the economic valuation of environmental improvements could make policymakers help design socially efficient coastal wetland restoration strategies. With a focus on mangrove area, biodiversity, and water quality, the study demonstrates how wetland restoration attributes, payment, and individual characteristics influence the public support for coastal wetland restoration in Ximen Island Special Marine Protected Area, China. The study employed the Choice Experiment (CE), and 201 randomly selected respondents in the wetland regions were interviewed, generating 1,608 observations. Though most of the respondents expressed positive and significant economic values from wetland restoration, the younger and better-educated respondents were more likely to provide support for the restoration. Moreover, regression results revealed that the size of the mangrove area was the most important attribute which needed to be considered in the restoration strategy design as it was highly valued by the respondents. The economic values derived for modest, moderate, and ambitious restoration measures were ¥302.30, ¥434.25, and ¥551.29 per respondent, respectively. The values could be used by policymakers to calculate the costs and benefits of the coastal wetland restoration projects or to calculate how much payment is needed for financing the projects. The values are useful in determining subsidy in case the costs exceed the benefits of restoration.

Lamsal et al. (2015) studied the socio-economic factors determining the participation of the local community in the conservation of the Ghodaghodi wetland in Nepal, as well as the value of ESs they derive from it. The study utilized a primary survey among 217 households in the wetland region and found that approximately 37 per cent of the indigenous households and 23 per cent of the migrant households received income from the wetland of between NPR5,000 (US$71) and NPR10,000 (US$142). The rest of the 4 per cent of indigenous households and 2 per cent of migrants received an income between NPR 10,000 (US$142) and 15,000 (US$214), respectively. On average, a sample household received annual benefits worth NPR4,379 (US$63), which is equivalent to 12.4 per cent of the households' gross annual income. It should be noted that the current income derived from the wetlands may be low due to poor quality of the wetlands. When the wetlands are restored, the income may go up considerably, which the study has not highlighted.

Baral et al. (2016) studied Jagadishpur Reservoir, a Ramsar Site, in Nepal to estimate its TEV. The study prioritized six values which include two *direct use values* (i.e. wetland goods consumption—fish, edible foods/fruits, tortoise—and tourism) three *indirect use values* (i.e. carbon sequestration, water supply, and biodiversity conservation), and the *option value* (i.e. conservation of the reservoir for future use). The study employed various market price and survey-based valuation techniques separately for the direct, indirect, and non-use values, to estimate the total value of the reservoir. The study found that fish was the main good consumed from the wetland, contributing more than 95 per cent of the total value of the wetland goods. The contingent valuation method (CVM) results reveal that, in addition to cash, the respondents were willing to contribute in terms of labour, which is an interesting finding in a developing country context. The study concluded by stating that out of the TEV, non-use values contribute more than half of the total value of the reservoir, followed by direct and indirect use values. This implies that the local community gives high importance to the future use of the wetlands, thereby laying more emphasis on adequate restoration and sustainable management.

The Buriganga River acts as a lifeline for Dhaka city but become polluted due to continuous dumping of domestic and industrial wastes and encroachment of riverbanks. Alam (2005) implemented a CV study with a hypothetical clean-up programme called Buriganga River Clean-up Programme (BRCP), which was proposed to be implemented for a ten-year period. The study area was restricted to Dhaka city (i.e. 360 sq. km based on the demarcation of the Dhaka City Corporation) and the study area was stratified into two parts, namely 'Buriganga River Area' (BRA) which is adjacent to the river, and 'Outside Buriganga Area' (OBA). A *payment card* elicitation format and an 'increase in water bill' as a *payment vehicle* were used in the survey design; nearly 400 households (from a total of 643016 households) in the city were interviewed in 2001. The results of the CV study suggest that from the sample of 400 households, 25.5 per cent were willing to contribute cash equivalent to Tk 51.91 for BRCP. Apparently, 32.75 per cent were willing to contribute 'time' for BRCP by providing their services in terms of physical labour, participating in campaigns and public awareness-building programmes, organizing meetings and rallies, contributing towards technical and non-technical office work, and providing consultancy services. It should be noted that more households were willing to contribute labour for the restoration programme, compared to the households willing to contribute cash. It was found that the annual per-capita income in Bangladesh in 2001 was only US$387, and 55 per cent of the residents in Dhaka city were living below the poverty line; however, they were still willing to pay for improving the environmental quality of the river by rendering their labour services. The study is silent on the measures adopted to minimize the *biases* and *errors* usually encountered in CV studies. Despite this issue, the study clearly shows two aspects in a developing country context: (1) in a poor country, people are willing to pay for restoration programmes but more in terms of labour which is abundant; and (2) the CV scenario employed should take into account the site-specific socio-economic, cultural, and political factors to arrive at useful results.

The Chilika wetland in Odisha is one of the largest coastal wetlands in India. Kumar and Patnaik (2012) focused on monetizing some of the important *use values* (using the market price method) and *non-use values* (using CVM) of the Chilika wetland. The market value of fish caught and the benefit generated in the ancillary industry using fisheries were Rs 768.82 million and Rs 215 million per year, respectively. Results of the travel cost method (TCM) reveal that domestic and international tourists enjoyed recreational benefits worth Rs 2,336 million per year. The navigation value provided by the wetland was estimated based on the revenue occurring to Chilika Development Authority, which is equivalent to Rs 0.72 million per year. The aquatic vegetation harvested by local communities was equivalent to 58,000 million tonnes, and its economic value was Rs 34.7 million per year. The aggregate *non-use values* of all the beneficiary households, estimated through CVM, amounted to Rs 858.78 million. The values clearly demonstrate how the coastal wetlands act as an important source of livelihood and address poverty as well as act as *natural capital* in enhancing regional sustainable development. However, this study also suffers from a double-counting problem due to combining the primary and secondary benefits, in addition to the problem of potential biases and errors in the CV estimates, adversely affecting the final results.

The Pallikaranai marshland in the Chennai Metropolitan Area (CMA) has been under enormous pressure from severe *negative externalities* such as encroachment and pollution. In 2011, the government of Tamil Nadu proposed to restore the marshland with an investment of Rs 157.5 million. Venkatachalam and Jayanthi (2016) quantified the ecosystem benefits enhanced by the proposed restoration measures. The results from a well-designed CVM conducted among 733 randomly selected households revealed that each household in the CMA would gain a restoration benefit worth Rs 2,096.59 annually during a five-year period starting from 2011. This translates into a total restoration benefit of Rs 2.34 billion per year (2015 prices). The expected benefits are significantly higher than the cost of restoring the marshland, which implies that the restoration can significantly enhance the welfare of the city population on a long-term basis.

When a wetland is converted into a protected area, what is the trade-off to its ecosystem services? How does the economic valuation highlight such a trade-off? The Ousteri wetland, jointly managed by the Tamil Nadu and Puducherry governments, was fully converted into a bird sanctuary in 2014, which resulted in preventing traditional stakeholders in ten neighbouring villages from using various ESs from the wetland. In the context of the above trade-offs, Venkatachalam and Zareena (2016) encountered only a limited number of ecosystem services—namely recreational services, groundwater irrigation, and biodiversity—for valuation. The recreational benefits estimated by using the TCM amounted to Rs 5.72 million per year; the agricultural benefits, estimated by using the *net income method*, amounted to Rs 11.5 million per year. The estimated value of groundwater used for irrigation was Rs 2,69,652 per year. The economic value of biodiversity conservation, elicited using a well-designed CVM, was Rs 2.44 million per year. The TEV of ecosystem services was Rs 19.67 million per year (in 2015 prices) and the *net present value* of the benefits (with the discount rate being 6) was Rs 82.89 million for a five-year period. The value turned out to be very meagre because the conservation measures have indeed reduced the use of many ESs, resulting in huge welfare loss. An important policy conclusion from the study is that involving people in conservation measures and allowing them to utilize various ESs would significantly enhance future ecosystem benefits and economic welfare.

14.6 Discussion and Conclusion

The review of limited empirical studies focusing on wetland valuation provides many interesting lessons. As Schroter et al. (2014) argue, the ES concept, which links ecosystem benefits to human wellbeing, concentrates more on the 'anthropocentric value' than the 'intrinsic value'. This is reflected in almost all the empirical studies we reviewed. The assumption behind these studies is that the monetary value expressed in terms of individual preferences does accommodate the *intrinsic value* as well, and therefore that the anthropocentric approach itself is sufficient to support the conservation and sustainable use of the environment. Another criticism is that the process of ES assessments involving monetary valuation tries to put a price on everything, making it unethical. However, the monetary valuation provides useful additional information in decision-making processes and the researchers are also using other techniques (e.g. *multi-criteria analysis*, *value*, and *approach*, etc.) that take into account other non-monetary values too. Along with monetary valuation, more biophysical and socio-cultural value indicators of ESs should be developed to improve management decisions (Schroter et al., 2014).

Wetlands generate a great variety of material and non-material ESs. However, the economic valuation practitioners at present focus mainly on material services. As Small et al. (2017) argue, significant efforts must be taken to include non-material services in the existing ES framework, because their inclusion will increase our understanding of human–nature interaction as well as enhance sustainable management of wetlands. There is a need to disaggregate beneficiaries of ESs using a place-based context to reflect how societies across the globe are composed of different communities, groups, and individuals with diverse competing needs and at different phases of life, and how each individual or group prioritizes different aspects of the ESs, trading them off against each other. It should be noted that when we deal with the ecosystem services with non-material characteristics, it is better to classify them as '+' services (non-monetizable) within the 'value+ approach' (Verma et al., 2019) developed to capture both monetary and non-monetary values.

Estimating the value of wetland-based biodiversity poses major challenges. Nunes and Bergh (2001) argue that, prior to economic valuation, adequate knowledge is essential on the biodiversity values in terms of instrumental versus intrinsic values, monetary versus biological indicators, direct versus indirect values, biodiversity versus biological resources, the value of levels versus changes of biodiversity, local versus global diversity, genetic versus other life organization levels, holistic versus reductionist approaches, and expert versus general-public assessments. These distinctions are important for making the valuation process more useful and for avoiding certain pertinent issues e.g. double-counting) encountered during economic valuation.

Many empirical studies we reviewed categorically demonstrate that wetlands, among all the biomes, generate highly valuable ESs, enhancing human wellbeing. However, these values are still seen as underestimated since many important ESs (e.g. carbon sequestration and biodiversity protection) were not fully monetized and included in the estimated values. Similarly, most of the studies have either not quantified the non-use values or have not separately identified these values. If the non-use values are also estimated as part of the TEV, then the marginal increase in the estimated values will be significant. The studies do not seem to capture the change in the future values of the wetlands either. For instance, temporal aspects such as the arrival of new bird species, the creation of recreational benefits, and mitigation of sea-level rise can shift the current values significantly, but they are not adequately represented in the valuation studies.

Another issue with most of the valuation studies is that the trade-offs between different ecosystem services are not properly taken into account in the process of valuation. For example, some of the wetlands have been declared as 'protected areas' or 'sanctuaries' for enhancing biodiversity, a highly valuable ES. However, such measures deny the traditional users their access to various other ESs that they utilized before such conservation efforts were initiated. Similarly, many multipurpose wetlands in India are now converted for a single use—for example for diverting drinking water under the National Water Policy 2002 directive—and such a measure deprives users of access to traditional ESs such as irrigation and fishing. The review clearly demonstrates that providing people with access to ESs and appropriately regulating their use can increase the benefits manifold. Another issue that has not been addressed adequately in the current literature is the valuation of *disservices* (e.g. invasive species) (Lyytimaki, 2015). The current valuation practices do not usually make a clear demarcation between the ecosystem *services* and the *disservices*; rather, they put all of them in one basket without clearly identifying the positive and negative values associated with the respective values. Similarly, the studies focus mainly on the benefit side and not much on the damage side; as a result, the values of the benefits are overestimated. In the future, the studies should consider estimating both the benefits and costs associated with the changes in ESs, separately.

Many of the studies using the BTM of valuation assume that the wetlands undervaluation could generate *all* types of ESs considered, and therefore they estimate all the values assigning maximum values to these wetlands. In reality, many wetlands suffering from various negative externalities can supply only a limited number of services. Similarly, the services delivered are assumed to be of high quality, so they assign a maximum value to these services. However, many services are of poor quality due to depletion and degradation of the wetland, widely seen in developing countries. As a result, the values estimated using the BTM are considered inflated. Similarly, some of the locally important ecosystem benefits (e.g. cow dung, fuel wood, etc.) are not included in the BTM. This leads to underestimation. Individual wetlands are also unique, and can generate a variety of diverse ESs. The BTM-based studies do not adequately capture the uniqueness and diversity of ESs of the wetlands, instead utilizing a 'standard global value' to estimate the benefits of all the wetlands uniformly; as a result, the 'per hectare values' estimated for all different types of wetlands are mostly constant, undermining the wetlands' uniqueness and the diversity. Support for this argument comes from the studies focusing on individual wetlands and using micro-valuation techniques, which report a wide range of values across the ESs and across the wetlands. Another related issue is that some of the ESs not used by human beings may not be subjected to economic valuation which is 'anthropocentric' in nature; these services in principle should be excluded from the valuation in order to avoid potential overestimation. Prior to valuation, a scientific understanding of the complex ecological and hydrological aspects of the wetlands should be the prerequisite for initiating an economic valuation exercise so that economic values adequately reflect the interdisciplinary aspects of wetland ecosystems.

The CVM is found to be a widely used method for wetland valuation, especially in developing countries. An important issue is that wetland-based ESs play a significant role in the lives of people in rural areas; however, these people state a lower WTP value due to income constraints and other institutional issues. This provides a misleading picture about the role of wetland ESs in explaining the welfare gained from them. To address this issue, the CV method should be combined with other economic valuation methods; the results will have to be interpreted by taking into account the prevailing social, economic, cultural, political, and institutional context; and the results should also be interpreted properly. Therefore, relevant qualitative data in sufficient quantity should be supplemented with quantitative data used in economic valuation. Another issue is that the developing-country CV practitioners do not seem to bother about *validity* and *reliability* issues encountered in the CV results. This being the case, the CV results may lead to wrong policy decisions. In order to address these issues, CV practitioners should strictly follow the standard CV guidelines (Venkatachalam, 2004) and should be willing to accept a higher transaction cost (arising from, for example, more time spent on testing the biases in the field) of conducting the survey to elicit the true value. In order to overcome these issues, more valuation studies should be initiated in a systematic and scientific manner for individual wetlands.

References

Alam, Khorshed (2005). 'Valuing the Environment in Developing Countries: Problems and Potentials'. Paper presented at the 49th Australian Agricultural and Resource Economics Society (AARES) Annual Conference, 9–11 February 2005, Coffs Harbour, NSW.

Baral, Sony, Basnyat, Bijendra, Khanal, Rajendra, et al. (2016). 'A Total Economic Valuation of Wetland Ecosystem Services: An evidence from Jagadishpur Ramsar Site, Nepal'. *The Scientific World Journal* (2605609), Hindawi Publishing Corporation, DOI: http://dx.doi.org/10.1155/2016/2605609.

Barbier, Edward E. (2013). 'Valuing Ecosystem Services for Coastal Wetland Protection and Restoration: Progress and Challenges'. *Resources*, 2, 213–230.

Barbier, Edward, B. (2011a). 'Wetlands as Natural Assets'. *Hydrological Sciences Journal*, 56(8), 1360–1373.

Barbier, Edward B. (2011b). 'Pricing Nature', *Annual Review of Resource Economics*, 3, 337–353. DOI: https://doi.org/10.1146/annurev-resource-083110-120115.

Bassi, Nitin, Kumar, Dinesh M., Sharma, Anuradha, and P. Pardha-Saradhi (2014). 'Status of Wetlands in India: A Review of Extent, Ecosystem Benefits, Threats and Management Strategies'. *Journal of Hydrology-Regional Studies*, 2, 1–19. DOI: https://doi.org/10.1016/j.ejrh.2014.07.001.

Brander, Luke, and Schuyt, Kirsten (2010). *Benefits Transfer: The Economic Value of World's Wetlands*. TEEB case, available online at: www.TEEBweb.org.

Campagne, Carol S., Roche, P. K., and Salles, J.-M. (2018). 'Looking into Pandora's Box: Ecosystem Disservices Assessment and Correlations with Ecosystem Services'. *Ecosystem Services*, 30, 126–136. DOI: 10.1016/j.ecoser.2018.02.005. hal-01945369.

Champ, Patricia A., Boyle, Kevin J. and Brown, Thomas C. (eds) (2017). *A Primer on Non-Market Valuation* (2nd edition), Springer, New York.

Costanza, Robert, d'Arge, Ralph, de Groot, Rudolf, et al. (1997). 'The Value of the World's Ecosystem Services and Natural Capital', *Nature*, 387, 253–260.

Costanza, Robert, de Groot, Rudolf, Sutton, Paul, et al. (2014). 'Changes in the Global Value of Ecosystem Services'. *Global Environmental Change*, 26, 152–158. DOI: https://doi.org/10.1016/j.gloenvcha.2014.04.002.

Costanza, Robert, de Groot, Rudolf, Braat, Leon, et al. (2017). 'Twenty Years of Ecosystem Services: How Far have We come and how Far do We still need to Go?' *Ecosystem Services*, 28, 1–16. DOI: https://doi.org/10.1016/j.ecoser.2017.09.008.

Davidson, Nick C., van Dam, A. A., Finlayson, Max, et al. (2019). 'Worth of Wetlands: Revised Global Monetary Values of Coastal and inland Wetland Ecosystem Services'. *Marine and Freshwater Research*, 70(8), 1189–1194. DOI: https://doi.org/10.1071/MF18391.

de Groot, Rudolf, Brander, Luke, Ploeg, Sandervander, et al. (2012). 'Global Estimates of the Value of Ecosystems and Their Services in Monetary Units'. *Ecosystem Services*, 1, 50–61. DOI: https://doi.org/10.1016/j.ecoser.2012.07.005.

Finlayson, C. M., Davidson, N. C., Spiers A. G., et al. (1999). 'Global Wetland Inventory: Current Status and Future Priorities'. *Marine & Freshwater Research*, 50: 717–727. DOI: https://doi.org/10.1071/MF99098.

Ghermandi, Andrea, van den Bergh, Jeroen C. J. M., Brander, Luke M., et al. (2008). The Economic Value of Wetland Conservation and Creation: A Meta-Analysis. *Working Paper 79*. Fondazione Eni Enrico Mattei.

IPBES (2019). 'Summary for Policymakers of the Global Assessment Report on Biodiversity and Ecosystem Services of the Intergovernmental Science-Policy Platform on Biodiversity and Ecosystem Services', Díaz, S., Settele, J., Brondízio, E. S. et al. (eds). IPBES Secretariat, Bonn, Germany. 56 pages.

Koch, Evamaria W., Barbier, Edward B., Silliman, Brian R., et al. (2009). 'Non-linearity in Ecosystem Services: Temporal and Spatial Variability in Coastal Protection'. *Frontiers in Ecology and the Environment*, 7(1), 29–37, DOI: doi:10.1890/080126.

Korsgaard, Louise, and Schou, Jesper S. (2010). 'Economic Valuation of Aquatic Ecosystem Services in Developing Countries'. *Water Policy*, 12(1), 20–31. DOI: https://doi.org/10.2166/wp.2009.124.

Kumar, Ritesh and Ajit K. Pattnaik (2012). *Chilika—An Integrated Management Planning Framework for Conservation and Wise Use*, Wetlands International South Asia, New Delhi, and Chilika Development Authority, Bhubaneswar, India.

Lamsal, Pramod., Pant, Krishna Prasad, Kumar, Lalit, et al. (2015). 'Sustainable Livelihoods through Conservation of Wetland Resources: A Case of Economic Benefits from Ghodaghodi Lake, Western Nepal'. *Ecology and Society* 20(1), 10. DOI: http://dx.doi.org/10.5751/ES-07172-200110.

Lele, Sarachchandra, Springate-Baginski, Oliver, Lakerveld, Roan, et al. (2013). 'Ecosystem Services: Origins, Contributions, Pitfalls, and Alternatives'. *Conservation and Society*, 11, 343–58. DOI: 10.4103/0972-4923.125752.

Lyytimaki, Jari (2015). 'Ecosystem Disservices: Embrace the Catchword'. *Ecosystem Services*, 12, 15, doi.org/10.1016/j.ecoser.2014.11.008.

MEA (Millennium Ecosystem Assessment) (2005). *Ecosystems and Human Well-being: Synthesis*. Island Press, Washington, DC.

Mitsch, William J., and Gosselink, James G. (2015). *Wetlands*. 5th edition. John Wiley & Sons, Hoboken, NJ.

Nunes, Paulo A. L.D., and van den Bergh, Jeroen C. J. M. (2001). 'Economic Valuation of Biodiversity: Sense or Nonsense?' *Ecological Economics*, 39, 203–222. DOI: https://doi.org/10.1016/S0921-8009(01)00233-6.

Russi, D., ten Brink, P., Farmer, A., et al. (2013). *The Economics of Ecosystems and Biodiversity for Water and Wetlands*. IEEP, London and Brussels; Ramsar Secretariat, Gland, Switzerland.

Schroter, Matthias, Crouzat, Emilie, Holting, Lisanne, et al. (2021). 'Assumptions in Ecosystem Service Assessments: Increasing Transparency for Conservation'. *Ambio*, 50, 289–300.

Schroter, Matthias, van der Zanden, Emma H., van Oudenhoven, Alexander P. E., et al. (2014). 'Ecosystem Services as a Contested Concept: A Synthesis of Critique and Counter-arguments'. *Conservation Letters*, 7(6), 514–523.

Small, N., Munday, M., and Durance, I. (2017). 'The Challenge of Valuing Ecosystem Services that have no Material Benefits'. *Global Environmental Change*, 44, 57–67. DOI: https://doi.org/10.1016/j.gloenvcha.2017.03.005.

Tan, Yonghua, Lv, Duian, Cheng, Jie, et al. (2018). 'Valuation of Environmental Improvements in Coastal Wetland Restoration: A Choice Experiment Approach'. *Global Ecology and Conservation*, 15, 1–8. DOI: https://doi.org/10.1016/j.gecco.2018.e00440.

TEEB (2010). *The Economics of Ecosystems and Biodiversity: Mainstreaming the Economics of Nature: A Synthesis of the Approach, Conclusions and Recommendations of TEEB*, Malta. https://www.teebweb.org/wp-content/uploads/Study%20and%20Reports/Reports/Synthesis%20report/TEEB%20Synthesis%20Report%202010.pdf.

United Nations (2021). The United Nations World Water Development Report 2021: Valuing Water. UNESCO.

Venkatachalam, L. (2022). 'Economic Valuation of Ecosystem Services of 80 Prioritised Wetlands in Tamil Nadu'. Report Submitted to Tamil Nadu State Wetlands Authority, Environment, Climate Change and Forest Department, Government of Tamil Nadu, Chennai.

Venkatachalam, L., and Jayanthi,M. (2016). Economic valuation of wetland ecosystem services: A contingent valuation approach. *Review of Development and Change*, 21(1), 89–110.

Venkatachalam, L., and Zareena Begum, I. (2016). 'Economic Valuation of Ecosystem Services: A Case Study of Ousteri Wetland, Puducherry'. *The Economics of Ecosystems and Biodiversity India Initiative*. GIZ India. 104 pages.

Verma, Madhu, Tiwari, Charu, Anand, Sumit, et al. (2019). 'Economic Valuation of Tiger Reserves in India: A Value+ Approach'. *Indian Institute of Forest Management*. Bhopal, India.

Whiteoak, Kim, and Binney, Jim (2016). 'Literature Review of the Economic Value of Ecosystem Services that Wetlands Provide'. Final Report Prepared for the Department of Sustainability, Environment, Water, Population and Communities, Marsden Jacob Associates, Perth.

Woodward, Richard, T., and Wui, Yank-Shuk (2001). 'The Economic Value of Wetland Services: A Meta-analysis'. *Ecological Economics*, 37(2), 257–270.

15

Climate Risks and Financial Management

K. S. Kavi Kumar

15.1 Introduction

Social cost of carbon is one of the most important inputs in formulating climate policies. The social cost of carbon is the present value of the incremental damage due to a small increase in carbon emissions, the main pollutant causing climate change. The social cost of carbon depends on the climate change-induced damage estimation besides temperature–emission linkages and assumptions about the social discount rate. Despite significant progress made in the assessment of impacts due to climate change across multiple sectors and geographical regions, there remains significant uncertainty. This is due to emerging understanding about the nature and manifestation of changes in the climate. Though there is considerable knowledge about the impacts due to gradual changes in climate on some of the important climate-sensitive sectors (such as agriculture), the evidence on impacts due to abrupt and sudden changes in climate is scant. The role played by adaptation further complicates the climate change impact assessment, and hence the estimation of the social cost of carbon.

Given the growing evidence of climate science and the slow pace of progress in greenhouse gas mitigation, it is widely believed that climate change impacts will exceed adaptation limits—at least in some contexts. The residual impacts are referred to in the literature as loss and damage. Currently, such residual impacts are observed in the context of climate-related events like cyclones, floods, droughts, salinization, etc. It is considered that the developing and the least-developed nations, in particular, bear relatively large impacts from such events.

K. S. Kavi Kumar, *Climate Risks and Financial Management* In: *Fiscal Policy and Public Financial Management.* Edited by: Pinaki Chakraborty and K R Shanmugam, Oxford University Press. © Oxford University Press 2024.
DOI: 10.1093/9780198930464.003.0015

Climate change impact assessments over time have started shifting focus from an academic to a more operational level. While the initial impact work focused on tracing incremental impacts due to gradual climate change (intended mainly to inform greenhouse gas mitigation policies), an emergent perspective assesses risk as shaped by both climate variability and climate change and seeks to support climate risk management (CRM) at different scales. CRM aligns disaster risk reduction (DRR)—which focuses on sudden-onset hydro-meteorological and geophysical events—with climate change adaptation, to address both slow-onset and sudden-onset climate-related impacts. The overall aim of CRM is to anticipate, avoid, prevent, and finance against risks, as well as absorb remaining impacts.

Current greenhouse gas mitigation efforts may not prevent global warming from going beyond the 2015 Paris Agreement's 2°C target. At the same time, despite increasing focus on climate change adaptation, climate-related risks may exceed adaptation possibilities of communities and countries. One of the notable features of the Paris Agreement was the endorsement of the Warsaw International Mechanism (WIM) for Loss and Damage (L&D). Despite several unresolved issues, including exact definition and policy framework, this endorsement established L&D as a distinct pillar of climate negotiations.

For several years now, the Parties to the UNFCCC (United Nations Framework Convention on Climate Change) have been struggling to address L&D amid fundamental disagreements about how the issue should be framed and understood. Science has remained mostly on the sidelines—most notably on attribution of impacts. This gap between science and policy, combined with the difficulties in finding common ground among the Parties, has led to a situation in which the L&D is one thing on paper, as outlined in the language on the Warsaw Mechanism, and another in the broader policy discourse. The COP (Conference of the Parties) decisions and the Paris Agreement focus mostly on risk management, but many governments are still keen on compensation.[1] Vulturius and Davis (2016) argue there is need for better understanding of the key traits of L&D, which include:

[1] It is pertinent to note that L&D found a place in the agenda of the 27th Conference of the Parties, held in Egypt on 6–18 November 2022.

1. **Attributability** If the WIM were to include a compensation scheme, attributing specific events and specific losses and damages to climate change could be very challenging, due to multiple uncertainties and social vulnerability, which is a key factor influencing the realized losses and damages.
2. **Irreversibility** The science distinguishes between physically and socially irreversible impacts. Physically irreversible risks often involve 'tipping points' in the Earth system. There is a growing body of evidence on tipping points and thresholds, on the global and local scales. The factors that make some impacts socially irreversible are, however, less well understood.
3. **Unavoidability** Focusing on 'hard' limits to adaptation might simplify the WIM mandate, as there is extensive evidence that adaptation finance and technology transfer fall far short of vulnerable countries' needs.
4. **Intolerability** An equity and/or human rights perspective is important in defining what is 'intolerable', to ensure that action under the WIM does not perpetuate inequalities that force poor and vulnerable communities to tolerate worse conditions than wealthier ones.

It is relevant to understand the interface of the above traits of L&D and development. For instance, it is possible that with development one can usually anticipate reduction in the share of irreversible and unavoidable losses, but at the same time development could increase society's intolerability towards losses and damages.

It is against this backdrop of L&D in the climate change context that one should analyse the physical and economic impacts due to climate extremes.[2] This chapter provides an overview of some aspects concerning climate extremes and their interface with Indian agriculture. The rest of the chapter is structured as follows: the next section (15.2) discusses

[2] L&D is usually the result of climate-related sudden-onset events (e.g. cyclones, floods, flash floods) and/or gradual changes (e.g. salinization, drought, heat stress) in interaction with a particular development path that either reduces or exacerbates the risk of L&D. Thus, the climate extremes cover a wide range of hydro-meteorological events in the L&D context. The discussion here, however, will be restricted to widely recognized events such as cyclones, floods, and drought. Further, while the term 'loss' refers to something irreversible, 'damage' is usually associated with reversible impact.

the trends in economic losses associated with cyclones and floods in India. Section 15.3 focuses on drought in India over recent decades and analyses the implications of drought on rice yield. This section further discusses the role played by crop diversity in ameliorating the adverse impacts of drought on crop yield. Section 15.4 provides a brief discussion on management of climate risk from Indian and global perspectives, and Section 15.5 provides conclusions.

15.2 Trends in Economic Losses due to Climate Extremes

Over the past six decades, India has lost approximately Rs 4.7 trillion worth of crops, houses, and other properties, and 1,695 lives on an average, per year, to floods. According to the Jal Shakti Ministry of India, India suffered a loss of Rs 95,736 crore in the 2018 floods—a three-fold increase on the previous year's loss. In the last two decades, extreme rainfall events have increased steadily in north, north-east, and south India, with a rise in sea surface temperature inducing floods (Mukherjee et al., 2018). With a rise in flood intensity, flood damage has also increased. The floods in Chennai in 2002, 2005, and 2015, and those in Mumbai (2005 and 2021), Kedarnath (2013), and Kerala (2018), are some of the most notorious flood events in the recent history of India. Moreover, cyclones have become a repeated annual event on the country's western and eastern coasts. In 2021, Cyclone Tauktae damaged the coasts of Kerala, Maharashtra, and Gujarat, and Cyclone Yaas submerged over 1,100 villages in West Bengal, displacing more over half a million people and damaging 3 lakh (300,000) houses. In 2020, India faced three deadly flooding events—one in West Bengal and Jharkhand due to Cyclone Amphan, one in Assam and Meghalaya due to extreme rainfall, and one in Bihar due to sudden downpour in Nepal. Similar trends are being reported in the context of other climate extremes such as droughts, heat waves, and cold waves. Following Gupta et al. (2021), Figure 15.1 shows trends in climate extremes over the period 1995–2020, divided into three subperiods, namely 1995–2004, 2005–14, and 2015–20.

In general, there are two determinants for occurrence of loss (and damage) from any climate extreme event: (1) climatic factors, to derive

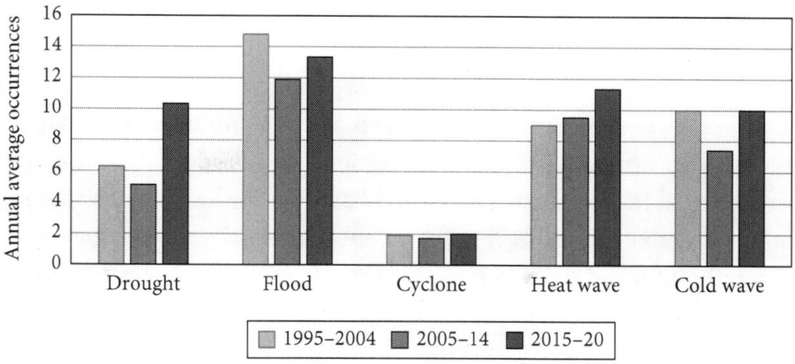

Figure 15.1 Annual average occurrences of climate extremes in India: 1995–2020.
Source: Adapted from Gupta et al. (2021).

the nature and intensity of extreme events; and (2) exposure and vulnerability due to socio-economic factors that largely determine *ex post* impact of an event (Schmidt et al., 2009; Neumayer and Barthel, 2011). Whereas the former capture the role of climate variability and anthropogenic climate change, the latter infers the sensitivity and adaptive capacity of an entity. Various studies have used 'normalization technique' to segregate the role of climate factors from that of the socio-economic factors in determining damages caused by the events. Adjusting the damage costs with socio-economic conditions of a particular year (known as the base year) could provide better estimation to design appropriate policy options to reduce potential damage costs. A substantial amount of empirical research has emerged in the last two decades across the globe in this context, mostly focused on the developed nations. The findings are mixed in nature—that is, they attribute the observed damages from various disasters to either socio-economic factors (Pielke et al., 2008), climate factors (Nordhaus, 2010), or both (Schmidt et al., 2010). In the context of India, while Raghavan and Rajesh (2003) report that socio-economic factors are mainly responsible, Bahinipati and Venkatachalam (2016) find that both climate (mainly natural climate variability) and socio-economic factors have influenced damages from extreme climatic events (cyclonic storms, floods, drought, etc.).

The loss (and damage) is usually calculated at two levels: *ex ante* or *ex post*. The former gives an indication about possible losses that are likely to occur in the near future due to an event under various scenarios of exposure and adaptation. This forecasts average annual losses from extreme events now and in the years to come, and ranks the entity (usually a geographical region, such as a district) based on the losses. Such ranking indicates the vulnerability level of an entity and assists policymakers in designing future adaptation policies. The latter, in contrast, estimates the actual losses (and damages) that occurred due to an event. Various state and national government agencies in India regularly carry out such assessments after an event, and use the estimates in either seeking or allocating the aid. While the reported (or actual) damages due to an extreme climatic event usually show an increasing trend, this could be due to higher values at risk in any geographical area. Here the discussion is confined to cyclonic storms hitting the coast of Tamil Nadu and the trend in the damages caused by those storms.

15.2.1 Losses due to Cyclonic Storms: Tamil Nadu

The state of Tamil Nadu is vulnerable to climate extremes and slow-onset disasters (e.g. cyclonic storms, floods, droughts, sea-level rise, temperature and rainfall changes, salinization, etc.). On an average, northern Tamil Nadu has experienced six cyclones (including depressions, cyclonic storms, and severe cyclonic storms) in each decade, and a higher percentage of cyclones occur in the north-east during monsoon season (i.e. October to December); this in turn has had significant effect on crops cultivated in the *kharif* season.

Figure 15.2 shows reported and 'normalized' economic damage costs due to cyclones over the past few decades in Tamil Nadu. Through the normalization procedure, the expected damage costs of a cyclonic storm are estimated as if it were to occur in the base year. Thus, the normalization controls all the socio-economic factors which could have influenced the impacts in order to detect the signals of climate variability. It can be seen from Figure 15.2 that while there is increasing trend in the reported damage costs, a declining trend is found for normalized economic losses. This suggests that the rising reported damage cost could be largely due to

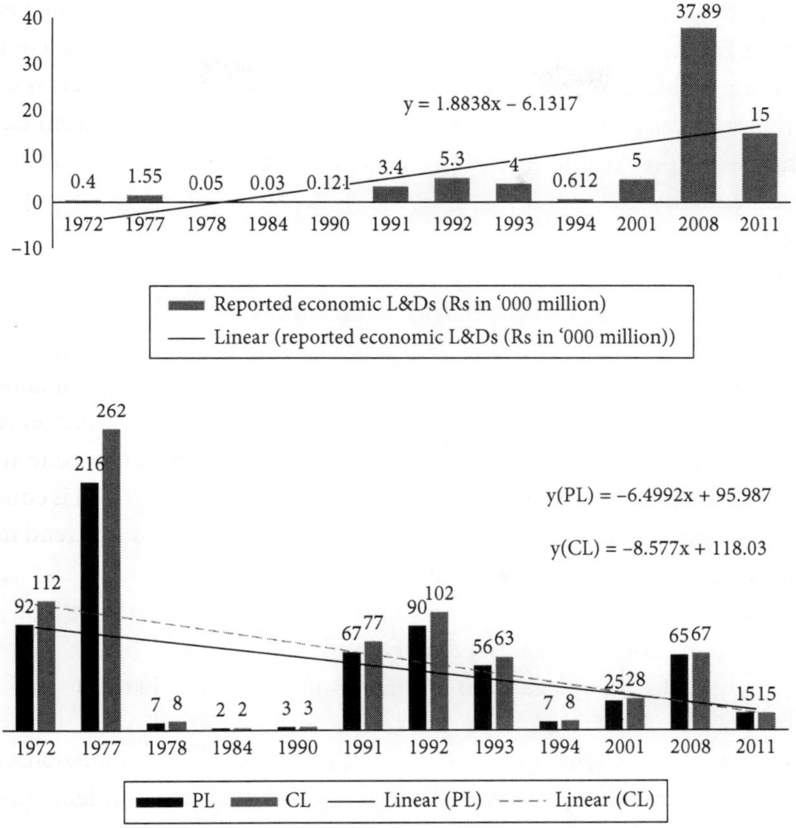

Figure 15.2 Reported and 'normalized' economic losses due to cyclonic storms in Tamil Nadu.
Source: Kavi Kumar et al. (2018).

increase in location-specific economic activity and population density. A similar pattern is observed in the context of reported and 'normalized' economic losses due to floods in Tamil Nadu.

Normalization that accounts for exposure suggests (in the case of cyclones and floods) that 'we are putting more in harm's way', in line with the general findings in the literature. However, the declining trend in the lives lost suggests that underlying vulnerability could be decreasing (or adaptation is increasing). Further, Tamil Nadu has witnessed a declining trend in cyclonic storms over the past 100 years, but severe cyclonic storms have registered an increasing trend over the same period, particularly over the northern part of the state. The intensity of the cyclonic storms over the past four decades has shown an increasing trend, in line with the increasing frequency of severe cyclonic storms. Overall, these trends suggest that future risks are likely to be significant due to increased exposure and increased intensity of storms, despite decreasing vulnerability.

15.3 Drought and Agriculture in India

Several studies have analysed the linkages between drought and agriculture in India. At aggregate level, Gadgil and Gadgil (2006) have analysed the impact of the inter-annual variation of the summer rainfall on gross domestic product (GDP) using data over five decades. Notwithstanding the decline in the contribution of agriculture to GDP over time in India, they estimate that severe drought lowered annual GDP by around 2 to 5 per cent during 1951–2003. In another study, Pandey et al. (2007) analysed drought in three eastern Indian states (Jharkhand, Chhattisgarh, and Odisha) and showed that household income reduced by 24 to 58 per cent in drought years compared to normal years. The drop in household income is shown to contribute towards increase in poverty headcount ratio in these states (12 to 33 per cent). This study also found that households adopted several strategies to cope with the loss in income caused by droughts, including cutting down expenditure on non-essential items (clothing, social functions, etc.) as well as on essential items (food and health). The study also showed that more than 50 per cent of farming households have undertaken extreme measures such as curtailing education of children, which could have long-term welfare implications.

Birthal et al. (2015) and Fontes et al. (2020) have analysed the influence of drought—a major constraint to sustainable improvements of agricultural productivity—on rice cultivation in India, and its resilience. Birthal et al. (2015) analysed the influence of drought on the rain-fed rice ecosystem. More specifically, the authors examined whether frequency, severity, and spread of droughts in India have had any influence on rice production in the country. They argue that nearly one-third of the area under rice cultivation in India is affected by drought that is of moderate intensity and that the frequency of such droughts has increased in recent years. However, based on analysis of nearly 200 districts over the period 1969–2005, they show that drought-induced losses in rice yields have reduced owing to improvements in farmers' adaptive capacity, attributable primarily to the expansion of irrigation facilities and increased availability of improved varieties for rain-fed production systems. Fontes et al. (2020) have categorized droughts into Types 1 and 2, based on above- and below-average cooling degree days, respectively. Using district-level data for India over the period 1966–2009, the authors argue that it is important to account for both types of droughts to accurately estimate drought impact on rice yield. They further argue that irrigation is a more appropriate adaptation strategy for addressing Type 2 droughts than Type 1 droughts.

Extending the discussion reported in Birthal et al. (2015) and Fontes et al. (2020), Kavi Kumar (2021) have further analyses the resilience of rice production in drought conditions across different regions of India. The scatter plots of temperature and rainfall deviations over the entire period of analysis (1966–2015) and for different decades show that the incidence of drought has increased over time, with the most recent decades reporting more instances of excess temperature and rainfall deficit compared to the long-term mean values. The drought categories show a similar trend over the decades, with the occurrence of severe droughts increasing over time.

To get a sense of the influence of drought on rice yield, for each district-year combination in the dataset the yield deviations from its long-term trend are plotted against the drought index. While there is clear negative correlation between the yield deviations and the drought index across all regions, the extent of influence of drought on rice yield is different in different regions. The northern and southern Indian regions exhibit relatively less adverse effects of drought on rice yield compared to the eastern, western, and central regions. Among other things, irrigation can help ameliorate the adverse effects of drought on crop yield. To see the role of irrigation in the context of rice yield, yield deviations and drought index are regressed on share of irrigated area under rice cultivation and the residuals are plotted against each other. Figure 15.3 shows the scatter plot of rice yield deviations and drought index after accounting for irrigation. As expected, the irrigation does moderate the adverse effects of

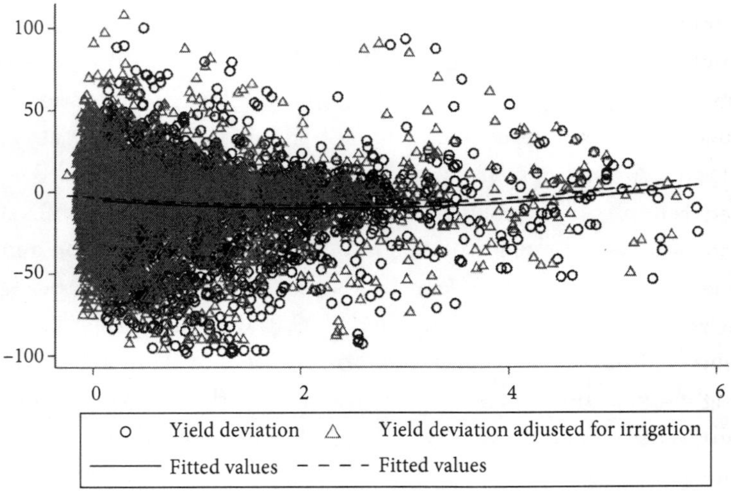

Figure 15.3 Relationship between rice yield and drought index—the role of irrigation.
Source: Kavi Kumar (2021).

drought on rice yield, with the black dashed line lying always above the grey solid line. However, the extent of moderation effected by irrigation varies with the severity of drought.

The modelling results reported in Kavi Kumar (2021) have suggested that while rice in general has become resilient to drought conditions in India, there is greater confidence about the resilience of rice yield to low and moderate droughts. Though the overall result is similar to that reported earlier, the results from this study are based on a different empirical strategy than that adopted by Birthal et al. (2015), and provide more robust estimates. The results also suggest that irrigation did play an important role in making rice crops less vulnerable to drought. However, irrigation is more effective in easing the adverse effects of low and moderate drought than those imposed by severe drought. For addressing severe drought conditions there is need to augment farm management strategies with the use of drought-tolerant rice cultivars.

The Government of India has taken several measures to enhance the resilience of agriculture to drought. These include policies/programmes to expand irrigation, use of better technology, development of drought-resistant cultivars, etc. However, wide gap exists in terms of the implementation of various programmes, including those aimed at drought management. Regarding technology uptake by Indian farmers, Palanisami et al. (2015) observed that farm-level adoption rate of water management technologies developed by research centres is only 22 per cent, and more than three-quarters of water-related farm practices are based on local and traditional wisdom. Despite resilience exhibited by some of the important crops such as rice to climate extremes like drought, the losses may increase substantially under climate change as constraints on further expansion of irrigation become more and more binding. Corroborating this, Zaveri and Lobell (2019), in their study on wheat yields in India over the past 40 years, argue that yield gains from irrigation expansion have slowed in recent years. In the context of the findings of the present study, this highlights the need to understand the behavioural and institutional factors constraining the technology adoption at farm level.

Crop diversification is an important adaptation strategy that farmers can implement to help withstand the adverse effects of extreme climate events such as droughts. Some studies (e.g. Auffhammer and Carleton, 2018) have demonstrated that diversification has indeed helped Indian farmers to mitigate the adverse effects on agricultural outcomes. Madhumitha et al. (2021) have attempted to explore the robustness of this finding under alternative characterizations of drought conditions and over a much longer period of time. In particular, the study used multiple datasets (i.e. the IAC and ICRISAT datasets) on district-level agricultural variables over the period 1966–2015 for the analysis. The main findings of Madhumitha et al. suggest that crop diversity provided a natural insurance against drought-induced losses on yield during the Green Revolution period in India. Further, the positive impact of diversity on yield during drought years is evident when drought is defined on the basis of rainfall deficit alone. The results from this study suggest that an increase in diversity level always corresponded to a fall in yield. Yield in terms of the quantity of physical produce was more responsive to changes in diversity, compared to revenue. Agricultural intensification and specialization oriented towards particular crops allowed for monoculture of those crops in order to provide better returns. But monoculture could also lead to long-term negative impacts since it is resource-intensive. Despite agricultural intensification providing better yield than diversification, during the no-drought years, intensification cannot be advocated as a coping strategy since it involves indiscriminate use of chemical inputs and leads to resource scarcity and environmental pollution (Yang et al., 2018).

15.4 Financial Management of Climate Extremes

In general, high-frequency/low-severity events can be managed better through risk-reduction measures, whereas low-frequency/high-severity events are usually more effectively managed through risk transfer. High levels of insurance penetration reduce the impact of natural disasters on economic growth and government revenues, and provide governments with greater flexibility to usher in fiscal stimulus in the aftermath of a disaster. Wolfrom and Yokoi-Arai (2016) have illustrated the role of insurance through an analysis of instantaneous and cumulative impact of disasters on economic growth. They simulate deviation of real economic growth from its trend due to a typical disaster event—without and with insurance, in the short and medium term—and argue that the economic impacts of disasters (including climate extremes) are significantly lowered by deeper penetration of insurance. However, between 2005 and 2014, insurance covered approximately 51 per cent of all losses in high-income countries, but less than 10 per cent of losses in developing countries. In the absence of insurance, vulnerable households have traditionally financed post-disaster recovery with a combination of savings and credit, informal kinship, government relief, and international donor support. Some examples of risk financing at different scales is shown in Table 15.1.

If insurance is seen as one of the important financial instruments in the context of L&D, then it is important to address the question, 'who pays the premium?'. Linnerooth-Bayer et al. (2019) outline three equity principles for organizing insurance:

1. **Mutuality**: the community at risk finances its own curative measures.
2. **Solidarity**: based on voluntary transfers for humanitarian reasons, without any liability.
3. **Accountability**: invokes the question of 'attribution' as well as some degree of culpability

Table 15.1 Risk financing at different scales—examples.

	Micro-scale Households, SMEs, farms	Intermediate scale Insurers, financial institutions, NGOs, etc.	Macro-scale Governments
Insurance instruments	Indemnity-based property, crop and life insurance, index-based property, livestock and crop insurance, weather hedges	Indemnity and parametric insurance for NGOs, co-ops; Re-insurance for direct insurance providers, catastrophe bonds	Sovereign risk transfer, contingent credit, regional catastrophe insurance pools
Solidarity	Government assistance, humanitarian aid	Government guarantees/ bail-outs	Bilateral and multilateral assistance
Savings and credit	Savings, micro-savings, micro-credit, fungible assets, food storage	Emergency liquidity funds	Reserve funds, post-disaster credit
Informal risk-sharing	Kinship and other mutual arrangements, remittances		Diversions from other budgeted programmes

Source: Linnerooth-Bayer et al. (2019).

For fulfilling the aspirations of Warsaw International Mechanism for L&D, it is important not to rely exclusively on markets and to recognize the critical role of international and public intervention in climate insurance provision—that is, move from 'mutuality' to 'solidarity', and further to 'accountability' as organizing principles. The interventions as such can include subsidies, technical assistance, provision of reinsurance, etc., to make insurance affordable to resource-poor and climate-sensitive stakeholders.

15.5 Conclusions

As things stand, climate impact assessments have not incorporated 'adaptation' comprehensively—at least in the context of economic assessments. Hence it is perhaps difficult to frame L&D as 'residual risk', as has been attempted in the literature and climate negotiations. It is more meaningful to frame L&D as impacts associated with sudden- and slow-onset hydro-meteorological events. This would complement understanding on climate change impacts as sudden- (and slow-) onset events, largely not yet covered in climate change impact assessments.

On methodological front (going by the above framing of L&D), one would need more accurate assessment of damages as well as the data-compilation process. There are political economy aspects closely intertwined with damage assessment (as they would influence fiscal transfers from centre to states). Some recent work (Pattanayak and Kumar, 2022; Kavi Kumar and Pattanayak, 2022) highlights the significant role played by partisan politics in fiscal transfers in the context of extreme events in India. Thus, one may need damage assessment to be carried out by independent bodies, to ensure the transparency needed for exploring global financing options.

Climate-compatible development depends on climate change actions being part of the mainstream development process, rather than being an isolated concern of climate change ministries/departments. Integrating climate change risks into mainstream policies requires more flexible, preventive, and forward-looking approaches, and will involve significant legal, institutional, and policy changes. Among the various mainstreaming approaches, climate-proofing of existing and planned developmental projects/programmes has gained importance. Climate-proofing aims to protect development interventions that have been planned in isolation without taking climate change into context. It makes the development interventions resilient to climate variability and climate extremes. Examples in the Indian context include climate-proofing watershed development initiatives of the National Bank for Agriculture and Rural Development. More widespread use of cost–benefit analysis and related tools is desirable to demonstrate that the climate-proofing is effective and economically viable.

As mentioned, four key traits are commonly associated with L&D in policy discourse—that it is *attributable* to human-induced climate change, *irreversible*, *unavoidable*, and *intolerable*. An equity and/or human rights perspective is important in defining what is 'intolerable', to ensure that action under the WIM does not perpetuate existing inequalities and force poor and vulnerable communities to tolerate worse conditions than their rich counterparts.

References

Auffhammer, M., and Carleton, T. A. (2018). 'Regional Crop Diversity and Weather Shocks'. *Asian Development Review*, 35(2), 113–130.

Bahinipati, C. S., and Venkatachalam, L. (2016). 'Role of Climatic Risks and Socio-economic Factors in Influencing the Economic Impact of Climatic Extremes: A Normalisation Study in the Context of Odisha, India'. *Regional Environmental Change*, 16(1), 177–178, doi: 10.1007/s10113-014-0735-4.

Birthal, P. S., Negi, D. S., Khan, T., et al. (2015). 'Is Indian Agriculture becoming Resilient to Droughts? Evidence From Rice Production Systems'. *Food Policy*, 56, 1–12.

Fontes, F., Gorst, A., and Palmer, C. (2020). 'Does Choice of Drought Index Influence Estimates of Drought Induced Rice Losses in India?', *Environment and Development Economics*, 25(5), 459–481. DOI: 10.1017/S1355770X2000011X.

Gadgil, S., and Gadgil, S. (2006). 'The Indian monsoon, GDP and agriculture'. *Economic and Political Weekly*, 41(47), 4887–4895.

Gupta, A. K., Chopde, S., Nair, S. S., et al. (2021). *Mapping Climatic and Biological Disasters in India: Study of Spatial and Temporal Patterns and Lessons for Strengthening Resilience*, Deutsche Gesellschaft für Internationale Zusammenarbeit (GIZ) GmbH India. (available at: https://nidm.gov.in/PDF/pubs/GIZNIDM_21.pdf).

Kavi Kumar, K. S. (2021). 'Rice Production Systems and Drought Resilience in India', in P. Dasgupta et al. (eds.), *Sustainable Development Insights from India*, Springer Nature, Singapore, 303–316.

Kavi Kumar, K. S. and Pattanayak, A. (2022). 'Fiscal Transfers, Climate Risks, and Partisan Politics: Does the Nature of Climate Risk Matter?' MSE Working Paper 227/2022, Madras School of Economics, Chennai.

Kavi Kumar, K. S., Sekhar Bahinipati, C., Das, S., et al. (2018). 'Climate-related Loss and Damage in India: Experiences from a Rapid Assessment in Tamil Nadu and Odisha', GIZ, New Delhi.

Linnerooth-Bayer, J., Surminski, S., Bouwer, L. M., et al. (2019). 'Insurance as a Response to Loss and Damage?', in R. Mechler et al. (eds) *Loss and Damage from Climate Change*, Springer Open (available at: https://link.springer.com/chapter/10.1007/978-3-319-72026-5_21), 483–512.

Madhumitha, S., Kavi Kumar, K. S., and Pattanayak. A. (2021). 'Crop Diversity and Resilience to Droughts: Evidence from Indian Agriculture'. MSE Working Paper 205/2021, Madras School of Economics, Chennai.

Mukherjee, S., Aadhar, S., Stone, D., et al. (2018). 'Increase in Extreme Precipitation Events under Anthropogenic Warming in India', *Weather and Climate Extremes*, 20, 45–53.

Neumayer, E., and Barthel, F. (2011). 'Normalising Economic Loss from Natural Disasters: A Global Analysis'. *Global Environmental Change*, 21(1): 13–24.

Nordhaus, W. D. (2010), 'The Economics of Hurricanes and Implications of Global Warming'. *Climate Change Economics*, 1(1), 1–20.

Palanisami, K., Suresh Kumar, D., Malik, R. P. S., et al. (2015). 'Managing Water Management Research: Analysis of Four Decades of Research and Outreach Programmes in India'. *Economic & Political Weekly*, 50(26–27), 33–43.

Pandey, S., Bhandari, H., and Hardy, B. (2007). *Economic Costs of Drought and Rice Farmer's Coping Mechanisms: A Cross-country Comparative Analysis from Asia*, International Rice Research Institute, Manila.

Pattanayak, A., and Kavi Kumar, K.S (2022). 'Fiscal Transfers, Natural Calamities and Partisan Politics: Evidence from India'. *Economics of Disasters and Climate Change*, 6, 375–392.

Pielke, R. A. Jr., Gratz, J., Landsea, C. W., et al. (2008). 'Normalised Hurricane Damage in the United States: 1900–2005', *Natural Hazards Review*, 9(1), 29–42.

Raghavan, S., and Rajesh, S. (2003). 'Trends in Tropical Cyclone Impact: A Study in Andhra Pradesh, India'. *Bulletin of the American Meteorological Society*, 84(5), 635–644.

Schmidt, S., Kemfert, C., and Hoppe, P. (2009). 'Tropical Cyclone Losses in the USA and the Impact of Climate Change: A Trend Analysis Based on Data from a New Approach to Adjusting Storm Losses'. *Environmental Impact Assessment Review*, 29(6), 359–369.

Schmidt, S., Kemfert, C., and Hoppe, P. (2010). 'The Impact of Socio-economics and Climate Change on Tropical Cyclone Losses in the USA'. *Regional Environmental Change*, 10(1), 13–26.

Vulturius, G., and Davis, M. (2016). 'Defining Loss and Damage: The Science and Politics around One of the Most Contested Issues within the UNFCCC', Discussion Brief, Stockholm Environment Institute, Stockholm. Available at: https://www.preventionweb.net/publications/view/51127 (accessed 1 February 2024).

Wolfrom, L., and Yokoi-Arai, M. (2016). 'Financial Instruments for Managing Disaster Risks related to Climate Change'. *OECD Journal: Financial Market Trends*, 2015/1.

Yang, X., Sui, P., Shen, Y., Gerber, J.S., Wang, D., Wang, X., Dai, H. and Chen, Y., (2018). 'Sustainability Evaluation of the Maize–Soybean Intercropping System and Maize Monocropping System in the North China Plain Based on Field Experiments'. *Agronomy*, 8(11), 268.

Zaveri, E. and Lobell, D.B. (2019). 'The Role of Irrigation in Changing Wheat Yields and Heat Sensitivity in India'. *Nature Communications*, 10: 4144, doi: 10.1038/s41467-019-12183-9.

16

Financial Analysis of Publicly Funded Investment Projects

I. Zareena Begum

16.1 Introduction

The state performs a variety of economic and social functions that necessitate relevant public investment decisions. However, these investments, which are supported by taxes and other taxpayer income, must adhere to strict economic rationality criteria, as well as good management principles and practices, in order to achieve the best results and/or socio-economic benefits at the lowest cost. In good financial management, the economy, efficiency, and effectiveness of public spending are critical issues to which all public financial decision-makers and managers must respond in order to avoid excessive pressure on public spending, which is a negative factor in the growth and development of society by its weight (Charbit and Michalun, 2009).

Economic analysis of projects will aid in resource investment decisions. When deciding to make a large investment in a future activity that involves risks of damage, whether predictable or unpredictable, one must be concerned about the possibility of losing one's own property. Economic analysis will provide information on the most effective and efficient investment alternative by comparing cost and benefit in a specific way and calculating the assumed risks.

A national government invests its limited resources to help improve its people's living standards. The government's resources include taxes levied on the people, which are then distributed into activities or projects for the benefit of the nation. Government investments must therefore be effective, efficient, valid, and accountable to the nation. Economic analysis will help to improve resource allocation in terms of economic

I. Zareena Begum, *Financial Analysis of Publicly Funded Investment Projects* In: *Fiscal Policy and Public Financial Management*. Edited by: Pinaki Chakraborty and K R Shanmugam, Oxford University Press.
 DOI: 10.1093/9780198930464.003.0016

efficiency. To evaluate the economic aspects of projects, there are two perspectives: 'national economic' and 'private economic' points of view. From the standpoint of the national economy, it must be determined that government investment should contribute to the development of the national economy and that the investment is used effectively and efficiently (Blöchliger and Petzold, 2009).

As stated in an Asian Development Bank guideline, 'for a project to be economically viable, it must be financially sustainable as well as economically efficient. Economic benefits will not be realized if a project is not financially sustainable. As a result, financial and economic analysis are two sides of the same coin that are complementary' (OECD, 2009c).

16.2 Identifying Project Benefits

A project's benefit is a comparison of without project and with project situations. The project benefit is defined as the incremental benefit (net benefit with project; net benefit without project) streamed into the flow during project life. The concept and examples of project benefits that may arise is represented in Figure 16.1. For an irrigation development projects, the net incremental benefit stream could be represented by the top-left-hand side or even the bottom-left-hand side.

16.3 Estimation of Project Benefit, Net Incremental Benefit, and Net Incremental Income

The basic procedure for estimating the benefits of a development project like the irrigation-specific scenario would be to (1) identify the area benefited, (2) comprehend the current situation, (3) develop a farming plan, and (4) price the benefits (Mizell and Allain-Dupré, 2013).

Net benefit is calculated by dividing gross output by production costs, which include costs for seeds, fertilizers, pesticides, machinery, labour, and so on. Family labour is an important aspect of farming. Family labour can be priced as part of the production cost, even though farmers do not pay cash for it. Machinery costs include depreciation, which is a special accounting arrangement. When calculating capital productivity,

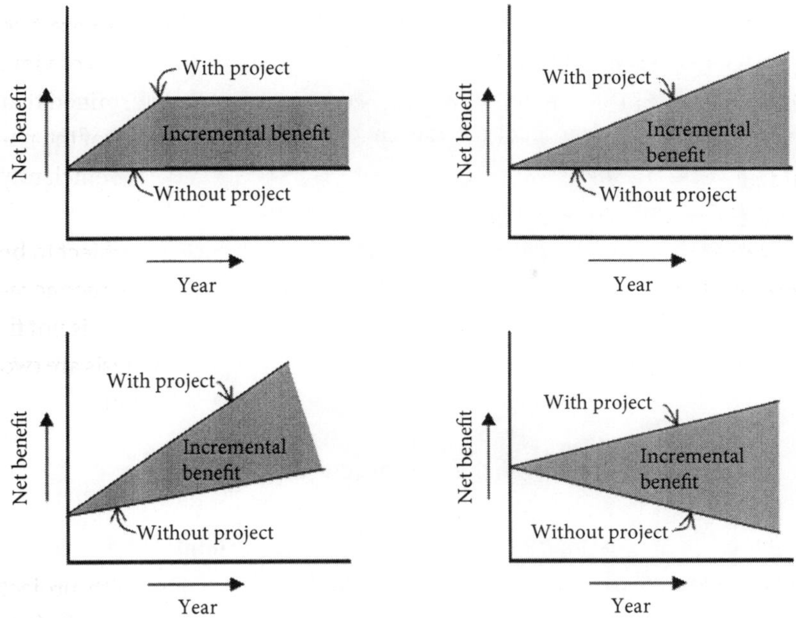

Figure 16.1 Sample of incremental benefit.
Source: Reproduced with permission from Garcilazo and Martins, 2013.

we should include the cost of family labour, though family labour is not a cash expense for farmers. Net income is defined here as the net benefit excluding family labour value. This will be used in financial analysis, while net benefit (including family labour values) will be used in economic analysis. Clearing and maintaining canals, and other maintenance costs, are accounted for in irrigation development projects. Because of the addition of new facilities, the benefit may become negative.

16.4 Financial Analysis

16.4.1 Process

The process of learning economic facts about a project based on an interpretation of financial data is referred to as financial analysis. The goal of financial analysis is to additionally consider operating expenses, capital costs, and revenue from operations. The analysis helps to steer the project's activities and conclusively establishes a relationship between the numerous project components. It also acts as a standard yardstick of worth for acquiring a precise knowledge of the project from a financial perspective.

For the purpose of valuing stocks and evaluating managerial programmes, a review of various financial tools serves as a crucial foundation. The understanding of financial statements requires the use of financial analysis. It can offer insight into two key management areas: return on investment, and the stability of the business's financial condition.

16.4.2 Significance

Financial analysis mainly focuses on the interpretation of the information contained in a project's proforma financial statements and the presentation of the information in a way that allows for a comparative evaluation of the projects. It actually cares about how the project's financial profile is developing. Its goal is to determine whether the project is compelling enough to attract the funding necessary for its many constituent activities and, after those funds have been attracted, whether the project can produce enough economic value to meet the goals for which it is intended to be executed. It addresses the project's operational as well as financial components.

16.5 Utility of Financial and Accounting Statements

Financial statements are essential for an enterprise's internal financial control. As a result, executives, bankers, creditors, and investors must construct, analyse, and interpret these documents correctly. The manager's ability to decide relevant financial data in order to plan profitability moves determines a company's future. The first step in any businessperson's attempt to learn financial management skills is to learn to read financial statements. The shift from elitist stock ownership to widespread public ownership has necessitated a corresponding shift in the entire process of reporting corporate financial results. The role of management in financial statement preparation is to add understanding to these statements, the fairness of which is to be viewed through the eyes of the user, while the accountant's role is to close the communication gap, and the auditor's role is to add credibility to the statements.

Accounting innovations are important in the development of a good economic information system. Without these, communication with the financial community would be difficult, current and future potential investors' interests would not be served, the company's ability to raise additional capital would be hampered, and the government's regulatory measures and policies would not serve the best interests of society. While a budget summary is useful, it is brief, only providing the undertaking's data for the year. Financial analysis tries to highlight the critical realities and connections concerning administrative execution, namely corporate effectiveness, monetary qualities, shortcomings, and the financial soundness of the venture.

Tariffs and fiscal support are two commercial issues that are relevant to this section. Financial analysis employs costs and revenues to assess the project from an investment standpoint, typically from the perspective of the private sector or a corporation (sometimes referred to as a special purpose vehicle or company (SPV or SPC)) created specifically for the project's execution.

The financial analysis is based on the standard methodology used by the private sector in the analysis of project feasibility, as well as by the public sector for private sector-oriented projects. Debt service, the commercial weighted cost of capital, and the return on equity are all used in the financial analysis, which is expressed in current terms (i.e. with inflation/escalation). As a result, it differs from the standard financial analysis employed by donor agencies and the public sector. It should be assumed, at least initially, that public–private partnership (PPP) projects will not require any financial support from the government, or that if such support is required, it will be targeted and minimized.

Based on its assumptions, the financial analysis can show:

- If the project is financially viable (or bankable, as a bankable project will always be financially viable, but a financially viable project may or may not be bankable), setting out the project's financial performance, including direct financial risk, over its life. It should be noted that all risks have a monetary component. The term 'direct' refers to the sensitivity of the project's financial performance to the variables used in the model, such as toll rates, demand, costs, and debt service, etc.

- What would be required to make the project viable (bankable or acceptable to the private sector) if it is only marginally viable; and
- A clear identification, approximate costing, and timing of any proposed project support measures, as well as the financial instruments through which this support may be provided, minimized, and scheduled.

16.6 Financial Model

16.6.1 Inputs

A financial model must be created in order to evaluate a project financially. This is usually more complicated than the economic analysis because (i) revenue streams and (ii) debt servicing must be detailed and projected based on a variety of scenarios and assumptions. Economic analysis of large multifaceted development projects, on the other hand, can be equally complex.

The following are the key factors that must be entered into a financial model:

- Financial project costs (construction, land, engineering, surveys, etc.), incurred by year
- Supply (traffic by type)
- Tariff escalation formula and first year tariffs (by type)
- Annual operating and maintenance costs (base year estimate plus inflationary increase, or can be related pro rata to inflationary revenue)
- Equity types
- Debt:equity ratio (usually varies between 80:20 and 60:40, commonly 70:30)
- Arrangements and costs for debt service (debt types and interest rates, grace and repayment periods)

- Weighted average (opportunity) cost of capital
- Tax rates (national corporate rates) permitted (national regulations)

The structure of the financial model, as well as these types of inputs, will be largely consistent across all publicly funded projects. Road projects have far fewer traffic groups than, say, airports or ports, which have far more revenue streams. Costs can be calculated by adding up direct, indirect, and overhead costs based on historical data, or as a percentage of project costs or revenue. It should be noted that historical/actual data is frequently unreliable, whereas the percentage (rule of thumb) basis is at least as good and much easier to generate at this stage. Forecasting difficulties affect all projects, and this should be kept in mind during both the modelling and risk-assessment stages, where inaccuracies in demand forecasts may significantly outweigh uncertainties in other model inputs/assumptions.

Project costs will be initially calculated in base year values (i.e. when the analysis begins), but a price contingency will be added for each construction year, and revenue and costs will be inflated by an appropriate index. The proposed index or tariff escalation rates that will be allowed under the contract should be included in the request for proposals (RFP). Tariff escalation should be a bidder procurement criterion, allowing bidders to compete on both initial and future tariffs.

16.6.2 Outputs

The model then generates the profit and loss statement and the cash flow statement, which provide estimates of the key data for each project year. Other supplementary accounting outputs, such as balance sheets, are typically required later. These statements show:

- the overall project cash flow; and
- the cash flow available to equity participants (investors).
- Profitability/viability: The financial internal rate of return/return on equity (FIRR/ROE projected). This is based on the same mathematical process as the economic internal rate of return (EIRR), but it considers financial costs and revenues over the course of the

project. Furthermore, it employs actual costs and revenues rather than incremental costs and benefits.

- Cost recovery: The number of years required to recoup the equity investment (the norm for commercial projects is 5–7 years, but infrastructure projects may require 10–15 years or more).
- Debt service coverage ratio (the projected cash flow must be sufficient to finance the projected debt service). Typically, the net cash flow must be at least 1.2 times (depending on the risk profile) the debt payment due in that year.
- Quantitative risk analysis is also becoming more common as a model output.

These constitute the majority of the quantitative bases of bankability, though other factors, such as non-quantifiable risk, can also be significant.

16.6.3 Evaluations

Models can be used to determine the following:

- contract length required to generate an acceptable return on equity;
- the financial impact of various types of debt and equity, as well as the optimal debt:equity ratio;
- early-year losses (if applicable) that must be met by the PPP concessionaire (and/or fiscal support/guarantees);
- any fiscal assistance that may be required (and used to calculate the cost of guarantees);
- the financial impact and optimal timing of the 'claw back' of subsidies (fiscal support);
- government revenue from corporate taxes (when profits are made);
- the effect of changing key variables such as tariffs, project costs, etc.;
- government returns if an equity participant (and if on terms different from the private sector, e.g. secondary equity).

As a result, key parameters are fed into the model, which generates financial estimates from which decisions on the publicly funded project can be made. A project is usually financially viable if it is economically viable. However, an economically viable project may or may not be financially viable due to insufficient revenue (traffic or tariff or both). Road projects, for example, generate significant economic benefits, but tariffs are set to be 'socially/politically' responsive.

16.6.4 Tariff Escalation

Tariffs and tariff escalation are typically set to ensure a reasonable rate of return on an efficient operation. However, a subsidy may be expressly permitted by the regulations and procedures, with such funding being paid by the government based on a lower toll rate based on estimates of the users' ability to pay concept. Several important subordinate principles are incorporated into the concept of an agreed financial return.

- If at all possible, full cost recovery (capital, operating, and financing costs) is required—that is, the user pays.
- Non-uniform tariffs (those determined by project and not sector) may be utilized.
- The proposed tariff escalation should also be project-based and spelled out in the concession agreement.
- If necessary, the tariff and/or subsidy should be determined through competitive bidding to ensure the best deal for the user/the lowest liability for the government.

What constitutes a proper or acceptable rate of return on equity (ROE) is not specified, but it could be around 18–20 per cent or more, depending on the circumstances and country. In determining a fair return, the macroeconomic situation, including inflation and returns available in other sectors (opportunity costs), should be considered. The government's role is to negotiate a contract that does not provide for (i) more or (ii) less than the approximate hurdle rate of return for the specific project at hand. The former would imply that the users would bear an excessive cost, while the latter would imply that the project would most likely not be implemented.

As a result, the government should be clear that by attempting to avoid what may be considered 'excessive' returns, it is not assuming unreasonable and/or excessive contingent liabilities and risks, nor is it dismissing legitimate commercial interest in the project. The government should further be sufficiently adaptable and agree to higher returns if the project or other relevant circumstances demand it. This balance should be recognized by the government as a difficult and somewhat delicate issue that requires adequate consideration (including consultation) in the pre- or full financial scenario study.

16.6.5 Concession Agreements

The concession agreement is a detailed contract between the parties in which the project is described in technical and financial terms, as well as concerning risk management. Many projects suffer from ambiguous contracts, but a contract that may last 30 years or more must anticipate all types of eventualities, at least in broad terms, in order to cover all potential problems.

The financial analysis enables the government to confidently draft the financial aspects of the concession agreement for inclusion in the RFP. The financial analysis and model can also be used later to model the tenders received in order to evaluate them for accuracy and realism.

16.6.6 Credit Enhancement

This term refers to actions taken to improve the risk–return profile of a project (which is economically viable) in order to attract financing and move it to 'financial closure'. The term can have several different meanings. In general, anything that improves a project's 'bankability' qualifies as credit enhancement. In broad terms, this may include (i) a solid, credible, and transparent cooperation programme; (ii) project identification and structuring that understands and addresses private-sector concerns.

It may include the three types of measures listed below:

- **Typical project finance techniques**: These include measures (e.g. escrow accounts, mezzanine financing, and securitization) that aim to reduce the common types of risk found in any cooperative project. They include measures agreed by the sponsors and developers (the equity participants) as well as the debt participants, and do not usually involve the host government directly. However, as part of their oversight and due diligence responsibilities in procuring and monitoring the desired infrastructure services, the contracting authority and other government agencies involved must be aware of and conversant with these techniques.

- **Government assistance**: This includes a variety of policies and measures (e.g. off-take agreements, revenue guarantees, and tax breaks) that the government can provide to reduce risk and improve project finances, or both, as perceived and analysed by the PPP concessionaire, and particularly the lenders.
- **Donors' backing**: The bilateral and multilateral donors can provide help to a country to develop its cooperation programme and bring projects to financial closure and implementation. These typically take effect when the overall country's risk is perceived to be high (making purely commercial financing difficult), despite the fact that individual projects may have sound financial and economic dynamics and merit to be implemented as cooperation projects.

16.7 Fiscal Support

The following section contains guidelines on government guarantees.

16.7.1 Evaluating Government Financial Assistance

The challenge, once it has been determined that a project requires assistance, is to evaluate the various types of support. Assuming that all types of assistance achieve the desired outcome, the goal is to select the assistance that provides the best value for money and is consistent with the government's fiscal framework.

16.7.2 Financial Rationale for the Provision of Government Fiscal Support

Several factors should be considered when evaluating government financial assistance. The objectives of the subsidy should be the starting point for government support assessment. The government should link the objectives to the project's financial performance, including its riskiness in the absence of any support.

16.7.3 Estimating the Expected Cost of Fiscal Support for a Publicly Funded Investment Project

Here we look at a method for estimating the government's expected cost or payout if it commits to a specific type of fiscal support. These types include:

- capital grant;
- minimum revenue or demand guarantee, including government-backed off-take or power purchase agreement;
- full debt service guarantee;
- revenue rights to other infrastructure facilities;
- tax honeymoon or vacation; and
- operating subsidy.

The method is primarily intended for contracting agencies, as they are the most knowledgeable about the commercial aspects of a publicly funded investment project. At this point, the contracting authority must justify any need for fiscal support for a publicly funded investment project. A cost–benefit analysis of the various types of fiscal assistance considered appropriate would be required by:

- the relevant line ministry's publicly funded investment cell, node, or unit;
- the publicly funded investment centre; and
- A ministry of finance's (MoF) publicly funded investment cell, node, or risk-management unit (RMU).

The evaluation would help the line ministry decide whether to submit the evaluated project to the central agencies. The publicly funded investment centre, in turn, would decide whether to negotiate with the RMU for fiscal support for the publicly funded investment project in question based on the contracting authority's due diligence.

16.7.3.1 The Method of Valuing the Future Cost of Fiscal Support

The approach is founded on a probabilistic model, specifically the expected utility model. It computes the present-day (present-value) cost of a specific type of fiscal contingent support. To simplify the analysis, it is assumed that the opportunity cost of a monetary unit is the same for all forms of fiscal support. The estimated present value (PV) of the support options is the result of this approach. By estimating the future (years 1 to *n* of the project) costs of each method of support, each type can be converted to PVs and compared using the appropriate discount rate. As a result, for each year, there would be a number of outcomes, each with a probability assigned to it.

16.7.3.2 Criteria for Fiscal Support to Publicly Funded Investment Projects

A set of criteria is proposed to help determine whether fiscal support should be provided to publicly funded investment projects. The criteria to be met are as follows.

- The assistance is in accordance with national laws.
- The proposed project has been prioritized as part of the national planning process.
- The company requesting assistance was chosen/procured through a fair, transparent, and competitive process with no conflicts of interest.
- The level of support meets the MoF's fiscal criteria.
- Alternative methods of assistance, policies, or other measures would not result in equivalent or greater socioeconomic benefits.
- The project adheres to sector strategy.

16.7.3.3 Procurement and Negotiating Strategy and Fiscal Support

The government must determine its procurement and negotiating strategy for fiscal support based on the above assessment. The feasibility study will have already indicated to the government whether assistance is required and how much it will cost. It is a critical principle that, following the study, the government decides whether or not to provide funding for that project, as well as the preferred type or types of funding.

As a result, discussions with the government and MoF must take place early in the project cycle to ensure coordination and that projects have not progressed to the study stage with little hope of support. The RFP can specify a maximum level of support, or none at all, and one of the bid criteria must be the minimization of support (or lack thereof) requested by bidders (Dabla-Norris et al., 2011).

16.7.4 Fall-back Strategy

Given that the actual agreed-upon level of support will be determined through negotiations with the private sector, the government must establish a maximum level of support that it will not exceed. As a result, the government must determine the fall-back negotiation position, or the point at which it believes the type/costs and/or risks of support are not justified.

16.7.5 Policy Guidelines on Government Support

The government needs more and better infrastructure while remaining fiscally responsible. However, if the project is risky and/or cannot generate enough revenue (demand is lower than expected and/or users do not pay enough), the government must make up the difference through the taxpayer. The government must determine whether it should contribute any assistance, and if so, how much, and when it should provide it. It is obvious that each project will have unique characteristics, and thus support will differ.

16.8 Conclusion

Project evaluation includes both the project's economic and financial analyses (it is also termed project justification). Technical, social, environmental, and economic and financial elements must all be considered in depth during the project-review process. However, in this chapter, the phrase 'project evaluation' has referred to both economic and financial analysis. As stated, though using economic prices is referred to as economic analysis, and using financial prices, financial analysis (OECD, 2009b), there is also debate over which benefits fall into which category. Economic analysis often focuses on the benefits that can be evaluated in money. However, there are two possible scenarios for financial analysis: one counting simply the benefit, which can be cash income for the private company; the other the benefit that might be valued in cash but which is not cash income.

In the budget, many Indian states have specified guidelines and forms. It should also establish the project value barrier below which the required assessment could be done. The amount of work put on return on investment (ROI)/cost–benefit analysis (CBA) should be in line with the planned expense. The project's economic analysis flow chart is outlined in Figure 16.2. The findings of project appraisal at a financial price will be presented initially as a sequence of calculations.

If the results do not demonstrate the project's viability, the implementation agency (e.g. the government) may deliberate, and the original plan should be evaluated once more. The analysis then moves on to project evaluation at economic price (economic analysis), translating financial price into an economic one, to examine the viability from the perspective of the national economy. This phase will be essential, particularly if the government plans to borrow money from other nations or international organizations.

However, there can be room for disagreement if the government is funding the project directly. In order to extract the efficiency of investment in a competitive market, project evaluation at an affordable cost will remove the effects of subsidies, taxes, and other charges. However, the government itself sets these tax and subsidy levels as a policy to steer the nation in a particular direction. If there are considerable subsidies, for example, it could be argued that EIRR's decisions contradict government policy.

The government may only need to consider a project's financial costs when making decisions if it wants to keep the impact of its policy. Comparisons between the outcomes of economic and financial prices

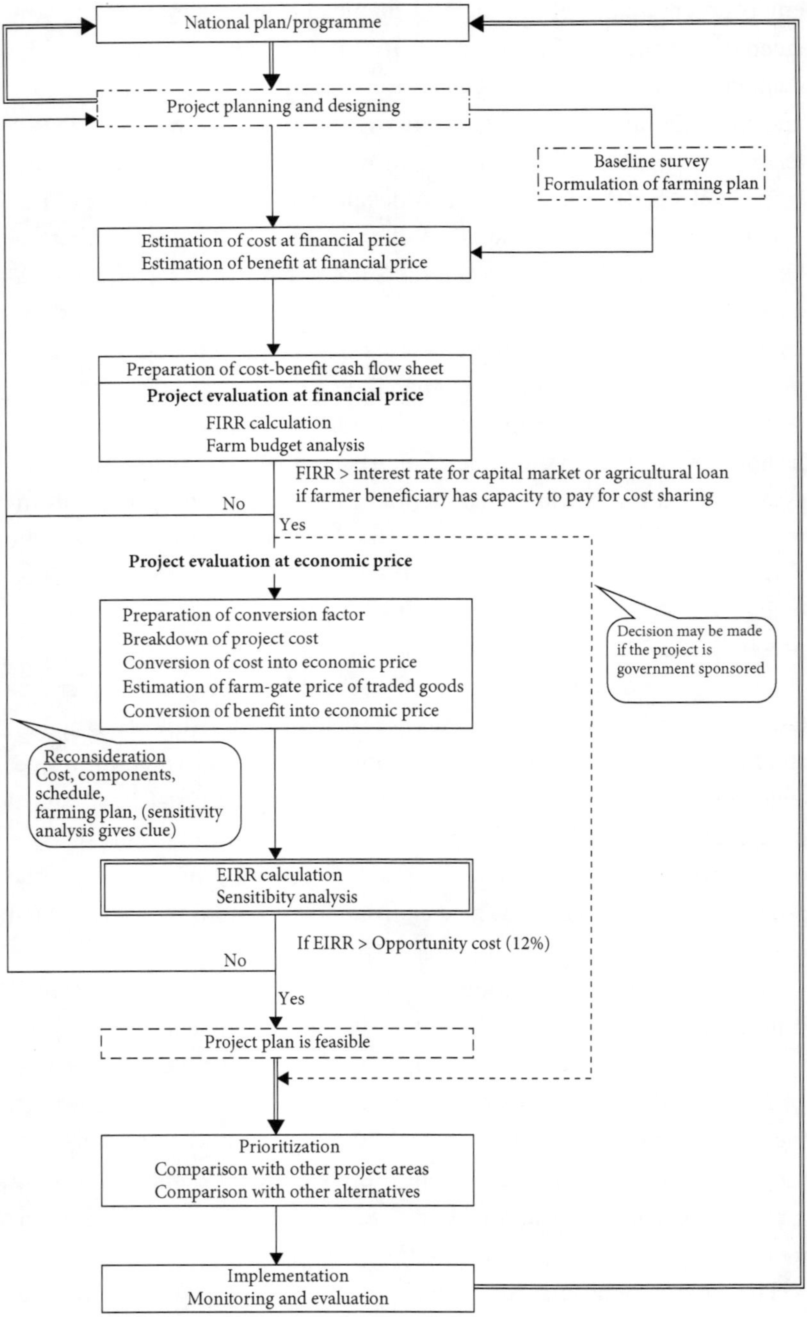

Figure 16.2 Flowchart of project evaluation.

might reveal market distortions and give the government insight into the need to reevaluate its policies. As a result, it is claimed that project evaluation at a reasonable cost is still beneficial for projects that are funded by the government.

References

Allain-Dupré, D. (2011). 'Multi-level Governance of Public Investment: Lessons from the Crisis', *OECD Regional Development Working Papers*, 2011/5, OECD Publishing, doi: 10.1787/5kg87n3bp6jb-en.

Blöchliger, H. and Petzold, O. (2009). 'Taxes or Grants: What Revenue Source for Sub-central Governments?', OECD Economics Department Working Papers, 706, OECD Publishing. http://dx.doi.org/10.1787/223111363085.

Charbit, C. (2011). 'Governance of Public Policies in Decentralised Contexts: The Multi-level Approach', OECD Regional Development Working Papers, 2011/04, OECD Publishing. http://dx.doi.org/10.1787/5kg883pkxkhc-en.

Charbit, C., and Michalun, M. (2009). 'Mind the Gaps: Managing Mutual Dependence in Relations among Levels of Government', OECD Working Papers On Public Governance, 14, OECD Publishing, doi:10.1787/221253707200.

Dabla-Norris, E., Brumby, J., Kyobe, A., et al. (2011). 'Investing in Public Investment: An Index of Public Investment Efficiency', IMF Working Paper 11/37, www.imf.org/external/pubs/ft/wp/2011/wp1137.pdf.

Garcilazo, E., and Oliveira Martins, J. (2013). 'The Contribution of Regions to Aggregate Growth', OECD Regional Development Working Papers.

Mizell, L., and Allain-Dupré, D. (2013). 'Creating Conditions for Effective Public Investment: Sub-national Capacities in a Multi-level Governance Context', OECD Regional Development Working Papers, 2013/04, OECD Publishing, doi: 10.1787/5k49j2cjv5mq-en.

OECD (2007a). *Linking Regions and Central Governments: Contracts for Regional Development*, OECD publishing, doi: 10.1787/9789264008755-en.

OECD (2009b). *Governing Regional Development Policy: The Use of Performance Indicators*, OECD Publishing, doi: 10.1787/9789264056299-en.

OECD (2009c). 'Investing for Growth: Building Innovative Regions', background report for the meeting of the Territorial Development Policy Committee (TDPC) at the ministerial level, 31 March 2009, http://www.oecd.org/regional/ministerial/42531915.pdf.

17

Project Appraisal and Alternative Sources of Funding

Some Perspectives to Improve Viability

L. Somasundaram

17.1 Introduction

Infrastructure finance has witnessed a transformation, having moved from the domain of grant finance to user-pay concepts. Infrastructure is important to achieve welfare targets and service delivery norms, and to provide support for businesses to thrive and generate employment. Moreover, a critical minimum investment in infrastructure is needed to sustain economic growth. Some of the emerging issues in project finance from a public finance perspective are its governance structure, the ability of users to repay, impacts on the environment and society, and the need for economic returns.

The Asian Development Bank estimates an investment requirement of US$ 1.7 trillion in the infrastructure sector in Asia through 2030 in order to maintain the current growth momentum and respond to climate change.[1] The challenge is not just investments, but the design and delivery of the projects have to take into consideration climate resilience and social protection while also being financially viable. The challenge is to make infrastructure projects bankable against the increasing costs related to land acquisition, raw materials, operations, and human resources. The role of project appraisal is specifically put in perspective in this context.

[1] Asian Development Bank, Meeting Asia's Infrastructure Needs, 2017.

L. Somasundaram, *Project Appraisal and Alternative Sources of Funding* In: *Fiscal Policy and Public Financial Management.* Edited by: Pinaki Chakraborty and K R Shanmugam, Oxford University Press.
 DOI: 10.1093/9780198930464.003.0017

17.2 Characteristics of Infrastructure Projects

Infrastructure projects have the characteristics of public goods—the consumption and subsequent derivation of utility by one individual does not prohibit the other(s) from deriving the utility from the same good/service. The justification for expenses is in the realm of providing public welfare and aimed towards justice and equity. An immediate issue is the question of pricing of the service: 'who pays?'. If the project does not envisage a user-fee model, then the relevant question is if the existing tax collections are sufficient.

The second important characteristic is that of impact—there could be both positive and negative impacts, termed externalities. The third characteristic is that it requires several appraisals—technical, social, economic, environmental, legal, and institutional. The financial appraisal should actually consider these costs. The economic environment is extremely dynamic as all nations move towards industrial and post-industrial stages of development. As a result, the realities of appraisals change rather faster and are often drastic.

Therefore, the emerging question is: Can we have an appraisal mechanism addressing all these concerns? In building the appraisal mechanism, it is imperative to understand the characteristics of an infrastructure project and the complexities involved. Project appraisals require, along with a financial management system, a complete governance system that can consider the following:

- **Variety of stakeholders**: The stakeholders in a typical infrastructure project are from diverse social and economic backgrounds. There are different groups of beneficiaries, some who pay the costs and some who may not pay for usage but still are to be served. The stakeholder group also includes the government resources at different levels of authority, from the central/state government to the head of the line departments to the authorities in the urban/rural local bodies.
- **Governance**: Timely decisions enable project completion within time and costs. At the same time, the governance mechanism should not lose sight of the need to adhere to legal and contractual requirements.

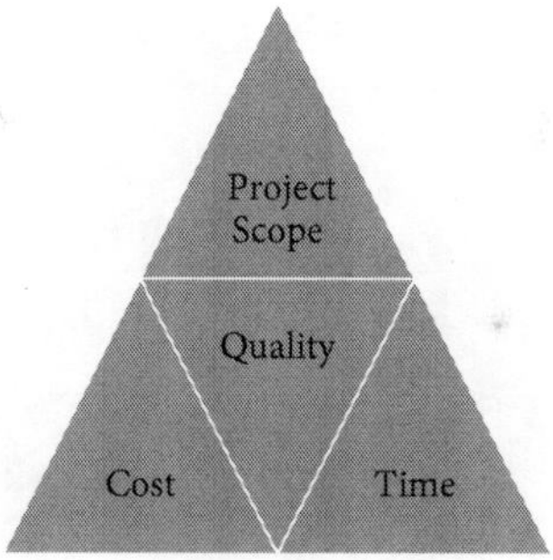

Figure 17.1 Interrelationship of factors in projects.
Source: Adapted by author based on Fabozzi and de Nahlik (2012).

- **Monitoring of progress and measurement of impacts:** Most projects today bring in the element of monitoring and evaluation (M&E) as an integral part. M&E is essential to understanding the operations and maintenance (O&M) costs and the progress of the project over the project timeline. A dashboard-based approach built into the management information system (MIS) is now the adopted mechanism to monitor different project-related data almost in real time. The dashboard needs to highlight time and cost overruns, missing any governance requirements in project progress, sharing of information with all relevant stakeholders, and enabling decision-making at appropriate levels (see Figure 17.1).

The traditional approach to project management involves an understanding of the flow of activities that can form a checklist of items in a project for successful management. Figure 17.2 presents such a flow chart.

17.3 Project Viability

What makes a project viable? A project has to earn returns on investment and cover the operational costs over its lifetime. Traditionally, the approach is to use cost–benefit analysis, considering the social costs and benefits along with the economic costs and benefits. Though the approach appears simple, complexities of various forms arise in real life.

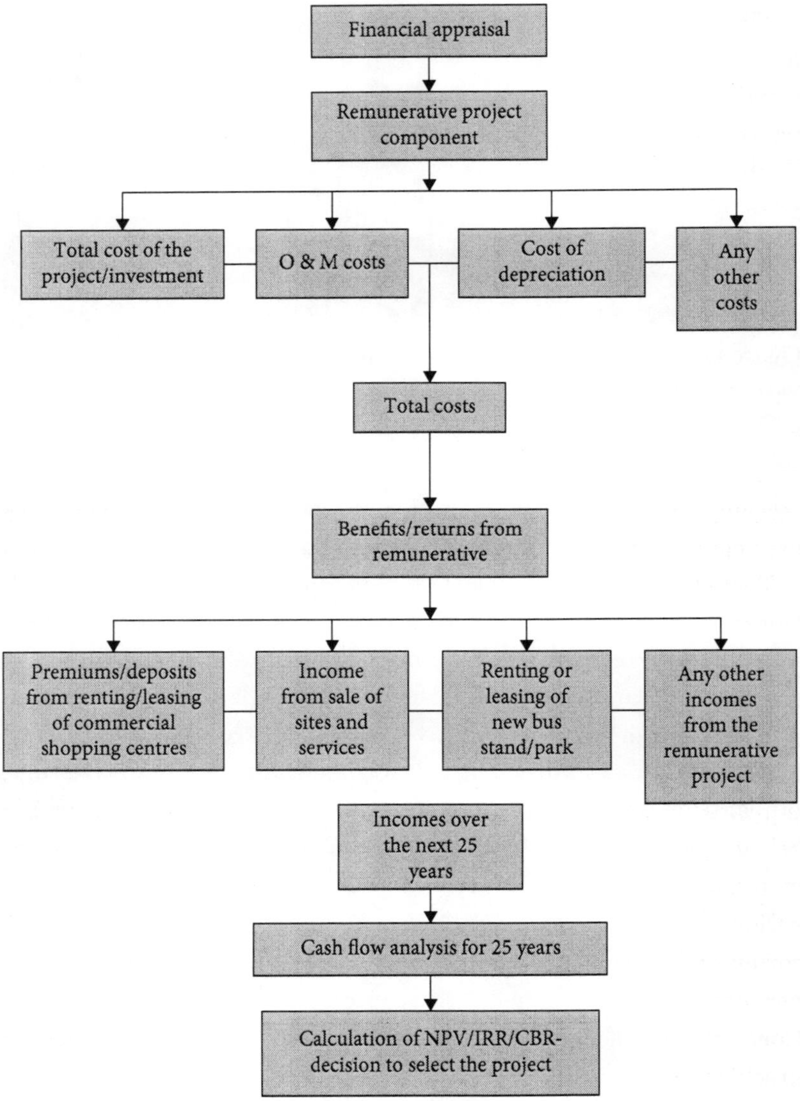

Figure 17.2 Checklist: Financial appraisal of an infrastructure development project, assuming a project lifetime of 25 years.

Source: *Handbook on Infrastructure Finance*, Administrative Training Institute, Mysore, unpublished.

First, the needs assessment is itself a challenge. The volume of demand for the project may not fructify. In projects such as transport, the demand could emerge over a period of time, and this could alter the project finance viability altogether. Second, the project funding faces challenges. For instance, the early railway projects were financed through a combination of subscriptions to bonds and equity, and these obligations were supported by mortgages or local city or state government (Jackson, 2014). Eventually interest rates increased, and the portfolio became riskier. In India, the North Bengal Company was set up to fund the railway projects but was not successful in raising the capital outlay, eventually requiring an Indian Government guarantee to complete the project. Third is the challenge of project delivery within time. Invariably projects exceed time schedules, and every additional day is a combination of cost overrun and revenue loss. Fourth, on the revenue side, there is always resistance to a user-pay model of cost recovery.

There has always been an effort to understand and address the challenges in project finance, and several changes to business models have evolved to solve specific issues. For instance, the public–private partnership (PPP) model has evolved to reduce various risk factors.

Yet, there have been failures, though at a lower rate. The PPP project failure rate in the developing world, as per the Private Participation in Infrastructure (PPI) database of the World Bank (ppi.worldbank.org), is below 4 per cent, for both the number of projects and associated investments. 292 PPP projects (out of 8,295 projects, or 3 per cent) failed in the period 1990 to 2020 in the developing world. In terms of investments, the corresponding numbers were US$71 billion out of US$1.99 trillion, or 3 per cent (Pratap, 2020). In India, initially the PPP model was successful. Contract management and risk management have contributed to failure to achieve financial returns in the projects (Kudtarkar, 2020).

To address this, the latest evolution is the hybrid annuity model (HAM) PPP. Contract management and risk management, cited above, have been addressed in the HAM PPP, which has the following features:

- financial risk sharing between the government and the private sector by injecting a portion of project costs;
- accepting the risk of revenue forecast and collection;

- hedging inflation by ensuring indexation of construction costs and O&M payments;
- flexibility in qualification criteria, which helped expand the market appetite and broaden the supply base beyond large companies;
- provisions requiring environmental and forest permits—and at least 80 per cent of site availability at commencement, to have achieved a high level of project readiness at the outset;
- the model offers flexibility to the private sector to promote innovation in construction and O&M, by focusing on performance-based service specifications for end users.

Key considerations for successful and bankable projects are as follows.

1. **Focus on credit risk**: Infrastructure projects generally have two phases (construction and operation), characterized by different risks and cash flow patterns. While the construction phase involves technological and environmental risks, the operation phase involves market risk and political risk, among other factors. These factors could contribute to credit risk in the project.
2. **Feasibility study**: There are a variety of feasibility studies that have to be undertaken before embarking on the project. The feasibility study shall be the key to understanding the operations and maintenance requirements, the demand factor, and the pricing.
   a. *Market feasibility*: Projects envisaging returns through user-payments need a comprehensive market feasibility study. When capacity utilization sees a shortfall, the revenues come down, impacting the cash flows and the internal rate of return (IRR). It must be noted that often O&M and other costs cannot come down for a given level of infrastructure capacity which has already been built.
   b. *Environmental feasibility and social-environmental impact studies*: This assesses the viability of a project from an environmental and a social perspective, identifying negative externalities that could impact the implementation of the proposed development. The environmental impact assessment (EIA) tries to forecast the impact that the project could have once it is completed. According to the United Nations Environment

Programme (UNEP), an EIA aims to predict environmental impacts at an early stage in project planning and design, find ways and means to reduce adverse impacts, shape projects to suit the local environment, and present the predictions and options to decision-makers. On the cost side, the project has to put in place an environment management plan to mitigate the negative effects which could incur further costs to the project. On the benefits side, an effective EIA considers social acceptance once the project is completed and also assesses positive spinoffs, which the project could leverage to enhance the IRR.

In India, On 27 January 1994, the then Union Ministry of Environment and Forests, under the Environmental (Protection) Act 1986, promulgated an EIA notification making environmental clearance (EC) mandatory for expansion or modernization of any activity or for setting up new projects listed in Schedule 1 of the notification. The Ministry of Environment, Forests and Climate Change (MoEFCC) notified new EIA legislation in September 2006. The notification makes it mandatory for projects to get environmental clearance.

However, unlike the EIA notification of 1994, the more recent legislation has put the onus of acquiring clearance for projects on the state government (depending on the size/capacity of the project). We shall revisit this in detail subsequently, highlighting its impact on the cost–benefit analyses.

3. **Risk assessment**: Hillsom (2003) suggested that the risk in infrastructure projects is divided into three levels: on the first, he differentiates among risks that result from (1) environment, (2) contractors, (3) clients, and (4) the project. Project risk pertains to the probability of uncertainties regarding the technical, schedule, and cost outcomes in a given project. Several risk-assessment methods have evolved over time. However, each type of infrastructure deserves close consideration and application of ground realities, and the relevant risk-assessment models should incorporate these parameters. Dey (2001) suggests an integrated project management model for the Indian petroleum industry . A risk-assessment framework using the analytical hierarchy process (AHP) model (Figure 17.3) is proposed.

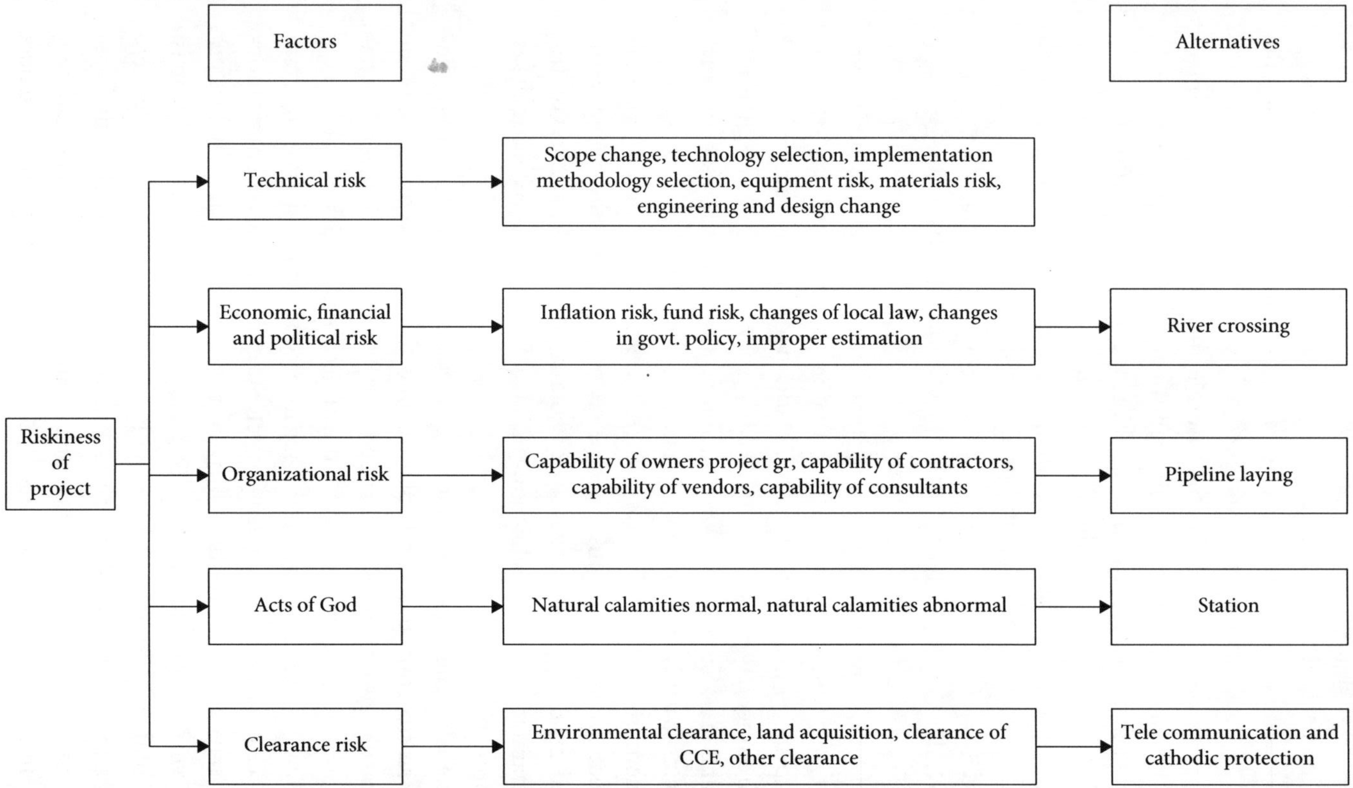

Figure 17.3 Analytic hierarchy process model for risk assessment of projects.

Source: Adapted by author based on Dey, 2001.

Table 17.1 Overview of three common approaches for project risk management.

PMBOK 2013	PRINCE2	Department of Defence (DOD) risk management
Plan risk management	Identify risk	Identify risk
Identify risks		
Perform quantitative risk analysis	Assess risk	Cluster analysis
Perform qualitative risk analysis		Risk-mitigation planning
Plan risk responses	Risk plan	Risk-mitigation plan implementation
Monitor and control risks	Implement and communicate	Risk tracking

Source: *Project Management Body of Knowledge*, Project Management Institute.

An important factor in project risk is the evolving nature of a project and the dynamic ecosystem after project completion. Infrastructure firms do bring in information technology (IT) systems for risk management. In practice, the most frequently applied methodology are the Project Management Body of Knowledge (PMBOK) guidelines proposed by the Project Management Institute (Rihar et al., 2019). The comparative features of three common risk-management approaches are presented in Table 17.1.

The risk-management plan and contingency planning have to consider risk factors in a systematic way, the challenge being to involve all the relevant stakeholders and to evolve a decision-making framework based on the complex data flow.

4. **Capacity-building for government authorities**: A number of governance failures relate to lack of capacity with the urban local bodies where the project is implemented. Though the aspect of capacity building has to be a common rather than a specific parameter for a project, this is a key consideration because in the emerging scenario of urban development and the growth of tier-two cities across India, active participation of urban local bodies will be a key determinant in how public finance is effectively utilized.

17.4 Review of Select Case Studies

There exists a large body of literature built up over a substantial period of time, which has considered geography and spread of sectors in its analysis of infrastructure projects. This section highlights some of the projects, with a focus on PPP, to put into perspective what has been learnt.

17.4.1 Case Study 1: Alandur Sewerage Project

The Alandur Sewerage Project was started in 1996 and completed in 2001. This project addressed some of the key issues identified above:

- Credit risk through securitization of future earnings
- Capital costs through a contribution from citizens
- O&M through user fee
- Compliance through stakeholder participation

Alandur forms a part of the Chennai Metropolitan Area (CMA) and is governed by the Alandur Municipality (AM) with a population of 165,000 people, with a mix of residential and commercial units. In 1996, when the Alandur Sewerage Project (ASP) was initiated, about 25 per cent of the population lived in slums. The township had individual septic tanks prior to 1996. The World Bank, in its report 'PPP Projects in India: A Compendium of Case Studies', notes that this project was transformational in the sense that the project was designed to provide a service with financial and management responsibilities being shared among the municipality, the residents, the private sector, and state government bodies.

The ASP had the following objectives:

- Improve the standard of living in Alandur (to be on a par with that of Chennai)
- 100 per cent coverage for the entire population of Alandur
- Eradicate the mosquito problem
- Avoid the recurring expenditure on septic tank cleaning
- Avoid groundwater contamination

The sewerage project was to be designed for the projected population of about 300,000 in 2027 and was planned to be completed within five years of its inception date. The project components included the following:

- a sewerage network consisting of the main sewer line, branch sewer lines, and manholes;
- construction of a sewage pumping station;
- A sewage treatment plant; and
- low-cost sanitation.

To plan this complex and politically challenging project, the AM worked in partnership with Tamil Nadu Urban Infrastructure Financial Services Ltd (TNUIFSL) and USAID's Financial Institution Reform and Expansion (FIRE) project. The total cost of the project was estimated at about Rs 45.31 crore and later revised to Rs 40.86 crore. The financial sources are listed in Table 17.2.

Fifty-nine per cent of financing was made through loans provided by the Tamil Nadu Urban Infrastructure Development Corporation (TUFIDCO) and TNUIFSL. The loan provided by TUFIDCO was payable over eight years after a two-year moratorium at an interest rate of 5 per cent per annum (as against prevailing market rates of 15 per cent at that time). TNUIFSL's loan was set at a rate of 16 per cent per annum, payable over a period of 15 years with a five-year moratorium. The term

Table 17.2 Sources of funds.

Source	Amount (Rs crore)
Grant from TNUIFSL	3
Loan from TNUIFSL	6
Loan from TUFIDCO	16
Grant from TUFIDCO	1
Deposits from public	12.4
Interest from deposits	2.46
Total	40.86

Source: World Bank Compendium of PPP Projects in India.

lenders stipulated an escrow account, where all the revenue receipts of the municipality (including property tax, stamp duty, and the grant from the Government of Tamil Nadu (GoTN)) as well as the sewer tariff were to be deposited in favour of TNUIFSL and TUFIDCO. Two points are noteworthy here:

1. This was a kind of securitization of future earnings towards repayment and a way to assure financial viability of the project.
2. The municipality also accepted limits imposed on future indebtedness, thus reducing the credit risk of the institution.

There was some grant support too. TUFIDCO provided a special grant from the Tamil Nadu urban development grant fund for this purpose, which worked out to nearly three per cent of the total project cost. The GoTN agreed in principle to bridge the gap in the sewer account during the life of the project, after providing for O&M expenses, debt servicing, and contribution to the sinking fund. Additionally, the GoTN agreed to fund the monthly operating costs of the system above Rs 150 per household sewer charge, to a maximum of Rs 30 per connection per month.

The most important part of the project was the users paying for the services rendered. There were two components of user pay. The first is the contribution to the capital costs, as presented in Table 17.3.

The municipality aimed to provide about 22,000 connections both for domestic and non-domestic categories of users by the end of 2004–05. This would yield an estimated income of nearly Rs 13 crore, which it proposed to put into a revolving fund for repayment of loans to the lenders.

Table 17.3 Contribution from users.

Category of user	Amount (in Rs)
Domestic	5,000 per house connection
Commercial	10,000 per connection
Industrial	10,000 per connection

Source: World Bank Compendium of PPP Projects in India.

Second component is the sewer maintenance charges at the rate of Rs 150 per month per connection from domestic users, Rs 450 per month per connection from commercial users, and Rs 750 per month from industrial users. The domestic monthly charges were proposed to be increased to 6 per cent annually till they reached a level of Rs 180 per month. Similarly, the commercial and industrial maintenance charges were proposed to be increased by 6 per cent annually up to the level of Rs 540 and Rs 900, respectively. These limits were later reduced on the basis of a willingness to pay (WTP) survey, and discussions with the citizens and officials concerned.

Stakeholder participation is a key part of the success of a PPP project. In this project too, the World Bank report notes that stakeholder participation, including the resident welfare associations in Alandur, was a key element of success for the project. Impact is a key consideration for successful projects and, as mentioned, impact measurement is imperative for successful projects in terms of social impact and environmental impact. The Alandur Sewerage Project's pre- and post-project impact is presented in Table 17.4.

17.4.2 Case Study 2: Mumbai Metro One Private Limited: Time and Cost Overruns

The Mumbai Metro One Private Ltd (MMOPL) project was delayed by 39 months due to frequent and substantial changes in project planning and timelines on account of uncontrollable factors such as a highly constrained rights of way. There were contractual risks leading to litigations. The Bombay High Court ordered the constitution of a Fare Fixation Committee (FFC) to recommend the fare to be charged. The FFC recommended a fare in the range of Rs 10 to Rs 110. The Mumbai Metropolitan Regional Development Authority (MMRDA) challenged this recommendation in the Bombay High Court, to retain the fares as per the provisions of the concession agreement. The Bombay High Court set aside the recommendations of the FFC and allowed the company to continue with the present fare structure (Rs 10 to Rs 40).

MMOPL resorted to filing various claims against the MMRDA on account of damages incurred due to delays to handing over unencumbered

Table 17.4 Impact of Alandur Sewerage Project.

Parameter	Situation before PPP intervention	Situation after PPP intervention
Urban service	No sewerage system for a population of 165,000	120 km underground sewerage system, pumping stations. and a sewage treatment plant of 24 million litres per day
Urban service	Water-borne sanitation facilities, septic/ holding tanks for disposal of night soil	Underground sewerage system with connection to each property
Urban service	Unregulated disposal of sewerage in storm-water drainage and low-lying areas	Modern sewerage treatment plant designed to international standards
Environment and health	Open storm-water drains stagnating in outer areas of town—environmental and health hazard	Underground sewerage system has eliminated risk of mosquitoes and related diseases for the citizens of Alandur and surrounding areas
Environment and health	Contamination of underground water sources due to open drains	Almost 100 per cent eradication of groundwater contamination through underground sewerage system and wastewater treatment plant
Public participation		Rs 12 crore out of the capital cost was through public contribution
Public participation		Collection of sewerage fee from the public (on a graded structure amounting to a weighted average of Rs 75 per connection) amounts to Rs 2 crore per month and covers both debt repayment and O&M costs of the Alandur Municipality

Source: World Bank Compendium of PPP Projects in India.

Right of Way and land, and additional costs incurred due to various changes in design to accommodate project encumbrances. The claims filed against the MMRDA as of 31 March 2019 aggregated to Rs 1,766.25 crore. The MMRDA has not accepted the said claims filed by MMOPL and hence MMOPL has initiated arbitration proceedings as per the provisions of the Concession Agreement.

The lingering credit risk materialized in June 2019. India Ratings downgraded the sponsor of the project Reliance Infrastructure's long-term rating to default grade. The Reliance group incurred a net loss of Rs 2,426.82 crore during the year ended 31 March 2019. The bank's loan of Rs 2500 to MMOPL was classified as a non-performing asset (NPA) in 2018.

The delay in land acquisition resulted in high time and cost overrun of the project during construction. The project revenue was increasing every year but was not sufficient to pay the interest and principal of the high debt, resulting in the project becoming an NPA. Due to a weak financial position, Reliance Infrastructure Ltd could not financially support MMOPL.

As noted in the previous section, risks have a cascading effect on project finances during both the construction and O&M stages. The land acquisition was the first trigger, and subsequently the project delays and contract-legal issues led to time and cost overruns.

17.4.3 Case Study 3: PNG Tollway Private Limited: Terminated Project

This project puts into perspective the role of market demand and the possibility of beneficiary payments. Stakeholder analysis was not conducted effectively. The project had registered considerably low toll volumes since the achievement of partial commercial operation date (COD) in October 2012. This was accentuated by local protests and diversion of traffic near the city of Nashik. The protests continued in the form of political agitations demanding exemption from toll for local people. Despite the Maharashtra state government being a party to the tripartite State Support Agreement, there was no support for additional security to toll plazas which would have aided full tolls.

The Bombay High Court had directed the District Administration to ensure law and order at the toll plaza and on the project highway, which were not implemented by the district administration, and the project SPV was forced to continue offering the discounted rates. Further, given that the toll rates notified post the partial COD in October 2012 were at around 30 per cent of the applicable rates, the average daily revenue collections were significantly lower than the initial estimates. Even after the toll revision in May 2014, average daily revenue collections had witnessed a sizable deficit compared to initial forecasts. As a result, the company had stopped paying the committed revenue share to the National Highways Authority of India (NHAI). The concessionaire faced a revenue loss of almost Rs 100 crore. In March 2016 the concessionaire, the consortium of Ashoka Buildcon, and L&T Infra served a termination notice to the NHAI on the grounds of prevailing force majeure conditions, citing 'lack of state support', and the toll and maintenance operations were taken over by the NHAI. As per its 2020–21 balance sheet, the company had an accumulated loss of about Rs 458 crore. The key takeaway is that political risks leading to beneficiary payment risks could lead to credit risk.

17.5 Infrastructure Projects: IRR and Emerging Public Finance Model

In sum, it can be seen that the rate of return can be impacted by several factors for any project. Since IRR is the key determinant for sustaining the project, in the emerging situation all these can impact the returns and thus impact public finance. It is imperative to consider the growth in citizen requirements in terms of solid waste management, effluents treatment, public sanitation, water supply, sewerages, transportation, and lighting of public spaces, all of which are under the purview of public finance. In the context of the urgent need to create projects that are not just economically viable, but also environmentally sustainable, the question arises whether public finance has to move to a larger ambit of financial model.

The emerging concept is 'blended finance'. Blended finance, according to the OECD, is the strategic use of development finance for the mobilization of additional finance towards sustainable development. The underlying logic is that the ultimate source of public finance is the citizens' contribution through taxes and loans. Both these have a negative impact on the larger economy—and in the context of developing economies, the problem is further accentuated by the pyramid structure of purchasing power. However, several strides have now been taken with collaboration from philanthropic funds, which is also driving the impact creation in the development sector.

Impact investment—wherein an investor is ready to accept lower than market returns for creating a social or environmental impact, usually measured in terms of the sustainable development goals (SDGs)—is seeing increasing momentum across the world. Blended finance is still evolving. According to the World Bank's Independent Evaluation Group report titled 'Findings from a Cluster of Project Performance Assessment Reports' (on projects that used blended finance) between 2010 and 2014, though there have been startup challenges, they showed good adherence to environmental and social standards. However, the project has to have a basic business case; the same report, in its analysis of later projects between 2012 and 2016, indicates that commercial viability was achieved along with impact creation. Figure 17.4 presents a framework of blended finance. Blended finance reduces the overall risk of the project, inducing investments.

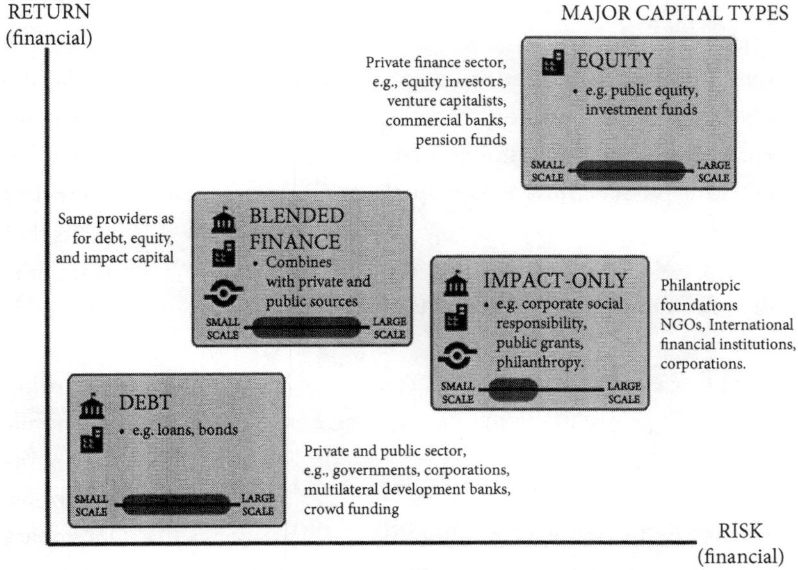

Figure 17.4 Risk–return versus capital types—the case for blended finance.
Source: Sumaila et al. (2021).

17.6 Impact versus Benefits and Systems for Impact Evaluation

Several public sector infrastructure projects create impact, such as solid waste management projects, water supply, treatment plants, and public sanitation. For impact investments to happen, impact has to be clearly measured and monitored. It can be measured and monitored, but may not be obtained from project data. A project has to create a strong baseline with stakeholder participation such that data can be sourced from the stakeholders. For example, in a public toilets project in a city, the beneficiaries are the travellers, but the impact is no open defecation. Open defecation is not an impact that can be 'measured' with the system data. Stakeholder and citizen participation are important for impact to be known. Thus, blended finance through impact investments could happen if there are robust systems to measure the impact, which can be achieved through an impact-evaluation framework—often termed the monitoring and evaluation (M&E) framework. The components of a robust M&E framework are:

- establishing measurable objectives, in line with the project development objectives;
- establishing structured indicators for impact;
- setting up appropriate data-collection mechanisms;
- developing an evaluation framework;
- setting up dissemination channels for reporting and use of the M&E system.

Effective monitoring will entail the following:

- routine collection of information;
- tracking project implementation progress;
- measuring efficiency.

There are three parts of monitoring, namely results monitoring (Figure 17.5), implementation monitoring (Figure 17.6), and project monitoring. These are interrelated and could be achieved in a single

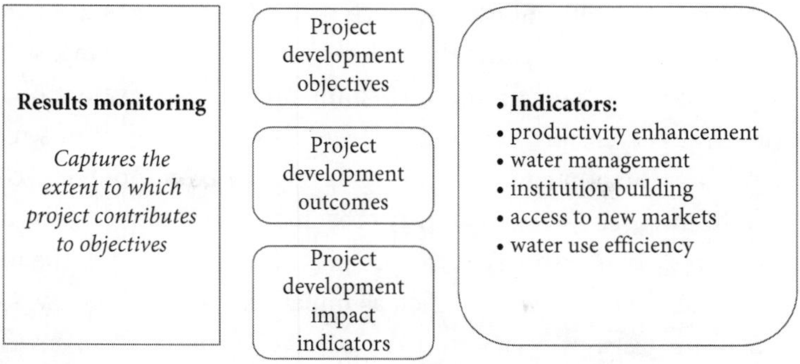

Figure 17.5 Results monitoring framework.
Source: Author.

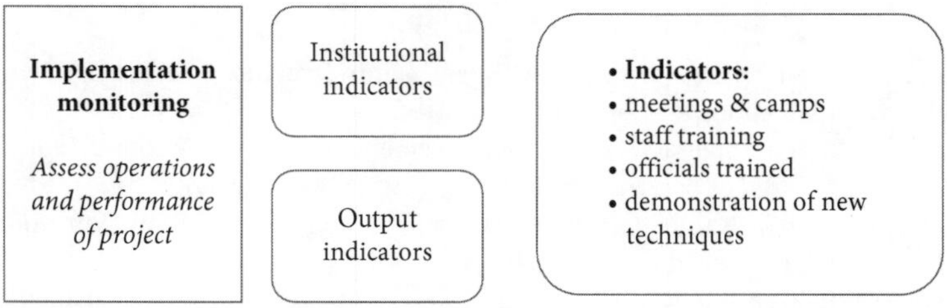

Figure 17.6 Implementation monitoring framework.
Source: Author.

project performance information system. Results monitoring could involve data from project administration as well as from a survey.

17.7 Conclusion

In the context of SDGs, the role of public finance as a source that can drive infrastructure and other public projects is reducing. Increasingly, projects have to be funded through user-pay models necessitating private participation in risk sharing and project delivery. Several evolutions have happened in the financial modelling of infrastructure projects. From ordinary PPP models to hybrid annuity model PPP, India has witnessed several changes in the delivery of public infrastructure. However, the factors that can push up project costs and thus reduce the IRR of a project are increasing.

Today, economic, social, and environmental impact evaluation are part of infrastructure project analysis. Multilateral organizations mandate impact evaluation and monitoring during the course of the project and its aftermath. A systems-based approach to achieve this can be utilized to address lower returns, if the projects accrue benefits in the form of impacts. SDGs could be identified as impact areas to attract investors and philanthropists. Projects could also involve a framework in environmental, social, and governance (ESG) reporting to attract impact investments and reduce the pressure on public finance.

References

Asian Development bank (2017). 'Meeting Asia's Infrastructure Needs', https://www.adb.org/publications/asia-infrastructure-needs.

Dey, P. K. (2001). 'Integrated Project Management in Indian Petroleum Industry'. *NICMAR-Journal of Construction Management*, 16(April–June), 1–34.

Fabozzi, F. J., and de Nahlik, C. (2012). *Project Financing*, eighth edition, Euromoney Institutional Investor PLC, Switzerland.

Hillson, D. (2003). 'Using a Risk Breakdown Structure in Project Management'. *Journal of Facilities management*, 2(1), 85–97.

Jackson, T. (2014). 'Project Appraisal Techniques', in J. Wang (ed.) *Encyclopaedia of Business Analytics and Optimization*, Hershey PA: IGI Global, 1922–1934. DOI:10.4018/978-1-4666-5202-6.

Kudtarkar, S. G. (2020). 'Failure of Operational Ppp Projects in India Leading to Private Developer's Apathy to Participate In Future Projects: A Case Study Based Analysis'. *Indian Journal of Finance and Banking*, 4(2), 17–27.

Nahlik, C. D., and Jackson, C. (2021). *Project Finance in Practice Case Studies.*

Pratap, Kumar V. (2020). 'Public–Private Partnership (PPP) project failures', *The Financial Express*, 10 December.

Rihar, L., Žužek, T., Berlec, T. et al. (2019). 'Standard Risk Management Model for Infrastructure Projects', in Nthatisi Khatleli (ed.), *Risk Management in Construction Projects*, chapter 1, 1–16, DOI: 10.5772/intechopen.80628.

Sumaila, U. R., Walsh, M., Hoareau, K. et al. (2021). 'Financing a Sustainable Ocean Economy'. *Nat Commun* 12, 3259. https://doi.org/10.1038/s41467-021-23168-y

World Bank (2020). The International Finance Corporation's Blended Finance Operations: Findings from a Cluster of Project Performance Assessment Reports. Independent Evaluation Group. World Bank.

18

Public Financial Management and Budget Credibility

Analysing Subnational Fiscal Marksmanship in India

Lekha Chakraborty, Pinaki Chakraborty, and Ruzel Shrestha

18.1 Introduction

Budget credibility, or a government's ability to accurately forecast macro-fiscal variables, is integral to public financial management (PFM). Fiscal marksmanship captures the extent of errors in budgetary forecasting. Fiscal rules can determine fiscal marksmanship. It is an effective fiscal tool that can help improve fiscal transparency and implementation of fiscal rules. Even logical and well-written fiscal rules require justification, given that constraining a government's ability to practise fiscal policy has obvious disadvantages as well (Auerbach, 2017). Against this backdrop, we analyse errors in budget forecasts in India at the state level.

Technically, the revenue and expenditure forecasts are initially made in the finance minister's annual budget speech as 'budget estimates'; these forecasts are revised after a year and published as 'revised estimates'. The finance accounts of the states, with a lag of two years, provide the actuals for audited revenue and expenditure. There is a high likelihood of huge deviations between these three stages.

We examine these deviations in macro-fiscal variables for 28 states (except Telangana) in India by employing a technique that estimates the magnitude and sources of forecast errors. The rest of this chapter is organized as follows. Section 18.2 reviews the fiscal marksmanship analysis. Section 18.3 explains the data sources and measurement issues. Section 18.4 carries out the application of the Theil's U techniques for the evaluation of fiscal marksmanship and identifies the systemic and

Lekha Chakraborty, Pinaki Chakraborty, and Ruzel Shrestha, *Public Financial Management and Budget Credibility* In: *Fiscal Policy and Public Financial Management*. Edited by: Pinaki Chakraborty and K R Shanmugam, Oxford University Press. © Oxford University Press 2024. DOI: 10.1093/9780198930464.003.0018 random components of forecast errors for all Indian states. Section 18.5 concludes and draws policy implications.

18.2 A Review of Fiscal Marksmanship Analysis

The political economy of budget deficits and other macro-fiscal variables started gaining attention in the 1990s (Alesina and Perotti, 1995; Blanchard, 1990). However, one of the earlier discussions of fiscal forecast errors was made by Allan (1965) in the case of Britain. According to Allan, fiscal marksmanship was important during that time because the margin for error was limited given the trade-off between inflation and full employment. In such a scenario, accurate predictions of budgetary estimates were important for meeting fiscal policy targets of full employment without undesirably high inflation. Davis (1980), following up on Allan's study, used a longer time series (from 1951 to 1978). The empirical evidence suggest that the forecast errors align with election cycles in Eurozone countries (Rullán and Villalonga, 2018; Strauch, Hallerberg, and Hagen 2004; Giuriato, Cepparulo, and Barberi, 2016; Pina and Venes, 2011).

There have been a number of fiscal marksmanship exercises in the case of India (Bhattacharya and Kumari, 1988). In one of the earlier attempts at analysing budgetary estimates in India (for the period 1956–64), Samuel and Rangarajan (1974) undertook an analysis of two components of the state and union budgets' capital expenditure on construction and industrial development (the analysis was limited to these two because of the scope of the subject matter they were dealing with). In this study, the analysis of forecasting errors was based largely on graphs plotting the actual expenditure and the budget estimates. In their analysis, it is stated that while in both components the central government's budget estimate was more accurate compared to the states', this difference was attributed to the difference in budgetary processes' efficiency.

Asher (1978) performed a more comprehensive fiscal marksmanship exercise for India for the period 1967–76 for both the revised and budget estimates. The study showed that during that period, both revenues and expenditures were consistently underestimated. However, it was observed that the extent of the error on the expenditure side was larger. Chakrabarty and Varghese (1982) used data from 1970–80. One of the major findings of that study was that both revenues and expenditures were underestimated. Pattnaik (1990) carried out a fiscal marksmanship exercise using Theil's index for the period 1951–89.

More recent studies on fiscal marksmanship in India have a different conclusion. A study by Nitin and Roy (2015) using data from 1990–2012 observed that while there is an attempt to have fiscal consolidation by controlling expenditure, the predictability of expenditure is quite low compared to that of revenue. In a similar study, Chakraborty and Sinha (2018) undertook a fiscal marksmanship exercise for the period 1990–2017 and came to a similar conclusion. Shrestha and Chakraborty (2019) is the only study that has examined fiscal marksmanship in the context of India's states. Their study focused on Kerala and identified forecast errors with respect to tax revenue projections.

In the recent empirical literature, fiscal forecast errors are analysed against the backdrop of fiscal rules. The political economy of fiscal forecasts at the subnational level depends on the tax autonomy and the nature of the intergovernmental fiscal transfer mechanism. Intergovernmental fiscal transfers may be progressive if the transfer is designed to offset the inter-state fiscal disabilities.

In India, the Finance Bill 2018 has incorporated a few clauses (clauses 207–210) to amend the FRBM Act of 2003, with special emphasis on the elimination of references to 'revenue balance' (i.e. revenue receipts = revenue expenditure) and using fiscal deficit as an operational parameter (Chakraborty and Chakraborty, 2018). Against these policy changes, it is pertinent to analyse the impact of fiscal rules on fiscal marksmanship of macro-fiscal variables in India. While Buiter and Patel (2011) analysed fiscal rules in India, the effect of fiscal rules on fiscal marksmanship in the context of India has not been analysed. As mentioned, Nitin and Roy (2015) analysed the normative fiscal assessments of India's Finance Commission, and realization of fiscal policy with regard to the central government's finances over the period 1990–2012.

The recent empirical literature on fiscal marksmanship is confined to the Indian national government's forecast errors (Chakraborty and Sinha, 2018; Nitin and Roy, 2015). There has been virtually no effort to undertake a fiscal marksmanship exercise at the state level. In this chapter, we attempt to carry out a fiscal marksmanship exercise at the state level for the period 2010–16, analysing the magnitude, and subsequently the nature, of the states' errors. This is done in two ways: first we check whether the errors are overestimates or underestimates, and then we check the extent of systematic and random components in these fiscal forecast errors.

18.3 Data and Measurement Issues

The data are organized from the finance accounts of various states and the Central Statistics Office (CSO). The forecast error is defined as the deviation between what is predicted as budget estimates (BE) or revised estimates (RE) and what is actual. The summary statistics usually used to measure forecasting errors in the empirical literature are from Cabanillas and Terzi (2012).

18.3.1 The Mean Error

The mean error (ME) refers to the average difference between the forecast and the actual. The ME has been calculated by taking the average of the difference between the predicted values (of both BE and RE) and the actuals over the period 2011–16. We have divided the ME by the sum of the actuals for the reference period. The ME is a crude measure of the forecast's quality, as positive and negative errors can offset each other, thereby not giving us the exact magnitude of error. However, the ME is an indicator of possible bias in the forecast.

18.3.2 The Root Mean Square Error

The root mean squared error (RMSE) is a measure of the relative size of the forecast error. In this chapter, to calculate the RMSE, the mean squared error (MSE) is taken over the reference period after which the square root of the MSE is calculated. While this will give us the magnitude of error, it will not give any information on the direction of the error (i.e. whether the error is positive or negative). We have taken the RMSE as a proportion of the sum of actuals of the reference period. It reflects the fact that large forecast errors are more significant than small differences.

18.3.3 Theil's Inequality Coefficients (U)

Theil's inequality coefficient (U) is used to analyse the measure of accuracy of the budget forecasts. Theil's inequality coefficient is based on the MSE (U_1). The forecast error of Theil (1958) is defined as:

$$U_1 = \frac{\sqrt{^{1/n}\sum (P_i - A_i)^2}}{\sqrt{^{1/n}\sum P_i^2} + \sqrt{^{1/n}\sum A_i^2}} \qquad (18.1)$$

Where U_1 = inequality coefficient, P_t = predicted value, A_t = actual value, and n = the number of years. This inequality coefficient ranges from zero to one. When $P_t = A_t$ for all observations (a perfect forecast), U_1 equals zero.

U_1 has been decomposed in order to indicate systematic and random sources of error. The systematic component is further divided into the proportion of the total forecast error due to bias and the proportion of total forecast error attributable to unequal variation. The derivation of Equation 18.2 is given in detail in Davis (1980).

$$1 = \frac{\left(\overline{P} - \overline{A}\right)^2}{^{1/n}\sum (P_i - A_i)^2} + \frac{(Sp - Sa)^2}{^{1/n}\sum (P_i - A_i)^2} + \frac{2(1-r)Sp.Sa}{^{1/n}\sum (P_i - A_i)^2} \qquad (18.2)$$

In Equation 18.2, P and A are mean predicted and mean actual changes, respectively; Sp and Sa are the standard deviations of predicted and actual values, respectively; and r is the coefficient of correlation between predicted and actual values.

The first expression on the right-hand side (RHS) in Equation 18.2 is the proportion of the total forecast error due to bias. It represents a measure of the proportion of error due to overprediction or underprediction of the average value. The second expression on the RHS in Equation 18.2 is the proportion of total forecast error attributable to unequal variation. In other words, it measures the proportion of error due to overprediction or underprediction of the variance of the values. The third expression on the RHS in Equation 18.2 measures the proportion of forecasting error due to random variation.

The first two sources of error are systematic; presumably they can be reduced by improved forecasting techniques, while the random component is beyond the control of the forecaster (Intriligator, 1978; Pindyck and Rubenfield, 1998; Theil, 1958).

18.4 Fiscal Marksmanship Analysis: Magnitude and Sources of Forecasting Errors

Our analysis showed that in 28 states the overestimation of revenue receipts amounts to 1.18 per cent of gross state domestic product (GSDP) with respect to the forecast deviation between BE and actuals. The same ratio is slightly reduced to 1.03 per cent for RE and actuals. The underestimation (negative deviations of BE and actuals) of revenue is, however, negligible (see Table 18.1).

The state's own tax revenue alone showed 0.40 per cent overestimation as a percentage of GSDP for all states with regard to forecast errors between BE and actuals. The errors were reduced to 0.22 per cent of GSDP for RE versus actuals. The state's own non-tax revenue was cumulatively overestimated by 0.11 per cent, while the central government's transfers were overestimated to 0.14 per cent of GSDP. It would be interesting to analyse the reasons for these forecast errors in the central government's transfers to all states. The design of cess and surcharges is an additional dimension for the reduction in the divisible tax pool transferred from the central government to the states. The cumulative forecast error/deviation between BE and actuals was relatively higher for grants than tax transfers to all states, at 0.66 per cent for BE versus actuals (Table 18.1).

The cumulative overestimation of revenue expenditure of all states over the period 2011–16 was 1.05 per cent of GSDP with respect to the forecast errors between BE and actuals (Table 18.2). Within the revenue expenditure, the overestimation of social services (0.53 per cent

Table 18.1 Deviation between BE/RE and actuals in revenue receipts (as a percentage of all GSDP).

	Revenue receipts		States' own tax revenue		State's own non-tax revenue		Share in central taxes		Grants from centre	
	BE:actuals	RE:actuals	BE:actuals	RE:actuals	BE:actuals	RE:actuals	BE:actuals	RE:actuals	BE:actuals	RE:actuals
Overestimation	1.20	1.05	0.40	0.22	0.11	0.08	0.14	0.12	0.67	0.66
Underestimation	0.00	−0.08	−0.04	−0.07	−0.04	−0.03	−0.02	−0.02	−0.02	0.00

Source: Finance accounts of states and state budget documents (various years).

Table 18.2 Deviation between BE/RE and actuals in revenue expenditure (as a percentage of all GSDP).

	Revenue expenditure (total)		Social services		Economic services		General services	
	BE:actuals	RE:actuals	BE:actuals	RE:actuals	BE:actuals	RE:actuals	BE:actuals	RE:actuals
Overestimation	1.05	1.29	0.37	0.53	0.19	0.39	0.34	0.17
Underestimation	−0.01	−0.10	−0.02	−0.05	−0.05	−0.02	−0.03	−0.05

Source: Finance accounts of states and state budget documents (various years).

with respect to RE versus actuals) is higher than those of economic services and general services. This is broadly giving an indication that against the backdrop of fiscal rules at subnational level, expenditure compression happens more with social sector spending. The cumulative overestimation of general services is 0.34 per cent for BE versus actuals and at 0.17 per cent for RE versus actuals. The cumulative overestimation of capital expenditure in the period under analysis was as high as 0.38 per cent of GSDP for both BE:actuals and RE:actuals (Table 18.3).

Analysing the ME and RMSE, we find that the values of MSE and RMSE (as a proportion of actuals) seem to be higher in the case of capital expenditure compared to revenue expenditure. This is true of almost all states. Only in the cases of Haryana, Karnataka, and Odisha is the MSE (as a proportion of actuals) higher for revenue expenditure compared to capital expenditure.[1] Furthermore, only in Himachal, Karnataka, Kerala, and Uttarakhand is the RMSE as a proportion of actuals higher in the case of revenue expenditure compared to capital expenditure. The MSE and RMSE (as a proportion of actuals) are higher in the case of non-tax revenue (including grants) compared to tax revenue (including tax transfers) at the all-state level. The all-state ME as a proportion of actuals for total tax revenue is 0.0496 and the all-state ME for non-tax revenues as a proportion of actuals is 0.2049. Similarly, in the case of RMSE, the all-state RMSE as a proportion of actuals for total tax revenue is 548.09 and the same for non-tax revenue is 1140.79. The main reason the ME and RMSE are higher for non-tax revenue is because the value of these two indicators is very high for the grants from the central government. The RMSE as a proportion of actuals for grants from the central government is 1157.62 and the RMSE for states' own non-tax revenue is only 372.02. Similarly, the states' ME for own-tax revenue is only 0.0544, whereas it is 0.282 for grants from the central government.

[1] The state-specific tables and figures are available on request.

Table 18.3 Deviation between BE/RE and actuals in capital expenditure (as percentage of all GSDP).

	Capital expenditure (total)		Social services		Economic services		General services	
	BE:actuals	RE:actuals	BE:actuals	RE:actuals	BE:actuals	RE:actuals	BE:actuals	RE:actuals
Overestimation	0.39	0.38	0.15	0.14	0.20	0.19	0.08	0.06
Underestimation	–0.02	–0.01	0.00	0.00	–0.05	–0.02	0.00	0.00

Source: Finance accounts of states and state budget documents (various years).

18.4.1 Forecasting Errors: Overestimate or Underestimate?

One of the limitations of RMSE is that we cannot find the signs of the error. In this section we attempt to calculate fiscal marksmanship indices that will help us assess whether the budgetary estimates are overestimates or underestimates. This ratio would give us information on whether the BE or RE is an underestimate or an overestimate. If the value of the ratio is above one, this indicates that, on average, the indicator has been overestimated. Conversely, if the value is below one, it can be said that it is an underestimate. In the case of BE, it can be observed that most of the categories are overestimated on both the revenue and the expenditure sides (Table 18.4).

On the total revenue receipt, all the states have overestimated the overall revenue, ranging from a maximum value of 1.36 (Meghalaya) to a minimum value of 1.01 (Rajasthan). The median value of total revenue receipt is 1.12 (Table 18.4). Correspondingly, both the tax revenue and non-tax revenue are generally overestimated. However, there are a few states where there has been underestimation of tax revenue and non-tax revenue. Tax revenue was underestimated in Karnataka and Orissa, and non-tax revenues were underestimated in Tamil Nadu and Rajasthan. An interesting observation from the data is that the standard deviation of this index for the non-tax revenues (for both states' own non-tax revenue and grants from the central government) was considerably higher than the tax

Table 18.4 Descriptive statistics of fiscal marksmanship ratio: Revenue and its components (BE:actuals).

	Total revenue receipt	Tax revenue	States' own tax revenue	Share in central taxes	Non-tax revenue	States' own tax revenue	Grants from centre
Median	1.115	1.029	1.003	1.056	1.210	1.120	1.332
Mean	1.118	1.039	1.097	1.038	1.241	1.156	1.325
Max.	1.360	1.223	1.072	1.166	1.698	2.191	2.121
Min.	1.012	0.916	0.952	0.866	0.839	0.828	0.803
Standard deviation	0.087	0.056	0.077	0.053	0.199	0.280	0.269

Source: CAG office finance accounts of states and state budget documents (basic data; various years).

revenues. In Table 18.4, the standard deviation for tax revenue is 0.053, whereas the standard deviation of non-tax revenue is 0.199. This shows that the ratio of BE:actuals is relatively more spread compared to tax revenues. An observation that is worth noting is that the higher standard deviation of the ratio of BE:actuals for non-tax revenue compared to tax revenue complements the fact that the ME and RMSE also had a similar trend. Coupling the results from this and the previous sections, one can conclude that while the BE is generally overestimated for both tax revenues and non-tax revenues, the errors are generally higher for non-tax revenues compared to tax revenues.

When we consider the expenditure side, we can observe that it is generally the case that both revenue expenditure and capital expenditure have seen different patterns. In the case of revenue expenditure, all the states except Nagaland and Assam have underestimates. In the case of capital expenditure, all the states excepts Karnataka, Uttar Pradesh, and Himachal Pradesh have overestimates. However, one trend that can be observed is that the range and standard deviation of capital expenditure is much higher compared to revenue expenditure (both overall and component-wise). The maximum and minimum of the revenue expenditure are 1.279 and 0.95, respectively, for revenue expenditure (Table 18.5). This is considerably lower compared to the maximum and minimum of this index for capital expenditure, which are 2.476 and 0.956, respectively (Table 18.6).

Table 18.5 Descriptive statistics of fiscal marksmanship ratio: Revenue expenditure.

	Revenue expenditure	Social services	Economic services	Non-developmental expenditure
Median	1.072	1.074	1.069	1.040
Mean	1.094	1.086	1.117	1.055
Max.	1.279	1.432	1.715	1.319
Min.	0.950	0.866	0.895	0.920
Standard deviation	0.084	0.122	0.174	0.088

Source: CAG office finance accounts of states and state budget documents (basic data; various years).

Table 18.6 Descriptive statistics of fiscal marksmanship ratio: Capital expenditure.

	Capital expenditure	Social services	Economic services	Non-developmental expenditure
Median	1.269	1.306	1.185	1.368
Mean	1.335	1.446	1.197	1.941
Max.	2.476	3.305	2.113	9.879
Min.	0.956	0.659	0.570	0.800
Standard deviation	0.359	0.555	0.330	1.765

Source: CAG office finance accounts of states and state budget documents (basic data; various years).

The standard deviation for capital expenditure is 0.359, which is around fourfold higher than the standard deviation of revenue expenditure (Table 18.6). As was observed in the previous section, the MSE and RMSE are higher for capital expenditure compared to revenue expenditure. Since most of the states had overestimates of both the revenue and capital expenditure, it can be concluded that the forecasting errors in capital expenditure tend to be higher compared to those in revenue expenditure.

18.4.2 Analysing the Forecast Errors using Theil's U

The U_1 of Theil's index has a lower limit of zero (which is the case of a perfect forecast) and an upper limit of one (which is the highest forecasting error). We will state some of the observations on the forecasting errors and elaborate on them using some basic statistical indicators.

In the case of the BE, the average forecasting errors in most of the revenue and expenditure are below 0.2. Furthermore, almost all of the variables (except revenue deficit) are positively skewed (since median < mean). This means that a lot of the observations are clustered to the left side of the interval of U_1 (i.e. 0 and 1) and most of them are below 0.2. One can observe that, on average, both revenue and expenditure variables have low forecasting errors. We observe that the all-state average for total revenue receipt is 0.09. The all-state average forecast error for the tax revenue is 0.074 and for non-tax revenue is 0.15. In the case of the expenditure variables, the all-India average is 0.08 for revenue expenditure and 0.177 for capital expenditure.

When we look at the error in estimating the fiscal deficit, the U_1 for fiscal deficit, on average, is 0.302. There are only four states that have fiscal deficit forecast errors greater than 0.5, namely Arunachal Pradesh (0.818), Assam (0.554), Mizoram (0.617), and Punjab (0.866). In the case of revenue deficit, the value of U_1 was higher, at 0.432. Seven states have a U_1 higher than 0.5, namely Andhra Pradesh (0.672), Assam (0.94), Goa (0.59), Jammu and Kashmir (0.861), Kerala (0.532), Uttar Pradesh (0.669), and West Bengal (0.636).

A very similar observation can be made regarding the revised estimates. The average forecasting errors for most of the revenue and expenditure variables are below 0.20. Similar to BE, all the variables are positively skewed. It is worth noting that, for most of the major revenue and expenditure variables, RE is better forecast than BE (on average). For all the macro-fiscal variables among the states, the value of U_1 in RE is lower than BE.

18.4.3 Decomposition of Forecast Errors

We have decomposed the error between the systematic and unsystematic errors. Systematic error is the sum of the ME and slope error. The systematic error can be improved by using better forecasting techniques. Within BE:actuals partitioning, more than 20 states showed that the source of errors was systemic for capital expenditure. Figures 18.1 to 18.7 report the source of errors.

One can observe that in merely seven and five states in the BE and RE, respectively, the *capital expenditure* variables have a random error of more than 0.5. The average of the random errors of the BE and RE is 0.31 and 0.24, respectively. Both the above observations tell us that the errors in capital expenditure are due more to systematic bias than to being random.

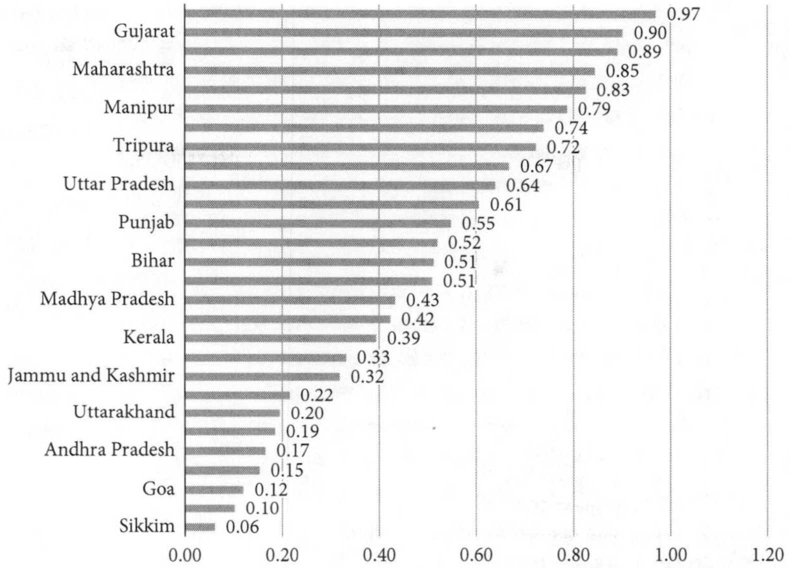

Figure 18.1 Randomness of errors in revenue deficit (BE:actual).
Source: CAG office finance accounts of states and state budget documents (basic data; various years).

In the case of BE, it can be observed that in most of the categories more than half of the states have a random error of over 50 per cent of the total error. In the case of all of the revenue and expenditure variables (except share in federal taxes, where four states have a systematic error of over 50 per cent), the former trend of random error over 50 per cent persists.

While there have been negligible improvements from the BE to the RE—that is, on average, the number of states having a systematic error of more than 50 per cent has changed marginally across the different categories of revenues and expenditure—the larger trend of the BE seems to persist. For instance, in categories such as tax revenue, states' own tax revenue, share in federal taxes, states' own non tax revenue, revenue expenditure, revenue deficit, and primary deficit, the number of states having systematic error of over 50 per cent of the total error has decreased. For the rest of the categories, the same have increased. However, in both cases, the change has been only marginal.

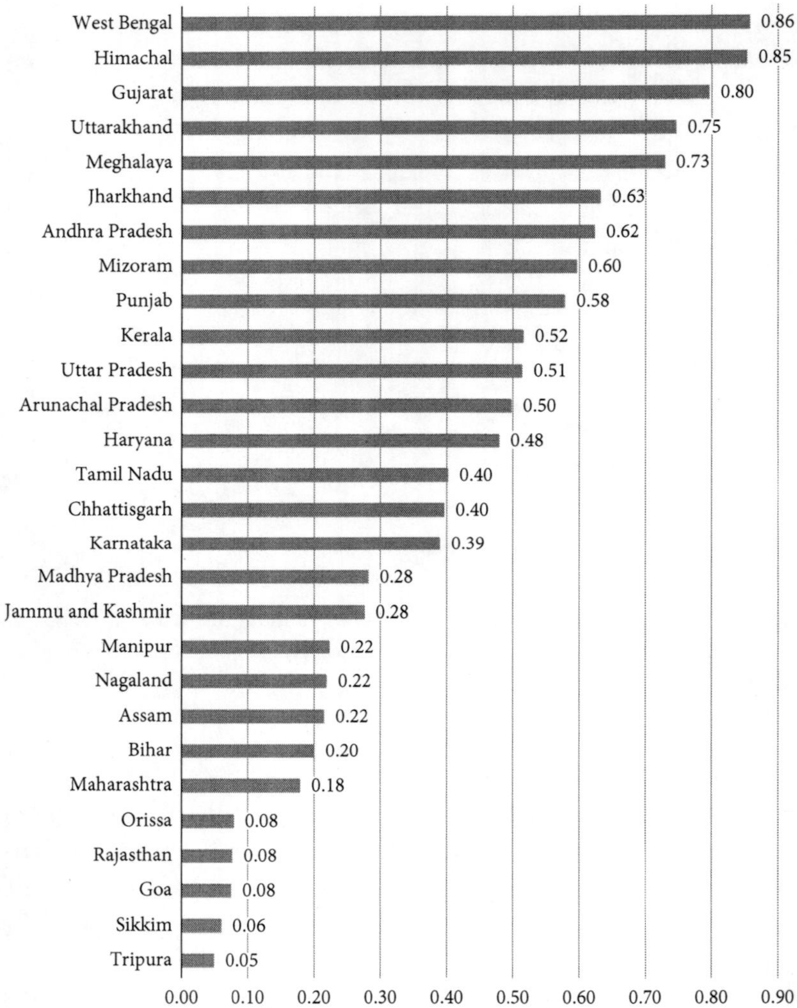

Figure 18.2 Randomness of errors in fiscal deficit (BE:actual).

Source: CAG office finance accounts of states and state budget documents (basic data; various years).

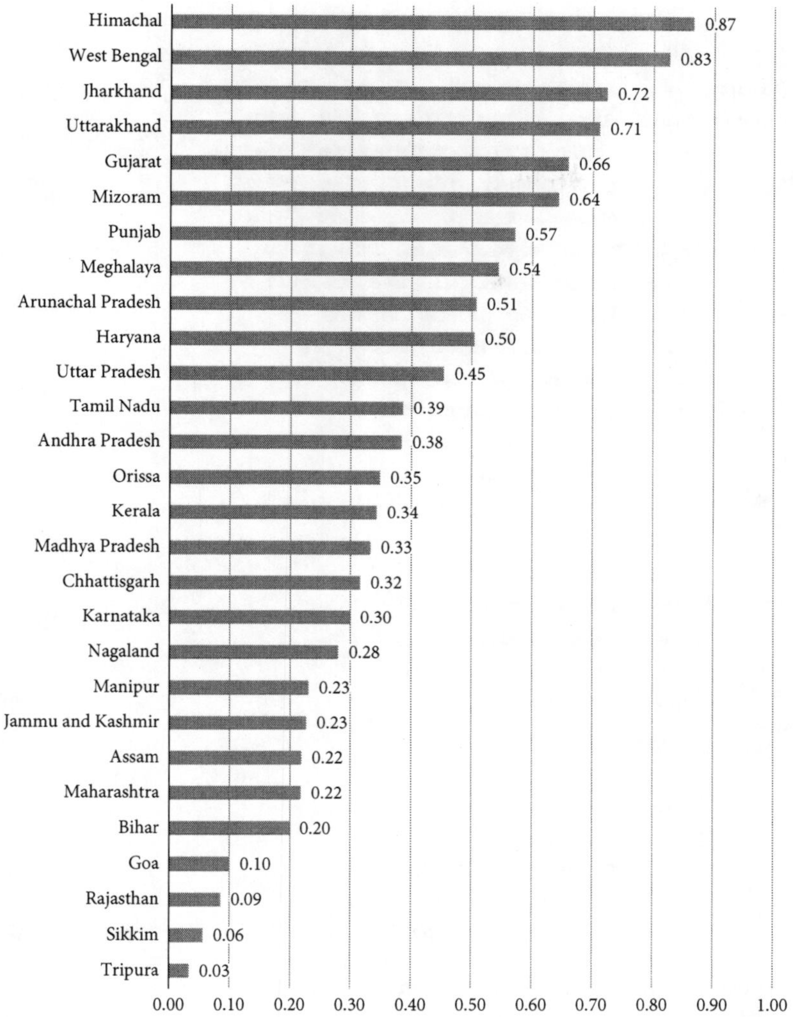

Figure 18.3 Randomness of errors in primary deficit (BE:actual).

Source: CAG office finance accounts of states and state budget documents (basic data; various years).

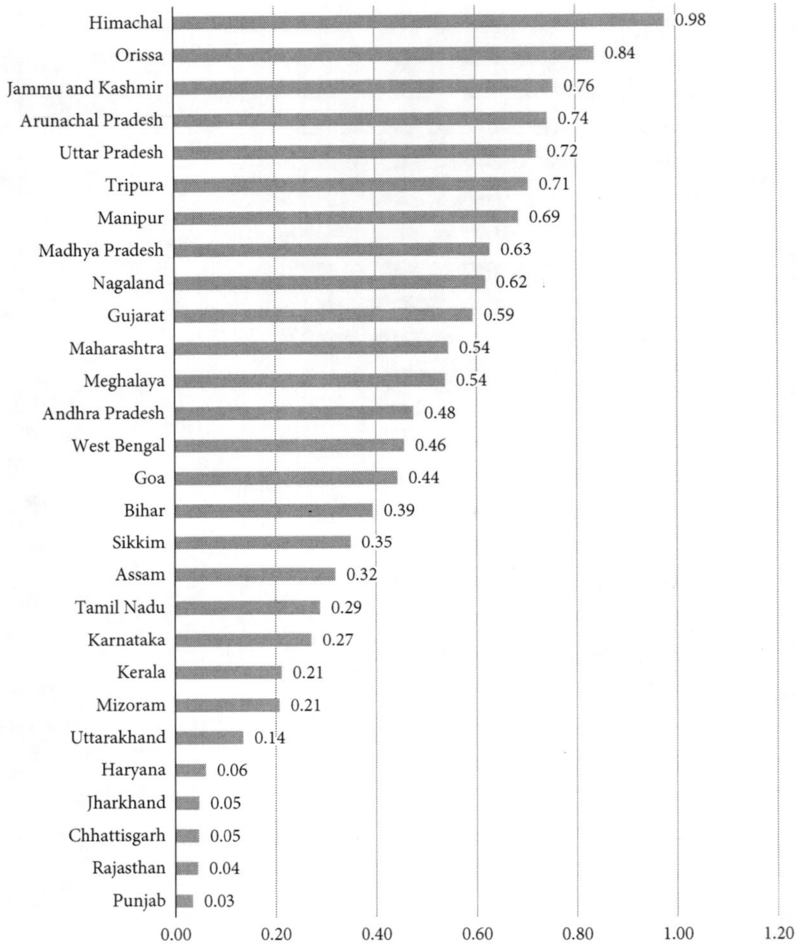

Figure 18.4 Randomness of errors in own tax revenue (BE:actual).

Source: CAG office finance accounts of states and state budget documents (basic data; various years).

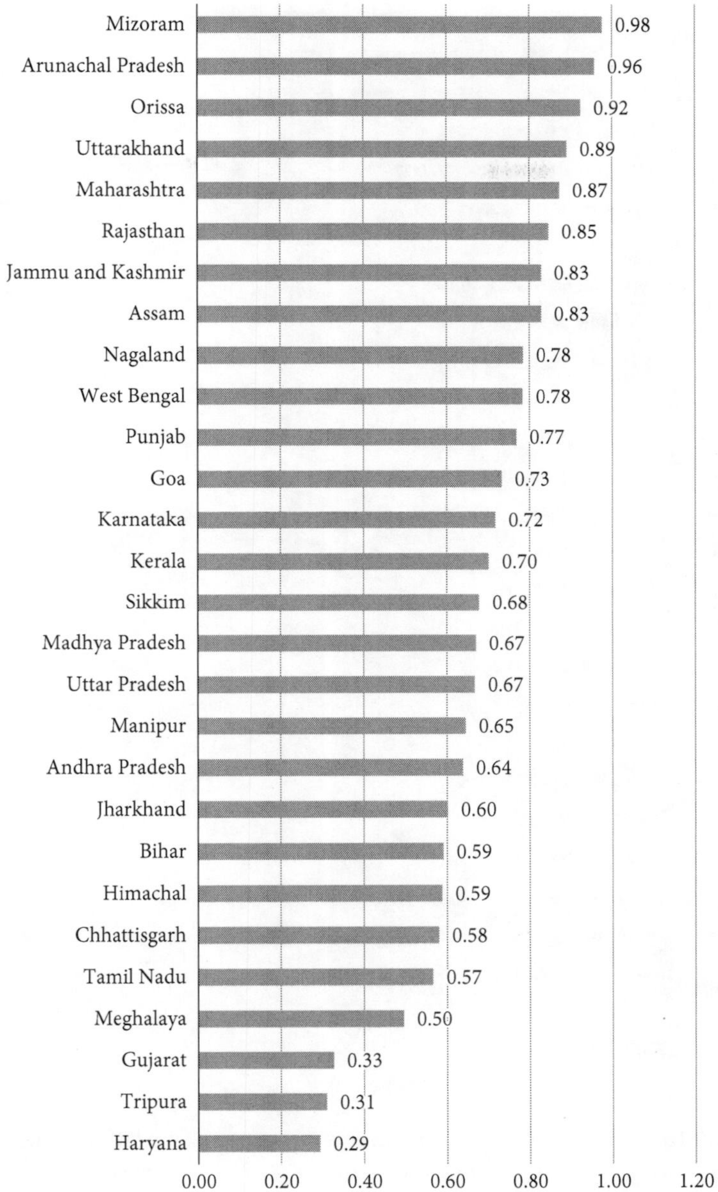

Figure 18.5 Randomness of errors in tax transfers (BE:actual).

Source: CAG office finance accounts of states and state budget documents (basic data; various years).

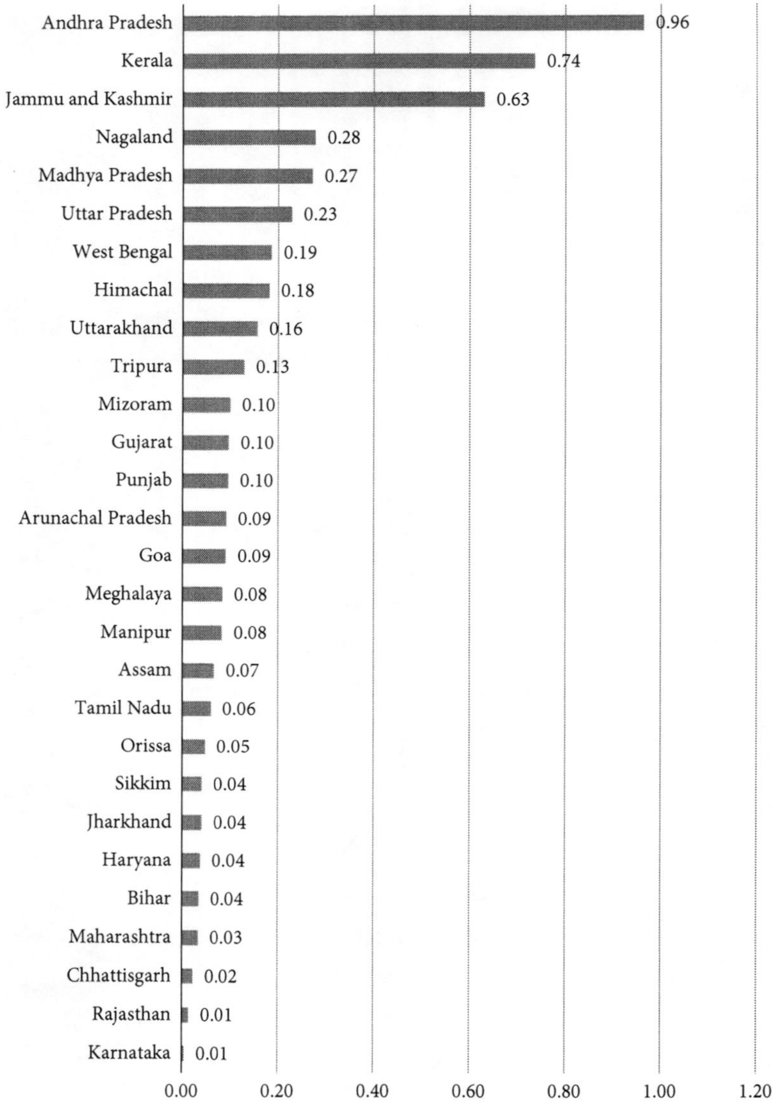

Figure 18.6 Randomness of errors in revenue expenditure (BE:actual).

Source: CAG office finance accounts of states and state budget documents (basic data; various years).

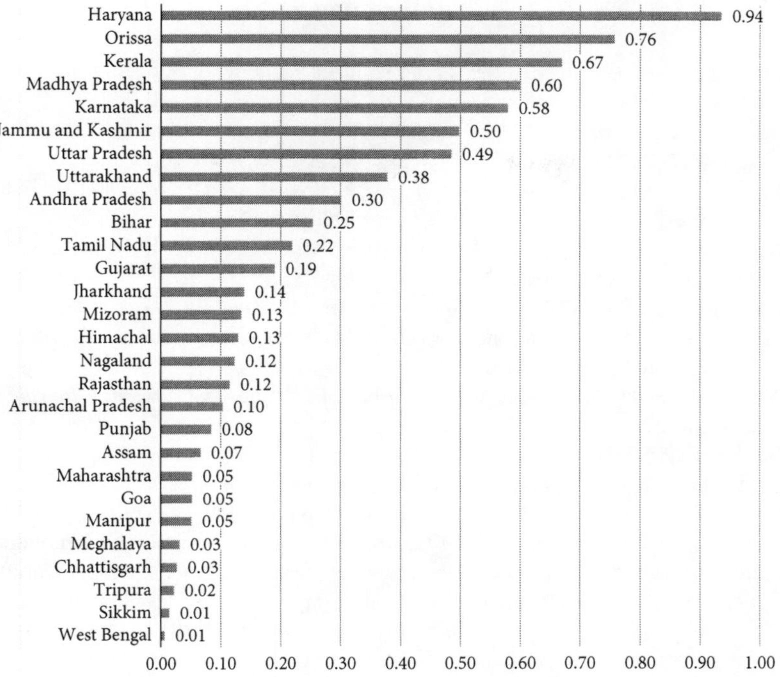

Figure 18.7 Randomness of Errors in capital expenditure (BE:actual).
Source: CAG office finance accounts of states and state budget documents (basic data; various years).

18.5 Conclusions

Applying Theil's U technique, we have tried to analyse the errors in the fiscal forecasts of India's subnational governments. The fiscal marksmanship analysis showed that the forecast errors in revenue receipts have been greater than those for revenue expenditure. Within revenue receipts, the forecast errors in grants is the highest. Within public expenditure, the errors of capital expenditure forecasts showed greater deviations than revenue expenditure. The analysis shows that in more than 20 states, the sources of error are systemic rather than random in the case of a few macro-fiscal variables, with negligible improvements from BE to RE.

References

Alesina, A., and Perotti, R. (1995). 'The Political Economy of Budget Deficits'. IMF Staff Papers 42(1), 1–31.

Allan, C. M. (1965). 'Fiscal Marksmanship, 1951–63'. *Oxford Economic Papers* (new series) 17(2): 317–327.

Artis, M. J., and Marcellino, M. (2001). 'Fiscal Forecasting: The Track Record of the IMF, OECD and EC'. *Econometrics Journal* 4(1): S20–S36.

Asher, M. G. (1978). 'Accuracy of Budgetary Forecasts of Central Government, 1967–68 to 1975–76'. *Economic and Political Weekly* 13(8), 423–432.

Auerbach, A. J. (2017). 'Fiscal Policy'. Paper presented in the conference on 'Rethinking Macroeconomics'. Peterson Institute of International Economics, Washington, DC, 12–13 October.

Auld, D. A. L. (1970). 'Fiscal Marksmanship in Canada'. *The Canadian Journal of Economics* 3(3): 507–11.

Beetsma, R. M. W. J., and Jensen, H. (2004). 'Mark-Up Fluctuations and Fiscal Policy Stabilization in a Monetary Union'. *Journal of Macroeconomics* 26, 357–376.

Buiter, W. H., and Patel, U.R (2011). 'Fiscal Rules in India: Are They Effective?' CEPR Discussion Paper Series No. 7810. Centre for Economic Policy Research, London.

Blanchard, O. (1990). 'Suggestions for a New Set of Fiscal Indicators'. OECD Working Paper No. 79. Organization for Economic Co-operation and Development, Paris.

Bretschneider, S. I., Gorr, W. L., Grizzle, G., et al. (1989). 'Political and Organizational Influences on the Accuracy of Forecasting State Government Revenues'. *International Journal of Forecasting* 5: 307–319.

Brück, T., and Stephan, A. (2005). 'Do Eurozone Countries Cheat with Their Budget Deficit Forecasts?' Postgraduate Research Programme Working Paper No. 2005.5. European University Viadrina Frankfurt (Oder), Frankfurt.

Cabanillas, L. G., and Terzi, A. (2012). 'The Accuracy of the European Commission's Forecasts Re-examined'. EC European Papers No. 476. European Commission, Brussels.

Cassidy, G., Kamlet, M. S., and Nagin, D. S. (1989). 'An Empirical Examination of Bias in Revenue Forecasts by State Governments'. *International Journal of Forecasting* 5(3), 321–331.

Chakraborty, L., and Sinha, D. (2018). 'Has Fiscal Rule Changed the Fiscal Marksmanship of Union Government?' NIPFP Working Paper No. 234. National Institute of Public Finance and Policy, New Delhi.

Chakraborty, L., and Chakraborty, P. (2018). 'New FRBM Framework: Time to Recast Union Government Expenditure Needs'. *Economic and Political Weekly* 53(9), 30–34.

Chakrabarty, T. K., and Varghese, W. (1982). 'The Government of India's Budget Estimation: An Analysis of the Error Components'. *Reserve Bank of India, Occasional Papers* 3(2), 175–190.

Davis, J. M. (1980). 'Fiscal Marksmanship in the United Kingdom, 1951–1978'. *The Manchester School* 48(2), 111–128.

Giuriato, L., Cepparulo, A., and Barberi, M. (2016). 'Fiscal Forecasts and Political Systems: A Legislative Budgeting Perspective'. *Public Choice* 168(1): 1–22.

Intriligator, M. D. (1978). *Econometric Models, Techniques, and Applications.* Prentice-Hall, Upper Saddle River, NJ.

Kopits, G. (2001). 'Fiscal Rules: Useful Policy Framework or Unnecessary Ornament?' IMF Working Paper No. 01/145. International Monetary Fund, Washington, DC.

Ministry of Finance. (2017). 'Fiscal Responsibility and Budget Management (FRBM) Committee Report'. Government of India, Ministry of Finance, New Delhi.

Morrison, R. J. (1986). 'Fiscal Marksmanship in the United States: 1950–1983'. *The Manchester School* 54(3): 322–333.

Muth, J. F. (1961). 'Rational Expectations and the Theory of Price Movements'. *Econometrica* 29: 315–35.

Nitan, K., and Roy, R. (2015). 'Finance Commission of India's Assessment: A Political Economy Contention between Expectations and Outcomes'. *Applied Economics* 48(2), 73–88.

Pattnaik, R. K. (1990). 'Fiscal Marksmanship in India'. *Reserve Bank of India Occasional Papers* 11(3), 1–20.

Pina, Á. M., and Venes, N. M. (2011). 'The Political Economy of EDP Fiscal Forecasts: An Empirical Assessment'. *European Journal of Political Economy* 27(3): 534–546.

Pindyck, R. S., and Rubinfeld, D. L. (1998). *Econometric Models and Economic Forecasts.* Irwin/McGraw-Hill, New York.

Rullán, X. O., and Villalonga, J. R. (2018). 'Determinants of Regional Budget Forecast Errors in Federal Economies: Spain 1995–2013'. *Review of Public Economics* 226(4): 85–121.

Samuel, P., and Rangarajan, C. (1974). *Short-Term Investment Forecasting.* Macmillan India, Noida.

Shrestha, R., and Chakraborty, L. (2019). 'Practising Subnational Public Finance in an Emerging Economy: Fiscal Marksmanship in Kerala'. NIPFP Working Paper No. 261. National Institute of Public Finance and Policy, New Delhi.

Strauch, R., Hallerberg, M., and Hagen, J. V. (2004). 'Budgetary Forecasts in Europe – The Track Record of Stability and Convergence Programmes', ECB Working Paper No. 307. Germany: European Central Bank (ECB)

Theil, H. (1958). *Economic Forecasts and Policy.* North Holland, Amsterdam.

Index

For the benefit of digital users, indexed terms that span two pages (e.g., 52–53) may, on occasion, appear on only one of those pages.

Tables and figures are indicated by an italic *t* and *f* following the page number.